Unpublished Fragments
from the Period of *Human, All Too Human I*
(Winter 1874/75–Winter 1877/78)

Volume Twelve

Based on the edition by
Giorgio Colli & Mazzino Montinari
First organized in English by Ernst Behler

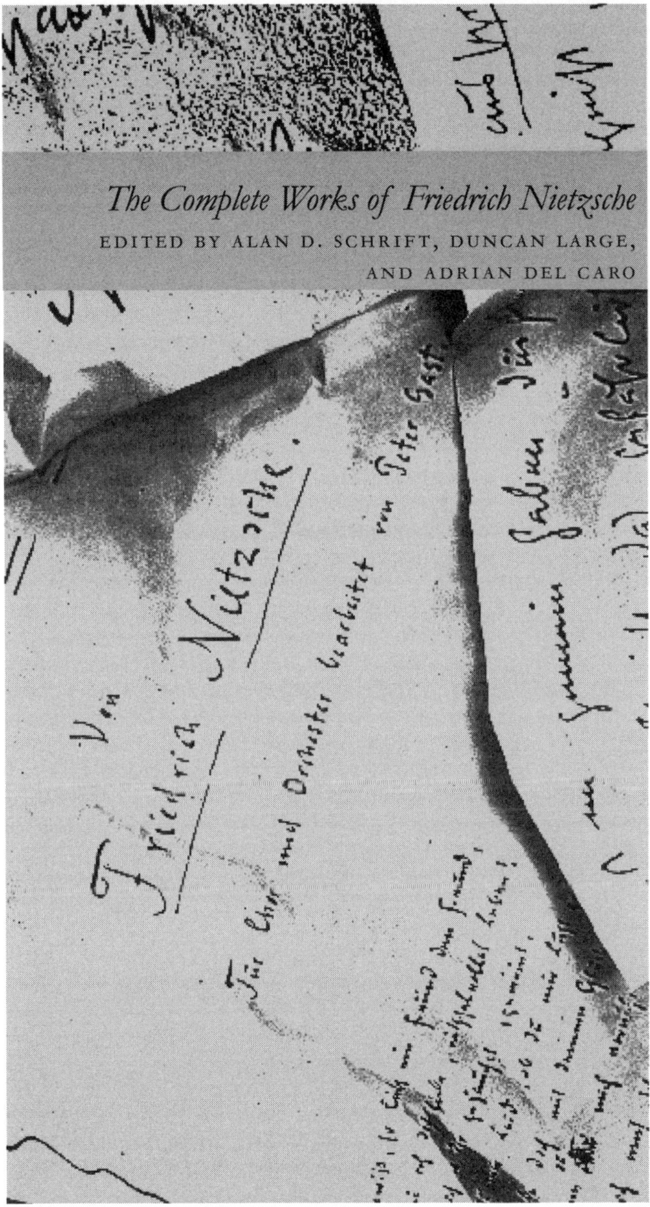

The Complete Works of Friedrich Nietzsche

EDITED BY ALAN D. SCHRIFT, DUNCAN LARGE, AND ADRIAN DEL CARO

Friedrich Nietzsche

Unpublished Fragments
from the Period of *Human, All Too Human I*
(Winter 1874/75–Winter 1877/78)

Translated, with an Afterword,
by Gary Handwerk

STANFORD UNIVERSITY PRESS
STANFORD, CALIFORNIA

Stanford University Press
Stanford, California

Translated from Friedrich Nietzsche, *Sämtliche Werke: Kritische Studienausgabe*, ed. Giorgio Colli and Mazzino Montinari, in 15 vols. This book corresponds to Vol. 8, pp. 9–474, and Vol. 14, pp. 555–605.

Critical edition of Friedrich Nietzsche's *Sämtliche Werke* and unpublished writings based on the original manuscripts.

Printed in the United States of America on acid-free, archival-quality paper.

CIP data appears at the end of the book.

In Memoriam

Helen Tartar
1951–2014

Contents

Reference Matter

A Note on This Edition

This is the first English translation of all of Nietzsche's writings, including his unpublished fragments, with annotation, afterwords concerning the individual texts, and indexes, in nineteen volumes. The aim of this collaborative work is to produce a critical edition for scholarly use. Volume 1 also includes an introduction to the entire edition, and Volume 19 will include a detailed chronology of Nietzsche's life. While the goal is to establish a readable text in contemporary English, the translation follows the original as closely as possible. All texts have been translated anew by a group of scholars, and particular attention has been given to maintaining a consistent terminology throughout the volumes. The translation is based on *Friedrich Nietzsche: Sämtliche Werke. Kritische Studienausgabe in 15 Bänden* (1980), edited by Giorgio Colli and Mazzino Montinari. The still-progressing *Nietzsche Werke: Kritische Gesamtausgabe*, which Colli and Montinari began in 1963, has also been consulted. The Colli-Montinari edition is of particular importance for the unpublished fragments, comprising more than half of Nietzsche's writings and published there for the first time in their entirety. Besides listing textual variants, the annotation to this English edition provides succinct information on the text and identifies events, names (except those in the Index of Persons), titles, quotes, and biographical facts of Nietzsche's own life. The notes are numbered in the text and are keyed by phrase. The Afterword presents the main facts about the origin of the text, the stages of its composition, and the main events of its reception. The Index of Persons includes mythological figures and lists the dates of birth and death as well as prominent personal characteristics. Since the first three volumes appeared, important corrections to the 1980 edition of the *Kritische Studienausgabe* have been noted, and these corrections have been incorporated into the translation that appears here.

ERNST BEHLER AND ALAN D. SCHRIFT

Unpublished Fragments
from the Period of *Human, All Too Human I*
(Winter 1874/75–Winter 1877/78)

[1 = N I 4. Winter–Spring 1875]

1[1]

Romundt[1] 9 January: 9–10 March his text must be finished no later than 10 April.

1[2]

Passage on Faust
Hölderlin
Conclusion Empedocles

1[3][2]

1875	4 5	Philologist. Wagner.
1876	6	Press.
1877	7 8	Religion. School.
1878	9 10	Social⟨ism⟩. State.
1879	11–12	My plan. Nature.
1880	13	Path of Liberation.

1[4][3]

Prelude. The Cultivated Philistine.[4,5]

1 History.[6]
2 Philosophy.[7]
3 Antiquity.[8]
4 Art.[9]
5 Religion.[10] 1876 Easter April May June

6	School.		July August September
7	Press.		October November December
8	State.	1877	January February March
9	Society.		April May June
10	A Man Such As I.		July August September
11	Nature.		October November December
12	Path of Liberation.	1878.	January February March
	1869 Easter–1876 Easter.		7 years at the university.
	Easter 1876–Easter 1878.		800 pages in 24 months,

24: 800 | 33, i.e., one page every day, 1 Unfashionable every three months.
72

I will then be done with the *Unfashionables* when I am 33 years old.

1[5]

13 years old–19 Schulpforta.
19–24 Bonn Leipzig.
24–31 Basel
31–33 ?

[2 = U II 8a. Up to the beginning of March 1875]

Notes for "WE PHILOLOGISTS"

2[1][1]

The seashell is curved on the inside, rough on the outside; when it rumbles while being blown, then for the first time do we have the proper respect for it. (Ind. Maxims ed. Böthlingk. I 335.)[2]

A wind instrument ugly in appearance: it must first be blown.

2[2]

Themes.

Theory of the ridiculous. With a set of examples.

Theory of the terrifying. With a set of examples.

Description of my musical experiences in reference to Wagner's.

The question in music.

I should lay out a large book for daily insights and experiences, plans, etc.: where scientific knowledge, too, is briefly recorded. Set all literary plans aside. *Mihi scribere.*[3]

2[3]

We Philologists.
Approximate Plan.

1. Genesis of contemporary philologists.
2. The contemporary philologist and the Greeks.
3. Effects upon nonphilologists.
4. Preliminary notes on the Greeks.
5. The future education of the philologist.
6. Greeks and Romans — and Christianity. Wolf's[4] separation.

Better:

a. Preference for the Greeks
b. Genesis of contemporary philologists.
c. Their effect upon nonphilologists.
d. Their position toward the real Greeks.
e. Future matters.

2[4]

Perhaps against the enemies of antiquity with Cicero in Piso. c. 30 "*Quid te, asine, litteras doceam? Non opus est verbis, sed fustibus.*"[5]

2[5]

There remains a great deal of *doubt* as to whether we can draw conclusions from *languages* about nationality and about *relationship* with other *nations*; a victorious language is nothing other than a frequent (not even a regular) sign of a successful subjugation. Where have there ever been autochthonous peoples? It is a completely unclear concept to speak of Greeks who did not yet live in Greece. What is characteristically Greek is much less the result of a natural disposition than of adapted institutions and likewise with the received language.

2[6]

I want to make short catechisms for my pupils, e.g.,
— on writing and reading.

— on Greek literature.
— main characteristics of the Greeks.
Greeks and Romans.
What we can learn from the Greeks.

2[7][6]

a. Preference for antiquity, its reasons and their refutation.
b. Genesis up to now of philologists, also their praxis.

2[8][7]

Klinger says "culture is the fruit of freer, more fearless feelings."

[3 = Mp XIII 6b. (U II 8, 239–200). March 1875]

Notes
for
We Philologists

3[1][1]

Go hence and conceal your good works and confess before the people the sins that you have committed.
Buddha.

3[2][2]

The eighth of April 1777, when F. A. Wolf invented the name *stud. philol.* for himself, is the birthdate of philology.

1.

3[3][3]

Against the science of philology there would be nothing to be said: but the philologists are also the educators. Therein lies the problem, whereby this science, too, comes under a higher law. — And would philology still even exist, if the philologists were not a teaching profession?

3[4][4]

It is hard to justify the *preference* with which antiquity is regarded: for it has emerged from prejudices:[5]

1) from lack of knowledge about the rest of antiquity,[6]
2) from a false idealization of humanitarian humanity[7] in general; whereas Indians and Chinese are in any case more humane,[8]
3) from schoolmasterly conceit,
4) from the traditional admiration that starts with the Romans,[9,10]
5) from opposition to the Christian church, or in support of it,[11,12]
6) the impression that the centuries-long work of philologists has made, and the manner of their work: it really must be a matter of gold mines, thinks the observer.
7) Skills and knowledge learned there. Preschool of science.[13]

In sum: in part out of *ignorance, false judgments* and *deceptive conclusions*, also through the *interest of a profession*, the philologists.

Preference for antiquity then, due to artists, who involuntarily make perceived measure and *sophrosyne*[14] into a characteristic of the whole of antiquity. Pure form. Likewise due to writers.

Preference for antiquity as an abbreviation of the history of humanity, as though there were here an autochthonous product from which all that is becoming could be studied.

Actually, *one reason after another for this preference*[15] is gradually being *set aside* now, and if the philologists should happen not to notice this, we still notice it outside of their circles as strongly as possible. History has had an effect; and then linguistics has brought forth the greatest diversion, indeed retreat, among the philologists themselves. All they have now is the schools: yet for how long! In the form it has had *up until now*, philology is *dying out*: its ground has been pulled out from under it. Whether a *profession* of philologists will be maintained at all is very doubtful: in any case it would be a dying race.[16]

3[5]

Our *terminology* already shows how much we are inclined to measure the ancients wrongly; the exaggerated sense for *literature*, e.g., or how Wolf speaks of the "inner history of ancient erudition," he also calls it "the history of the *learned enlightenment*."[17]

3[6][18]

How much scorn for "humanistic" studies[19] is implied by the fact that they were also called *belles lettres* (*bellas litteras*)!

3[7]

Wolf's reasons for why we may not place Egyptians Hebrews Persians and other nations of the Orient on a single line with Greeks and Romans: the former raised themselves "not at all or only a few steps above the form of cultivation[20] that we should call *bourgeois policing* or *civilization*, in contrast to *genuine higher spiritual culture*."[21] He defines this immediately afterward as spiritual or *literary*[22] "in an auspiciously organized people, this can commence earlier than order and tranquility of the external life"[23] ("civilization"). Then he contrasts the farthest east of Asia ("similar to the sort of individuals who do not lack cleanliness, propriety and comfortableness in their residences clothes and all other surroundings, but never feel the need for higher enlightenment"[24]) to the Greeks ("with the Greeks, and also with the most cultivated Attic peoples, the opposite often occurred to an amazing extent and they neglected as insignificant what we generally, thanks to our love of order, tend to regard as the basis of spiritual refinement"[25]).

3[8][26]

"Toward the end of his life, there came over Markland, as so many[27] of those like him before, an aversion to all scholarly fame, to the extent that he in part scattered, in part burned a number of long-planned works."

3[9][28]

"In Winckelmann's youth, there was really no study of antiquity other than in the common service of bread-earning disciplines — one read and expounded upon the ancients at that time in order to prepare oneself better for the explication of the Bible and of the *corpus juris.*"[29]

3[10]

F. A. Wolf one time recalled[30] how frightful and feeble the first steps were that our forefathers made toward the formation of science, how even Latin classics had to be smuggled like suspicious wares, under pretexts, into the market of the universities; in the Göttingen lecture catalog for 1737 J. M. Gesner announces *Horatii Odas "ut in primis, quid prodesse* in severioribus[31] studiis *possint, ostendat.*"[32]

3[11][33]

Newton was astonished that men such as Bentley and Hare wasted their time on a book of comedies[34] (because both of them were theological dignitaries).

3[12]

It is so hard to empathize with anything at all from antiquity, we must be able to wait until we manage to hear something. The *humanness*[35] that antiquity shows us is not to be confused with *humaneness.*[36] This opposition must be very strongly emphasized, philology grows ill from wanting to impute humaneness; it is only because of this that we lead young people toward it, so that they become humane. I believe that in order to attain that, a lot of history is sufficient: brutal self-confidence is demolished when we see things and valuations changing so much. — The humanness of the Hellenes lies in a certain naïveté by which the human being shows himself among them, state, art, society, martial and international law, sexual intercourse, education, party: it is precisely humanness that shows itself everywhere, among all peoples, but with them in an unmaskedness and inhumanity that is indispensable for instruction. Moreover, they created the greatest number of individuals — in this are they so instructive concerning *human beings*; a Greek cook is more of a cook than another.

3[13][37]

Christianity overcame antiquity — yes, that is easily said. First, it is itself a piece of antiquity, second, it conserved antiquity, third, it is not at all in conflict with the pure ages of antiquity. Instead: so that Christianity could be preserved, it had to let itself be overcome by the spirit of antiquity, e.g., by the imperial idea, the community, etc. We suffer from the uncommon impurity and obscurity of *humanness*, from the witty *mendacity* that Christianity brought upon human beings.

3[14]

Greek antiquity as a whole has not yet been appraised; I am convinced that if it did not have this traditional radiance around it, contemporary humans would reject it with disgust: the radiance is therefore not genuine, of gold paper.

3[15]

A great advantage for a philologist is that his science has prepared so much in order to place it in the possession of heirs, if he *is capable* of this — especially to take up the *appraisal* of the whole Hellenic way of thinking. As long as one fiddled with details, it led to a *misunderstanding* of the Greeks; the *steps of this misunderstanding* can be labeled. (Sophists of the second century, the philologist-poets[38] of the Renaissance, the philologist as school-teacher of the upper classes) (Goethe-Schiller).[39]

3[16]

Imitation of antiquity: whether not finally a refuted principle?

Flight from reality to the ancients: whether the conception of antiquity is not thereby falsified?[40]

3[17]

One sort of observation is still in arrears: to *comprehend* how the greatest products of the spirit have a terrible and evil background; the *skeptical* observation: Hellenism to be examined as the most beautiful example of life.

Judging correctly is hard.[41]

3[18][42]

That we can attain cultivation *only* through antiquity is not true. But we *can* attain some of it from there. However, not the kind we now call cultivation. Our cultivation can construct itself only upon a completely castrated and mendacious study of antiquity.

In order to see now how ineffective this study is, just look at the philologists: for they must have been *educated the best by means of antiquity*.

2.

3[19]

How little reason rules among humans, how much chance does, is shown by the almost regular disparity between what we term[43] the calling in life and the disposition thereto:[44] the happy cases are exceptions, like the happy marriages, and even these are not brought about by reason. A human being *chooses* his vocation when he is not yet capable of choosing; he is not acquainted with the various vocations, he is not acquainted with himself; he passes his most active years, then, in this vocation, expends all of his reflection upon it, becomes more experienced; if he does reach the summit of his insight, it is generally then too late to begin something new, and wisdom on earth has almost always had something of elderly feebleness and a lack of muscular energy about it.

The task is most often that of once again making up for, more or less rectifying, what was lacking in talent; many will recognize that the later part of life displays an intentionality that has emerged from an original disharmony; living is hard. At the end of life, however, we are used to it — then we can err about our lives and praise our stupidities: *bene navigavi cum naufragium feci*,[45] and[46] even begin to sing a song of praise for "providence."[47]

3[20]

I ask now about the emergence of the philologist and assert:

1) the young person can hardly even know yet[48] who the Greeks and Romans are,

2) he does not know whether he is suited for research about them

3) and really not even to what extent he is suited to be a *teacher* with this knowledge. What determines him, therefore, is not insight into himself and his science, but instead

a) imitation,

b) convenience, in that he carries on what he pursued in school,

c) gradually the intent to earn his bread, too.

I believe, 99 out of 100 philologists *should* not be one.

3[21][49]

Stricter religions demand that humans understand their activity only as a means to a metaphysical plan: a miscarried choice of vocation, then, lets itself be accounted for as a test of the individual. Religions keep their eye only upon the salvation of the individual: whether he be slave or free man, tradesman or teacher, his life's goal does not lie in his vocation and therefore a false choice is no great misfortune. This may well serve to comfort the philologist; but {is} a denuded insight for the genuine philologists:[50] what becomes of a[51] science that is pursued by such a 99? This really unsuited majority puts the science in order and adjusts its demands to the capacities and inclinations of the majority: it thereby *tyrannizes* those who are really capable, that hundredth person. If it holds education in its hands, it *educates* them consciously or unconsciously according to its *own* pattern: what becomes then of the *classicness* of the Greeks and Romans![52]

To be proven

A) the disparity between philologists and the ancients.

B) the incapacity of the philologists to *educate* with the assistance of the ancients.

C) *the falsification of science due to the incapacity of the majorities, the false requirements, denial of the real goals of this science.*

3[22]

How does one come *most suitably* to this *appraisal*? — Not, in any case, if one is trained to be a philologist like now. It must be said to what extent the means here make the final purpose impossible. — Therefore the philologist himself is *not* the goal of philology. —

3[23]

Leopardi is the modern ideal of a philologist; the German philologists cannot *do* anything. (Voss is to be studied in this regard!)

3[24]

Vanity is the involuntary inclination to act as if one were an individual,[53] whereas one is not; that is, as independent, whereas one does depend. Wisdom is the reverse: it behaves as if dependent, whereas it is independent.

3[25]

A great value of antiquity lies in the fact that its *writings* are the only ones that modern humans still *read precisely*.

3[26]

Overstraining of *memory* — very common among philologists, lesser[54] development of judgment.

3[27]

In the education of the contemporary philologist, the influence of linguistics should be mentioned and judged; for a philologist, pretty much to be declined: the questions concerning the primal beginnings of the Greeks and Romans should not concern him at all: how we can also spoil our theme in this way.

3[28]

In the philologists I note:

1) lack of respect for antiquity,
2) flabbiness and fancy rhetoric, perhaps even apology,
3) simple historicizing,
4) conceit about themselves,
5) underestimation of the gifted philologists.

3[29]

Bergk's literary history,[55] not even a tiny spark of Greek fire and Greek sense.

3[30][56]

I am glad to read in Bentley:[57] "*non tam grande pretium emendatiunculis meis statuere soleo, ut singularem aliquam gratiam inde sperem aut exigam.*"[58]

3[31]

Horace is placed by Bentley before a judgment seat that he would have had to reject. The admiration[59] that a sharp-witted acute man harvests as a philologist stands in relation to the rarity of sharp-wittedness among philologists.[60] — How he proceeds with Horace has something schoolmasterly about it, only that it is not Horace himself who should be censored, but instead his transmitters; in truth and on the whole, however, it concerns Horace. It is now established for me that having written a single line that deserves to be commented upon by the scholars of a later time outweighs the merit of the greatest critic.[61] There is a deep modesty that lies in the philologist. Improving texts is an entertaining task for scholars, it is rebus-solving; but we should regard it as not a very important matter. A bad thing, if antiquity were to speak less clearly to us because a million words stood in the way!

3[32][62]

A schoolteacher said to Bentley: "Master, I will make your grandson into just as great a scholar as you are." "How so?" said Bentley. "When I have now forgotten more than you ever knew?"

3[33][63]

Bentley, says Wolf, as *litterator*,[64] just like as a human being, has been throughout the greatest part of his life misunderstood and persecuted, or rather, praised with malignity.

3[34]

Wolf calls it the flower of all historical research, raising oneself to the great and universal views of the whole and to the profoundly comprehended differentiation of the progress in art and in various styles.[65] But Wolf concedes that Winckelmann[66] lacked that more common talent, philological critique, or that it did not come into operation correctly: "a rare mixture of spiritual coldness and a petty, restless concern for a hundred things trivial in themselves, with an all-inspiriting, particularity-devouring fire and a talent for divination that is an annoyance to the uninitiated."[67]

3[35][68]

"Criticism often demonstrates its best expression of energy precisely there, where it points out reasons for what degree of conviction can be attained on both sides and why an expression or a passage is irreparable. It seems to us that doctors, with whom critics sometimes compare themselves, know quite similar triumphs in their art."

3[36]

Amid the often so deeply obtrusive *uncertainty* of *divination*,[69] a sickly *mania* asserts itself from time to time, to want at any price to *believe* and be *certain*: e.g., with regard to Aristotle or in detecting numerologies — with Lachmann[70] almost an illness.

3.

3[37][71]

It will no longer be surprising now that the cultivation of our time, with such teachers, is worth nothing. I will never shirk from making a portrayal of such uncultivation. And to be sure, precisely in relation to the things where we *must* learn from antiquity, if we even could (e.g., writing, speaking, etc.).

3[38]

Besides the great number of unqualified philologists, there now exists conversely a number of born philologists, who are hindered by some circumstances or others from becoming them. The most important hindrance, however, that deters these born philologists is bad representation of philology by the incompetent philologists.

3[39]

The untruthful enthusiasm for antiquity in which many philologists live. Actually, antiquity assails us when we are young with an abundance of trivialities, and we especially believe ourselves to be beyond ethics. And Homer and Walter Scott — who indeed attains the prize? If one is honest! If the enthusiasm were great, we would hardly seek our vocation in it. I mean: only *late* does it begin to dawn on us what we can have in the Greeks: only after we have experienced a lot, thought through a lot.

3[40]

Where does the effect of antiquity show itself? Not even in language, not in the imitation of anything, not even in a perversion like the French have displayed. Our museums fill themselves up; I always feel disgust when I see pure naked figures in the Greek style: toward the thoughtless philistinism that wants to devour everything.

3[41][72]

We actually[73] compare our time with the Periclean age in school programs, we congratulate ourselves on the reawakening of national feeling, and I recall a parody on the funeral oration of Pericles by G. Freitag, where this poet born with an erection portrays the happiness that 60-year-old men now feel. — All pure *caricature*! Thus the effect! Deep sorrow and scorn and seclusion remains for one who has *seen* more of it.

3[42]

They have forgotten how to speak to other human beings, and because they cannot speak to older people, they cannot speak to young ones either.

3[43]

They lack the real desire for the strong and energetic characteristics of antiquity. They become eulogists and thereby become ridiculous.

3[44][74]

Wolf says, "everywhere, there is truly mostly little that is gained for spiritual nourishment from well-digested scholarship."

3[45][75]

"Only the readiness to write according to the manner of the ancients, only our own productive talent enables us to understand completely foreign productions of the same kind and to comprehend therein more than certain subordinate virtues."

3[46][76]

Wolf calls our attention to the fact that antiquity knew only theories of oratory and poetry that made production easier, τέχναι and *artes*[77] that really shaped orators and poets; "while today we will soon have theories in accordance with which an oration or a poem can as little be made as a thunderstorm in accordance with a brontology."[78]

3[47][79]

"In the end, only those few are permitted to attain to genuine, complete connoisseurship who are born with artistic talent and equipped with learning, make use[80] of the best opportunities, acquire the necessary technical knowledge practically and theoretically." Wolf. True!

3[48]

The ancients are according to *Goethe* "the despair of emulators."[81]

Voltaire said: "if the admirers of Homer were sincere, they would admit the boredom that their darling so often causes them."[82]

4.

3[49]

If I say, the Greeks were *in summa*, however, *more moral* than modern humans: what does that mean? The entire visibility of the soul in action already shows that they were without shame; they had no bad conscience. They were more open, more passionate, like artists are; a sort of children's naïveté accompanies them, so that they have amid everything bad a streak of purity in them, something close to holiness. a remarkable amount of individuality, shouldn't a higher morality lie therein? If we think that their[83] character emerged slowly, what is it, though, that finally produced so much individuality? Perhaps *vanity* among one another, competition? Possible. Little desire for the conventional.

3[50]

Consider how differently a science propagates itself, how differently a special talent in a family. Physical propagation of an individual science is something quite rare. Do the sons of philologists become philologists easily? *Dubito.*[84] No accumulation of philological capabilities emerges in this way, as in Beethoven's family, perhaps, musical capabilities. Most begin from the beginning, and are facilitated, of course, by *books*, not by travels, etc. But education, to be sure.

3[51]

The *Hades shadows* of Homer — what sort of existence are they really painted from? I believe it is the description of the *philologist*; it is better to be a day-laborer[85] than such a lifeless[86] memory of what is past — great and small. (To sacrifice many sheep.)[87]

3[52]

The stance of the philologist toward antiquity is *apologetic* or even prompted by the intention of pointing out in antiquity what our time esteems highly. The correct starting point is the opposite one: namely, starting from the insight into modern perversity and looking backward — much that seems quite offensive in antiquity then appears as profound necessity.

We must make it clear to ourselves that *we* look completely *absurd* if we defend and embellish antiquity: what are we!

3[53]

Every religion has for its highest images an analogue in a state of the soul.[88] The God of *Mohammed* the solitude of the desert, far-off roaring of lions, the vision of a fearsome fighter. The God of *Christians* — everything that men and women think with the word "love."[89] The God of the *Greeks*: a beautiful dream-shape.

3[54]

Someone who has no sense for the *symbolic* has none for antiquity: this sentence to be applied to sober philologists.

3[55]

It is the affair of the *free man* to live for his own sake and not with regard to others. Therefore the Greeks held artisanal work to be unseemly.

3[56]

Not much can be attained with industriousness if the head is dull. Philologists who stumble upon Homer believe they could attain it. Antiquity speaks with us when it pleases, not when we do.

3[57]

The excellent daughter Joanna commiserated with Bentley for having expended so much time and talent on the critique of foreign works instead of his own independent compositions. "Bentley remained silent for a while, as if communing with himself; finally he said, her remark was quite right; he himself felt that he perhaps ought to have applied his natural talents differently: nonetheless, he had earlier done something for the honor of God and for the benefit of his fellow human beings (he means his *Confutation of Atheism*);[90] but afterwards, the genius of the ancient heathens attracted him, *and in despair of raising himself to their height by any other route*, he had climbed upon their shoulders in order to look over their heads in this way."[91]

3[58]

"The moderns are indebted above all to the Greeks that for those who always sought the beautiful behind the useful, not all knowledge was neatly packageable, that the better culture was not completely turned back into the service of civilization, that even various studies that had to remain unrecompensed as a sort of luxury were at least not forbidden to anybody who renounced the assistance of the state."[92]

3[59]

Noteworthy is Wolf's judgment about the connoisseurs of philological knowledge: "they found themselves equipped by nature with talents that were related to the spirit of the ancients or[93] were receptive to an easy displacement into foreign ways of thinking and situations of life, so they of course attained through such half-familiarity with the best writers more of the wealth of those energetic natures and great models in thought and action than most of those who offered themselves up to them for their whole lives as translators."[94]

5.

3[60]

Just as humans stand in relation to their vocations, skeptical-melancholic,[95] so should we position ourselves in relation to the highest vocation of a people: in order to *comprehend* what *life* is.

3[61]

My consolation holds good especially for tyrannized individuals, too — these may simply treat all those majorities as their assistants, and they may likewise put to use the prejudice that is still widespread in favor of classical[96] instruction; they need *many* workers. But they need to have unconditional *insight into their goals.*

3[62]

Philology as a science concerned with antiquity naturally has no eternal duration, its subject matter can be exhausted. Not to be exhausted is the ever-new accommodation of every age to antiquity, measuring oneself against it. If one sets the philologist the task of understanding *his* age better by means of antiquity, then his task is an eternal one. — This is the antimony of philology: we have actually always understood *antiquity* only *from out of the present* — and are now supposed to understand the *present from out of antiquity*? More precisely: we have explained antiquity from out of experience, and from the antiquity attained in this way we have *appraised*, depreciated experience. *Experience* is admittedly the unconditional prerequisite for a philologist — that means, however: first be a human being, only then will someone be fruitful as a philologist. From this it follows that older men are suited to be philologists, if in the time of their lives richest in experience they were *not* philologists.

But after all: only through knowledge of the present can we acquire *the drive toward classical*[97] antiquity. Without this knowledge — how then is the drive supposed to emerge there? If we look at how few philologists there are, apart from those who live off it, we can conclude how it basically stands with regard to this drive to antiquity, it *almost* does *not* exist; for there are no unselfish philologists.

So the *task* is to be posed thus: to conquer for philology its generally educational effect. *Means*: limitation of the philological class, doubtful whether to make young people acquainted with it. Critique of the philologist. The worth of antiquity: it is sinking with you: how deeply must you have sunk since it now has so little worth!

3[63][98]

Most humans clearly do *not* take themselves to be *individuals at all*; their lives demonstrate this. The Christian demand that *everyone* have his salvation and this *alone* in view has as its opposite general human life, where everyone lives only as a point between points, living not just wholly as the result of earlier generations, but also only with regard to coming ones. Only in three forms of existence does a human remain an individual: as philosopher, saint[99] and artist. Just look at the way in which a scientific human beats his life to death: what does the teaching of Greek particles have to do with the sense for life? — So we see here, too, how countless humans really only live as preparation for a real human being: e.g., philologists as preparation for the philosopher who understands how to make use of their labor of ants in order to make a statement about the *value of life*. Admittedly, if there is no *direction*, the *greatest part* of that labor of ants is simply *nonsense* and superfluous.

3[64]

Most humans are clearly in the world *accidentally*: no necessity of a higher form displays itself in them. They pursue this and that, their talent is mediocre. How strange! The way in which they live now shows that they think nothing of themselves, they expose themselves by throwing themselves into shabby activities (be it petty passions or the *quisquilia*[100] of their profession). In the so-called "vocations" that everyone is supposed to choose lies a touching *modesty* of humans: they say thereby, we are called to benefit and to serve those like us, and the neighbor likewise and his neighbor, too; and so everyone serves the other, none has as his calling being there for his own sake, but instead again and again for the sake of others; so we have a turtle that stands on top of another and this one again on top of another and so on. If everyone has his purpose in someone else, then *all* have *no purpose in themselves for existing*; and this "*existing for one another*" is the most comical of comedies.

3[65]

The happiest and most agreeable form of political-social circumstances is least to be found among the Greeks; that goal hovers before our dreamers of the future. Horrible! For we must judge it according to the measure: the more spirit, the more suffering (as the Greeks demonstrate). Therefore also: the more stupidity, the more agreeableness. The cultivated philistine is the most agreeable creature that has ever seen the light of day; he will have a fitting stupidity.

3[66]

It is a false conception to say: "there has always existed a caste that managed the cultivation of a people"; consequently *scholars* are necessary. For scholars have only the knowledge about cultivation (even this only in the best case). Doubtless there will also exist among us more cultivated humans, hardly a caste; but these can be *very few*.

3[67]

{Is} the preoccupation with bygone cultural epochs gratitude? In order to explain to ourselves present cultural conditions, we look backward: we will certainly not be too panegyrical toward our conditions, but perhaps we must be, in order not to be too *hard* against ourselves.

3[68]

My goal is: to generate complete enmity between our present-day "culture" and antiquity. Anyone who wants to serve the first must *hate* the latter.

3[69][101]

A very precise process of recollection leads to the insight that we are a multiplication of many pasts: how then could we also be the final purpose? — But why not? Most often, however, we don't want to be that at all, line ourselves up once again, work on a tiny corner of things and hope that it won't be completely lost for those to come. But that is really the tub of the Danaïds:[102] it does not help at all, we have to do everything again for ourselves and only for ourselves and, e.g., to measure science against ourselves with the question: what is science *to us*? But not: what are we to science? We really make life too easy for ourselves if we so simply take ourselves historically and put ourselves in its service. "Your own welfare matters more than anything," we should say to ourselves: and there is no institution that you should respect more highly than your own soul. — But now the human being is getting to know himself: he finds himself pitiable, despises himself, rejoices in finding something worth respecting besides himself. And so he throws himself away in that he aligns himself somewhere, strictly does his duty and atones for his existence. He knows that he does not work for his own sake; he will want to help those who dare to be there for their own sakes; like Socrates. Like a host of rubber balloons most humans hang in the air, every breath of wind agitates them. — **Consequence:** *the scholar must be one out of self-knowledge, therefore out of self-contempt: that is, he must know himself to be the servant of someone higher, who comes after him. Otherwise he is a sheep.*

3[70]

People believe it is over with philology — and I believe it has not yet begun.

The greatest events that philology has encountered[103] are the appearance of Goethe, Schopenhauer and Wagner: we can with them cast a glance that reaches further. The 5th and 6th centuries are now to be discovered.[104]

3[71]

I recommend cultivating Greek style in place of Latin, especially from Demosthenes: simplicity. Leopardi to be referred to, who is perhaps the greatest stylist of the century.

3[72][105]

"*Graiis — praeter laudem nullius avaris*"[106] says Horace. He calls their primary activity *nugari*[107] (*Ep.* II 93), characteristic for the Romans.

3[73]

Wolf "it is in any case a prejudice to believe that the history of world affairs becomes more credible to the degree[108] that it comes closer to our days."[109]

3[74]

Primary points of view with regard to the later worth of antiquity.

1) It is nothing for young people, for it displays humans with a freedom from shame.
2) It is nothing for direct imitation, but instructs as to the way in which up to now the highest cultivation of art has been attained.
3) It is only accessible for few and there should be a moral police, as there should be for bad pianists who play Beethoven.
4) These few measure our present against it, as critics of the former, and they measure antiquity against their ideal and are thus critics of antiquity.

5) The contrast between Hellenic and Roman and in turn between old Hellenic and late Hellenic to be studied. — Clarification of the various forms of culture.

3[75]

I want to say for once all that I no longer believe — also what I believe.

In the great whirlpool of energies stands the human being and imagines that that whirlpool is rational and has a rational purpose: error!

The sole rational thing that we know is the bit of reason of humans: they must strain it greatly and it always turns out to ruin them if they want to give themselves over, say, to "providence."

The sole happiness lies in reason, the whole world besides is *triste.*[110] But I see the highest reason in the work of the artist, and he can feel it as such; there may exist something that, if it could be brought forth with consciousness, would produce a still greater feeling of reason and happiness: e.g., the course of the solar system, the procreation and cultivation of a human being.

Happiness lies in the quickness of feeling and thought: all the rest of the world is slow, gradual[111] and stupid. Whoever could feel the flow of a ray of light would be very blessed, for it is very quick.

Thinking in itself gives little happiness: but if we have much happiness in this, it lies in the fact that we are not basically thinking of ourselves, but of our ideal. This is far away and only the quick one attains it and rejoices.

An association of a great center of humans for the procreation of better humans is the task of the future. The individual must become used to such demands so that, in affirming himself, he is affirming the will of that center, e.g., with regard to the choice that he makes among women, the way in which he raises his child. Up to now no individual, or only the rarest of them, was free; they were determined by such conceptions, too, but by bad and contradictory ones. Organization of the individual intentions.[112]

3[76]

If we look out toward the *Greeks* from the disposition and morality of the *Catholic Middle Ages*, they do admittedly shine in the splendor of a higher *humanity*: for everything for which we reproach them, we must to a much greater extent reproach the Middle Ages themselves. So reverence for the ancients in the Renaissance period is completely honorable and right. We have now gotten much further in some things, precisely on the basis of that awakening ray of light. We have overtaken the Greeks in the *elucidation* of the world, through natural and human history, and our knowledge is much greater, our judgments more moderate and more just. A milder humaneness is widespread, too, thanks to the age of Enlightenment, which has *weakened* human beings — but this weakness looks very good transformed into morality and does us honor. Humans now have a great deal of freedom, it is their affair that they have made so little use of it; the fanaticism of opinion is much moderated. That we finally prefer, however, to live in this rather than another time is essentially the service of science, and surely there has not been for any generation such a sum of noble joys as for ours — even if our generation does not exactly have the stomach and palate to be able to feel much joy. — Now we can live well amid all of this "freedom" only if we want simply to comprehend, not to take part — that is the modern catch. Those who take part seem less attractive than ever; how stupid they must be!

Thus emerges the danger that knowledge takes its revenge upon us, as not knowing[113] took its revenge on us during the Middle Age. With religions, which believe in gods, in providences, in rational orderings of the world, in miracles and sacraments, it is all over, and certain kinds of holy life, of asceticism are over with, because we readily[114] infer a damaged brain and sickness. There is no doubt, the opposition between a pure, incorporeal soul and a body has nearly been set aside. Who still[115] believes in an immortality of the soul! All things blessed and fateful, which consequently rested upon certain erroneous physiological assumptions, are untenable as soon as these assumptions are recognized as errors. What scientific assumptions are right now allows just as easily for interpretation and utilization as something stupefying-philistinistic, indeed, as something bestial, as for interpretation into something blessed and inspiring. Our foundation is new by comparison with all earlier ages, hence we can still experience something of the human species. — With *regard to culture* this means: up to now we were acquainted with only *one* perfect form, that is the civic culture of the Greeks, resting upon their mythical and social foundations, and *one* imperfect one, the Roman, as decoration of life, borrowing from the Greek one. Now all foundations have changed, mythical and political-social; our supposed culture has no durability, because it is built upon unsustainable, already almost vanished conditions and opinions. — Completely comprehending Greek culture, we therefore perceive that it is over. Thus the philologist is the *great skeptic* amid our conditions of cultivation and education: that is his mission. — Lucky if he, like Wagner and Schopenhauer, has a presentiment of the promising energies in which a new culture is stirring.

[4 = N I 3b. Spring 1875]

4[1]

To attend to:

Books to procure and exchange.
Historians, e.g., all of Ranke.
Geographers, e.g., Peschel Atlas[1]
Biographers, e.g., Cardanus.
Church authors in translation.
Bible in a recent translation.
Greek-Roman classics, e.g., Aristotle.
Schopenhauer.[2]
Natural science library.[3]

4[2][4]

To excerpt: *Die Bevölkerung der Alpen* {"The population of the Alps"} by Rütimeyer, in *Jahrbuch des Schweizer Alpenclubs*, first year of publication 1864.

Then: *Vom Meer bis nach den Alpen* {"From the sea to the Alps"}, by L. Rütimeyer, Bern 1854. Dalpsche Bookstore.

4[3]

Up to 1876.

Summer 1875. "Philology."
Autumn and until Christmas. Preliminary studies for "Wagner."
Summer 1875. Literary history.

Winter 1875–76. *Choephorae*[5] along with criticism and hermeneutic.
Summer 1876 — — —
Burckhardt's notebook to be finished.[6]

4[4]

Difficulty of the genesis of the artist.

1) The unnaïve element in education — limited concept of nature.[7]
2) Where should the artist classify himself? Music{:} a language that can only be understood {as} in hostility toward the rest of culture. Uneasiness of the artist in official positions.[8]
3) How does he protect himself against misunderstanding? When he writes, who is his audience?
4) He takes play seriously (Cervantes the chivalric novel, W⟨agner⟩ the theater),[9] the pathos seems wasted if it is not considered a waking call and symbol for equivalent energies.
5) He clings with more pleasure to existence than other humans.
6) A present-day artist must have *intentions*.[10]

4[5]

School of the Educator.

Where is
the doctor
the naturalist
the economist
the cultural historian
the expert in church history
the expert in the Greeks
the expert in the state.

[5 = U II 8b. Spring–Summer 1875]

5[1]

Starting from the beginning is always a delusion: even what drove us to this ostensible "beginning" is the effect and result of what preceded it. But such a strong and decisive break will be a sign of a strong and extreme advance at some time in the past. The radicalism of our opinions and our truth is the consequence of the radicalism of our errors and mistakes. The great law of *reaction* — therein lies all so-called "progress." The moral judgment must always be basically the same. But now understanding and experience are increasing, the moral quality is always only being converted. In the end, however, we esteem a doctrine according to its *effects*, e.g., whether it has killed or warped many people; that is not fair. —

5[2]

To construct antiquity in writing — a still completely unsolved task.

5[3]

The belief in individuality — whether we could think it away! In any case, we are facing times in which human opinions may become very uniform; but with this the individuals become more alike, yet ever more separate. Animosity then displays itself all the more sharply amid slight differences.

5[4][1]

We must juxtapose precisely against one another why the Greeks and philologists *must* scarcely understand one another: in so doing, the characterization of the Greeks is given as well.

5[5]

All religions, though, rest in the end upon certain physical assumptions, which are there *from before* and adapt themselves[2] to the religion. E.g., in Christianity the opposition of body and soul, the unconditional importance of the earth as the "world," miraculous occurrences in nature. If the opposite views someday become predominant, e.g., strict natural law, the helplessness and superfluousness of all gods, the narrowest conception of the spiritual as a bodily process — *then it is all over*. Now *the entire Greek tradition rests upon such views.*

5[6]

With Thucydides, the comfortable feeling with which we turn a key in a lock: gradually giving way with difficulty, but methodically and always closer to attaining its goal.

With Aristotle one sees the bare bones.[3]

5[7]

The tyrants of the spirit, too, were almost always murdered and have only sparse progeny.[4]

5[8]

Transmission of motion is inheritance: we should say that in connection with the effect of the Greeks upon[5] philologists.

5[9]

Yet how can we exalt and praise an entire people! It is the individuals, among the Greeks, too.

5[10]

There is a lot of *caricature* among the Greeks, too, e.g., the concern for one's own happiness among the Cynics.

5[11]

All that interests me is the relationship of the people to the education of the individual; and there is in any case among the Greeks something very favorable for the development of the individual, yet not out of the *goodness* of the people, but instead out of the struggle of evil drives.

Through fortunate discoveries, we can educate the great individual quite differently and more highly than he has up to now been educated through accidents. There lie my hopes: breeding of significant human beings.

5[12]

Greek history has up to now always been written optimistically.

5[13]

The wish to have anything at all certain in aesthetics misled {us} into the worship of Aristotle; I believe it can gradually be proven that he understands nothing about art and that it is only the clever conversations of the Athenians whose echo we admire so much in him.

5[14]

The Greeks are interesting and extravagantly important because they have such a crowd of great individuals. How was that possible? That must be studied.

5[15]

With the vanishing of Christianity a good part of antiquity has also become less comprehensible, especially the completely religious basis of life. For that reason alone, an imitation of antiquity is a false tendency; the philologists who are still thinking about this are deceivers or deceived. We live in the period when various conceptions of life stand beside one another: hence the age is so instructive, as any have rarely been, hence so sick, because it suffers at one and the same time from ills from every direction. Future human: the European human.

5[16]

Knowing history now means: to recognize how all humans who believe in providence have made it too easy on themselves. There is none. If human affairs go along in a wild and disorderly way, do not believe that a god is thereby aiming at something or that he is allowing it. We can almost perceive that the history of Christianity upon earth is one of the most terrible parts of history and that it *must* one day be over and done with. Admittedly, it was precisely in Christianity that antiquity also extended into our time; and if it fades, the understanding for antiquity will fade even more. Now is the best time to recognize it; no prejudice in favor of Christianity directs us anymore, but we do still understand it and in it antiquity, too, insofar as it stands in a single line.

5[17][6]

The decline of the philologist-poets lies in large part in their personal decay; their kind flourishes further later on, as e.g., Goethe and Leopardi[7] are such manifestations. The pure philologist-scholars plow along after them. The whole kind begins with the sophistry of the second century.

5[18]

At the exit from antiquity, there still stand completely unchristian figures that are more beautiful, more pure and more harmonious than all Christian ones, e.g., Proclus; his mysticism his syncretism are things for which precisely Christianity dare not reproach him. In any case, it would be my wish to live together with *them*. In relation to *them*, Christianity seems only to be arranged like the crudest coarsening for the multitudes and the wicked.

5[19][8]

All directions of history have tried themselves out in antiquity; the **critical** observation alone still remains. Only we must not understand that as conjectural and literary-historical critique.

5[20]

To bring the unreason in human things to light, without any *shamefulness* — that is the goal of *our brothers and comrades*. Then we will have to distinguish what in it is fundamental and unimprovable, what can still be improved.[9] But every "providence" is to be kept at a distance: for that is a concept whereby we make things too easy for ourselves. I wish for the breath of *this* intention to infuse science. To advance the *knowledge of human beings*! What is good and rational in the human being is accidental or apparent or the reverse of something very irrational. Someday there will be no thought at all except for *education*.

5[21]

Resignation to *necessity* is not what I teach — for we would first have to know it as necessary. Perhaps there exist multiple necessities; but even so it is still in general a lazy person's bed.

5[22]

Signs and *miracles* are not believed; only a "providence" needs something like that. There is no help, not in prayer, nor in asceticism, nor in visions. If all of this is religion, then there is no religion anymore for me.

My religion, if I am still permitted to call anything by that name, lies in working for the begetting of genius; education is everything to be hoped for, everything comforting is called art. *Education* is *love of what has been begotten*, an excess of love over and above self-love. Religion is *"loving over and above ourselves." The work of art is the image of such a love over and above oneself and a perfect one.*

5[23]

The stupidity of the will is Schopenhauer's greatest idea, if we judge ideas according to their power. We can see in Hartmann, how he immediately conjures this idea away again. Nobody would call something stupid God.

5[24]

That is therefore what is new in all of the world's future affairs: we are no longer permitted to *dominate* humans with religious representations. Will they then show themselves to be *worse*? I do not find that they behave well and morally under the yoke of religions; I do not stand on the side of Demopheles.[10] The fear of the beyond and then the religious fear of divine punishment in general will hardly have made humans better.

5[25]

Where something great appears with somewhat longer duration, there we can perceive that there has previously been a careful breeding, e.g., with the Greeks. How did so many humans among them attain freedom?

To educate educators! But the first ones must educate themselves! And for these, I write.

5[26]

The denial of life is no longer so easy to attain: one could be a hermit or a monk — what is denied there! This concept is now becoming more profound: it is above all *a knowing denial, a denial wanting to be just, no longer of a single piece.*

Anyone who would want to be good and holy today would have it harder: he would not be permitted, in order to be good, to be as *unjust* against *knowledge* as the early saints were. He would have to be a knower-saint: binding together love and wisdom; and he could no longer dare to have anything to do with a belief in gods or demi-gods or providences; as Indian saints likewise had nothing to do with that. He would have to be healthy, too, and to keep himself healthy; otherwise he would have to become mistrustful toward himself. And perhaps he would look not at all like an ascetic saint, perhaps even a man of the world.

5[27][11]

All the ways of dealing with history have already been tried upon antiquity. Above all, however, we have experienced enough now in order to make use of the history of antiquity — without coming to ruin upon antiquity.

5[28]

The German Reformation distanced us from antiquity: did it have to do that? It uncovered anew the old contradiction "heathenism, Christianity"; it was at the same time a protest against the *decorative culture* of the Renaissance; it was a triumph over the same culture that had been defeated with the beginning of Christianity.

5[29]

With regard to "worldly things," Christianity has conserved precisely the cruder views of the ancients. Everything nobler in marriage, slavery, the state is unchristian. It *needed* the distorted traits of worldliness in order to prove *itself*.

5[30]

I dream of a fellowship of humans who are unconditional, know no consideration, and want to be called "annihilators": they hold up to everything the measuring stick of their critique and sacrifice themselves to the truth. What is bad and false should be brought to light! We do not want to build prematurely, we do not know whether we can ever build and whether it is not the best thing not to build. There are lazy pessimists, resigners — we do not want to belong to them.

5[31][12]

Oddly important position of philologists: an entire class to which the youth are entrusted and which has to do research on a special antiquity. Clearly we place the highest worth upon antiquity. But if we have falsely appraised antiquity, the foundation for the exalted position of philologists would suddenly be lacking. In any case we have appraised antiquity quite *variously*: and each time adjusted the assessment of philologists accordingly. This professional class has drawn its strength from strong prejudices in favor of antiquity. — This is to be depicted. — It now feels that if these prejudices were finally to be fundamentally contradicted and antiquity were to be purely portrayed, that favorable prejudice for philologists would immediately vanish. *It is therefore a professional class interest not to allow purer insights about antiquity to arise: especially the insight that antiquity makes {us} unfashionable in the deepest sense.*

It is, second, a professional class interest of the philologists to allow no higher view about the teaching profession to arise than the one that they can match.

5[32][13]

Hopefully there exist some who feel it as a problem, why it is precisely the philologists who are supposed to be the educators of the nobler youth. Perhaps it will not always be so. — In itself, it would really be much more natural that we instruct the youth in geographical natural-scientific national-economic social principles, that we gradually lead them to observation of life, and finally, late, bring in the most noteworthy pasts. So that *knowledge of antiquity* would belong to the last things that someone acquired; is *this position* of *antiquity* in education the more *honorable* one for antiquity, or the usual one? — It is used now as propaedeutic for thinking, speaking and writing; *there was a time when it was the essence of worldly knowledge and when one wanted to attain by learning it precisely what we would now attain through that just described plan of study (which has been transformed precisely according to the advanced knowledge of the age).* Hence the inner *intention* in philological teacherdom has been completely changed, once this was the *material* instruction, *now only the formal one.* —

5[33]

The connection of *humanism* and *religious rationalism* is well emphasized by Köchly[14] as Saxon: the prototype of this philologist is *G. Hermann.*

5[34][15]

Is it true that the philologist, insofar as he makes use of antiquity for the sake of *formal cultivation*, is himself *formally cultivated*?

But what an opposition! formal and material! Here is material knowledge, facts. Formal the way in which we think speak write, therefore *how* we obtain knowledge and spread it.

5[35]

If the task of the philologist were *to educate formally*, he would have to teach how to walk, dance, speak, sing, behave, converse: and that is approximately what one learned with the formal educators of the second and third centuries. But in this way we are always thinking only of the education of the *scientific human being* and there "formal" means: to think and to write, scarcely to speak.

5[36][16]

Selected points from antiquity: e.g., power fire verve in ancient musical feeling (through the first Pythian Ode),[17] purity of historical feeling and gratitude for the blessings of culture, fire festivals, harvest festivals. The ennobling of jealousy, the Greeks the most jealous people. Suicide, hatred toward old age, e.g., toward poverty. Empedocles upon sexual love.

5[37][18]

I *lament* an *education* in which understanding Wagner has not been attained, in which Schopenhauer sounds raw and unharmonious; this education has failed.

5[38]

There is an old struggle of the Germans against antiquity, i.e., against ancient culture: it is certain that in this precisely what is best and most profound in the Germans is resisting. But the main point, however, is this: that resisting is right only if we mean Romanized culture: but this is already the falling off from a deeper and nobler one. The German wrongly resists the latter.

5[39]

I see in philologists an *association conspiring to educate youth about ancient culture*; I would understand it if we criticized this association and its intentions from all sides. It would matter a lot, then, to know what these philologists *understand* ancient culture to be. — If I saw, e.g., that they were educating against German philosophy and music, I would oppose *them* or even oppose *ancient culture*, the first perhaps by showing that the philologists have not understood ancient culture. Now I see 1) great change in the appraisal of ancient culture among the philologists 2) something profoundly un-ancient in them themselves, unfree 3) unclarity as to *which* ancient culture they mean 4) in the means, much that is perverse, e.g., scholarliness 5) amalgamation with Christianity.

5[40]

Healthier, more agile bodies, a purer and deeper sense in observation of the very nearest things, free masculinity, belief in good race and good education, martial proficiency, jealousy in ἀριστεύειν,[19] pleasure in the arts, respect for free idleness, a sense for free individuals, for the symbolic.

5[41][20]

A colloquium on "System of Culture."

1. The finally clearly recognized goal of culture.
2. History of goals and their errors.
3. Means of culture.

5[42]

Plans for life.

Unfashionable Observations. For my thirties.
The Greeks. For my forties.
Addresses to Humanity. For my fifties.

5[43]

If the *Gymnasium*[21] is supposed to prepare students to do science, then now we say: no preparation for any science can exist anymore, so comprehensive have the sciences become. In consequence, we must prepare generally, i.e., for all sciences, i.e., for *scientific characterization* — and classical studies *serve* for that! — Strange leap! A very desperate justification! What now exists is supposed to be right, even after it has clearly been seen that the previous right upon which it rested has become not right.

5[44]

With regard to the simplicity of antiquity, it is like the simplicity of style; it is the highest thing that we recognize and have to imitate, but also the ultimate one. Consider that the classical prose of the Greeks is a late result, too.

5[45][22]

The foundation upon which the general esteem for antiquity still rests consists of prejudices: if these are done away with, the esteem might be transformed into a fundamental hatred. Now, do the philologists also shelter these prejudices? But then they do not know antiquity. If they do not shelter them — how does it stand then with their honesty! Where is it shown, however, that they intentionally destroyed them?

5[46][23]

Do philologists know the present? Their judgments about it as Periclean, their errors of judgment when they speak of Freitag's spirit as of one congenial to Homer etc., their chasing after while the literati run on ahead. Their renunciation of the heathen sensibility, which Goethe was precisely the one to have uncovered in Winckelmann as the antique.

5[47]

Our *position toward classical antiquity is basically the deep cause of the unproductivity of modern culture*: for we have this entire modern concept of culture from the Hellenized Romans. We must *make a separation* in antiquity itself: in learning to know its sole productive age, we also *condemn* the entire Alexandrian-Roman culture. But *likewise we condemn at the same time our own entire position toward antiquity and our philology*!

5[48]

There is a way of occupying oneself philologically and it is frequent: we throw ourselves or are thrown senselessly upon any region at all: from there we seek to the right and to the left, find many a good and new thing — but in an unguarded hour we nonetheless say to ourselves: what the devil exactly does all of that matter to me? Meanwhile we have grown old, have habituated ourselves and continue on, just as in marriage.[24]

5[49]

On the whole, contemporary philology has lost its guiding thread: those who directed it previously are denied; but on the whole, the whole effect and appraisal still rest upon the fame of that earlier guidance, e.g., that of humanitarianism.

5[50]

There are things about which antiquity instructs, on which I would not like to express myself lightly in public.

5[51]

It is almost ridiculous to see how almost all the sciences and arts in the modern age are once again growing from seeds that were blown this way out of antiquity, and how Christianity here seems only like a bad frost from a long night, in which we are supposed to believe that it is over forever with reason and the honesty of humans. The struggle against the natural human being has made the unnatural human being.[25]

5[52]

How we make young people acquainted with the ancients has something contrary to respect: even worse, it is unpedagogical; for what is the point of being acquainted with things that a young person cannot possibly consciously admire! Perhaps he is supposed to learn to *believe*; and therefore I do not wish it.

5[53]

Those who say: "but antiquity nonetheless still always remains as an object of pure science, even if all of its educational intentions are denied," are to be answered: what is pure science here! Actions and qualities are to be *judged*, and the one judging must stand above them: therefore, you should first take care *to overcome antiquity*. Before you do that, your science is not pure, but instead impure and confined: as can be perceived.

5[54][26]

How it stands with the philologists is shown by their indifference at the appearance of Wagner. They could have learned more than via Goethe — and they have yet to cast a glance that way. That shows: they are directed by no strong need: otherwise they would have a feeling for where their nourishment is to be found.

5[55]

Plan for Chapter 1.

Philology of all sciences up to now[27] the most favored: the greatest number, for centuries, promoted among all peoples, the guardianship of the nobler youth and therewith the most beautiful occasion for propagating itself and awakening *respect* for itself. How has it attained this power?

Enumerating the various prejudices in its favor.

How then, if these were recognized as prejudices? — Would philology indeed still remain if we made allowance for the interest of a class, of a way of earning bread? If we were to say the truth about antiquity and its fitness for educating the present?

Chap. 2.

In order to answer this, look at the education for becoming a philologist, his genesis: he does not emerge at all anymore, if that interest ceases to exist.

Chap. 3

If our public world were to find out what an unfashionable thing antiquity really is, philologists would no longer be appointed as educators.

Chap. 4

Only the alliance between the philologists who neither *want* nor *are able to* understand antiquity and public opinion, which is directed by prejudices about it, still gives to philology its strength.

Chap. 5

The future philologist as skeptic about our entire culture and thereby also as annihilator of the class of philologists.

5[56][28]

Would philology still exist as a science if its servants were not educators with salaries? In Italy such ones did exist. Who puts a German beside, e.g., Leopardi?

5[57][29]

Effect on nonphilologists exactly null. If they were to become imperative and contradictory, oh how they would be persecuted! But they humble themselves.

The Greeks really and their diminution by the philologists.

5[58][30]

All of history up to now has been written from the standpoint of success, and indeed, with the assumption of rationality in the success. Even Greek history: we do not yet possess any. But so it stands in general: where are historians who regard things without being dominated by general tricks? I see only one — Burckhardt. Everywhere broad optimism in science. The question: "what would have happened if this and this had not occurred" is refused almost unanimously, and yet it is precisely the cardinal question whereby everything becomes an ironic thing. Just look at our lives. If we look for a plan in history, we are looking for it in the intentions of a mighty human being, perhaps in those of a family, a party. Everything else is a muddle. — In natural science, too, there is this idolization of *what is necessary*. —

Germany has become the breeding ground for historical optimism: for that, Hegel may be partly to blame. But nothing has made German culture work more disastrously. Everything repressed by success is gradually rebelling; history as the scorn of the victor; a servile way of thinking and submissiveness to the fact — "sense for the state" we now call it: as if it still needed to be implanted![31] Anyone who does not grasp how brutal and senseless history is will also not understand at all the inducement to make history meaningful. Look at how rare is a meaningful knowledge of one's own life such as Goethe's: what kind of rational thing is now supposed to occur out of all these veiled and blind existences when they are working chaotically with and against one another.

It is especially naïve, then, if Hellwald, the author of a cultural history, waves aside all "ideals" because history has always laid them aside one after another.[32]

5[59][33]

Greeks and Philologists.

The[34] Greeks do homage to beauty	Philologists are babblers and triflers.
they develop the body	ugly enclosure.[35]
they speak well	stutterers.
religious transfigurers of the everyday	dirty pedants.
listeners and observers	hair-splitters and night owls.
for the symbolic	incapacity for the symbolic
free masculinity	fervently slaves of the state
clear view of the world	confused Christians
pessimists of thought	philistines

5[60][36]

It is true, humanism and the Enlightenment have led antiquity into the field as their ally: and so it is natural that the opponents of humanism are hostile toward antiquity. Only the antiquity of humanism was a badly known and completely falsified one:[37] seen more clearly, it is proof *against* humanism, against a fundamentally good human nature, etc. The opponents of humanism are in error if they oppose antiquity along with it: they have there a strong ally.

5[61][38]

I understand religions as *narcotics*: but if they are given to peoples such as the Germanic tribesmen, they are pure *poisons*.

5[62][39]

What condition did only the Greeks take as the model for their life in Hades? Bloodless, dreamlike, weak: it is the repeated intensification of *old age*: where memory dwindles further and the body even more. The old age of old age — so do we live in the eyes of the Hellenes.

5[63]

How *realistic* the Greeks were even in pure inventions, how they composed poetry upon the basis of reality, did not yearn to be beyond it.

5[64]

Education is first of all instruction about *what is necessary*, then about *what changes and what varies*. We lead the youth into nature, show him everywhere the rule of laws; then the laws of civil society: already here the question is set in motion: *must* it be this way? Gradually he has need of history in order to hear how that has come to be as it is. But with that, he is learning that it can also be otherwise. How much power over things does the human being have? this is the question in all education. Now, in order to show how completely different it can be, we might point, e.g., to the Greeks. We need the Romans in order to show how it *became* as it was.

5[65][40]

The Greeks as the only *people of genius* in world history; even as learners[41] this is what they are, they understand this the best and do not know merely how[42] to decorate and to adorn with borrowed things: as the Romans do.

The constitution of the polis is a Phoenician invention: even this the Hellenes copied. For a long time, they learned like joyful dilettantes from everything all around; just as Aphrodite is Phoenician, too. Nor do they deny at all what had immigrated and was not-original.

5[66][43]

The Egyptians are *much more* a *literary* people than the Greeks. This against Wolf.[44]

5[67][45]

The first grain in Eleusis, the first grapevine in Thebes, the first olive tree, fig tree.

5[68][46]

Egyptians had essentially lost their mythology.

5[69][47]

The *embodied appearance* of gods, as in Sappho's invocation to Aphrodite,[48] is *not* to be understood as poetic license, it is frequently hallucinations. Much, like the *wish to die*, too, we comprehend superficially, as rhetorical.

5[70]

Greeks the *genius* among peoples.[49]

Childish nature. Credulous.[50]

Passionate. They are living unconsciously the procreation of genius. Enemies of constraint and dullness. Pain. Imprudent behavior. Their form of intuitive insight into misery, along with a golden genial-joyous temperament.[51] Thoughtfulness in comprehending and exalting what is nearest at hand (fire agriculture). Mendacious. Unhistorical. The cultural significance of the polis instinctively recognized; center and periphery favorable for great human beings. (The surveillability of a civic community, also the possibility of addressing it as a whole.)[52] The individual intensified to its highest energy by the polis.[53] Envy, jealousy as with ingenious people.

5[71][54]

The relaxation of the Spartans consisted of festivals, hunting and war: their everyday life was too hard. On the whole, however, their state is a caricature of the polis and a corruption of Hellas.

The production of the perfect Spartan — but what kind of great thing is he, that producing him required such a brutal state!

5[72]

Greek culture rested upon the relationship by which a class few in numbers held mastery over 4–5 times as many unfree people.[55] *Proportionately*, Greece was a land inhabited by barbarians. How can we even find the ancients to be *humane*! Opposition of genius to the wage-earner, part draft-animal[56] and part beast-of-burden. The Greeks believed in a difference of race: Schopenhauer is surprised that nature did not choose to invent two separate species.[57]

5[73]

The barbarian is related to the Greek like "what mobile or indeed winged animals are to mussels cemented to a rock that have to wait for anything chance might bring their way."[58] Schopenhauerian image.

5[74]

"The basic feature of the genius is always to see the universal in the particular"[59] Schopenhauer. Think of Pindar, of the Προμηθεῖα,[60] etc. "Clarity of mind,"[61] according to Schopenhauer, has its roots chiefly in the *distinctness* with which the Greeks perceive the world and themselves and thereby come to consciousness of these things.

5[75]

The "increasing separation of the will and the intellect"[62] describes geniuses, and also the Greeks.

5[76]

"The *melancholy* accompanying genius is due to the fact *that the will to life perceives the misery of its condition* more clearly, *the brighter the intellect it finds itself illuminated by.*"[63] Schopenhauer. Cf. the Greeks!

5[77]

How the Romans in their dry seriousness contrast against the ingenious Greeks! Schopenhauer: "the solid and practical attitude of taking life seriously called *gravitas* by the Romans presupposes that the intellect does *not* leave the service of the will to launch forth toward things of no concern to the will."[64]

5[78]

The *moderation* of the Greeks in their physical consumption, eating and drinking and their pleasure in these things: the Olympic games and their worship — that shows what they were.

5[79]

With the genius, "his intellect will exhibit the same errors to which every instrument tends when used in a manner for which it was not constructed."[65] "It very often leaves its will in the lurch at the wrong moment: so the genius is more or less useless for life and in fact in his behavior is sometimes reminiscent of madness."[66]

5[80]

"If the full brunt of that abnormally heightened cognitive power is suddenly directed to the affairs and miseries of the will — it will magnify everything in too vivid a manner, in colors that are too harsh, a light that is too bright, to a hideous extent; then the individual is driven into extremes."[67]

5[81]

The Greeks lack sobriety. Excessive sensibility, abnormally heightened neural and cerebral life, vehemence and passion of willing.[68]

5[82]

The happiest lot that can fall to the genius is a release from ordinary hustle and bustle with plenty of leisure:[69] and thus did the Greeks know to appreciate things. A blessing upon work! *nugari*[70] is what the Romans called all the struggling and striving of the Hellenes.[71]

The course of his life is not a happy one, he stands in contradiction and conflict with his age. Thus the Greeks: they strove tremendously, instinctively to provide themselves with a secure shell (in the polis). Finally everything in politics went to ruin. They were forced to stand firm against the outside: that became ever more difficult, finally impossible.

5[83][72]

By changing a single word of Bacon of Verulam[73] we can say: *infimarum Graecorum virtutum, apud philologos, laus est, mediarum admiratio, supremarum sensus nullus.*[74]

5[84][75]

The *childlike character* of the Greeks was sensed by the Egyptians.

5[85]

The *intensification* of *what exists now* into something *colossal and eternal*, e.g., in Pindar.

5[86]

The unmathematical swaying of the column in Paestum,[76] e.g., is an analogue for the modification of tempo: animation instead of being moved like a machine.

5[87]

It is the work of all education to transform conscious activities into more or less unconscious ones: and the history of humanity is in this sense its education. Now the philologist exercises a multitude of activities unconsciously in this way: I want to investigate for once how his energy, i.e., his instinctive action, is the result of once conscious activities, which he gradually hardly feels as such any longer: but *that consciousness consisted of prejudices. His present* energy depends *upon those prejudices*, e.g., the esteeming of the *ratio*,[77] as in Bentley, Hermann. Prejudices are, as Lichtenberg says,[78] the *aesthetic drives of humans.*

5[88]

Skills are what we expect from occupying oneself with the ancients: formerly, e.g., being able to write and to speak. But what do we expect now! — to think and to infer: but we do not learn this *from* the ancients, but at most *at* the ancients, by means of science. Besides, however, all historical inference is very limited and uncertain: we should prefer the natural scientific kind.

5[89]

Proclus, who worships the rising moon in a festive way.

5[90]

The inherited training of the contemporary philologist: a certain infertility of the basic insights has resulted; for they promote the science, but not the philologists.

5[91]

The political defeat of Greece is the greatest failure of culture: for it has brought forth the horrible theory that we can only take care of culture if we are at the same time armed to the teeth and provided with boxing gloves. The rise of Christianity was the second great failure: raw power there, stupid intellect here triumphed over the aristocratic genius among peoples. To be a philhellene means to be an enemy of raw power and stupid intellect. To that extent Sparta was the ruin of Hellas, insofar as it forced Athens to work federally and to throw itself completely into politics.

5[92]

On the whole, what stands as certain is the *increase* in the *military strength of humanity*. The triumph of the *stronger* nation: gradually it is not only the measuring stick of corporeal, but even more so of *spiritual being-stronger*.

5[93]

In *Socrates* we have a *process of consciousness lying* open before us, as it were, from which the *instincts of the theoretical human* later emerged. That someone prefers to die rather than become old and weak in spirit.[79]

5[94]

With Christianity, a religion that corresponded to a pre-Grecian condition of humans attained predominance: belief in miraculous occurrences anywhere and everywhere, bloody sacrifices, superstitious fear of daemonic punishments, despair about oneself, ecstatic brooding and hallucinating, human beings themselves having become a playground of good and evil spirits and their battles.

5[95]

It would have been much *more fortunate* if the *Persians* rather than precisely the *Romans* had become masters of the Greeks.

5[96]

The magnificent sense for *order* and organization has made the state of the Athenians immortal. — The ten generals in Athens![80] fantastic! far too much of a sacrifice upon the altar of jealousy.

5[97]

Statute of the Society of the Unfashionables.

Everyone has to submit four times a year a written report about his activity.

O. R. G. B. N.[81]

5[98]

For the introduction to a collected edition of the "Unfashionables."

Sketch their emergence: my desperation because of Bayreuth, I see nothing anymore that I do not know to be full of fault, I discover upon deeper reflection that I have come upon the most fundamental problem of all culture. Sometimes I lack any desire to live on. But then again I say to myself: if ever life should be lived, then now. — I actually held Strauss to be too insignificant for me: I did not want to do battle with him. A few words of Wagner's in Strasbourg.

5[99]

Now, if the Romans had disdained Greek culture: it would perhaps have gone radically to ruin. What would have awakened it again? Christianity and Romans and barbarians — that would have been an assault. Completely effaced. We see the danger under which genius lives. Cicero is thus already one of the greatest benefactors of humanity. — There is no providence for the genius: only for ordinary human beings *en masse* and their distresses does such a thing exist; they find their satisfaction, later their justification.

5[100][82]

Out of reciprocal deadly enmity grow the Greek πόλις[83] and the αἰὲν ἀριστεύειν.[84] Hellenic and philanthropic were opposites, although the ancients flattered themselves sufficiently.

5[101]

Homer, in the world of Hellenic discord, the Panhellenic Greek.

The contest of the Greeks is also displayed in the *symposion*,[85] in the form of spirited dialogue.

5[102]

The genius makes all half-gifted people tributary: thus even the Persians sent their embassies to the Greek oracles.

5[103][86]

Much spirit belongs to a Greek polytheism; admittedly we treat spirit more frugally if we have only a single ⟨god⟩.[87]

5[104][88]

Morality does not rest upon religion, but instead upon the πόλις.

There were only priests for individual gods, not representatives for the entire religion: therefore no class. Likewise no sacred document.

5[105][89]

The "easy-living gods" is the highest embellishment that has been allotted to the world; in the feeling of how hard it is to live.[90]

5[106][91]

Have there been *many gifted philologists*? I doubt it; for reason breaks a path too slowly with them (counting manuscripts, etc.) — Word- and object-philology[92] — stupid conflict! — and then the exaggerated esteem for any sort of clever man among them!

5[107]

What he deemed humanistic was energetically cultivated by Charlemagne, whereas he proceeded against what he deemed barbaric with the harshest coercive measures. Ancient mythology was diffused, the German treated like a crime. I believe that at bottom here lay the feeling that Christianity had already dispensed with ancient religion: one did not fear it, but made use of the culture of antiquity resting upon it. One did fear the German world of gods. — A great *superficiality* in the conception of antiquity, practically just the esteem for its formal completeness and its knowledge *had to be* implanted here. Forces can be named that stood in the way of a deepening of the insight into antiquity. First of all 1) antique culture is used as *a means of attraction for the adoption of Christianity*: it is, as it were, the earnest money for conversion. The sweetener for the sipping of that poison. Then one requires the remedy of ancient culture, 2) as a *weapon* for the spiritual defense of Christianity. Even the Reformation could not do without classical studies in this sense. Now, in contrast, the Renaissance begins classical studies with a *purer* sense, but also one thoroughly inimical to Christians; it shows an awakening of *honesty* in the south, like the Reformation in the north. Admittedly, they could not abide each other, for a serious inclination toward antiquity makes one unchristian. The Church was on the whole *successful* in giving classical studies an *innocuous* turn: *the philologist was invented*, as scholar, who is moreover a priest or some such thing: and even in the realm of the Reformation it succeeded likewise in castrating the scholar. Hence Friedrich August Wolf is remarkable, because he *freed* the class from the discipline of theology: but his action was not fully understood, for an aggressive, active element, as adhered to the poet-philologists of the Renaissance, was not developed. The liberation benefited science, not human beings.

5[108][93]

The *unpopulist element* of the new Renaissance culture! A frightful fact!

5[109]

What is antiquity still *at present*, as against modern art and science and philosophy? No longer the treasure house of all knowledge, in knowledge of nature and history it has been overcome. The suppression by the Church has been broken. A *purer* knowledge of antiquity is now possible, but also, to be sure, a *less effective*, weaker one? — That is correct: if we know the effect only as *mass effect*; but for the production of the greatest spirits antiquity is stronger *than ever*. Goethe as *German poet-philologist*;[94] *Wagner* as a still higher stage: clear sight for the only worthy position of art; never has an ancient work had such a powerful effect as the *Oresteia* upon Wagner.[95] The *objective-castrated philologist*, who in other respects is a cultivated philistine and an opponent of culture, and works at pure science on the side, is admittedly a melancholy figure.

5[110]

Bentley was likewise *defensor fidei*;[96,97] and Scaliger was at the same time an enemy of the Jesuits and very much attacked.

5[111][98]

There is no contradiction between *our* highest art and philosophy and the *truly* apprehended **older** antiquity: they support and sustain one another. Here lie my hopes.

5[112]

There exist areas where *ratio* will produce only nonsense, and the philologist who has nothing more than this is thereby lost and can never see the truth, e.g., when observing[99] Greek mythology. Naturally a visionary has no claim either: we must have Greek imagination and something of Greek piety. Even the poet does not need to be consistent in himself: in general, consistency is the last thing for which the Greeks would understand themselves.

5[113]

Almost all the Greek divinities are assembled ones, one layer on top of others, sometimes misshapen, sometimes cemented in a makeshift way. To scientifically pick one thing from another out of this seems to me hardly possible: for there can be no good method for doing so: the miserable conclusion of the analogy is already a very good conclusion here.

5[114]

How far away from the Greeks must one be in order to attribute to them such a narrow-minded autochthony as O. Müller does! How Christian, with Welcker[100] to take the Greeks for the original monotheists! How philologists exercise themselves with the question as to whether Homer wrote,[101] without grasping the much higher principle that Greek art had a long, inner enmity toward writing and did not want to be read.

5[115][102]

The Greeks were horribly plagued by the desire to fabricate fables.[103] Even in everyday life it was hard to keep them away from the "mythical," from swindling: as every poetic people takes this sort of pleasure in lying, along with their innocence in doing it. The neighboring peoples no doubt found that maddening.

5[116]

To live upon mountains, to travel a great deal, to leave a place quickly — therein we can now equate ourselves with the Greek gods. We also know what is past and almost what is to come. What would a Greek say if he were to see us? —

5[117][104]

The gods make a human being even *worse*; such is human nature. When we do not like someone, we wish for him to become worse and then we rejoice. This is part of the gloomy philosophy of hatred, which has not yet been written because it is everywhere the *pudendum*[105] that everyone feels.

5[118][106]

The Panhellene Homer took pleasure in the frivolity of the gods; but it is astonishing how he can then attribute dignity to them again. This tremendous soaring, however, is Greek.

5[119]

Thucydides on the *state*.[107]

The *tyrannical* element is well nourished in every aristocrat: that betrays itself in prayers (Xenophon, Socrates).[108] They held one another within limits: the people in turn held all of them together within limits, as much as possible.

5[120][109]

Where, then, does *envy of the gods* originate? one does not believe in any calm, peaceful happiness, but instead only in an arrogant one. The Greeks must have been dispirited, their soul was all too easily wounded: it embittered them to see a happy person. That is *Greek*. Wherever there was a distinguished talent, the throng of jealous people may have been exceptionally large: if he encountered misfortune, they said, "aha! he was too arrogant." And everyone would have behaved the same if they had had the talent, arrogantly; and everyone would gladly have played for a bit the god who sends misfortune.

5[121]

The Greek gods required no alteration of the senses and were in general not so annoying and importunate: thus it was also possible to take them seriously and to believe. In Homer's times, moreover, the Greek essence was complete: a frivolity of images and of the imagination is necessary in order to somewhat soothe and to liberate their excessively passionate disposition. When their understanding speaks, oh how bitter and cruel life seems! They do not deceive themselves. But they playfully surround life with lies: Simonides advised taking life like a game: they were all too familiar with seriousness as a source of pain. The misery of humans is a pleasure to the gods, when it is sung to them. The Greeks knew that only art could transform misery itself into pleasure, *vide tragoediam*.[110,111]

5[122][112]

The genuinely *scientific people*, the people of literature, are the Egyptians and not the Greeks.[113] What seems to be science among the Greeks springs from there and later returns to Egypt in order to reunify itself with the ancient stream. Alexandrian culture is an amalgamation of the Hellenic and Egyptian ones: and if the modern world is tied to the culture of the ancients, then it has — — —

5[123][114]

The *seer* must be full of love, otherwise people will not trust him: viz. Cassandra.

5[124]

Classical philology is the hearth of the most superficial enlightenment: always employed dishonestly, gradually having become completely ineffective. Its effect is one illusion more upon modern humans. It is actually only a case of an educator-class that does not consist of clerics: herein lies the interest of the state.

Its utility is completed used up; whereas, e.g., the history of Christianity still displays its strength.

5[125]

From the discourse about philology, when it springs from philologists, we learn nothing, it is the purest chatter, e.g., Jahn ("The Significance and Position of Classical Studies in Germany").[115] No feeling at all for what is to be defended, what to be protected: so speak people who have not at all considered that someone could attack them.

5[126][116]

It is not at all true that the Greeks had their sight directed only upon this life. They, too, suffered from fear of death and hell. But no remorse and contrition.

5[127][117]

"The wanton reciprocal annihilation (unavoidable as long as a single πόλις still wanted to live), their envy toward everything higher, their avarice, the derangement of their morals, the enslaved position of women, the lack of conscience in oaths, in murder and manslaughter." B⟨urckhardt⟩.

5[128][118]

Tremendous energy of self-overcoming, e.g., in the citizen, in Socrates, who was capable of any evil.

5[129]

We come across the qualities of ingenious people without ingenuity in the average Hellene, basically all of the most dangerous qualities of disposition and character.

5[130][119]

The "patient endurer" is Hellenic. Prometheus, Heracles.

The *hero-myth* became *Panhellenic*; a poet admittedly was part of this.

5[131][120]

Wagner cultivates the inner imagination of humans; later generations will be witnesses of plastic works of art. Poetry must lead the way for plastic art.

5[132]

"Classical education"![121] What do we see in it! A thing that brings about nothing except — liberation from military burdens and doctoral titles!

5[133]

To feel the class of philologists to be a problem.

5[134]

Wagner respects his art far too highly to stick himself in a corner like Schumann. Either he subjects himself to the public (*Rienzi*[122]) or he subjects it to him. He is training it upward. Even the small ones want a public, but they seek it through inartistic means, perhaps the press, Hanslick, etc.

5[135]

Philologists who speak about their science never touch on the *roots*, they never represent philology as a problem. Bad conscience? or thoughtlessness?

5[136]

"Enlightenment" and Alexandrian cultivation are — in the best case![123] — what philologists want. Not Hellenism.

5[137]

The *consistency* that we prize in the scholar is, as concerns the Greeks, pedantry.

5[138]

Classical cultivation! Even if it were only at least as much heathenism as Goethe found and extolled in Winckelmann — it was not so very much. But now the whole untrue Christianity of our times along with it, or in the middle of it — that is too much for me and I must help myself by venting for once my disgust with it. — People really believe in magic with regard to this "classical cultivation"; but naturally those who still have the most of antiquity, the philologists, also have to have the most of this cultivation: but *what* in them is classical!

5[139][124]

Formerly people attributed their temptations and desires to the devil or to evil spirits: that is now considered as a fairy tale. So it will also be a fairy tale to thank a god for one's good impulses and successes. Both are modes of alleviation, one made oneself comfortable by doing so. To be proven, how *religion* has been especially concerned about *comfort*: easily available and ready-made excuses and subterfuge.

5[140][125]

Five-year silence. Student nurse educator.

5[141][126]

What is talent? — Wanting a lofty goal and the means for attaining it.

5[142]

Philologists are people who make use of the stifling feeling of modern human beings about their own insufficiency in order to earn money and bread from it.

I know them, I am one myself.

5[143][127]

German scholars and so-called thinkers, standing far off from real history, have made history into their theme and, as born theologians, attempted to prove its rationality. I fear that a later time will recognize this German contribution to European culture as the unholiest dowry: their history is false!

5[144]

We treat our young people as if they were already instructed, mature men when we present the Greeks to them. *What* then of the Greek essence really is suited for youth? In the end, it remains entirely a matter of *formalities*, of presenting *individual things*. Are those observations for young people? —

Do we offer the best and highest total representation of the ancients to young people, though? Or not? The *reading* of the ancients is emphasized in this way.

I believe that occupying oneself with antiquity is misplaced into a *false* stage of life. At the end of one's twenties it begins to dawn.

5[145]

To *make clear* for once all of the difficulties of historical study through the greatest example.

To what extent our young people are not suited to the Greeks.

Consequences of philology: arrogant anticipation
cultivated philistinism
overestimation of reading and writing
lack of thoroughness
alienation from the people and popular distress.

The philologists themselves (and historians and philosophers ⟨and⟩ jurists, all smoked through with haze).

There are *real* sciences to be imparted to youth.

Likewise *real* art.

Thus will, at a more advanced age, a desire for *real* history also be present.

Philologist, emergence generally and now.
Youth and the philologist.
The consequences of philology.
Task for philology: downfall.

Inhumanity: even from the *Antigone*, even from the Goethean *Iphigenia*.
The lack of *enlightenment*.
Political matters not understandable for youths.
The poetic — a bad anticipation.

5[146]

Critique of Development.

False assumption of a *natural* development.[128]

Degeneration is behind *every* great appearance; at every moment, the onset of the ending is present. Degeneration lies in facile imitation and superficial understanding of the great exemplars: i.e., the exemplar stimulates vainer natures to imitate and do likewise or outdo it.[129]

The chain from one genius to another is rarely a straight line: and so in no way between Aeschylus and Sophocles. A multitude of developmental paths still lay open *after* Aeschylus; Sophocles took *a single one* of them.

Something fateful in all great talents: they sweep one away and lay waste around them, as Rome lies amid a desert. Many energies, still embryonic, are thus stifled.[130]

To be demonstrated, how *preponderant* degeneration is even in Hellas, how rare and short anything great, how deficiently (from the false side) assessed.

How stiff must the beginnings of tragedy have been with Thespis! i.e., the aesthetically appropriate re-formations of the native orgies. Thus prose was at first very stiff in relation to real speech.

The dangers are: we take pleasure in the content or we are indifferent toward the content and aspire to sensual stimulation of sounds etc.

The agonistic is also the danger with all development; it overstimulates the drive to create. — The most fortunate case in development, when several geniuses keep one another within limits.[131]

Aren't very many splendid possibilities stifled in germ? Who would, e.g., have taken Theocritus still to be possible in his time if he had not been there?

The greatest fact is always that **Homer** was *Panhellenic* at such an early point. Yet everything good springs from him: but at the same time he remained the most powerful limit that existed. He *leveled things*, hence the more serious ones struggled so against him, in vain. Homer always triumphed.[132]

The *suppressing element* of the great spiritual powers is visible here too, but what a difference: Homer or a Bible as such a power!

The pleasure in *intoxication*, the pleasure in *craftiness*, in *revenge*, in envy, in *abuse*, in *obscenity* — all of this was *acknowledged* by the Greeks, as human, and on that basis they found a place for it in the structure of society and morality. The wisdom of their institutions lies in the lack of any separation between good and evil, black and white. Nature, as it manifests itself, is not denied, but instead only *has a place found for it*, limited to specific cults and days. This is the root of all broad-mindedness of antiquity; one sought a moderate discharge for natural forces, not an annihilation and renunciation. — The entire system of a new order, then, is the *state*. It was constructed not with an eye to specific individuals, but instead with an eye to regular human qualities: manifest in its foundation is *acuity of observation and a sense for the factual*, especially for the typical-factual, what made the Greeks capable of science history geography etc. It was not a limited priestly *moral code* that gave orders at the foundation of the state. Where did the Greeks get this freedom? Already, indeed, from *Homer*; but where did he get it? — The poets are not the wisest and most logically cultivated beings; but they take pleasure in individual realities of every kind and do not wish to deny them, yet nonetheless to moderate them so that they do not murder everything.[133]

5[147][134]

The necessity of discharge, of κάθαρσις,[135] a fundamental law of Greek being.[136]

Accumulation and discharge in powerful, temporally separated impacts. Can *tragedy* be explained from this?

5[148]

Philosophical minds have to take this up and to produce for once a total accounting for antiquity. As soon as this has been produced, it will be overcome. We are much too strongly dependent upon antiquity in everything defective, in what torments us, for us still to be dealing mildly with it for much longer. The most colossal blasphemy of humanity, that Christianity could become possible as it became possible, is the *fault* of antiquity. Along with Christianity, antiquity will also be cleared away. — As of now, it is very close behind us, and to be just certainly not possible. It is used in the most abominable way for repression and has sustained religious repression by being masked with "cultivation." The best joke was: "antiquity has been overcome by Christianity"! This was a *historical* fact and so busying oneself with it became innocuous. Indeed, it is so plausible to find the Christian ethic "more profound" than Socrates! With Plato, one could already admit it. It is a repeated cud-chewing of the same battle that played out in the first centuries. Only now a completely pallid specter has stepped into the place of the antiquity that was then quite visible, and admittedly even Christianity has become quite spectral. It is a battle *after* the decisive battle, an after-tremor. In the end, all the powers of which antiquity consists came to light in Christianity in the crudest form, there is nothing new, only quantitatively extraordinary.

5[149]

Ah, it is a lamentable history, the history of philology! The most disgusting erudition, lazy, inactive sitting-off-to-the-side, anxious subjection. — Who then has had something free?

5[150][137]

The *religious cult* can be traced back to the *buying* or *begging* of favor from the divinities. It is a question of where we fear their disfavor. — Hence, where we cannot or will not achieve success *by means of our own energy*, we seek supernatural energies: hence with a view to *relief from the effort of life*. Where we do *not* want or are *not* able to make up for something *through action*, we beg the gods for mercy and forgiveness, hence, with a view to *relieving an oppressed conscience*. The gods were invented for the *convenience* of humans: finally, in addition, their cult, the sum of all *relaxations and delights*.

If we take them away: then all burdens are heavier, and there is much less easiness. — Where the Olympians receded, Greek life was gloomier. — Where we *investigate* and work, there the Greeks celebrated festivals. They are the *celebrators of festivals*.

They do not see the gods above them as masters, nor themselves as servants, as did the Jews. It is the conception of a happier and more powerful caste, a mirror image of the most successful specimens of their own caste, hence an ideal, not an antithesis of their own being. They feel thoroughly related to one another. There exists an interest on both sides, a sort of *symmachia*.[138] We think nobly of ourselves when we create such gods in poetry. And so, too, the *begging* and *buying of their favor* also has something *noble* about it. It is a relationship like that of lower to higher nobility; whereas the Romans have a real peasant-religion, anxiety about goblins and spectral occurrences.

5[151]

I want to make myself master of literature sufficiently well that I can, e.g.,

compare the ἀναγνωρίσεις[139]
the prologues in drama, etc.

5[152][140]

Outline for 18 Lectures

9. *Honors* among cities, princes, festivals, sacrificial victims, etc. Tyrants.
18. *Forms of death.*
10. *Groups of association*, of the same aspiration.
11. *Diffusion through the student body.*
12. *Rebellious students.*
6. *Non-Greeks* and Greeks, geographical share.
7. *Slaves and wholly lesser* people.
8. *Very noble people.*
13. *Personal enmities*, contests.
17. *Influence upon the state* and standing aside.
14. *Silence.*
15. *Devaluing and not* understanding predecessors.

16. *Diffusion through lecture, travels*, book-trade, libraries.
2. *Our losses*, greatness, reasons for the loss.
5. *Works of art for all* and those for a specific circle.
3. *Some principles* for the study of literature.
1. *Critique of development*, absolute worth.
4. *Falsifications.* Literary-historical mythology.

5[153]

A prince is always a caricature, something pretentious; and if a people still needs princes, it is proof that the political drive of the individual is still too weak. Anyone who has tasted better thinks with disgust about looking-upward, and with regret about those who have to position themselves as if they were looking downward "from above."

5[154]

When I see how all states now promote classical cultivation, I say, "how innocuous it must be!" And then "how useful it must be." It gains for these states the reputation of promoting "free cultivation." Now look at the philologists in order to assess this "freedom" correctly.

5[155]

In the religious cult, an earlier stage of culture has been retained, they are "vestiges." The ages that celebrate them are not those that invented them. The contrast is often very colorful. The Greek cult leads us back into a pre-Homeric state of mind and morality, is almost the most ancient thing that we know about the Greeks: older than the mythology that the poets essentially remodeled in the way that we know it. — *Can* we call this cult *Greek*? I doubt it. They are completers, not inventors. They *conserve* by means of this beautiful completion.

5[156]

It *separates us* forever from *ancient culture* that its *foundation* has become utterly *untenable* for us. A critique of the Greeks is accordingly at the same time a critique of Christianity, for the foundation in a belief in spirits, in the religious cult, in the enchantment of nature is the same. — There exist even today numerous *backward* stages; but they are already at the point of *decaying*.

This would be **a task**, to *characterize ancient Greece as irrecoverable* and *thereby also Christianity and the foundation up to now of our society and politics.*

5[157]

Task: the *death of ancient culture* unavoidable: to characterize the Greek one as prototype and to show how all culture rests upon representations that are decaying.

Dangerous significance of *art*: as guardian and galvanizing of dead and dying representations. Of *history*, insofar as it wants to displace us back into feelings that have been overcome. To feel "historically," "to be just toward the past," is only possible if we are at the same time *beyond* it. But the danger with the appreciation required here is great: let us, however, let the dead bury their dead:[141] thus we do not take on ourselves the scent of corpses.

5[158][142]

The death of ancient culture.

1. Meaning up to now of classical studies, unclear, deceitful.
2. As soon as they apprehend their goal, they condemn themselves to death: for their goal is to describe ancient culture itself as one to be annihilated.
3. Collection of all representations out of which the Hellenic culture grew. Critique of religion, art, society, the state, morality.
4. The Christian one is disavowed along with it.
5. Art and history — dangerous.
6. Replacement of classical studies, which have become untenable for the education of youth.

Thus the task of the science of *history* is accomplished and it has itself become superfluous: if the whole internally cohesive circle of past attempts has been *condemned*. Into its place must step the science about the *future*.

5[159]

The teacher of reading and writing and the *proofreader* are the first types of the philologist.

5[160]

Our philologists are related to real educators as the medicine men of savages to real doctors. What astonishment a far-off time will have!

5[161]

Everything with critique.

2. Literature.
2. Religious representations.
2. Moral representations.
1. Education.
1. Intercourse, of the sexes, of countries etc. of classes.
2. State.
1. Art of language, concept of the cultivated and the uncultivated.
2. Philosophy and science.
1. On classical philology and antiquity in the modern age.
1. On the Greeks and Romans.

After 5½ years, i.e., autumn 1975–Easter 81.
Easter 82 + 7½ = 89½, e.g., 45–46 years old.

5[162][143]

Poets are backward beings and a bridge to completely far-away times, really always epigones. Are they therefore necessary? They can be reproached for what religion is reproached for, that they provide *temporary reassurance* and have something palliative about them. They keep people from working toward genuine improvement because they themselves suspend and discharge the passion of dissatisfaction.

5[163][144]

The remedies against pain that humans employ are frequently *narcotics*. Religion and art belong to the category of narcotics by means of mental representations. They balance things out and pacify; it is a stage of *the lower healing art* for spiritual pains. *Eliminating* the *cause of suffering* by means of a supposition, e.g., if a child has died, to suppose it is still living, more beautifully, and some day reunion will occur. Thus religion is supposed to exist for the poor, with its consolation.

Is tragedy still possible for someone who does not believe in any metaphysical world? We must show how even the *highest* of humanity up to now has grown on the basis of that lower healing art.

5[164]

We look back upon humanity across a pretty considerable time; how will a humanity appear that one day looks at us from just as far away? That finds us still to be completely drowned in the vestiges of ancient culture. That finds its comfort only in "being helpful and good"[145] and rejects all other consolations! — Does beauty also grow from ancient culture? I believe our *ugliness* depends upon our metaphysical vestiges; our confusion about morality, our badness with regard to marriages, etc. is the cause. The beautiful human being, the healthy and moderate and enterprising human being shapes what is around him into beauty then as well, into his image.

5[165][146]

In the Greeks' divine beings and cult we find every sign of a coarse and gloomy primeval condition, amid which the Greeks would have become something quite different if they had had to remain stuck in it. *Homer* freed them with the peculiar frivolity of his gods. The reshaping of a *savage, gloomy religion* into *a Homeric one* is, however, the *greatest event.*[147] Now consider the countercurrents, the self-revelation of the ancient representations, the taking up of related, foreign ones.

1. Coarse and gloomy primeval times. Fetish-worship. Human sacrifice etc. Fear of death and worship.
2. Spectacles of the cult.
3. Later movements and revivals of the most ancient gloomy religion.
4. The relief and frivolity of religion. The Ionian poets.
5. Narcotics[148] and evasions against the pain and difficulties of life.
6. Falsely explaining and poetizing upon myth, reconciliation and blending.
7. Disbelief.
8. Art as backward and against enlightenment, as it works on the whole.
9. The state seeks its foundation, in what is religious. Likewise the society.
10. Religion, in order to entertain the people, to preserve against distress and boredom.

Cult.

1. Prayer. (Curse, oath.)
2. Sacrifice.
3. Ecstasy and its means. Divination. Oracle. Taking oaths. Magic. The priest.
4. Orientation. (Temple f⟨orm⟩)
5. Purification. (Mysteries.)
6. Complicated forms: festivals with spectacles.
   a) State-cult
   b) Gent⟨ile⟩[149] cult
   c) Domestic cult
   d) Death-cult

5[166]

On Religion

I Love the *trick* of Christianity in its ambiguity.[150] (Sexual love in antiquity purely conceived in Empedocles.)

II Christian love, on the basis of contempt.

III The activity of the Christian in opposition to Buddhist calmness.

IV No religion of revenge and righteousness! the Jews the *worst* people.[151]

V Concepts smuggled in: death by proxy.

VI The priests' state. Hypocrites. Aversion to serious conception of every problem. (Cult of sacrifice, compelling the gods.)

VII The greatest sin against the rationality of humanity is historical Christianity.

VIII God completely superfluous.

IX The decline of humanity: nothing eternal.

X Contemptibility of all motives, impurity of thought, fundamental mistakes of all kinds, classes, aspirations.

XI Either to live among illusions alone: or in the difficult way, without hope, without deception, without providence, without salvations and immortalities: but with a glance filled with compassionate love toward oneself. Separation of two worldviews, that of the everyday and that of the rarest moments of feeling and thought. (Contempt and love, insight and feeling equally powerful.) This conception of religion requires science (as tool of the contempt-filled insight into the weakness and purposelessness of humans.) It increases steadily, the higher the knowledge of the world ascends. — The struggle with necessity[152] — the one principle of life. The insight into the deceptiveness of all purposes and compassion for oneself — the other.[153]

5[167]

To *overcome* ancient Greece through action would be the task. But for that we would first have to know it![154] — there is a thoroughness that is only a pretext for inactivity. Think what Goethe understood of antiquity; certainly not as much as a philologist and yet enough to struggle fruitfully with it. We *should* not even know more about something than we could also create. Moreover, it is itself the sole means of truly *knowing* something, if we attempt to *make* it. Try to live in the way of antiquity — we immediately come a hundred miles closer to the ancients than with all scholarship. — Our philologists do not show that they *emulate* antiquity in any way whatsoever — therefore *their* antiquity is without effect upon the pupils.

Study of **rivalry** (Renaissance, Goethe) and *study of* **despair**!

5[168]

There is *not much* at stake in a correctly emended author.

5[169]

The false image of being occupied with the ancients inhibits even the best.

5[170]

The sciences will perhaps some day be pursued by women: men should *create* spiritually, states laws works of art etc.

5[171]

We should study only the *exemplary* antiquity, as we study an *exemplary human being*: thus, imitating as much as we comprehend and if the exemplar is far off, pondering the paths and preparations and *discovering* the middle stages.

The *measure* of study lies in this: *only what stimulates to imitation, what* will be taken up with love and demands to be reproduced further should be studied. That would be *the most correct*: a *progressive* canon of *exemplars, suitable* for *younger young* and *older* people.

5[172]

In *this* way did Goethe apprehend antiquity: always with a competitive soul. But who else? We see nothing of a pedagogy thought through in this way: who knows that there exists knowledge of antiquity that is incommunicable to young people!

5[173]

The *boyish* character of philology: invented for pupils by teachers.

5[174]

Ever *more general* form of the *exemplary*: first human beings, then institutions, finally orientations intentions or the lack of them.

Highest form: *overcoming of the exemplar* with the reverse movement from tendencies to institutions, from institutions to human beings.

5[175][155]

The *advancement of a science at the expense of human beings* is the most damaging thing in the world. The spoiled human is a step backward for humanity; he casts his *shadow* forward across all time. It debases the disposition, the natural purpose of the individual science: it is itself finally ruined by this; it stands there, advanced, but does not affect life, or does so immorally.

5[176]

Do not use human beings as *things*!

5[177]

There went forth from a very imperfect philology and knowledge of antiquity a stream of freedom, our highly developed kind subjugates and serves the idol of the state.

5[178][156]

The better the state is organized, the feebler the humanity.

To make the individual *uncomfortable*: my task!

Attractiveness of the liberation of the individual in battle!

The spiritual height has its *time* in history, inherited energy belongs to it. In the ideal state this is over and done with.

5[179][157]

The spiritual culture of Greece an aberration of the enormous political drive toward ἀριστεύειν.[158] — The πόλις highly dismissive toward new education. *Nevertheless* culture did exist.

5[180]

Highest judgment about life only from the highest energy of life, the spirit must be as far away as possible from *feebleness*.

In the *middle* of world history, judgment will be the most correct, because the greatest *geniuses* exist there.

Engendering of genius as the only one who can truly *esteem* and *deny* life.

5[181][159]

Walter Scott loved society because he wanted to tell stories; he practiced, like a virtuoso practices the piano for seven hours.

5[182]

Save your genius! should be shouted to the people, liberate it! Do everything in order to unchain it!

5[183]

The feeble ones, the spiritually poor *are not permitted* to judge life.

5[184][160]

When good friends etc. praise me, I am often seemingly pleased and grateful out of politeness and good will; but in truth, I am indifferent to it. My real nature is quite lethargic toward this and cannot thereby be moved a single step away from the sun or the shade in which it lies. — But people want to cause pleasure through praise and we would distress them if we did not take joy in their praise.

5[185][161]

We must not expect from the future of humanity what certain past ages engendered, e.g., the effects of religious feeling. Perhaps the type of the saint is possible only along with a certain constraint of the intellect, which is now over and done with. Even the *high point* of intelligence has perhaps been reserved for one age of humanity. Tremendous energy of the will, carried over to spiritual exertions (aberration) — only possible as long as that wildness and energy were bred on a large scale. It comes closer, perhaps, to the goal of humanity in the middle of its path than at the end. — Forces upon which art depends could die out, e.g., the pleasure in lies, in obscure symbolic things, etc., intoxication, too, could come to be disdained. And basically: if life is organized within the ideal state, then no poetry of the *present* is possible anymore: in the best case, it looks back with longing to the times of the unideal state.

5[186][162]

Childhood and boyhood has its goal in itself, is not a *stage*.

5[187]

I wish for a book about the *lifestyle of the scholar*.

5[188][163]

Goals

The value of life can only be measured by the *highest intellect* and the warmest[164] heart.

How are the highest intelligences to be engendered? —

The goals of *human welfare* generally speaking are completely *different*: than engendering the highest intelligence. Living well counts much too highly and is taken completely superficially, also school and education.

The ideal state of which the socialists dream destroys the *foundation* of the great intelligences, the strong energy.

We must wish that life maintain its *violent* character, that *savage* forces and energies be called forth. The judgment about the value of existence is the highest result of the most powerful *tension* amid chaos.

Now the warmest heart longs to eliminate that violent, savage character; even though it itself came forth from this! It wants to do away with its foundation! That means, it is not intelligent.

The highest intelligence and the warmest heart cannot coexist in any single person. The highest intelligence is *higher* than everything good, even *the latter* is only something *to be discounted* in the total reckoning of life, the sage stands above it.

The *sage* must *resist* the idea of an unintelligent goodness, because he is concerned with the re-engendering of his type. At least, he *cannot promote* the ideal state. — Christ promoted human stupidity, he held up the engendering of the great intellect. Consistent! His reverse image, perhaps, will obstruct the engendering of Christ. — *Fatum tristissimum generis humani!*[165]

5[189]

Proœmium[166]

If I were already *free*, I would not need the whole struggle, but would turn instead to a work or a deed on which I could try out all of my energy. — Now I may only hope gradually to become free; and I perceive up to now that I am becoming more and more so. So my day of real *work* is still coming, and the *preparation* for the Olympic games is *done*. —

5[190][167]

It still lies before me to express views that *are considered disgraceful* for those who hold them; even friends and acquaintances will become shy and nervous then. Through this fire, too, I must make my way. I will belong more and more to myself then. —

5[191][168]

Anyone who became aware of how genius has been engendered and also wanted to put into practice nature's procedure would have to be as malicious and ruthless as nature itself.

5[192]

I find Xenophon's *Memorabilia* very interesting. We still have to acknowledge Socrates's example: it is still immediately inimitable. The ἀνδραποδισταὶ ἑαυτῶν[169] pique me.

5[193][170]

Plato's Socrates is a *carricatura* in the real sense, something overloaded.

5[194][171]

Mistreat human beings, drive them to extremes, and do it for centuries — then the genius springs forth all at once, through an *error* of nature, through the flying spark of the terrible energy that has thus been ignited. — So history tells me. Frightful visage! Woe! I cannot bear you! — [172]

5[195][173]

The *Greeks* of the *age of the Caesars* are *feeble* and may very well appear to be the types of future humanity. They seem to be humanitarian, especially in contrast to Rome, detest gladiatorial combats, etc. — It is completely false to draw from that conclusions about the time of their youth.

5[196][174]

Homer is so much at home in the humanized world of divinities and so at ease as a poet that he must have been deeply unreligious. He deals like the sculptor does with his clay and marble.

5[197][175]

The Greek polis resists cultivation, its political drive was in this direction highly crippling and stabilizing. There should be no *history* no *becoming* in cultivation, it should be firmly established once and for all time. So Plato, too, later wanted it to be. Higher cultivation emerged *despite* the polis: indirectly even through it, because the ambition of the individual was raised by it to the highest level. If a Greek entered on the path of spiritual distinction, he went to the furthest extremes.

5[198][176]

Original inhabitants of Greek territory: Mongolian descent with tree and snake cults. The coast trimmed with a Semitic strip. Here and there Thracians. The Greeks assimilated all of these constituent parts in their blood, also all of the gods and myths along with them (much Mongolian in the Odysseus fables). The Doric migration is an *afterthrust*, after everything had already gradually been flooded over before. What are "racial Greeks"? Isn't it sufficient to assume that the Italic people, paired with Thracian and Semitic elements, became *Greeks*?[177]

5[199][178]

If we think of the tremendous mass of slaves on the mainland, *Greeks* were always only to be found sporadically. A *higher* caste of do-nothings politicians etc. Their *enmities* held them in physical and spiritual tension. They held on to their *superiority* in *quality* — that was their magic spell upon the masses.

5[200][179]

The *oration* of *Pericles* a grandly optimistic deception, the sunset amid which one forgets the horrible day — night comes along afterwards.

[6 = U II 8c. Summer 1875]

6[1]

Imitation of antiquity.

The means, philology, make imitation impossible for the philologist. Knowing without being able to do.

Hence: either having become purely historical —

or philology having gone to ruin (Schiller).

Even the historical knowledge of antiquity is mediated through reproduction, imitation.

The Goethean version of the ancient Greek world (the Greek σωφϱοσύνη[1] in art carried over to the moral human being).

6[2]

Greek antiquity as classical collecting of examples for explaining our entire culture and its development. It is a means *to understand ourselves*, to direct our time and thereby to overcome it.

The pessimistic foundation of our culture.

6[3]

Socrates, just to confess it, stands so close to me that I am almost always fighting a battle with him.

6[4]

Science and wisdom in conflict.

Science (NB. *before* it is habit and instinct)[2] emerges

1) when the gods are not thought to be good. Great advantage to know anything at all as *certain*.
2) egoism impels the individual to seek his advantage in certain activities, e.g., sailing, through science.
3) something for people of high rank who have leisure time. Curiosity.
4) the individual wants a firmer foundation in the wild back-and-forth of the people's opinions.

How does this drive to science differentiate itself from the general drive to learn and to take up something? Only through the lesser degree of egoism or by stretching it further. *First*, a losing of oneself in things. *Second*, a selfishness extended beyond the individual.

Wisdom shows itself

1) in illogical generalization and flying to the final goal.
2) in relating these results to life.
3) In the unconditional importance that we attribute to our souls. One thing is necessary.[3]

Socratism is *first* wisdom in taking the soul seriously.
second science as fear and hatred toward illogical generalization.
third something specific through the demand for conscious and logically correct actions.

From this emerges damage for science, for the ethical life.

6[5]

Science and wisdom in conflict,
exhibited by the ancient Greek philosophers.

6[6]

1) How is the world shown to be colored in these ancient Greeks?
2) How do they behave toward nonphilosophers?

3) Much depends upon their *persons*: to guess this is the significance of my observation of their doctrines.
4) Science and wisdom in conflict among them.
5) Ironic news: everything is false.[4] How human beings cling to a balcony.

6[7]

There is also a way of telling this history *ironically* and *filled with melancholy*. I want in any case to avoid the earnest-indifferent tone.

Socrates *upsets* the *whole* at a moment when it had approached *most closely* to the truth; that is especially *ironic*.

Everything to be painted upon the background of myth. Its limitless uncertainty and fluctuation. We yearn for what is certain.

Only where the beam of myth falls does the life of the Greeks light up; elsewhere it is gloomy. Now these philosophers rob themselves of myth; so how do they endure this gloominess? —[5]

The individual, who wants to stand *on his own. For that, final knowledge*, philosophy, *is necessary*. The other humans require slowly increasing science.

Or rather: a belief is necessary in order to possess such final knowledge. A degree of credulity about one's own knowing such as those ancient Greeks possessed will never exist again: but the difficulty and danger of knowing did not yet stand before their souls; they had a sturdy belief in themselves, with which they overcame all of their neighbors and predecessors. The happiness in possessing the truth was never greater in the world, but never, too, the harshness, the arrogance, the *tyrannical*. In his secret wishing every Greek was a tyrant; and in general, everyone was that whenever he could be, perhaps with the exception of Solon, inferring from his own poems.[6,7]

Even independence is only apparent: in the end, everyone is joined to his predecessors. Phantasma to phantasma. It is comical to take everything so seriously.

All ancient philosophy as a curious *maze*-way of reason. It is to be tuned to a key of dream and fable.

6[8]

Aristotle in his aesthetic judgment.

against Empedocles.
with regard to tragedy.
Demosthenes.
Thucydides.
plastic art.
music.

6[9]

The development of Greek *music* and *philosophy* go alongside each other. Compare both, insofar as both make statements about Hellenic existence. The music, admittedly, is known to us only from out of its precipitation as lyric.

Empedocles — tragedy	Sacred monody
Heraclitus — Archilochus	Xenophanes sympotic.
Democritus — Anacreon	
Pythagoras — Pindar	
Anaxagoras — Simonides.	

All comparison of persons is cockeyed and stupid.

6[10][8]

The *philosophers* are *Hades shadows* in relation to Greek life: they reflect it back, but as if in a cloud of smoke.

We must follow closely after such human beings until they are once again re-created by a poet: the supplementary inventiveness of many must be at work here.

They are too rare for us to allow them to run away. How little lets itself be attained with critique and the turning around and shaking out of every written note![9]

6[11]

Introduction.	1st Chap.	Comparison of ancient Greek[10] philosophers with the sect-philosophers after Socrates.
	2nd Chap.	The temporal relationships of the ancient philosophers.

Story

So much depends upon the development of Greek culture, since our entire occidental world received its impetus from there: fate wanted it such that the more recent and degenerate Greek world showed the most historical force. On that point, the ancient Greek world has always been judged falsely. We have to know the more recent one exactly, in order to differentiate it from the ancient one.

There still exist very many possibilities that have not yet been discovered: because the Greeks did not discover them. Others *discovered* the Greeks and later *covered* them *over* again.

6[12]

These philosophers prove *what dangers Greek culture contained within itself:*

myth as a lazy person's bed for thought	— by contrast cold abstraction and strict science. Democritus.
the soft comfortableness of life	— by contrast moderation, strict ascetic conception in Pythagoras, Empedocles, Anaximander.
cruelty in battle and conflict	— by contrast Empedocles with his reform of sacrifice.
lying and deceit	— by contrast enthusiasm for what is true despite any consequence.

pliancy, exaggerated sociability — by contrast Heraclitus's pride and solitude.

6[13]

These philosophers display the vitality of that culture, which engendered its own corrective.

How does this age die out? Unnaturally. Yet where then are the germs of decay hidden?

The *flight of the better ones from the world* was a great misfortune. From Socrates on: all at once the individual took himself to be too important.

Pestilence came in addition, for Athens.

Then they were *destroyed* by the *Persian wars*. The danger was too great and the triumph too exceptional.

The death of great musical lyric and of philosophy.

Socrates is the *revenge for Thersites*: the magnificent Achilles slew the ugly man of the people, Thersites, wrathful about his words upon Penthesilea's death;[11] the ugly man of the people, Socrates, slew the *authority* of the wonderful myth[12] in Greece.

6[14]

Ancient Greek philosophy is the philosophy of *genuine statesmen*. How miserable it is with our statesmen! That, moreover, differentiates the pre-Socratics and the post-Socratics the most.

With them, we do not have "the indecent pretension to happiness,"[13] as from Socrates on. Everything does not revolve around the condition of their souls: for about that one does not reflect without danger. Later the γνῶθι σαυτόν[14] of Apollo was misunderstood.

Nor did they *chatter* and *curse* so much, nor did they *write*.

The enfeebled Greek world, Romanized, coarsened, become decorative, then accepted as decorative culture by an enfeebled Christianity, as its ally, propagated with violence among uncivilized peoples — that is the history of occidental culture. The trick is performed, and Greek and Papist brought together.

I want to add together Schopenhauer Wagner and the ancient Greek world: it provides a perspective upon a magnificent culture.[15]

6[15]

Comparison of ancient philosophy with the post-Socratic.

1) the ancient is related to *art*, its solution of the world-riddle let itself be inspired again and again by art. Spirit of music and plastic art.
2) it is *not* the negation of the *other* life, but instead *grew* out of it like a rare blossom; it expresses the secrets of that. (theory — praxis)
3) it is *not* so *individual-eudaemonological*, without the indecent pretension to happiness.[16]
4) these ancient philosophers themselves have a higher wisdom in their lives and not cold-clever righteousness. Their image of life is richer and more complicated, the Socratics simplify and banalize.

6[16]

The three-jointed history of the *dithyramb*:

1 the Arionic — from that, ancient tragedy
2 the agonal state-dithyramb — parallel to domesticated tragedy
3 the mimetic, genial-dissolute.

6[17]

Again and again among the Greeks a *more ancient* form is the *higher one*, e.g., with the *dithyramb* and *tragedy*. The danger for the Greeks lay in *virtuosity* of every kind; with Socrates begin the virtuosos of life, Socrates, the newer dithyramb, the newer tragedy, the *discovery of the rhetor*!

The rhetor is a Greek discovery! of the later age. They discovered "form in itself" (and also the philosophies for that).

How is the battle of Plato against rhetoric to be understood? He *envies* their influence.

The ancient Greek world *revealed its energies in the line of philosophers*. With Socrates this revelation *breaks off*: he attempts *to engender himself* and to discard all tradition.

My general task: to show how life philosophy and art can have a deeper and kindred relationship to one another, without philosophy becoming flat and the life of the philosopher deceitful.

It is magnificent that the old philosophers could live *so freely, without thereby becoming fools and virtuosos*. The freedom of the individual was immeasurably great.

The false opposition between *vita practica*[17] and *contemplativa*[18] is Asiatic. The Greeks understood it better.

6[18]

We can represent these ancient philosophers as ones who feel the Greek atmosphere and customs as *constraint* and *limit*: hence self-liberators (struggle of Heraclitus against Homer and Hesiod, Pythagoras against secularization, all of them against myth, especially Democritus). They have a gap in their nature, with regard to the Greek artist and, indeed, the statesman as well.

I conceive of them as the **precursors of a reformation** of the Greeks: but not of Socrates. Instead, their reformation did not arrive, with Pythagoras it remained sectarian. A group of appearances bear all of this reformation-spirit — the *development* of *tragedy*. The *failed reformer* is **Empedocles**; when he failed, only Socrates still remained. So the enmity of Aristotle toward Empedocles is quite comprehensible.

Empedocles — free state — transformation of life — popular reform — attempt with the help of the great Hellenic festivals. —

Tragedy was likewise a means. Pindar?

They did not find their philosophers and reformers, compare Plato; he is a deviation through Socrates. Attempt at a characterization of Plato *without* Socrates. Tragedy — deep apprehension of love — pure nature — no fanatical renunciation:

the Greeks were clearly *about* to discover *a still higher type* of human being than the earlier ones were; then the scissors cut in between. What remains is the *tragic age* of the Greeks.

6[19]

1. Image of the Hellenes with regard to their dangers and corruptions.
2. Reverse-image of the tragic currents in contrast. New interpretation of myth.
3. Beginnings of the reformers. Attempts to attain the *world-image.*
4. The decision — Socrates. The *deviated Plato.*

6[20]

The passion in Mimnermus,[19] the hatred against *old age.*

The deep melancholy in Pindar: only when a ray comes from above does human life light up.

To understand the world from *out of suffering* is the tragic element in tragedy.

6[21]

Thales — the unmythical.

Anaximander — passing away and emergence in nature moral, as guilt and punishment.

Heraclitus — lawfulness and justice in the world.

Parmenides — the other world behind this one; this as a problem.

Anaxagoras — world-architect.

Empedocles — blind love and blind hatred; the deeply irrational element in the most rational things in the world.

Democritus — the world is completely without reason and drive, all shaken up together. All gods and myths useless.

Socrates: nothing remains there for me except myself; anxiety about oneself becomes the soul of philosophy.

Plato's attempt to think everything to the end and to be the redeemer.

6[22]

The personalities are to be depicted: just as I have depicted Heraclitus. The historical element to be woven in.

6[23][20]

In the entire world *gradualness* rules, with the Greeks it went forward quickly, but also downward frightfully quickly. Once the Hellenic genius had created its highest types, the Greek then sank as rapidly as possible. An interruption had to occur only once, and the great life-form will no longer be made complete: it was over with immediately; just as with tragedy. A single powerful contrarian like Socrates — then the tear was irreparable. In him the self-destruction of the Greeks fulfills itself. I believe it matters that he was the son of a sculptor.

If these plastic arts would ever speak, they would seem superficial to us; in Socrates, the son of the sculptor, their superficiality came out.

6[24]

Humans became *more witty*[21] during the Middle Ages; calculating by two measures, the subtlety of conscience, the interpretation of writing were the means. This way of *sharpening the intellect* through the pressure of a hierarchy and theology was lacking for antiquity. Instead, the Greeks, in reverse fashion, were credulous and superficial amid the great freedom of thought; one began wherever one wished and ceased wherever one wished in believing something. Hence they lack the pleasure in contorted acuteness and thus the favorite form of wit in the modern age. The Greeks were not very *witty*; that is why they made such a fuss about the irony of Socrates. I find Plato often somewhat clumsy in this.

6[25]

With Empedocles and Democritus, the Greeks were on the best path *to appraise correctly* human existence, its irrationality, its suffering; *they never attained that.* Thanks to Socrates.

The dispassionate gaze upon humans is lacking in all Socratics, who have in their heads the dreadful abstractions "the good, the just." Read Schopenhauer and ask yourself, why did the ancients lack such a deep- and free-gaze — *had* to lack it? I do not understand it. On the contrary. Through Socrates they lose their unaffectedness. Their myths and tragedies are much wiser than the ethics of Plato and Aristotle; and their "*stoic* and *epicurean*" humans are *poor* compared to their ancient poets and statesmen.

6[26]

Socrates's effect: 1) he destroyed the dispassionateness of ethical judgment,
2) annihilated science,
3) had no sense for art,
4) tore the individual out of historical association,
5) promotes dialectical nonsense and loquacity.

6[27][22]

I no longer believe in the "natural development" of the Greeks: they were much too gifted to be *gradual* in the step-by-step manner that the stone and stupidity are. The Persian wars are the national misfortune: the success was too great, all of the bad drives broke out, the tyrannical desire to rule all of Hellas came over individual men and individual states. With the domination of Athens (in the spiritual realm) a host of energies were stifled; just think how unproductive Athens was for philosophy for a long time. Pindar would not have been possible as an Athenian. Simonides shows it. And Empedocles would not have been, either, nor Heraclitus. Almost all the great musicians come from outside. The Athenian tragedy is not the highest form that we could conceive. The heroes therein are far too lacking in the Pindaric element. Really: how terrible was it that conflict had to break out precisely between *Sparta* and *Athens*

— that cannot be regarded deeply enough. *The spiritual domination of Athens was the obstacle to that reformation.* We must for once think ourselves into the place where this domination did not yet exist at all: it was not necessary, it first became so in consequence of the Persian wars, i.e., after it displayed physical political power. Miletus, e.g., was much more gifted, Agrigentum, too.

6[28][23]

The tyrant who can do whatever he pleases, i.e., the Greek who is held within limits by no power, is a completely measureless being: "he overturns the customs of the fatherland, does violence to the women and kills people arbitrarily."[24] Just as unbridled is the tyrannical free spirit, of which the Greeks were likewise afraid. Hatred of kings — sign of the democratic sentiments. I believe: the reformation would have been possible, if a tyrant had been an Empedocles.

With his demand for the philosopher to be upon the throne, Plato expressed a *thought possible* at that time: the idea came to him after the time to realize it had passed. Periander? —

6[29]

Without the tyrant Pisastratus, the Athenians would have had no tragedy: for Solon was against it, but the pleasure in it had been awakened. What did Pisastratus want with these great stimulations of grief?

Solon's aversion to tragedy: think of the limitations upon the festivities of mourning in cases of death, the forbidding of threnoi.[25] Among the Milesian women, μανικὸν πένθος[26] was mentioned.

According to the anecdote, it is *pretense* that displeases Solon; the inartistic nature of the Athenians shows itself.[27]

Kleisthenes, Periander and Pisistratus the promoters of tragedy as a popular entertainment, the pleasure in μανικὸν πένθος. Solon wants moderation.

6[30]

The centralizing tendencies, emerging from the Persian wars: Sparta and Athens seized upon them. In contrast, from 776–560 {BCE} none of this existed: the culture of the polis was blossoming; I believe, without the Persian wars they would have obtained the idea of centralization from a *reformation of the spirit* — Pythagoras?

At that time, what mattered was the unity of the festivals and the cult: here, too, the reform might have begun. *The idea of a Panhellenic tragedy* — a still infinitely richer energy would have developed there. Why didn't it come about? After Corinth Sicyon and Athens had developed this art.

6[31]

The greatest loss that can befall humanity is when the highest life-forms do not come into existence. Something like this happened at that time. A sharp parallel between this ideal and the Christian one. To be used, Schopenhauer's remark: "Excellent, noble human beings soon become aware of this education through fate and gratefully submit to be formed by it; they realize that instruction, but not happiness is to be found in the world . . . and in the end say with Petrarch: '*altro diletto, che 'mparar, non provo*.'[28] It can even happen that they only pretend to pursue their wishes and aspirations and merely behave frivolously with them, so to speak, but actually, in their heart of hearts, they expect only instruction, which then imbues them with a contemplative, ingenious, sublime touch." — *Parerga I*, 439.[29] Compare with this the *Socratics* and the hunt for happiness![30]

6[32][31]

The horrible parley of the Athenians with the Melians in Thucydides! With such sentiments, the Hellenic had to come to ruin, through *fear* on all sides. E.g., when the Athenians say: "As for what concerns the benevolence of the gods, we will not be at a disadvantage; for we require and do nothing that lies outside of the human way, neither in relation to beliefs in the gods nor also in what humans wish for themselves."[32]

6[33][33]

Luther: "I have no better work than wrath and zeal: for if I indeed want to compose, to write, to pray and to preach, then I must be wrathful, since all of my blood is refreshed, my understanding sharpened and all reluctant thoughts and oppositions give way."

6[34]

It is a beautiful truth that for someone for whom self-improvement or knowledge have become life goals, all things serve for the best. But still only true in a limited sense: someone who wants knowledge is forced into the most exhausting work, someone improving himself is enervated and ruined by illnesses! On the whole it may hold true: the apparent deliberateness of fate[34] is the act of the individual, who puts his life in order and learns how to suck knowledge from everything, as the bee does from honey. The fate that befalls a people, however, befalls a whole that cannot reflect thus upon its existence and be provided with goals; and so deliberateness for peoples is a swindle of brooding minds, nothing is easier than to show nondeliberateness, e.g., in that an age in fullest blossoming is suddenly struck by a snowfall, so that everything dies. It is in this as completely stupid as in nature. Up to a certain degree, every people[35] does indeed make its way even under the most unfavorable conditions to something that calls to mind its talent. But in order for it to be able to accomplish its *best*, certain mishaps must not occur. The Greeks did not accomplish their best.

The Athenians, too, would have become something higher without the political furor after the Persian wars: think of Aeschylus, who comes from the pre-Persian era and who was dissatisfied with the Athenians of his era.

6[35]

Due to the unfavorableness of the situation of the Greek cities after the Persian wars, many favorable conditions for the emergence and development of great individuals were eliminated: and so the creation of the genius depends, to be sure, upon the fate of peoples. For the starting points for genius are quite frequent, but very rarely do all of the essential favorable factors come together.

This reformation of the Hellenes, as I dream of it, would have been an amazing basis for the engendering of geniuses: one such as has never yet existed. That would be something to describe. There we have lost something indescribable.

6[36]

The higher *moral* nature of the Hellenes shows itself in their wholeness and simplification; by showing us human beings *simplified*, they please us as the sight of animals does.

6[37]

The striving of the philosophers goes toward *understanding* what their fellow humans only live. While they interpret their existence to themselves and understand its dangers, at the same time they also interpret to their people its existence.

A *new world-picture* in place of the *popular* one is what the philosopher wants to posit.

6[38][36]

Thales's league of cities: he saw the destiny of the polis and saw myth as the foundation of the polis. If he broke myth, then perhaps also the polis. Thales as statesman. Struggle against the polis.

Heraclitus's position toward the Persians: he was clear about the danger of the Hellenic and barbaric.

Anaximander as founder of colonies.

Parmenides as lawgiver.

Empedocles the democrat, who bears social reforms upon his shield.

6[39][37]

Words are the seducers of philosophers; they struggle in the nets of language.

6[40]

The *power of the individual* is exceptional in Greece: to found cities, to give laws.

6[41]

Science investigates the processes of nature, but can never *command* human beings. Inclination love pleasure displeasure elation exhaustion — with all of that, science is not acquainted. What human beings live and experience, they must *interpret* from out of somewhere; thereby appraise it. Religions have their force ⟨in that⟩ they are *standards of value*, measuring sticks. Seen within myth, an event appears differently. The interpretation of religions has this going for it, that it measures human life according to humanlike ideals.

6[42]

Aeschylus lived and struggled in vain: he came too late. That is the tragic element in Greek history: the *greatest*, like Demosthenes, come too late to elevate the people.

Aeschylus also attests to a loftiness of the Greek spirit that dies out with him.

6[43]

We are amazed now by the gospel of the tortoise — ah, the Greeks moved too swiftly.[38] I do not seek happy times in history, but the sort that offer favorable ground for the *engendering* of genius. There I find the times before the Persian wars. We cannot get to know them precisely enough.

6[44]

1. These philosophers isolated by themselves.
2. Then as witnesses for the Hellenic. (Their philosophies Hades-shadows of Greek existence.)[39]
3. Then as fighters against the dangers of the Hellenic.
4. Then in the course of Hellenic history as unsuccessful reformers.
5. Then in opposition to Socrates and the sects, and to the *vita contempl⟨ativa⟩*, as attempts to attain a *life-form* that has *not yet* been attained.

6[45][40]

Many humans live a *dramatic* life, many an *epic* one, many an unaesthetic and confused one. Due to the Persian wars, Greek history has a *daemon ex machina*.[41]

6[46]

In Anaxagoras: the νοῦς[42] is an ἄθεος *ex machina*.[43]

6[47][44]

Attempt at a culture of the people.

Waste of the most precious Greek *spirit* and Greek *blood*! From that can be shown how humans must learn to live much *more prudently*. The tyrants of the spirit in Greece were almost always murdered and had only sparse progeny.[45] Other ages have displayed their energy in thinking to the end and pursuing in all of its possibilities a single great thought: e.g., the Christian one. But for the Greeks, attaining this predominance was too hard; everything there was in enmity with everything else. Civic culture alone *demonstrated* up to now — we still live off it now.

Civic culture

World culture

People's culture: how weak among the Greeks, still really only Athenian civic culture, faded.

6[48][46]

1. There no doubt comes for everyone an hour when, with amazement at himself, he asks: How does one even live! And yet one does live! — an hour, when he begins to comprehend that he possesses an inventiveness of the same kind that he admires in plants, which wind and climb and finally gain by force some light for themselves and a bit of soil besides and thus create for themselves their share of joy on inhospitable ground. In the descriptions that someone makes of his life, there is always the sort of point where one is astonished at how a plant can still live here and how it carries on with an unshakeable courage. Now, there are paths of life where the difficulties have grown into something colossal, those of the thinker; and here, where something of this is to be related, we must listen attentively, for here we perceive something of the *possibilities of life*, just hearing of which brings happiness and energy, and pours light down upon the lives of those who come later; here everything is[47] so inventive, sensible, audacious, despairing and full of hope, rather like the voyages of the greatest world-circumnavigators and also, in fact, something of the same kind, circumnavigations of the most remote and most dangerous regions of life. The astonishing thing about such paths of life lies in the way that two hostile drives, pressing in different directions,[48] are here forced to proceed under a single yoke, as it were; someone who wants to know must forsake again and again the ground upon which human beings live and venture into what is uncertain, and the drive that wants life must grope its way again and again to a more or less secure place[49] upon which it can stand; we are reminded of James Cook, who with a nautical plumb in his hand had to grope through a chain of reefs, three months running: and whose dangers often grew so great that he would gladly have sought protection again even in a position that shortly before he had held to be one of the most dangerous. Lichtenberg IV 152.[50] That struggle between life and knowledge will be so much the greater, that proceeding under a single yoke so much the stranger, the more powerful

both drives are, therefore the fuller and more flourishing the life is, and in turn, the more insatiable knowing is and the more insatiably it presses toward all adventures.

2. Hence I never get my fill of setting before my soul a row of thinkers, each one of whom has in him that incomprehensibility and must awaken that astonishment at how he found precisely his own possibility of life: the thinkers who lived in Greece's most energetic and fruitful age, in the century before the Persian wars and during them: for these thinkers even discovered *beautiful possibilities of life*; and it seems to me that the later Greeks have forgotten the best of these: and what people up to now could say that it has rediscovered them? — Compare the thinkers of other ages and other peoples with that row of figures that begins with Thales and ends with Democritus, indeed, put[51] Socrates and his pupils and all the leaders of sects in later Greece beside those ancient Greeks — now we want to do that in this written work and hopefully others will do it even better: nevertheless, I believe that every observation will end with this cry: How beautiful they are! I see no distorted and desolate figures among them, no priestly visages, no emaciated desert-hermits, no fanatical prettifiers of present-day things, no theologizing counterfeiters, no depressed and pale scholars:[52] nor do I see among them those who take as so important the "salvation of their souls" or the question: what is happiness, that they forget with this the world and their fellow human beings. — Who could rediscover "*these possibilities of life*"! Poets and historians[53] are supposed to brood over this task: for such human beings are too rare that we could let them get away. Instead, we should not let ourselves rest until we have re-created their images and painted them a hundred times upon the wall — and if we have gotten this far — then, admittedly, we will not really let ourselves rest. For our so-inventive age is still lacking precisely the discovery that the ancient philosophers must have made: where else did their marvelous beauty come from! whence our ugliness! — For what is beauty, if

not the mirror image[54] glimpsed by us of an exceptional joy in nature over the fact that a new, fruitful possibility of life has been discovered? And what is ugliness, if not its discontent with itself, its doubt as to whether it still really understands how to entice art into life?[55]

3. Greek philosophy seems to begin with a nonsensical notion, with the proposition that water is the source and the womb of all things; is it really necessary, we might ask ourselves, to stand still and to reflect seriously upon this? — Yes, and for three reasons: first, because the proposition does assert something about the source of things, second, because it does this without imagery and mythical fabling, and finally third, because in it, even if only in the state of pupation, is contained the thought: Everything is one. The first-mentioned reason leaves Thales still in association with religious and superstitious elements, the second takes him out of this society and shows him to be the first natural scientist, on the basis of the third Thales counts as the first Greek philosopher. In Thales, the scientific man triumphs for the first time over the mythical one, and the wise man, in turn, over the scientific one.

6[49][56]

How was it possible for Thales to renounce myth! Thales as statesman! Something must have happened here. If the polis was the focal point of the Hellenic will and if it rested upon myth, giving up myth means the same as giving up the old concept of the polis. Now we know that Thales recommended the founding of a league of cities, but did not prevail: he ran aground on the ancient, mythic concept of the polis. At the same time, he had a presentiment of the colossal danger for Greece, if this isolating power of myth held the cities apart. In fact: if Thales had brought about his league, Greece would have been spared the Persian wars, and thereby also the Athenian triumph and ascendancy. All of the ancient philosophers worked toward the transformation of the concept of the polis and creation of a

Panhellenic sensibility. Heraclitus seems even to have torn down the barrier between barbaric and Hellenic in order to create a greater freedom and to move narrow views forward. — The significance of water and of the sea for the Greeks.

6[50][57]

Thales: what drives him toward science and wisdom? — Above all, however, the fight against myth. Against the polis, which is founded upon it. Sole means for protecting the Hellenic; for warding off the Persian wars. In all the philosophers a Panhellenic purpose.

Anaximander. Fight against myth, insofar as it enfeebles and makes superficial and thus brings the Greeks into danger.

Heraclitus. Fight against myth, insofar as it isolates the Greeks and opposes them to the barbarians. He reflects upon a world order that is supra-Hellenic.

Parmenides. Theoretical diminishment of the world, as a delusion. Fight against what is fantastic and fluctuating in the whole worldview: he wants to give humans peace from political passion. Lawgiver.

Anaxagoras. The world as irrational, yet still temperate and beautiful: thus should humans be and thus he found them in the ancient Athenians, Aeschylus, etc. His philosophy a mirror image of ancient Athens: law-giving for humans who need none.

Empedocles. Panhellenic reformer, Pythagorean life, scientifically grounded. New mythology. Insight into the irrationality of both drives, love and hate. Love democracy community of property. Comparison with tragedy.

Democritus: the world is irrational, not temperate and beautiful either, but instead only necessary. Unconditional putting aside of everything mythic. The world is intelligible. He wants the polis (in place of the Epicurean garden); that was one possibility for Hellenic life.

Socrates. The tragic hastiness of the Greeks. The ancient philosophers were not effective. The virtuosos of life: the ancient philosophers always think *like Icarus*.

6[51]

The Greeks have certainly never been *overestimated*: for then we would have had to appraise them as they deserve; but precisely that is impossible. How should we be able to be just in our appraisal of them! We have only appraised them *falsely*.

[7 = Mp XIII 6a. 1875]

7[1]

The reverence for classical antiquity, as the Italians displayed it, that is, therefore, the only serious, unselfish, devoted reverence that antiquity has found up until now, is a magnificent example of Don Quixotism: and therefore philology is in the best case something like that. Already so with the Alexandrian scholars, so with all the Sophists of the first and second centuries, with the Atticists, etc. They imitate something purely chimerical and go running after a miraculous world that never existed. This sort of trait already runs through antiquity: the way in which they copied Homeric heroes, all of their dealings with myth have something of this. All of ancient Greece itself has gradually become a Don Quixote object. We cannot understand our modern world if we do not perceive the colossal influence of what is purely fantastic. Now, opposite to this stands: there can be no imitation. All imitation is only an aesthetic phenomenon, directed therefore at appearance; something living can take on manners, thoughts, etc. through imitation, but it can *engender* nothing. A culture that runs after the Greek one can engender nothing. Admittedly, the creator can borrow from and nourish himself everywhere. And so, too, only as creators will we be able to have something of the Greeks. Wherein, though, would philologists be creators! Some unclean trades do have to exist, knackers; also proofreaders: are philologists supposed to represent that sort of unclean trade?

7[2]

Emergence of the philologist. At the appearance of the great work of art, there will always stand opposite a spectator who not only feels its effect, but also would like to eternalize it. So, too, with the great state, in short, with everything that elevates human beings. So the philologists want to eternalize the effect of antiquity: they can do that only as *re-creating artists*. Not as still-living hum⟨ans?⟩

7[3][1]

Emergence of philology. (Did antiquity need a class of representatives?)
Present-day emergence of the philologist.
His relationship to the Greeks.
Their influence upon nonphilologists.
The philologists of the future — whether any such will exist?

7[4][2]

Friendship goddess hear with favor the song
that we now sing to friendship
Wherever the eye of friends gazes
brimming over with the happiness of friendship:
approach us helpfully
dawn in your gaze and
true pledge of eternal youth in the holy laws.[3]

7[5][4]

In examining the history of philology, it is striking how few really talented people have participated in it. Among the most famous are some who have destroyed their understanding with erudition, and among the most intelligent are those who knew how to do nothing with their understanding other than to strain at gnats. It is a melancholy history, I believe, no science is so poor in talents. They are the lame in spirit, who have found their hobbyhorse in hairsplitting.

I prefer to write something that deserves to be read as the philologists read their writers, rather than to crouch over a single author. And after all — even the least of creating stands higher than the discourse about what has been created.

7[6][5]

That there exist scholars who occupy themselves exclusively with the investigation of Greek and Roman antiquity is found by everyone to be proper, indeed praiseworthy, and above all comprehensible, assuming that they approve generally of investigating the past: that these same scholars, however, are at the same time the educators of the nobler youth, of the rich classes, is not as easily understood: here lies a problem. Why exactly *them*? That is not self-evident, as when the scholar of the healing art also heals and is a doctor. For if these were the same, occupying oneself with Greek and Roman antiquity would have to be the same as "science of education." In short: the relationship between theory and practice in the philologist is not so quickly perceived. How does he come to the claim to be the teacher in a higher sense and to educate not only all scientific people, but all cultivated ones generally? — The philologist would therefore have to acquire this educating force from antiquity; so then we ask with astonishment: how do we come to attribute to a distant past such value that we can only be cultivated with the help of its knowledge? — Really, we do not or only rarely ask this: instead, the domination of philology over the educational process is almost undoubted, and antiquity *has* that worth. To that extent, the situation of the philologist is more favorable than that of every other adherent of science: admittedly, he still does not have the greatest mass of human beings who have need of him; the doctor, e.g., has many more. But he has selected human beings and, indeed, youths at the time when everything is budding; those who can expend time and money upon their higher development. As far as European cultivation now extends, people have employed a Latin-Greek foundation for secondary schools, as the first and highest means. Philology has thereby found the right and best opportunity to propagate and to awaken respect for itself: no other science stands here in so favorable a position. On the whole, all of those who have gone through such institutions also hold firmly to the excellence of the arrangement; they are unconscious conspirators in favor of philology; if a single word against it resounds from those who have not taken this path, denunciation follows as unanimously and as quietly as if classical cultivation were a sort of magic, producing blessedness and proving itself through this blessedness to every individual; they do not even polemicize, "they have experienced it."

Now, there exist many things to which humans have so accustomed themselves that they take them for purposeful; for habituation mixes sweetness into all things and humans mostly assess the rightness of a thing according to pleasure. *Pleasure in classical antiquity*, as it is felt at present, should now be tested for once and analyzed as to how much of it is that pleasure in habituation, how much pleasure in dishabituation: I mean that inner, active, new and young pleasure, how it awakens a fertile conviction from day to day, the pleasure in a higher goal, which also wants to be the means to it: whereby we come further, step by step, from one unaccustomed thing into another unaccustomed thing: like a mountain-climber.

On what basis does the great esteem for antiquity in the present rest, that we construct the entirety of modern cultivation upon it? Where is the origin of this pleasure? Of this preference for antiquity?

In performing this investigation, I believe that I have come to realize that all of philology also rests upon the same basis as that upon which the impression of antiquity as an important means of education rests, I mean all of its present existence and force. The philological profession as teaching profession is the exact expression of a predominant view about the value of antiquity and about the best method of education. Two propositions are included in this thought; first: all higher education must be a historical one, second: it is different with Greek and Roman history than with all others, namely, *classical*. So one who knows this history becomes a teacher. Here we do not investigate the first proposition, whether a higher education must be historical, but instead the second: *to what extent classical?*

Concerning this some prejudices are very widespread.

First, the prejudice that lies in the synonymous concept "*humanistic* studies": antiquity is classical, because it is the school of what is humane.

Second: "antiquity is classical because it is *enlightened*."

7[7][6]

Il faut dire la vérité et s'immoler.[7]
Voltaire.

If we once assume that there might exist freer and more superior spirits, who would be dissatisfied with the cultivation that goes along now in full swing and would lead it in front of their tribunal: how would the defendant speak to them? Above all, thus: "whether you have a right to accuse or not, in any case do not take hold of me, but of my creators; they have the duty to defend me and I have a right to remain silent: I am after all nothing but their creation." Now we would lead in the creators: and among them would also see one entire class, that of the *philologists*. This class consists on the one hand of people who use their knowledge of Greek and Roman antiquity in order to educate with it young people from 13 to 20 years of age, and thus also of those who have the task of cultivating ever anew their teachers, therefore of being the educators of educators; the philologists of the first kind are teachers in gymnasia, those of the second professors in the universities. To the first we turn over selected young people, those in whom talent and a nobler sensibility are visible early, and upon whose education the parents can amply expend time and money; if we turn over to them still others who do not meet these three conditions, it lies in the hands of the teachers to turn them away. The second kind, consisting of the philologists of the university, receive the young men who feel themselves dedicated to the highest and most demanding occupation, that of the teacher and creator of the human species; it lies in turn in their hands to put aside false intruders. Now if the cultivation of any age is condemned, then the philologists are in any case severely assailed: that is, either they, in the confusion of their senses, want precisely that bad cultivation, because they take it to be something good, or they do not want it, but are too weak to impose the one that they perceive to be better. Their guilt, therefore, lies either in the defectiveness of their insight or in the impotence of their will. In the first case, they would say they did not know any better, in the second, they could not do any better. But since the philologists educate primarily with the help of Greek and Roman antiquity, the defectiveness of their insight presumed in the first case could point to the fact that they *do not understand* antiquity; in the second, however, to the fact that antiquity has been set down by them in the present by mistake, supposedly as the most important resource for education,[8] because it does not educate at all or no longer does so now. If on the contrary we make the impotence of their will into the reproach, then they would certainly be completely right if they do ascribe that educational significance and energy to antiquity, but they would not be the suitable tools through which antiquity could express this energy: that is, they would be teachers mistakenly and would live in a false position: but how then did they come to this? Through a deception about themselves and their vocation. In order therefore to grant the philologists their share in the contemporary bad cultivation, we could condense the various possibilities in this sentence. *The philologist must understand three things if he wants to prove his innocence, antiquity, the present, himself: his guilt lies in not understanding either antiquity or the present or himself. First question: does the philologist understand antiquity?* — — —[9]

[8 = U I 6b. Summer 1875]

8[1]

Books for 8 years.

Schopenhauer.
Dühring.
Aristotle.
Goethe.
Plato.

8[2]

Against lyric poetry among the Germans. Then I even read that *Mörike*[1] is supposed to be the greatest German lyric poet! Isn't it a crime to be stupid, if someone therefore feels or wants to feel Goethe[2] *not* to be the greatest? — But what must be rattling around there in people's heads, what idea of lyric poetry? I thereupon had another look at this Mörike and found him completely weak and unpoetic, with the exception of 4–5 things in the German folk-song manner. Above all, clarity of perception is completely lacking. And what people call musical in him is not very much so: and shows *how little* people know about music: which is *more* than this sort of sugary-flimsy sing-song and cling-clang! — Of ideas, now, he has none at all: and I still tolerate only poets who, along with other things, also have ideas, like Pindar and Leopardi. But in the long run, what can this boyish vagueness of feeling, as it expresses itself in the German folk song, be for anyone! There I give thanks instead to Horace, on account of him being quite precise and placing his little words and ideas like a mosaic.

8[3][3]

In turn:

Dühring The Value of Life.[4]
Dühring Course in Philosophy.[5]
Reis[6] Mathematics.
Physics, etc.
Natural scientific library.
Political economy.
Hygiene.
History.

First hour of the day dedicated to learning.
Then preparation of the lecture course.
In the seminar *Prometheus*?
Choephori?
Alcestis?

8[4]

Plans of every kind:

1) the series of lectures on Greek existence.[7]
2) collection of huge empirical material about the knowledge of human beings. For that purpose, ancient works of history, novels, etc. to be read, also letters.
3) Dühring, to be studied thoroughly and to be seen as the attempt at doing away with Schopenhauer and to see what I have in Schopenhauer, what not. Afterwards, Schopenhauer to be read once again.[8]
4) gradual continuation of my *Unfashionable Observations*, first of all "Richard Wagner in Bayreuth," "the philologists"[9] "on religion."
5) to pursue my philological works, so that they do not completely escape from memory. To publish the first

volume of a collection of philological works, containing: "The *Choephori* of Aeschylus" "on rhythm" "Hesiod's and Homer's contest" "*diadoche*[10] of philosophers."

6) with my students Baumgartner and Brenner, the preparatory studies for a theory of style.[11]
7) in the pedagogical seminar: Plato *Iliad* theory of modes Aeschylus's *Agamemnon*.

8[5][12]

Goethe is above all an *epic poet*, much more than some sort of lyric poet. Completely false to see in him the *greatest* lyric poet.

8[6][13]

Aeschylus is, like all poets, unreligious.

8[7][14]

One of the most harmful books is *Don Quixote*.

8[8]

It is not at all necessary to have "beautiful weather" for nature to appear beautiful. Much of nature even *requires* bad {weather} for this.

[9 = U III 1. Summer 1875]

9[1][1]

The Value of Life by E. Dühring. 1865.

Dühring's preface to the "Value of Life." He expects enmity from all sides, believes he has given offense to school-philosophy, first because he takes into consideration the economic future of humanity, then because he traces the concepts of justice back to revenge. Otherwise he knows himself to be in *complete accord with the spirit of the age* and believes that the attempts to push him aside will run aground precisely on this spirit. Bad style, lack of composure and loftiness, spoiled manner of conciseness ("materialist viewpoints," "nation distances itself from the dreamworld, in which the center-point of its existence fell," "anticipation," "consideration," "colossal dimensions that thinking must adopt"). In the language is something illogical, yet in no way the illogic of enthusiastic reflection, but rather a blend of uncleanliness (slovenliness), sobriety and lack of practice in style.[2] I am not supposed to think of Schopenhauer, even what concerns ethics. — "World-despair" — pretty word — is therefore not recommended. He describes himself as the "most decided antagonist" of Schopenhauer; yet he has "high esteem for his striving and his accomplishments"! — He traces back to Feuerbach "the young, lively, energetic direction that now understands how to preserve a part of the dignity of philosophy by confronting obscurification with energy and success." Berlin 1865.

Introduction.

— "the strength of optimism consists in overlooking and ignoring"[3] the disharmonious elements in this world, pessimism "piles two systems upon each other," "does not know the force of unified thinking."[4] — So optimism would therefore be the philosophy of the *more logical* human beings — which has to do with conclusions drawn from the material presented, but they intentionally present an incomplete material and disregard the rest. The solution of pessimists is an illogical one, they place two logically irreconcilable worlds beside each other: because for them the higher order of things is not supposed to explain the lower one, but instead to cancel, to annihilate it; they often assume blind unreason directly as cause for the existence of the real world. It is not a logical necessity, but instead a poetic one, that engenders pessimism. While it is in general not practical necessity that engenders optimism: they feel comfortable and only begin to construct a system out of it and to justify themselves logically when they are forced to do so by pessimists. So optimism is essentially *self-defense of the happy ones against the assertions of the pessimists, pessimism is aggressive and has necessity as its mother*. It is *older* and more originary *than optimism*, productive, so that it *itself still* calls to light *its opposite*. Ego.

In the field of practical judgments and values there is no pure judgment, no pure knowledge.[5] In the constitution of our *striving*, our *intentions* lies the root of all of our assenting or rejecting judgments concerning life. This as critique of Schopenhauerian philosophy. Certain representations are not possible at all *except* in relationship to a will. Every *drive* is a need and already contains the *representation of the existence of an object of satisfaction*; thus the drive is formative of ideas.

The *opposition* of purely theoretical judgments and practical valuations is this: a theoretical judgment sets forth agreement with a purely theoretical concept, the practical valuation, agreement with an aspiration, i.e., with an object that *already has* some measure of what *ought to be*.

The total judgment about the value of life is the resultant of the elementary determinations; there can be no theoretical concept that would establish in advance how life would have to be constituted in order to have our approval. Absurd standpoints are therefore ones such as: misfortune[6] is to be denied, for it is really misfortune only from the standpoint of a human. Or with Spinoza: nothing is objectionable in itself; first the will of human beings stamps this as good, that as evil. If we thus give up what is human generally, we lose every measure for practical valuation. Moreover we lose the moral judgment (we are no longer permitted to speak of good and evil, indeed every not purely theoretical decision would have to be designated as an illusion). — Therefore the value of things is measured by *striving*, for someone *who does not strive at all*, there are *no values*, for the pure knower all good and evil, all assent and rejection, are absent. Someone who does not strive at all produces only purely theoretical judgments. It therefore seems to me that all loftiness of judgment about the value of life would depend upon the loftiness and strength of the striving, i.e., first upon the goal, and second upon the degree of pushing, of running toward the goal.

Every affirming valuation is a striving toward something, every negation a striving against something. Every practical judgment goes back to inclination or disinclination.

Perhaps even everything *purely theoretical* belongs under the fundamental form of the practical. Understanding gives the law as to what is in accordance with understanding and what is not: hence what is supposed to be and what not: it assents to what is in conformity with its own being.

The judgment about the value of life is, put succinctly, an emotion[7] — either craving for or satiety with life. Dühring denies hatred for life: it would be an impulse of life that moves against life itself.

The consideration of the unalterable element in the subjectivity of human beings is therefore the preparatory work: with the question: is the entire design of the life of sensations and emotions perhaps irreconcilable with a harmonious unfolding of existence?

Whether this world is the best one is an absurd question: we have no conception at all of different possibilities.[8]

Dühring sets forth his task thus: "the adverse sides of existence should find their elucidation in the harmony of the whole" (disgracefully expressed!) "Misfortune does not let itself be reminted as something good." "Pain remains pain, whatever consequences it may have." "Although the world fully satisfies neither understanding nor drives, we nevertheless have no means at all for investigating according to the understanding why life includes misfortunes."[9] "World and life are given facts, our reconciliation with their adverse sides can only be a factual one."[10] "This reconciliation therefore itself exists only in the form of a *striving*." We seek the resultants of the individualized emotions and utilize these as force of resistance against the manifold impressions. Thus we attain to what is still harmony, even if not free of discordance. The reconciliation with the individual is drawn from the consideration of the whole. The theoretical impossibility of inquiring into the basis of the factual is in itself already disharmony. There remains for our understanding only "the idea of overcoming the individual hardship through the conception of a greater coherence,"[11] to modify the individual conception through the totality of the others.

But the theoretical reconciliation does not suffice; if thinking were in a position to provide undisturbed calm, then contemplative wisdom (like everything that promises to satisfy simply through theory, e.g., art) would merit the exclusive interest of humans. But it is not the means for becoming master over misfortune. Philosophy must acknowledge precisely that mere arrangement of ideas does not suffice when it comes to coping with misfortune. The fact and consciousness of the fact must be added; the real change of sensations must give a different foundation to the conceptions, the mood must be changed.

Even a theory that proceeds toward a harmonious perspective on the world cannot do without the presupposition that energy of action is necessary against misfortune. *Only, what is firmly established for human beings as* **unalterable**, *can prompt them simply* to *adjust their ideas.*[12] Where human intervention can still change things, actions are most important. Optimism is frequently despicable because it extenuates misfortune due to its *laziness*, and a great part of philosophers has assumed unalterability where human energy of action does still have a prospect of success. "The judgment about the value of life will fall out in different ways according to where one draws the line between what is unalterable and what human beings can shift."[13,14,15]

Those are the thoughts in the introduction.

In short: out of many individual valuations results as a sum the actual view upon the value of life. In the case of no valuation is it a matter of pure knowledge, all are emotions; that sum is also nothing but an emotion. I want, however, to add that it would be more correct to call all such judgments *impure knowledge*: the impurity lies 1) in the way in which the material is available, e.g., very incompletely 2) in the way that from this the sum is constructed: so that, e.g., a false generalization is made (the sum of our experiences *can never* justify a judgment about life), therefore the logical expression of that summation is false 3) in that every individual piece of the material is once again the result of impure knowing; and indeed, quite necessarily: no experience, e.g., of a friend can be complete, so that we would have a *logical* right to a total valuation. All valuations are premature and must be so. So then the measure with which we measure is our being, no unalterable magnitude, we have moods, etc., we would have to know ourselves in order to assess fairly the relationship of anything whatsoever to ourselves.

If, then, all judgments about the value of life have developed unjustly and illogically: would it follow from this that we should *not* judge *at all*? But if we could only *live*, without appraising, without aversion and attraction! For all aversion is connected to a valuation, just as all attraction. A drive *without* any accompanying knowledge (about what is beneficial, what is harmful) does not exist at all. — We are from the beginning illogical and therefore also *unjust* beings **and can recognize this!** That is one of the most monstrous *disharmonies* of existence![16] Yet we bear within ourselves a measure with which we measure existence here and which is completely immovable: it is, no doubt, the principle of identity. And in turn, this measure is precisely the sole *harmony* that we know. It seems to us that the disharmonious world exists, but that harmony in the principle of identity is nothing but a theory, a representation. But can we think of what is self-contradictory as *real*? The so-called reality-philosophy recommends itself by this word to the popular prejudice about real and unreal. But if, e.g., it were established that without the concept of a harmonious reality things could not be assessed at all, not even falsely, then judging, determining values is indeed itself nothing other than measuring the "real" world according to one that counts for us as **more real**.

Therefore: the differentiation of two worlds, of which the one is the worse one, the more unreal one, in comparison with a *more real*, better one, *the thesis consequently of pessimism* is the fact that precedes all value-assessing; it lies in the constitution of the judging understanding, which proceeds from the identity of the world accessible to it. The emergence of the understanding and its constitution is not to be derived from the practical relation to things, the understanding is not a formation coming from the temperament. Instead, all inclination and aversion already presume the understanding and in it the principle of contradiction; *without logic*, no sensation either, no mood, no representation.

I. *Life as the aggregate of sensations and emotions.*

It is a question of the *totality* of affections; those brought forth by dreams are also to be taken into account. In general it does not matter whether an affection rests upon truth or error.

Life is *not only* the sum of stimulations that enter into consciousness. Their kind and degree are too different. The systems of the ancients extracted only one kind and made it into the exclusive measure of judgment: the Epicureans sensation, the Stoics abstract consciousness. So in practice they reached false maxims. The former pursued pleasurable sensations and underestimated the mighty power of abstract representations upon the temperament; the others feigned a triumph over sensation and affect, fell into affectation and so directed themselves externally toward the pattern of the catechism, without having triumphed inwardly: grimaces and play-acting. — Not even the life of animals consists purely of sensations; in the higher stages it has emotions; it has, e.g., grief. *The human always sinks below the animal, if at any time he sinks.* There is always a degeneration linked to the renunciation of certain elements of the complete life. — Does there exist a view that makes the emotions into the exclusive measure of value? By contrast, not only stoicism, but all of modern morality has placed the center-point of existence in abstract representations: in the agreement with completely abstracted maxims, which are *not* supposed to have their source in the affects. But motives for action and affection that would not have their root in sensation and affect do not exist. The play of affects makes comprehensible all expressions of life up to the production of the most abstract ideas. The passions belong to life, we dare not throw suspicion upon them as the disturbers of happiness. Existence becomes a bleak desert without love and hate. Humans do not at all want a uniform calm, they seek stimulation and excitement. They challenge pleasure and pain, so to speak. Nothing great is brought to completion without passion, says Aristotle. Life itself is that great thing, which is not brought to completion without passion. To abstract from the passions leads on the one side to asceticism, on the other side to well-calculated, insipid sensual pleasure; there everything that bestows value upon life is annihilated. The human being sinks in the second case below the animal, in the first he becomes a repugnant monster ("he touches the root of all striving without distinction"[17]). There one turns against a part of the conditions of life, here against its complete content. The ordinary suicide is something relatively guiltless compared to beginning to kill the essence of the species itself, not only a single individual. Even murder can seem like a smaller crime than the dark work of people who poison life with their complaining. — And so the shameless abusiveness proceeds; therein occurs: "the uprooting of everything great and noble, mockery of and enmity toward all humane sensations and feelings"[18] — ; "bound up with dissoluteness and the deadened living out of life" — "then a supposed philosophy sets out boldly to sow hatred of life and of what is alive."[19] Just think of Buddha and Christ, etc., in this regard! "The individual may be excused if he turns to the cloister; it cannot become the general doctrine without assuming the character of an intellectual crime."[20] That must mean: the individual in his practical renunciation may be excused: but not the individual who makes a theoretical general maxim out of it, that would be a crime against the intellect. "If the bond of humanity were tied more tightly, those melancholy exceptions would also cease, the temperament would not be bound only to its own self-interested endeavor, the individual fate would not be powerful enough to smother affects related to a greater whole, to humanity. The force of passion would maintain itself; the force of love and hate would escape the deadly power of the particular fate."[21] But there everything is upside down! In the first place, he assumes everywhere that ascetics are ascetics precisely as egoists, that only the individual destiny brings them to hate existence. In the second place, he feels nothing of the generally helpful pathos of asceticism, which is effective for everyone; in its highest form, it is precisely death and suffering for everyone. In the third place, he confuses blaséness and disgust with turning away from life. When he says "if the bond of humanity were tied more tightly, those melancholy exceptions, that spiritual suicide, would cease."[22] He therefore means in all seriousness that a life in solitude could never be a life for humans, and that turning away from life would be turning away from humans. Now, it is actually the reverse; I would like to know what sort of higher bonds would tie human to human generally, if we wanted to take away the work of the solitary ascetics of every kind! And spiritual suicide even! Think of Empedocles and Schopenhauer, Leopardi, who appear here as "criminals against the intellect," of Luther and of how many others. It does not seem to be precisely the "spirit" that is stunted by this way of considering life!

Now, the self-tormenting teachings are derived from powerfully artificial relationships ("the mood must deviate significantly from the normal attitude"[23] — the popular insinuation about the madness of all ascetics and ascetic philosophies!). Therefore this "caricature of the human" should not be such a dangerous opponent. — (And yet the most serious human beings have lived and taught according to completely monstrous religions!)

More dangerous would be the morality that sacrifices to abstractions.

I want to add that an intellectual *error* (concerning body and soul, concerning the body as seat of the affects, as in Plato) is perhaps necessary for the emergence of asceticism; but this error, however, is related only to the *representation* of how a human being gets free from the *will to life*; the drive to get free from it in general has nothing to do with it, is not to be derived from the intellect. That such a drive can emerge precisely among the more noble human beings is, however, a measure of value for existence, we do not get away from it even by insulting it; even *if* a monstrous error lay therein, still the possibility of such an error belonged once again to the dark features of existence. Dühring is especially enraged about the aforementioned lack of affect; yet if someone renounces pathos and understands how to become completely ἦθος, that counts *for us* much more highly and the possibility of such behavior is precisely for us an object of longing. The advocate of pathos looks bad as a glorifier of life. If nothing great emerges without pathos (which can be doubted —) an uncanny light falls upon life; it suffices to see something tragic in every emergence of something great, indeed, to see in life itself a tragedy. "Our morality is[24] an idolatry that sacrifices living motives to empty abstractions."[25] Injustice, e.g., the greatest misfortune that the world knows (I doubt it!); abstinence from it the first presupposition of a contented state of temperament. It does not have this quality because an abstract rule designates it as repugnant; a drive has created the concept of injustice, the drive for requital, revenge; the fading concepts of justice and duty refer back to this affect,

Morality wants to determine the value of different kinds of behavior: for that it needs a measure. This lies in the involuntary determinations that nature has given, the foundation is laid in drives and affects. The purely theoretical understanding can bring forth no obligation. A morality that condemns the entire realm of immediate feelings is vain hypocrisy.

"Thus the false principles of *moral* valuation are opposed to a proper appreciation of life."[26] He tries now to discredit the balance of the soul as if it were of no importance, it is a matter of the forces that are found to be in balance here. Kind and measure of the sensations and emotions that are connected to one another are what we have to thank when a balance emerges; the abstract force is related only to the determination of the individual factors, not that of the whole. — All of this is unclearly thought or expressed.

The degeneration of systems of morality is attached to neglect of the difference between those emotions that are related to humans as individuals and those related to the behavior of humans toward one another. Someone thought of as a solitary in the world would be lacking a primary source of pleasure and pain: know nothing of the sympathetic affections, nothing of love and hate, envy and revenge. Injustice and disloyalty would be inconceivable to him. The human being requires not only nature, he requires his equal. The depth of woe (in the injuring of one human being by another) corresponds to the height of bliss (in satisfaction from love honor fame). The room for play between them is exceptionally large: that is a result of the fact that the entire human being can become an object for another person;

not individual instances of good and ill that we experience from one another, but instead the disposition, as the expression of which we understand everything individual, moves us so much, down into the depth of our being. The purely egoistical needs of life and those emerging from intercourse with humans, egoistical pleasure and the joys of sympathy, are not at all equal. Infamous, to stamp self-sacrifice as selfishness and to deny the disinterested feelings! Compassion and love have their center-point in the representation of an alien being, revenge and envy seek the preservation of one's own self. Certain arrogant doctrines do admittedly try to find an isolated subjectivism and in addition an abstract unity of all affections: these install an empire of egoism. Spinoza cannot be absolved of this. In contrast, Kant displays an initial inkling of what is involved: separation of the morality that is concerned with simple purposiveness according to the viewpoint of human needs and the morality that keeps its eye upon the considerations of one human being to another. He disdained the former kind as simple technique of life; that is his one-sidedness. In contrast, Dühring: "the higher insight into the essence of life depends upon whether we know how to differentiate the misfortune that is the consequence of an unjust injury from the hardship that chance and necessity impose upon us."[27] "Everything that the viewpoint of our own advantage has stamped as vice and virtue vanishes in comparison with the significance of the behavior in which human beings benefit or injure their equals."[28] "The sensations of temperament of one or the other class are *completely different*." "This is the basis for our admittedly regretting the most acute offenses against our own well-being, yet not feeling them with the thorn that accompanies the feeling of injustice."[29]

II. *Difference as the genuine object of feelings.*

Pleasure in life strives for an impact-like transition from one state to another. Indeed, the uniformity of mood is itself perhaps nothing other than a great multitude of impacts that individually are imperceptible. But we desire the unevenness of impacts, their high energy, amid all variations; we place the variation where the high point of sensation lies. It is *essentially only the variation that is sensed.* Tension of opposites is necessary for the emergence of every stronger sensation. The eye senses the variation of light-stimulation more strongly than its continuance: we say there that *habit deadens.* Physiologically, the deadening depends upon the repetition of the same sudden impression, interrupted by empty intervals. A lattice that allows rays of sun through it; the eye does not put up with the sudden change of brightness and darkness, with strong stimulus and the almost complete lack of it. All sensation in the form of a uniform rhythm, which almost alternates emptiness and fullness like at the lattice. Hence fatigue. A long sound eventually very burdensome: we cannot look for too long at one picture. Thus we feel the beginning of an affection more strongly, because the continuing stimulation brings our fatigue along with it: therefore habit is the expression for a certain fatigue; extended still further, it produces satiety.

Boredom: to be explained as the absence of life-stimuli, where the same activity is always repeating itself; in the fortunate case, it turns into satiety and finds its end there. But the life-drive is often too weak to produce the intensity of boredom that leads to the negation of the state: the worst form of displeasure! Otherwise it is an impelling power; it condemns the present activity of the mind and stimulates it to transition into a new state. It is therefore life-numbing only where lethargy of the life-drive is already present. (He says this against Schopenhauer: but what sort of nonsense is that, "*leth*argy of the life-drive"[30]). "Where the energy for emotion has been annihilated forever, there is disharmony among the representations of the still-active understanding and the few life-stimuli that are still accessible to the *deadened* temperament."[31] He means the ascetics and philosophers of asceticism: they would be bored; therefore in a state of "partial deadening of the capacity for life"; in this case he advises that one arrange oneself artificially and restrict oneself mainly to the abstract faculty of representation; for an old man, the stimulus of the faded images of affections begins, also where a "premature using up of the life-energies"[32] makes it like being old. There we should *beware of nothing more so* than "regaining the fresh stimulus of life"; "existence would become stunted by the futility of the striving."[33] Here, one must renounce: then the supposedly life-numbing character of boredom ceases. It is then a more restricted sphere of life in comparison to the complete whole life.

It is always only difference that is sensed, we must know the measure of the efforts in order to judge about existence and the magnitude of satisfaction.

If human beings did not consider continuing situations with indifference, they would also perceive that there can be happiness in unhappiness. It depends entirely upon the frame of life, once that has been drawn: inside of it, there either is or is not satisfaction. The state that stimulated us most forcefully becomes a matter of indifference afterwards and forms the new indifferent basis of the new life-pleasure.

The entrance into life is also a transition: the wholly new stimulus distinguishes itself in the strongest way from the relative emptiness and indeterminacy of the life-impulse. Every individual is a new standpoint, which allows a new world to enter into consciousness.

(Well now, that, too, is mythology, and mysticism and certainly badly *believed*!)

III. The basic form in the succession of life-stimulations.

Alternation of rising and sinking, the *wave* is the simplest type. The wave-form in almost all processes of nature: in it, movements transmit themselves. Rhythm rules the entire so-called dead existence.

Waves are alternating accumulation and diminution of the otherwise uniformly distributed material. Its basic form is: alternation in drawing together and spreading out. Risings and sinkings of the energy of feeling follow in continual alternation, the constant states are a uniformly recurring rhythm, the particular pulse of which we do not discern. Thus we sense light- and sound-impressions as *constant*, whereas they are rhythmic. Now sensation as such is not a movement. If we attempt to represent it to ourselves as such, then we are once again imagining this force in a reverse way. The unconstrained movement of a mass in empty space is not represented as force from the standpoint of our sensation. Movement belongs entirely to the formal side of our thinking, has nothing to do with sensation. Movement must first vanish, i.e., lead to a static effect, before it solicits our sensation. Sensation is the sign of a movement that has been made statically perceptible, i.e., abolished. The ordinary representation, that sensation is the direct expression of a movement stimulated in us, is false. We do not sense movement as such.

Therefore: in the constant states of sensation there is an elementary rhythm. But in interrupted sensations? Does there exist an equally periodic alternation? Within every class of sensations, rising and sinking are completely visible. But various states of temperament seem to follow irregularly. The high points of life have the appearance of isolated peaks.

A certain disharmony, i.e., a mixture of attunement and conflict seems to be the actual form of life. Movement below the threshold of the completely harmonious is what bestows its charm upon play. Here Dühring draws a lot upon the analogy between music and life; his doctrine, moreover, is symbolically-mythologically also contained in my conception of the Dionysian and Apollonian. The Dionysian is then the disharmonious ground that longs for rhythm, beauty, etc. The rhythm of organic life — how fully does it adapt itself to the form of the impressing stimuli? The opposite can be sensed at first, up until the complete annihilation of the sensation, on the other hand, at least for a while the rhythm of organic life can give in entirely to the impressing stimuli, pass over into it — all of this is the Dionysian phenomenon. In contrast, the moderate behavior in the presence of impressing stimuli, the maintenance of one's own rhythm, the arranging of two forms of rhythm into each other, finally the transference of one's own rhythm to the impressing stimuli (= beauty) the Apollonian phenomenon.

Why did Schopenhauer respect music so much? Dühring explains it thus. Sensation binds itself immediately to sound (music is a "means of expression"). If it is a question of contraction of the world of sensation and temperament, in which the *objective* representations are of no consequence, then music is the longed-for abstract realm. Now, Schopenhauer derives all of the blame for the stunting of existence from objectification. He gazes with mystical longing toward an empire that corresponds to the unboundedness and freedom of the world of sounds.

IV. The course of a human life.

Knowledge is what unifies life's experiences into a unitary consciousness and, in spreading itself across the individual life, apprehends the general fate and makes the distress of the moment within it *fade away*. Thus it becomes philosophy and leads to belief in the value of life. (Must it really do so? Knowledge of our *general* fate — couldn't it therefore "make" the present and individual distress "*fade away*" only because it weighs and hurts so much more intensely, therefore deadens only as the more intensive pain by comparison with the much smaller one? Isn't the belief in the nonvalue of existence a narcotic against individual things, as well as the belief in its value?)

If we were limited to our own memory and expectation, we would not know birth and death at all: just as the entire species of human beings does not know them. (Origin completely concealed, with regard to the future, doubt as to whether humanity has a goal or not.) If we had knowledge of how the population of a cosmic body perished, our consciousness of the world would be vastly increased. If we were once to experience something like that, therefore also about the goal that was put into our species, the center-point of our endeavors would be altered; we would no longer believe in achieving something of *eternal* significance in science art and social institutions. (I think in connection with this of how such illusions of individual peoples have already been recognized as such; the Greeks believed that with every Olympic victory the whole world was watching such an event, the gods included.) The limitlessness of prospect would be lacking, everything would have to become more practical. The immortality of the species is the silent presupposition of all of our higher representations. (I would like to investigate what humanity owes to imaginings, to impure thinking, indeed, whether a higher life is possible after skepticism once gains mastery here, e.g., is art still possible?)

The basic form of the *child's* life is the present; the entire increase of pleasure and pain that the persisting representation brings with it is lacking; that is lucky! Hunger and thirst are certainly much stronger feelings than at a later age. The entire life of the child has a shorter rhythm; to the restlessly working development corresponds restlessness of sensation. With regard to nourishment the organism has not only to maintain the *balance* of the metabolism, but to manage an increase: that must incite sensation to visible pains; as the signs also indicate. — Crying precedes laughing; it outweighs it in any case. — If we think of a needy and helpless situation as the opposite of a conscious representation that feels the impotence of its efforts to alter the state, there we will measure how fortunate it is that nature does not illuminate all of its states with the light of knowledge. (And yet knowledge in the philosopher reaches such a degree that the individual human being in his helplessness against the general ἀνάγκη[34] would appear to himself precisely like a *child that has become conscious*!)[35]

Playing is the real work of the child and likewise a need for him, like creative activity for a riper age. (We can infer completely his later activity from the way in which a child plays.) Play is the most serious concern for a child, not something amusing-superfluous, as adults often judge it to be. Indeed, one has explained our entire, so serious existence as play; how could anything other than simply an arbitrary arrangement of the conditions of life arise out of a mere nothing? So existence would have the character of a freely chosen amusement, obstacles created only in order to be overcome. Dühring takes the idea as insipid: it was, moreover, Plato's idea[36] that we are the plaything of the gods. "Life is no game, for it includes genuine pains";[37] as though that weren't also true of children's play!

Every stage of life has its own right to be respected, we should not treat the earlier ones only as means for the later ones. The purpose cannot always lie only outside the present.[38]

The child is much more than a simple object for education. Pedagogues always think only about what they *have to make* out of the child: the child lives in the present, that is the contrast.

Learning and playing are to be strictly separated. School must display sober seriousness that prepares for life. The overcoming of obstacles and the perception of our capacity is bound up with a joy that exceeds in strength that of play. With regard to certain artificial situations, those who view school as the beginning of the stunting of life are right: it was a prison existence. But the work of learning can become a joy and satisfaction, it is accidental, alterable states that make of it the opposite.

Foolish principle, that it would only be a question of learning to work and exercise of the energies! Dühring is right to say that it would be an irony upon the nature of life. (The failure of pedagogy generally conceals itself behind this, e.g., in the gymnasium.) This maxim abstracts from success, stunts the natural relationship of effort and reward and leads to a pain to which no satisfaction corresponds. Moreover, it is comical in the first place to want to make of life a race with obstacles. Nature has connected satisfaction not to effort, but to the success of effort: this feeling would dwindle and give way to an aversion toward an essentially useless occupation.

The disposition of the child finds its limit in house and family; whatever good or ill befalls him here is much increased by this limitation of the entire field of vision. The greatest misfortune is the injustice in the injuring of one human being by another,[39] the greatest happiness the one that grows out of every sort of inclination. How important, whether the child experiences parental love or not! Parental love is in the first place a drive independent of the understanding, rooted in the sensual; therefore it can be disturbed by opposed drives, it requires a supplement in accordance with the understanding. Justice toward the child cannot be replaced by love. The child has the sharpest instinct for what is just, for this desire for justice is rooted in the natural drive, is related to the need for revenge. The childish temperament hates, in such cases, even the parents.

Later experiences tend rather to deaden one against certain kinds of injustice. Now, the household authority is rarely the pattern for just conduct. Moreover, what is aimed at in the family is subordination, not a just equality of arrangements.

The differentiation of justice and injustice is very easy for those who are the suffering part, but causes difficulties for those who practice injustice; the concept of justice arises from the one who is suffering. In taking their revenge, the suffering ones become the teachers of justice for all. The power of resistance of those who suffer injustice is presupposed; equal right only with equal power, therefore among equals. Everywhere that nature has created inequality, it goes badly for making subjective justice valid. A certain justice should be practiced even in such circumstances, but this does not have the usual source, it is involuntary. One borrows the concept of just conduct from where it has been most generally cultivated; this abstractly arisen feeling for justice is, however, weaker and more indeterminate than the other, the kind that arose out of a drive. Justice is undoubtedly worst off in *school*: there, even the love that rules in families is absent. The thought of an abstract purpose is the only protection here. A teacher who is a pedant of justice is relatively speaking still good fortune for the adolescent in comparison with a teacher who behaves according to mood and whim. — We forget with the most difficulty the injustice that befalls the pupil. It is even the sign of a noble disposition when the stimulation of an immature age leaves behind enduring traces.

Until the stirrings of sexual life, boys and girls lead a relatively placid existence. Now the feeling of life increases to the highest of heights. Competitions for honor, the passions of communal life are soon added. Nature and social world divide themselves now in human beings, with the first, they get caught up in love, with the latter, in honor; around this further existence gravitates.

What is *honor*? First of all, we have to set aside a multitude of caricatures. — For one thing, honor means the same as justice, and then distinguishing recognition. Offenses of honor, insults are offenses to justice, encroachments upon a different sphere of will. In favor of the duel, Dühring says: "crude offenses, one concedes, should be revenged; but should offenses of a more subtle and spiritual kind be considered as nothing? Would that not lead to deadening of the feeling of justice?"[40] —

Self-defense is the original form of all justice; this original foundation can never completely cease to exist. Public justice is only organized self-defense for the purpose of avenging injustice. Thus we should not be surprised if self-defense, as the engendering reason, supplements its organization when it does not suffice. The punishment for injuries in no way satisfies the natural consciousness of justice. Perhaps a part of the antipathy against public settlement of offenses to honor would vanish, if a sort of trial by jury were to replace an administrative judiciary. Yet there always remain cases where only private redress is possible (i.e., for deadly offenses that are not suited precisely for public handling).

The Germanic form of our concept of honor was remote from the ancients. But we should not forget that the natural representation of the necessity of taking revenge for injustice had not yet been crippled among them by an opposed principle. Communal life then stepped into the foreground and so private relations remained protected from an artificial exacerbation of the concept of justice.

A human being remains, as soon as he is willing to wager his life, master of his justice and his honor.

Honor, which stands open to injury, is a negative concept. — Completely different from it the acknowledgment of special prerogatives and services — something positive! With its magic, it passes through every stage of life. The representation of the opinion that others have of us exerts the greatest power upon our conduct. This honor is nothing but the approbation that our doing and being find among others. Everyone strives for it: what is uncommon needs objective acknowledgment to a higher degree: even in the form of posthumous fame. (This seems to me what is most important: our works and actions are the highest expressions of our self and all together represent our ideal: to this we want to grant a life for itself that would have not only the duration of a human lifetime. We ourselves treat our works as having a force and magnitude that stand outside of us, from which we can draw comfort and courage.) It is a need for sympathetic affection, not the lack of one's own judgment, one's own conviction; we feel ourselves elevated when we attain assent (above all we feel ourselves *more fruitful*! all love and affection indicate fruitfulness.)

Dishonor (ἀτιμία) is disapproval and disdain for our being and doing, not some offense against honor (ὕβρις). A dismissive judgment.[41] Acknowledgment and disdain the greatest moral powers in communal life. We uproot human nature if we cast suspicion upon the concept of honor. The most important objection is that a special distinction, however, could only be attained at the cost of others: honor a motive that makes humans into enemies; they seek their own pleasure in damaging others. So it ought to be incompatible with a noble *modest* disposition. — But that is sophistry, to unjustly stamp the mere nonexistence of special honor as prejudice against the multitude. Injustice may frequently infiltrate itself into the competition for honor, but it does not lie in the striving itself to measure one's own excellence against that of others. The painful feeling from failing in a competition *does* not *have to* be bound up with hatred toward fellow competitors, such enmity would not be rooted in honor, but in envy. If the failure were just, only the consciousness of an earlier error and a vain attempt should manifest itself: but every human must be accustomed to that. If in some unjust way merit is not acknowledged, then the feeling of having incurred an offense is added. But anyone who does not understand how to overcome injustice and injuries ought to renounce honor[42] not only on the practice ground, but in life itself. He ought to become a hermit and thus limit his sympathetic affections to the smallest extent. (A pretty judgment about life, that Dühring lets fall in such an offhand way!)

Dühring takes honor, next to love, for the reason that makes life worth living.

— We should guard ourselves from exceeding nature with our fantasy and wanting to make death into the petrifying gorgon of life. People who speak of the penance for the pleasure in life through the pain of death do not hit the mark about the naïveté of nature. (There he is right, for nature is far too stupid and blind and cruel to be able to conceive such a thought.)

We have not considered exceptional disturbances in the course of life, e.g., unusual illnesses. But these misfortunes amount to a quickly passing pain and have a subordinate significance. (Highly absurd, Dühring!) "Indeed, one would feel tempted to assume that even painful overcoming of obstacles heightens the charm of the goal and the satisfaction of success."[43] (Here he is himself only a step away from the "insipid" conception that life is a game and that suffering has its point in artistic dissonances. And he comes to this precisely with regard to illnesses! Does he not know their crippling and depressing influence, where someone has to renounce or has to fear renouncing his highest goal in life on their account? Not to mention that he knows nothing of the utility of being ill for meditative purification, for becoming kind and good!)

V. Love

No form of love is without sensual foundation; always something involuntary. Not to be brought forth by simple intent and good will. The commandment for universal love for human beings is only a *metaphor of love*, we call up the memory of a familiar sensation for help in order to indicate what goal the *understanding would have to set in general intercourse* with human beings. It is not even an analogy for love. Universal love for human beings is a stipulation in accordance with the understanding, growing upon the ground of feeling (memory of passing individual stimulations, plus an abstract striving for something more general). Opposite of the Uranian and the pandemian Aphrodite[44] right for all times and peoples. A human being can abstract from the full essence of his nature, give himself over to momentary pleasure. Much more offensive is calculating conduct. The *involuntariness* of nature does not know the separation of what is coarsely sensual from what is more noble. What is sensual, what is spiritual! Anyone who thinks only of the coarsest elements of sensuality can differentiate like Plato.

A *widespread opinion* imagines an opposition between the sensual and the spiritual in love: so that where the satisfaction of the sensual needs is *obstructed, denied* is where the more noble kinds first manifest themselves; without an unsatisfied desire it would never attain the sublime lyric of the pain of love; creative energy can obtain the one effect only at the expense of the other. Where the desire is fulfilled in its original direction, it will never let itself to be satisfied by mere ideas. So the abnormal disturbance would be the creatrice of the high feeling of love.

But the form in which love enters into humans immediately disenchants a world of sweeter ideas and impulses, long before there can be talk of an abnormal blockage. (This reply allows for a further reply.)

Why is there something *painful* in every sensation that corresponds to a drive and need? Feeling first becomes torturous in connection with abnormal obstructions. That is the strengthening of the first seed. A slight excitation is not sensed as pain, but instead as perception, which seeks its own intensification.

Think of taste, of the various degrees of sourness. We speak there of pleasure: and yet just a quantitative intensification would already produce pain.

Schopenhauer takes pleasure for the negative, pain for the positive in sensation: an ingenious theory on the basis of the most superficial point of view. In every need a lack, therefore all sensations that are attached to need are stamped as something negative. But the general movement goes from pain toward pleasure, that is the positive direction. Admittedly, pleasure also dwindles in the direction of a point of indifference; but it would be perverse to allow satisfaction to strive for need, rather than need for satisfaction. (To be sure, Faust says "and in pleasure was a pining for desire."[45]) But rather, need vanishes in pleasure. The negative must be sought in the emergence of need. (In contrast, I say: every pleasure is an excitation that turns into pain with an intensification of the stimulus; every pain is only quantitatively different from a pleasure and there exists a degree of transition from pleasure into pain. This individual pleasure is not always still sensed as such; for we live in a state of countless individual pleasurable excitations, the feeling of well-being of the whole human being is the expression of this. A minimal degree of excitation and pain is perceived as pleasure: thus need, lack, the demand for excitation also lie in every pleasure; pain is simply the *excess* of satisfaction of this lack and need. So both pleasure and pain are positive, that is, abolishing a lack, but pain at the same time creating a new need demanding decrease of the excitation. Pleasure *longs* for an increase of the excitation, pain for its decrease: in this regard both are negative. Need is their common source.) It would be thorough nonsense to say pleasure is nothing other than a subsiding pain; so that we would have to congratulate ourselves if life turned out to be rich with pains; the abundance of pain, of course, opens a tempting prospect of a similar abundance of pleasure.

Dühring differentiates between the feelings of love, which emerge fully normally with the first blossoming of that affect, and those that are obstructed and richly tempered with pain: he rails against the latter; only from a perspective contrary to nature would they be celebrated as the summit of spiritual transfiguration. To be sure, lyrical sublimity seems to gain from yearning sorrow. Love preserves its genuine nature only where it is capable of dramatic representation. But what is the point of inactive longing in connection with the active life? The poets prove nothing: it is easier and often more attractive, too, to present an impactful expression of unnature than of nature; poetic sensibility indulges in many follies. It is a weak reaction when striving, *instead of battling real obstacles*, yields to a luxury of feelings and ideas. For we can explain the enjoyment of pain only by the fact that sensation, lacking an energy directed toward the goal, seeks in reproductions and extravagant intensifications a subjective closure and respite from itself. Where an unalterable fate confronts someone, sensation often turns against its bearer and destroys his temperament. If simple indolence retreats in the face of obstacles, then the play of affects is not especially serious and puts the subject to sleep.

Sensual friendship in blameless form, its distortion now almost only what is known. It shows the absurdity of the highest infatuation and a noble self-sacrifice unto death among the Greeks, e.g., in Plato. Love objectified not only as Aphrodite, but as Eros:[46] Eros is in no way the ideal of the love of a woman for a man, but instead the ideal of that second form. It seems to be the close relationship of what is female with the gentle blossoms of the other sex: and everywhere that an opposition exists through difference of age or character, as between man and woman, he would like to preserve an expression in sensation as well. Dühring recalls the friendships of earliest youth with their more sensual character; the difference in age slight, the natures strongly different. Relations in advanced age are, according to Dühring, supposedly either degenerations of a natural drive or a bond of inclination remaining from the earliest youth.

Erotic love demonstrates the excess of feeling *independently* of natural purpose. According to Schopenhauer, the passion of love is supposedly only the expression of the striving of nature to live on in a second individual. (Dühring calls this "striving for utilization of a favorable conjuncture."[47]) But Eros, too, spurs on to every kind of action, would not shy away from death — can we speak there of an error of nature? It would have achieved the accomplishments of passion only by mistake?

Parental love, too, an essentially sensual power. Motherly love as instinct, as involuntary affect. The love of the child for its parents is only a *reactive* sensation; not an instinctive inclination. It is gratitude as reply to disposition. This love is sensual, admittedly not originally, but of the same kind as parental inclination.

Schopenhauer's view of love. Anyone who disdains life must also disdain love. Reality is not supposed to accomplish what sensation promises, love supposedly a delusive madness. Sensation and feeling as such never a delusion. Humans can charge with deceptiveness only the web of ideas that is attached to sensation. Representation is always active, anticipating the future of sensation. Herein delusion is possible, indeed unavoidable. The understanding allows the dimension of sensation to grow limitlessly according to prior experience for the future, too, as long as sensation is still growing; the belief in the transience of sensation is impossible for it. First love believes in the *eternal* significance of itself. The poets have so exalted it and not taken into consideration ordinary understanding, which alone knows external experience. — *Delusion* therefore *lies not in the laws of sensation, but instead in the laws of the understanding.* Do we want to lament that there exist *originally unavoidable errors*? (I think so!) The power of feeling, which conjures forth a dreamworld, is a higher and nobler force than the one that only recognizes passively and receptively. *Creating stands higher than apprehending.* Even if that magic creates only a world of poetry, it is nonetheless an image of the potency working at the basis of things. Sensation corresponds to those extravagant ideas, because these are first created by sensation: here there is no deception. (Schopenhauer's indictment of love would therefore be an indictment of its *art*ificial character; it would be a polemic, like that of Plato against art.)

Where then would the disillusionment be, if feeling changes into a more peaceful rhythm and marriage emerges from this: because of habit, the persistent inner inclination cannot remain present to feeling, but the high degree of the in-a-certain-sense latent love emerges, as soon as disruptive powers threaten. What the bond of the family signifies, e.g., shows itself also only when a rip emerges. The love of a spouse might not be inferior to passionate love.

It is not entirely usual to consider marriage as a product of nature and as a creation of love. It is supposedly a social arrangement with all sorts of purposes (procreation and upbringing of children): those, however, are not conscious purposes, but effective causes that push toward structures that the understanding does not immediately grasp. Instinct has worked more on the *social* world than we believe; not the conscious intentions.

In the most ancient times of peoples, marriage is a legal institution, related to property; the woman is under the mastery of the man, without will, as a thing. With marriage, the owner changes, previously it was the father or grandfather. The wife is worth the same in Roman law with regard to inheritance as the daughter. Among other peoples, the imitation of a business transaction displays itself in the consummation of a marriage. Originally, therefore, marriage was not entered into by two persons, marriage comes over the woman like a fate, the woman has no part in the shaping of marriage.

Marriage precedes the complete family, it must rest upon instinct: what, now, is the instinct that would be sufficient to hinder promiscuity?

Lower sensual pleasure is ruled by the law of *change*. It therefore seems that nature aimed at *nothing* less than at marriage. We also try to explain it as actually a formation of need, as a striving to exclude the injuries and disturbances that are attached to competition in promiscuity. But how did it come about that the woman did not then become simply the slave of the man?

So that she could be sold: whereas the wife in marriage, when rejected, returned into the old paternal authority. One might be tempted to make the nobler form of love into the foundation of the formation of marriage: but polygamy speaks against this. Marriage is therefore the realization of love, to be sure, but as much of love for the wife as love for the children. (This passage is weak.)

What do those people want who consider the possession of a woman as the grave of their hopes? They rail against nature because they have fallen in love with unnaturalness. "With the girdle, with the veil, the beautiful illusion is torn in two":[48] the blame for this idea lies in artificialized sensation; it stems from the gloomy conception of life. Schopenhauer and the poets, too, think with abhorrence about the sensations that accompany sensual enjoyment. We believe we are raising ourselves above nature by dis-ennobling it. — Dejection is supposedly the unavoidable consequence and at the same time the judgment upon the preceding sinful pleasure. Here in Dühring the "natural humor" becomes active. That would only be the consequence of debauchery or would display itself in lower animal life (among bees, e.g.). The cloister concocts its theories in the sense of unnaturalness. It is the same with celibate metaphysics, which makes us believe that sickly overstimulation and its fate is the law of healthy nature.

Another interpretation is the transfer of Darwinian natural selection onto this territory. If human beings were to strive with deliberation for the improvement of the type, they would have to behave like nature; it would be even better provided for if an instinct ruled here. Schopenhauer sees it in *individual* love. The highest intensifications of love, with contempt for fate and death, are a means for the thinker to attain an especially favorable conjuncture for procreation. Nature is indifferent toward the fate of individuals; it drives them into distress and death in order to gain new forms of existence. Now what is more beautiful and nobler awakens love in a higher degree: where love is not reciprocal, two opposed judgments of nature result; from one standpoint, the opportunity for improving the species seems quite favorable, from the other not. It would therefore require a two-sided judgment in order to proclaim the will of nature. (In truth! so it is!) The fate of love is not a game concerning purposes that lie outside of individual satisfaction. Could nature be so foolish as not to respect what is individual and to sacrifice it in order afterwards only to attain something individual, too? (But in order to attain *duration* in what is individual.) If we want an interpretation, then the excess of sensation is the premonition of universal, limitless life, which promises to attach itself to the fulfillment of that desire. (Everything is weak; and he has completely left aside the deep insight of Schopenhauer into the nature of illusion in everything instinctive.)

VI. Death

If death is nothing other than mere absence of life, we would not have to concern ourselves with it at all; as indeed we stand in relation to nonexistence before birth. The sensations of life spread a deception over what is no longer life. In every dream we can learn how the natural relationship between representation and sensation can be reversed; a painful pressure upon the heart, and dreams become alarming. All affects fabricate representations where they do not come across them in reality. The beyond is decorated with images, which are in part the creations of immediate fear, in part reactive affects that long for a better existence and for justice. Since the subject is annihilated, we have nothing to hope from death, nothing to fear. But what does this self even matter! We know for certain that living and suffering go on; but who is it then really who is affected by that living and suffering? Is it an absolute nothing, before which the surprise is impending of becoming the bearer of existence? Then we ought to have some sympathy for this nothing, we are in fact that nothing, to which the expectancy of future life is connected. What we have just met with in living we will meet with again (this "we" in the sense of a completely indeterminate subject). Dreams of metaphysics do not help us get any further here, to be sure, though all the instincts that are related to the following generations do.

In that case, our interest in the future rests upon the law that representations lead involuntarily to practical affections. One wants to know, e.g., that one's cadaver not be subjected to anatomical procedures. Think of the meticulous arrangement of gravesites during people's lifetimes. Or even concern for the family, for posthumous fame, for the probable next destinies of our species. What does matter to us from everything after death is the fate of those who continue our existence, but not the empty space at the borders of individual consciousness.

Death is now to be considered as subjective experience: here begin the accusations. Mortality is supposedly a punishment for original sin; all that emerges deserves to be destroyed;[49] the pleasure of life is supposedly to be paid for with the final great pain. — But the fully natural death is no pain at all, a peaceful, gentle passing away; does nature here, therefore, seem to renounce having the torment of death as atonement for the pleasure in life? If we had to choose between a quiet life with euthanasia at the end — and a turbulent one with a death-struggle at the end, instinct would take the second. If we assume that someone does not know of his imminent death, he will take the pains of the death-struggle for the same as what precedes an alarming loss of consciousness. It is not the prospect of this torment that poisons existence, alarming are only the "giant shadows of our own fears."[50] Death first becomes frightful due to the background that we give it. As love engenders a blissful dreamworld, so fear a hellish dreamworld. The misled understanding engenders the fears. We should not indeed overcome death, but learn to endure it.

Dreams exert a power like what is real, their shadows lie upon the day; they often outdo even the sensation of what is real. We may refer to the pain of sensation in accusing life, but we have no right to take into account false theoretical judgments.

The meaning of death is to be judged according to what it annihilates. The hardest death is that of mature old age; with pain because of the uncompleted task, with worry for those left behind. It is the *untimeliness* that makes death so bitter here. Dying is an act of life. Only someone who preserves a noble and firm bearing in life will die with dignity.

If we want to indict life because of the premature death to which it almost always leads, we must turn not against the fact of life, but instead the mastery of *chance*. The ordinary concept of chance has complete truth.

Now, it is precisely the highest charm that is based upon testing the chances of existence. Human beings love under certain circumstances to actually play with life and death; the successes that are gained from the highest wager are considered the highest satisfaction. Chance is no unfortunate law of the world. Existence is not the playing out of a performance at which we would only be spectators.

We should consider death instead as a certain *reconciliation* of all of the otherwise unconquerable misfortunes of the individual existence. The thought of the ephemerality of everything sensed and felt is the final refuge. Death is the final *deus ex machina* in every case. What death is for the survivors: the worse misfortune: here we could rather indict the order of things. The individual is in the strict sense irreplaceable. The single person must direct his gaze toward what is generally human. The single person always has a right to complain about such losses, but the species cannot lament the pains of a single member, because it is precisely through this that sympathy for the higher and more general character of life is kept alert. The individual will is wronged by chance, the general sensation of the meaning of life increased. We would better accuse a world in which nothing could truly be lost, but then nothing could truly be won either. Meaning of the *irreplaceable* losses.

The *voluntary* death seems to contain a general reproach against the order of things in which it occurs; moreover, it is connected with great pain. Anyone who prefers to suffer death rather than the pain of lost love or honor concedes such significance to a single element of life, in order to consider the loss of it exactly like the loss of life. The loss is essentially already there. The voluntary death need not include any condemnation of life. It is the love of life itself that prefers the loss of existence to the feeling of lacking, of an essential lack.

Schopenhauer[51] has connected two mutually contradictory thoughts about suicide with each other. In the first place, it is a self-defense of nature, to be compared with the awakening with which the too highly intensified fear of the dream comes to an end. But then the person who has decided to die is supposedly striving for a repeated testing of the chances of life, but detesting life under certain circumstances. — But if life is a dream, it is constantly and everywhere the opposite of the longed-for waking state, it is a contradiction to allow the one dying voluntarily to depart from the entire dream for a higher reality (waking) and still at the same time to allow him to slip back into the old kind of dreaming. According to Schopenhauer, someone who throws away existence does not at all attain the higher purpose, the fruit of existence; he will be reborn in order to learn about freeing himself from the pleasure of life in a new existence and its pains. So suicide is an offense against the eternal order of salvation. "Who does not know that trivial idea, that life is the preparation for a beyond? Who would not have heard of testing, training and such things?"[52] says Dühring.

It is a great blunder to judge suicide according to the measure of a general representation, without regard for its special content. The voluntary death can be a great action or the expression of a completely ordinary misery or a repugnant distortion of nature. It can appear as morally indifferent, but then again as utter forgetting of duty and shocking injustice toward the survivors.

Death is an annihilation whose nature we can recognize from what has been annihilated. Life is the measure of death. Even more important the reverse: death is the measure of life. How much merit the striving and struggling of humans can include within itself reveals itself first when death draws near. The highest energy of life deploys itself where the play of success and failure turns into a testing of life and death. Hence the *tragic* form of life is the most meritorious, it raises itself to those heights where life and death border upon each other. The seriousness of the great passions confirms itself in death. The dark horizon is necessary so that the flame of life may shine in its complete glow.

If tragedy among all arts shakes us the most powerfully, it is also true that life itself receives its highest expression in the tragic form. — The charm, moreover, lies more in the possibility of tragic form than in its reality, in the bold movement up to those borders. Death cannot be lacking in the whole of life, otherwise a stale, boring activity would come of it. Death is not the enemy of life in general, but instead the means through which the meaning of life is made visible.[53]

VII. Communal life

When the reproaches against the individual life are set aside, we turn to *social* misery, which holds out the prospect of an even more dreadful future. A growing culture supposedly only increases the distress of life; it supposedly brings with it a multitude of unknown misfortunes and does not even satisfy the ordinary necessities of the species; finally everywhere overpopulation and painful existence. The recommended remedies give the accusers of life cause for new imprecations. So social misfortunes seem to be something that can be combated only through greater misfortune and essentially cannot be overcome at all.

We would have to *renounce every justification for existence*, if disharmony existed between the demands of subjective life and the objective possibilities for satisfying them. If it were possible, e.g., that the prospect of overpopulation was certain, such a disharmony would exist. No experience can make such an antinomy demonstrable for us. We correctly imagine that the capacity for the increase of individuals is subjectively linked, to be sure, to certain limits in its rate, moreover would be limited only by objective obstacles. Now, suppose a law, according to which the subjective force itself were to diminish toward a specific limit, i.e., in the gradual course of the species would actually imply a gradual vanishing. Reproduction would eventually have to limit itself to simple replacement. There are many analogies for such a thought. In cosmic as in individual formations, the law of the diminution of the creative energies and of the transition into an almost steady persistence of change repeats itself.

There are only three possibilities: either the capacity for additional increase remains; then the surface of the planet must become greater (otherwise someday the land would be lacking upon which humans could even stand). Or there are annihilating objective powers corresponding to the additional increase. Or diminution of the creative force. Apart from the first case, a limitation of the increase is absolutely necessary. Experience speaks against the assumption that the subjective force would diminish: up to now, this shows neither increase nor diminution, but instead constancy. The increase is an expression of the same force combined with the magnitude of the *temporal* periods, upon which the rate of increase finally depends. How would we think of a change of the periodicity?[54] So we have to anticipate the constancy up to now for the future, too. So the third possibility remains "the objective boundaries of the unlimited drive,"[55] already demonstrated, moreover, by experience. That is what was on the mind of *Malthus*, the pessimist of social philosophy. But he knows only how to speak of the misfortunes of population increase and forgets that for human beings there is no higher good than, once again, human beings. In an overpopulated world, human beings would become stunted by manifold deprivations and be destroyed. There sexual life would supposedly then become a privilege that is divided up according to the measure of possessions:

We should differentiate 1) the Malthusian law 2) its disposition 3) its ghost. The law states that the increase in population occurs more rapidly than the increase in subsistence (he increases population geometrically, subsistence arithmetically, with a constant summand). With regard to the arithmetical increase of subsistence he asserts too much, he holds out the prospect of an objective increase of the means *without limits*; but there the material itself would have to increase for this to be possible: there must be a point where the increase in human energy remains completely unsuccessful and not the slightest further amount can be extracted from the ground. — We can concede that the tendency to create subjects of necessities outstrips the actual state of subsistence; but the necessity of satisfaction must always precede. Now, Malthus therefore expects asceticism from a great part of society; and he certainly thereby takes the part of the property-owners and well off. For their benefit, the greater number should perform their work like beasts of burden outside of the familial bond. I would think that a nobler disposition would have to regard all the misfortunes that will emerge from overpopulation as trifling things compared to the great *injustice* of the doctrine toward the proletarians. A needy condition is bad, a way to spoil life, an unjust one is worse. Politicians have no confidence in individual morality, they want to derive from that doctrine morals and rights for a limitation upon entering into marriage — that is the practical consequence of that doctrine. The highest injustice of the minority against the majority! Bad alternatives among the miseries of overpopulation and among the remedies from a Malthusian disposition! —

With real overpopulation, where it does show up, we either have ⟨to⟩ turn the people's energy outward or ⟨to⟩ clear away the obstacles to greater development of energy. Birth pains are unavoidable here, too, here with internal and external wars. War is in no ⟨other⟩ sense a misfortune than pain in general is. It is objectionable only when it is not the consequence of a necessity. Sometimes certain potencies have to be seen as lost energies in the mechanism of the social machinery so that an action might be possible at all. In the struggle for the right to life, it is a means without any scruples. There is no other guarantee of justice than[56] the employment of physical force (if the justification for life does not change here into something atrocious and bestial, then I am blind!). The consciousness of justice is truly established for the first time in battle (not in the beginning of human intercourse). Unless we renounce generally the implementation of justice (— !), the use of power cannot be avoided. (And this same Dühring moralizes previously in the most edifying way against Malthus on behalf of the unhindered sexual drive.)

Now, we could set a point where no increase in power would any longer be in a position to transform a certain state of overpopulation into a more livable existence. In these cases, Dühring implies, mass murder is to be recommended more than asceticism ("a partial annihilation of the life that has attained development more fully is better than the dismal repression and restraint of life-energy"[57] — by the way, I find that chastity is one of the most powerful promoters of life-energy).

Life, then, supposedly becomes *richer in content* in that the resistances to it increase: for if the single person wants to succeed amid overpopulation "the play of individual effort becomes more meaningful." (O idiocy!) "The weighing of justice becomes more important than it could ever have become before."[58] (I am thinking of half-starved people on a ship off course in the sea, with the problem of who should be eaten first: there, admittedly, the concept of justice becomes more subtle than ever!)

Dühring sees in the social discontent of today only a salutary spur to overcoming indolence; social misfortune seems to him from time to time not yet even to be great enough to goad the indolence of the people's energy. — Nor would we have the right to claim an unlimited amount of time, as Malthus does.

VIII. Knowledge

To what extent can the higher or lower degree of knowledge become a source of joy and suffering?

Knowing is based upon a need. The "pure joy of knowledge" is nothing other than the satisfaction at having cleared away obstacles. A striving must always come before; as in everything practical. Here, too, work is the mediating term between need and enjoyment.

The "pure subject of knowledge" is a chimaera. For all expressions of human nature, actions or thoughts have success and failure in common. In the field of theory, misfortune makes its appearance in the form of error. The purely theoretical disillusionment is not to be considered as a misfortune.

Is error in itself really a misfortune? Isn't it perhaps only the practical consequences of false representations? A representation, as long as it is held to be true, cannot be at all differentiated from a genuine truth in its effect upon the temperament. Prejudices can just as well make us happy as unhappy; think of the blissfulness that results from superstitions.

We could take many a rapturous delusion as more valuable than the truth, e.g., that of a benevolent and loving god. But the belief has in our mind an unshakeable foundation, we have only to exclude what is theoretically erroneous from it. Only the rationalist fiction of the belief, not the belief, runs into danger from critique.

In the end, there is agreement in the truth alone, error always leads to conflict. Hence it is a misfortune. Error could only leave us indifferent, if the striving for truth were lacking in our nature.

Error becomes a subjective misfortune first when it is recognized as such. Hence there will always also be an element of satisfaction along with it.

The false idea of the immobility of the earth had no consequences at all before; now it would be a very bad thing if the true astronomical system were to be lost once again, like after the times of Aristarchus. A free science could not persist at all without that cornerstone; the true cosmic representations have today a significance for the mind, they point humans toward modesty. Nature does not seem to have set out to lead us immediately everywhere to the truth; at times, it seems, it requires errors. That erring is something human still does not suffice to cast suspicion upon existence. Only where the error becomes moral, poisons the conception of life, does it become questionable.

The more limited our representations are, the more easily they come into contradiction with real experiences.(!) The impartial human being very soon sets his ideas into balance with the objective course of human affairs.(!) We cherish no sympathy for disillusionments that spring from a pedantic morality. (Ugh!)

Absolutist morality can be compared with grammar, as governesses conceive of it: as a power in and of itself. We can only master language via grammar if we have previously been watching for it in language. So morality must first be obtained from the motive powers and the basic character of life, before we dare advance with it toward life.

Morality is there because of life, not the reverse. — We have to guard carefully against unfounded presuppositions; we should instead give ourselves over to the character of life. Thus we harvest lasting satisfaction.

Many deluded hopes are based upon exaggerated presuppositions about our fellow human beings. In suffering injustice, in fact, it is our nature whose consequences we suffer. An alien disposition that disregards our fates is, moreover, frequently only appearance; humans are occupied with their own needs, there they have no eyes for others.

How can a human being despair about the salvation of the species! Even if he reproaches them for all sorts of vulgarity and vileness, he himself still remains. Humans with great volition believe in the possibility of their conceptions and therefore do not accuse other humans in a desperate way.

The truly miserable despair is where we ourselves feel that we represent what we ⟨do not⟩ wish for.[59] A great part of psychic pain is not really to be attributed to the malicious actions of humans, but instead to the power of unfortunate accidents to occur.

Nonetheless, pain remains. Injustice, as the greatest misfortune, if not exactly also as the ruling power. We can think of no development of human affairs without presupposing need as a spurring motive. No wisdom exists that would be allowed to call the connection according to *purposes* a fabrication. Every action of nature is in accordance with the understanding, it realizes not simply a multiplicity, but instead an infinity of understandable considerations. The causal and also the final connection extend as far as our understanding cares to follow them. What we know in clear consciousness is only a reflection of that *infinite concatenation*: this and human insight do not belong in the same class. There is in things not only understanding, but something that lies beyond all understanding. The synthesis of this infinite enchainment forever remains for us an unreachable beyond. So understanding can never have the capacity to justify the absolute merit of existence. It is not the agreement or the conflict in the system of things, but instead the *totality of the impression* that life makes upon the subject, that remains the measure. Sensations and feelings never err, because they do not yet differentiate between representation and object. *Feeling* is something transcendent for the understanding, *it is therefore capable in a certain sense of representing the absolute nature of what is real.*

Understanding could even be realized in the richest measure in the most wretchedly deformed creatures of the world. — It is a matter of the measure and *not* the fact of the suffering. — The immediate judgment about the value of existence must have the form of feeling, that is: it will be a *belief.*

IX. The Belief in the Value of Life

If the limited survey of which we are capable strengthens[60] us in the belief of finding things also under further investigation to be in accord with the requirements of our being: thus emerges belief in the value of existence.

Disturbances in this can exist. For the individual, confidence in life can be completely upset by terrible fates. "The cloister and generally avoiding the dealings of the world sometimes make good sense."[61] (Now, the awfulness of the general fate is certainly greater than every "individual" —)

The normal constitution of the disposition is thereby destroyed. We have no right to expect of it that it strive with its own energy toward reconciliation with life. The instrument is damaged.

But what is justified for the individual is not for the whole, it dare not invite humanity to curse existence. If humanity were a conscious whole, it would not make much fuss about the suffering of the individual member. (On the contrary! Just think of toothache etc. in a human being.) (Could precisely that collective consciousness be imagined as a perpetually suffering one?)[62] Insofar as it is possible to have affections, the center-point of which falls in other beings, the individual sensation allows itself to heighten into a general sympathy: and from this the individual fate is to be mastered and reconciled (what!? because we learn to take part in so many other and greater sufferings! the heavier pain overpowers the lesser!)

Of what concern to the bearer of individual consciousness is the fate of the world! The sympathetic affects are the mediators. Without the thought of a certain solidarity, no satisfaction, no reconciliation is possible. (ego: That is a half-and-half figure of speech: no human being can completely feel the fate of humanity, it is a very vague overlap from the individual into the general that brings about reconciliation here. A stronger one would completely suppress the individual. The *narrowness* of head and heart makes existence tolerable!) Self-interested isolation is the degeneration of what is human. The most terrible tormentor is the thought of relinquishment and surrender. Human beings mislead themselves mutually in the belief in a better human nature, out of vanity, out of the titillation of showing themselves to be especially cunning and unnatural. It is only an *appearance* if egoism is considered to be the governing rule of human intercourse. (Here Dühring lapses into infantilism. I wish he were not trying to fool me here! Really, all agreement ceases here: if he seriously believes in his proposition, he may hope heartily for all socialisms.)

The belief in the value of life must also believe in the *good human being* by nature: (otherwise it cannot be endured, thinks Dühring). It has to do first with the subjective nature of our species and then with the conformity of the tendency of greater nature with the needs and purposes of human existence. In both directions he is looking for confirmation of his incomplete conceptions.

If anything is capable of tuning the temperament to philosophical calm, it is the consideration of a world whose significance extends infinitely beyond human fate (what then do we know of a "significance"! in such a case, for whom does it still signify something!) — There is no more bitter enemy of philosophical belief than ideologism (which no longer knows, of course, the strict concept of a real objectivity, it effaces the difference between belief and knowledge).

Insofar as we have the need to verify the general conceptions overlapping with *what is known* by us through new experiences and investigations, we find ourselves in a state of *belief.* But it has a factual basis, includes a knowledge, although a limited one, and differentiates itself thereby from authorized belief. (Moreover, religions have always known quite well how to resort to an "although limited" knowledge and never completely disdained it. That would therefore remain the same; only that Dühring makes *what is known* into the foundation upon which the fiction is then raised: whereas in religions fiction is ordinarily the basis against which something known is then occasionally leaned, more in order to support than to be held, but still not in order to serve completely as foundation.)

Appendix.
Theoretical idealism and the unity of the system of things.

We can never infer practical idealism, a practically ideal stance of those who profess it, on the basis of theoretical idealism. On the contrary, a sturdy life-realism can sometimes be paired with idealistic basic views, as the example of Schopenhauer demonstrates to a certain degree. For Schopenhauer, practical idealism is an absurdity. The noblest sides of human nature were dragged by Schopenhauer into the dirt of the commonest apprehension. (Everything utterly false and mean. Herr Dühring! I thought the *practical* idealism of Schopenhauer gleamed more brightly than the sun. And then such a wise lad still has to renounce him quite explicitly.)

The transcendent satisfaction of revenge.

The feeling of justice is a *ressentiment*, goes along with revenge: the representation of an *other-worldly justice* also goes back to the feeling of *revenge.*

Justice consists of retaliation (injuring someone back), to the injury a counter-injury must correspond: *talio.*[63] This, the primeval and still always popular conception. From another side, one sought for a reason and hit upon a purposeful basis for public justice: preventing injury through deterrence.

The intelligence directed by practical motives knows of no justice without the feeling of revenge.

In criminal law, two classes: first, simple expediencies (has therefore nothing to do with justice), and then the considerations that one human owes to another; the hostile injury.

This holds good in civil law, too. Only insofar as disrespecting or disturbing a state would be an injury does the concept of nondisturbance become a legal concept. The law never prescribes positive conduct.

Transcendent retaliation: what is good should garner blessing, what is evil, execration. The drive for gratitude is the basis of the representations of reward: as the drive for revenge is of justice. Thus hatred and love also have their worlds beyond.

Is then Schopenhauer's "eternal justice" something to be taken so seriously and respected so emphatically! The unrestrained drive for revenge, which even fashions transcendent ideas! Those who call upon the criminal court of eternity show their own image in the mirror. — We have to attend not only to the relationship and opposition of ideas, but above all to what incites to the whole game, the power of drives and feelings. Dreams are ⟨not⟩ only[64] the causes, but also the effects of our states of temperament: fictions on the basis of drives and feelings. And like dreams, so the whole representing world of ideas.

The representation of a transcendent criminal court is a fiction and conflicts then with the nobler stance of consciousness, as product of the feeling of revenge. We lay claim to the arm of the gods the most when we are indignant about having suffered injustice.

Here stands the final support of wavering belief: the moral world is ostensibly in need of a supplement, otherwise no satisfaction would be provided for our desire for a just order of things. For that, there would have to be an eternal justice standing above earthly things. For that, God was brought in as demand for the retaliatory drive: the retaliator, the representative of eternal justice. For that, individual immortality. The presupposition for an actual metaphysical requital is metaphysical guilt, and this is unthinkable without *metaphysical freedom*. The second presupposition of a metaphysical requital is the metaphysical living-on of the guilty one; the third — a metaphysical judge and executor. This is the *religion of revenge*. Thus did Kant understood religion. The most subtle turn is the Schopenhauerian one. World history the world court, yet so that beyond the physical meaning of the course of events there stands still another, metaphysical one. A mystical causality of the world process. We see only the execution of the judgment before us, and indeed in the form of the world process, of an existence playing itself out deterministically: injustice and guilt lie beyond the existence of the world in general. "Humans are in fact all too poetic when it is a question of weaving the bad luck of their enemies into their true or supposed guilt."[65] It is precisely cowardice and impotence that tend to be most successful in discovery of so-called "criminal courts." It is an annoying consequence of all revenge to interpret events in the sense of an alleged justice.

We increase the misfortunes of the world even more with transcendent ghosts; let's not invent metaphysical caricatures of things! The natural image of world corresponds to the deeper being of our nature even where it leaves us unsatisfied. —

End.

Concluding observation, from me.

The belief in the value of life is based upon impure thinking. It is only possible when sympathy for the general life and suffering of humanity is very weakly developed. If we understand how to direct our attention principally toward the rarest human beings, the exalted talents, the pure souls, if we take their becoming as the goal and rejoice in their works, then we may believe in the value of life. Likewise, if we keep our eye upon just a single class of drives among all human beings, the less egoistical ones, and excuse them with regard to the others: then we can have hope for humanity.

It seems to me, on the contrary, much more certain that human beings endure life and believe in the value of life precisely when they want and assert only themselves and do not step outside of themselves: so that everything extrapersonal is noticeable only like a weak shadow.

Therefore, the value of life for ordinary active human beings lies in taking themselves as more important than the world: and the reason why they take so little part in other beings is the great lack of imagination, so that they cannot think themselves into other beings. Anyone who can do that and who has a loving heart must despair of the value of life; unless he invents a mystical significance for the whole affair.[66]

If someone were even able to apprehend within himself a collective consciousness of humanity, he would break down with a curse against existence. For humanity has no goals. Consequently he cannot find his comfort and support by considering the whole of humanity, even if he were capable of this:

but instead, his despair. If he sees in everything that he does the ultimate aimlessness of humanity, his work takes on the character of *wastefulness* in his eyes. I believe that nothing is comparable to feeling oneself as humanity as wasted as we see the individual buds of nature wasted. Everything was necessary and is necessary in us. Only that *we* are supposed *to see* the spectacle! There everything really comes to an end.

The *woe* in the world has caused human beings to suckle from it in an ingenious way a sort of happiness for themselves.[67] The view of life of those who want *knowledge* alone from existence, of those who *surrender* and resign themselves, of those who *rest* and of those who *struggle* — everywhere a little happiness, too, springs up along with it. But it would be terrible to say that with this happiness the suffering itself would be compensated. In general, no compensation at all should even be possible! Or rather: what does to compensate mean here? We cannot undo the suffering, so that happiness follows later. Pleasure and displeasure cannot at all cancel each other out.

Now I want finally to set forth my gospel. It goes thus.

That we do not love the one whom we respect, that is known. And he would love most purely who had not to respect the beloved thing at all, but to despise it. Contempt is a thing of the head.

The one who could *love* himself *completely purely* — therefore in completely purified self-love — would be the one who could at the same time despise himself. Love yourself and nobody besides you — because you can know yourself alone; and love the others if you can, i.e., if you are in a position to know and to despise them completely, like yourself.

This is the position of Christ toward the world. It is *self-love* out of pity, the core of Christianity, without all of the shell and mythology.

Self-knowledge originates in justice toward oneself; and justice is basically the feeling of revenge. If someone has suffered enough from himself, injured himself enough, in sinfulness — then he begins to perceive the feeling of revenge against himself:

his penetrating self-observation and its resultant self-contempt is the result. For many people even *asceticism*, that is, *revenge upon themselves* in the violence of repugnance and hatred. (In much haste and work the same tendency manifests itself —)

That despite all this human beings still love themselves appears then like a miracle of grace. This is not the love of greedy, blind egoism. Ordinarily we attribute such a refined and inconceivable love to a god. But we are ourselves the ones who are capable of such a love. It is self-pardoning. Revenge is done away with. Along with it, self-knowledge as well. We act once again and live on. But all the ordinary motives that otherwise direct us appear transformed. Here is the difference between what is Buddhist and what is Christian. The Christian acts out of that self-love; and if he is not always capable of this, he nevertheless still has "self-compassion." All *com*passion is, like humans are, weak. — But Christ despised himself and loved himself and saw humans as like him.

The Christian acts and takes acting as unavoidable: in return, he comforts himself with the prospect of the world's downfall. He does not esteem any earthly striving very highly, it is for naught. Now, if we know that humanity is done for, the expression of aimlessness lays itself upon all human striving. Moreover, we can figure out the fundamental errors in all striving and exhibit them: impure thinking lies at the base of all of them. What do all parents do, e.g.? — they procreate without responsibility and educate without knowledge of those they are educating — in every case, they do injustice and go about things the wrong way in an alien sphere — but they *have* to do it — that is part of the wretchedness of existence. And so human beings become, in all that they do, full of dissatisfaction and have compassion for themselves.

A human seems to be a multiplicity of beings, a union of multiple spheres, each one of which can gaze upon the others. — [68]

End.

9[2][69]
The Conservation of Energy. By B. Stewart.

The universe — a machine that is composed of atoms and a sort of medium between them: the laws of energy are the laws that govern the working of this machine.

Chapter I.
Our lack of knowledge about individual beings, whereas we often know the laws that determine collectives. When the temperature is very low, mortality in London is much greater. That is certain, but not how a given case of death would be caused by the lower temperature. After a bad harvest, a large import of grain takes place; we cannot give an account of the path of the individual particle of flour. There is a continual flow of air toward the equator; but nobody can give an account of the movements of a single particle of air. So in the system of planets, in the politics of nations. The natural law of all individual beings is very complicated, whether these are living beings or lifeless particles of material; a great battle rages, the battlefield is often concealed from us; what the individual beings do there, we do not see, but the outcome of the battle we can judge, often even predict. That total result attainable by the collective is determined by *simple laws.*

We suppose that a great number of illnesses are caused by organic germs; our lack of knowledge of these is complete. The air swarms with them, they fight with one another, we are the prey of the stronger ones. Thus we are connected in the most intimate ways with a whole world of creatures and know them no better than the inhabitants of Mars.

Yet we do know some characteristics of these robber-states, e.g., that cholera is chiefly an illness of the lowlands, that we have to pay attention to drinking water. — Vaccination regulates the devastation by means of pustules, but we are like prisoners who have to mutilate themselves in order to make themselves worthless for their triumphant opponents; so that they leave them alone.

Even greater our lack of knowledge of the molecules of inorganic matter.

A molecule of sand is the smallest thinkable thing that still possesses all the qualities of sand; a further division, if it were possible, would decompose it into its chemical constituents, silica and oxygen. In any case, the disintegration does not continue into infinity. If we increase a drop of water to the circumference of the entire earth: an individual molecule[70] would be somewhat larger than a musket-ball, somewhat smaller than a cricket-ball. We will never succeed in making the final molecules visible; the very greatest masses in the cosmos have in common with the very smallest that they retreat from human senses: the former too far away, the latter too small.

These molecules in constant movement and in battle colliding with one another: until a blow is powerful enough to separate two or more simple atoms, out of which a molecule[71] is composed. Then a new state of things arrives. The basic atom is immortal, but continually moved. This is a new limit for our knowledge, it does not sit still.

Equality of Effect and Countereffect.

In every system that is left to itself, strong inner forces may be operative among the various parts, but effects and countereffects balance each other out, the system persists at *rest.* A hollow glass bowl with numerous actively moving goldfish, set very lightly upon wheels, stands still, even if the table surface were a smooth plane of ice: it is a system. Another is a rifle with power and lead: while the ball is projected forward, the musket-butt is thrown backward. If the musket weighs 3000 grams, the ball 30 grams, and the ball is projected forward at 300 meters per second: then the rifle is thrown backward at a speed of 3 meters. Therefore 3000 gr x 3 m = 30 gr x 300 m. — If I throw a stone from a slope toward the earth, the movement seems to have only one direction, in truth it is the result of a reciprocal attraction of stone and earth. The earth really moves upward, toward the stone, but quite imperceptibly: but, since the mass of the earth is quite large in comparison with the mass of the stone, the speed must be exceptionally slight. st wt x speed downward = wt of earth x speed upward. In general: if A exerts its attracting or repelling force upon B, then B in turn attracts or repels A. Despite our lack of knowledge of the individual entities, this law can be known.

"Magnitude of movement" is the product of mass and speed. With the musket, the magnitudes of movement are therefore the same in both directions. Yet what here differentiates the musket-ball and the rifle-butt? The musket-ball can overcome resistance: this penetrating force is the sign of a substance endowed with very great speed. Let us call this capacity energy: it stands in relation to the weight or to the mass of the body. It is the same, whether a ball of 60 gr weight moves with a speed of 100 meters per sec or 2 balls, each of 30 gr. — But the energy does not stand in simple relation to the speed; it increases much more quickly with the speed. If the speed of a ball is doubled, its energy increases almost fourfold. If the speed is

2 (fold), then the energy 4 (fold)
3 (fold), then the energy 9 (fold)

The energy changes according to the square of its speed.

Now, how should we measure work? As unit of weight the kilogram (2 pounds), as unit of length the meter (= 3.186 Rheinish feet).

Now, if we lift a kilogram 1 meter high, we expend energy: this we consider as a unit of work: kilogram-meter.

If we multiply the lifted weight (in kilogr) by the vertical height (in met.) by which it is lifted, we obtain as result the work performed (in kilogram-meters). Energy is proportional to the square of speed, whether we measure energy according to the thickness of the boards that it[72] can penetrate or the height to which it[73] can climb against the force of gravity.

[10 = N I 6. Summer 1875]

10[1][1]

Anyone who enjoys the supreme moment, *is blinded.*

10[2]

A love that is still quite young — cow-warm.

10[3][2]

You should love (and certainly not fear) God above all things and trust in him.

10[4][3]

The *Flying Dutchman* element in Wagner's will. Annihilation-curse.

Inhibited will. Jealousy wrath.

10[5][4]

King of Bavaria. Evening shadows. Shelter.

10[6]

Mathematics.
Mechanics (with history).
Physics.
Chemistry.
Descript⟨ive⟩ natural sciences.
Physiology.
Cosmos.

Geography.
History.
Political economy.
Philosophy.

10[7][5]

With the most energetic steps of life, death resonates.

10[8][6]

Writer. Speaking-style. Before enemies. Restless rhythm now and then compelling. Broken dialectic. Emphasis on the authoritative.

10[9][7]

Servant and friend, Kurwenal.

10[10][8]

Christianity, a form of antiquity thought through and pursued with excessive diligence to its logical conclusion. The Alexandrian — the direction has remained. Taking the power and giving for it — the culture of the powers dominating up to now.[9]

10[11][10]

The communicative inventive-talent. Fitting of thought into given circumstances. Writing also belongs to that (out of necessity, since the example was not possible).

10[12][11]

The *element of fellowship* in the B⟨ayreuth⟩ undertaking.

10[13]

The future of art (if humanity comprehends its *end*).[12]

I could imagine a *forward*-gazing art, too, that seeks its images in the future. Why does such a thing not exist? Art is tied to *piety*.

10[14][13]

Those who hold themselves back out of desperation, like Jacob Burckhardt.

10[15][14]

Every art goes *to weeds*, at a certain height of development.

10[16][15]

How W⟨agner⟩ first loosens the tongue and breaks[16] the limbs of music.

10[17][17]

Opposition of the peak of art and the miserable *male choral* music. Among the Greeks, the *state* looked after that.

10[18][18]

Depiction of the main characters.
Survey of the kinds.
Abundance.

10[19][19]

Musicians — poets — writers — actors.

10[20][20]

Greeks.
Philologists, *caste*-teachers (of a higher caste).
Wagner.
Religion.
Public education.
Man and woman.
State.
Health and illness.
Universities, the scholars.
Workers and aristocrats.
Commerce.

Press.
School of educators.

10[21][21]
I am ready.

[11 = U II 9. Mp XIII 4, 6–8, 47. Summer 1875]

Preliminary work for "Richard Wagner in Bayreuth"

11[1][1]

35. On *Wagner*. The struggle with ἀνάγκη;[2] all progress is based upon forgetting to take some sort of thing for necessity. Wagner has taken the desperation of modern humans, as if they always only had to be epigones. Whereas instead we are indebted in everything to *ancient* culture, with state society religion: he brings to light the human being who is *in* us *prior* to all culture and thereby throws off the heavy burden.

11[2][4]

36. He senses the *opprobrium toward modern art* within modern society, the contradictions of the demands, he cannot bear to stay quietistically in the corner, but instead he demands for art as an artist its public dignity and becomes revolutionary in everything. Everything in him is prophetic. The word-scholars have nothing more to say. The art of writing and poetry is recognized and disdained for the first time. Though he animates Christian and Nordic myth, he does not express anything at all dogmatic and is not behind the times, as the poet otherwise is. The gospel of love toward power, convention, the spirit of commerce and of money and of contracts. He has sense for the poor and neglected in our culture, he discovers the mimes

and musicians. He softens hearts and moves them deeply. And within the circumference of centuries, he absorbs all interest into himself and is the turning point. The *greatest* artist.

11[3]

Character of the new culture: *knowledge* its foundation, *utility* its soul. From where do we now take the hopes for a nobler humanity? From where is love of our fellow humans supposed to come? Religion[4] can no longer be of use for ennobling the individual, his sense of truth is outraged. The "love for God" is a phrase. So would culture then be over and done with? Utility bestializes and[5] knowledge mummifies. And the vengeful desires of the previously oppressed humanity! What binds together? Where is something in common? Hasn't everything been a means for oppression, art above all? Hatred and the desire to annihilate are only too comprehensible. — Here now is the artist Wagner, a symptom of the opposite. The spirit of *negating what has previously existed* speaks forth from him; likewise, however, a feeling of the deepest compassion, of *bene*volence, which takes up the struggle with necessity: the *Promethean element* of the artist. He would almost have lost his art in this struggle: the *disgust* was so great. "You heroic sages, give your heart's blood for that."[6]

Compassion that presses toward complicity!

11[4][7]

34. There are elements present in Wagner that appear *reactionary*: the Middle-Ages-Christian, the princely posture, the Buddhist; the miraculous. From these, he may have gained many adherents. These are his *means of expressing* himself, the language that is still understood, but has acquired a *new content*. These things are to be taken artistically, not dogmatically, in the artist. Even the *national-German* is part of this. He is seeking analogies for what is to come in what has been, so the German of Luther, Beethoven and himself, the German character and its great princes, seem to him like guarantees that something

analogous to what he takes to be necessary in the future did once exist; courage loyalty simplicity goodness self-sacrifice, as he summarized all this in the magnificent symbolism of his "Imperial March" — this is his Germanness. He is seeking the *contribution* that the Germans will give to the coming culture. That is admittedly not the "historicism" of the scholars of Germany, as Hillebrand believes.[8] For that is really reaction and the spirit of deceit and optimism. *Instead, in the great unsatisfied heart that is much greater than one nation* — that is what he calls German: in a vulgar way, we call it the cosmopolitan element of the German, but that is only caricature. The Germans *are* not national, but also not cosmopolitan, the *greatest* Germans; only their enemies have inoculated them with the stupid delusion that we must be limited.

11[5]
32. The *love* in *Tristan* is not to be understood as Schopenhauerian, but instead as Empedoclean, it completely lacks any sinful element, it is the sign and guarantee of an eternal unity.

11[6]
33. There are in Wagner **dangerous tendencies**: the *lack of measure* (how easily his genius would have been able to splinter itself![9] But it is like with the Greeks, as artist he is σώφρων,[10] as human being not), the *tendency toward pomp and luxury* (stimulated by continual renunciation, the fate of all artists), *jealousy* (he is forced into measuring himself against all modern[11] forces, especially artists, in order to discover in them the Wagnerian element, however embryonic, and so to feel himself as *necessary* after all; but if he assigns necessity to the development *up toward him*, he sees the *other* developments as byways and side ways, and even wrong ways, as withdrawn energies, as squandering, and *is annoyed* about it; he is also annoyed about the fame that has followed such errant stars, because it takes the sunshine from his path and the fruitfulness from his works), the *greatly agile, widely understanding*

(reading in alien individuals, surveying hardly allows for proper human intercourse, just as we also cannot associate with a wise man. Only love comes near him, but this blindly, whereas he *sees*. So he accustoms himself to letting himself be loved and thereby to govern: he helps others against despair.) *Cunning and art of deception*, countless pretended motives, evasions, expedients, as it were, in the drama of his life; which he finds and applies lightning-quick. *Always to be right*, his wrongness is related at most to the form, the degree, or the entire material was unknown to him. — All these dangers are the dangers of the *dramatist*, increased especially by his struggle, which does not allow itself to be embarrassed about the means. He has something of his *heroes*, they do not sin. — Now the *religion of music* lies around his entire being: he feels it, how contracts power splendor struggle and triumph do not make one happy, how all powerful willing makes one unjust, and he calls *love* the highest thing. The Empedoclean.[12] He wants indeed *to help, to be of use, to save* — and this *condemns* him to such a life of passion and of dissatisfaction.

11[7]

28. In the drama his **passion breathes slowly** and has the shape of an arc, ascending, swiftly descending; he is not so idyllic and spreads himself out like a placid lake. He moves restlessly, as if upon hidden, jagged rocks,[13] convulsive, and suddenly, he gradually falls into a movement sweeping him away, the turbulence has been transformed into a *calming of the quick, wide*[14] *movement* and now he plunges downward into the depths, splendid and powerful. The *pleasure in passion*, something of the ocean's pleasures in the surf and in bad weather.[15]

11[8][16]

29. The **many-headed passion** in drama his element: it is the psychic process in a *group* of persons, which he feels *at the same time*. His orchestra is the expression of *intermingled* passion, symbolic, without end; human beings of all eras will recognize

themselves here. He has a means of expression that is far beyond language convention gesture; or rather: word, gesture serve for *clarification* of the inner, agitated world of temperament.

11[9][17]

30. The **populist element:** highly remarkable, since as a writer he is not simple, not direct, but instead exerts himself to speak a language unnatural to him. The one he speaks is of the *highest cultivation*, but of the *ancient, unpopulist, scholarly-abstract*; as soon as he comes into his element, he throws all of this off from himself. Also the *maxim*: we are restored to the state where people *still composed poetry and almost did not yet think*: in the age where language emerged.

31. We see how *populist* he is in comparison with Goethe. The entire *Faust problem* is quite understandable for us who have barely gotten away from the Middle Ages; apart from this temporal relationship, it is the *least understandable* poetry. Goethe himself knew it, but made use of the "barbaric advantages."[18] How must a people have been prepared in order for it to appreciate Faust as populist piece! Goethean songs are *modeled on* the popular song, but do not offer a model for singing it: as the great poet does.

11[10][19]

Final act of the *Twilight of the Gods*: everything evening-red, summer breeze, late summer, deep glow, sorrow woven into everything. Siegfried narrating the touching memory of his deeds.[20] Tragically quickly night falls.

11[11][21]

How I felt in Nirmsdorf,[22] in the golden meadow! the moon has risen.[23] In Plauen[24] at the brook beneath butterflies in the spring. In Pobles,[25] when I cried over my lost childhood. In Röcken, when I found the colorful snail shells. Near Naumberg,[26] when I dug for lime-spar and gypsum. In Pforta when the fields were empty and fall came. When grandfather explained Hölty's "Wunderseliger Mann"[27] to me.[28] Near Bonn where the Wied (?)[29] flows into the Rhine, I was overcome once again by the feeling of childhood.[30] Then in the Neugasse,[31] where I forever heard the admonishing voice of my father. — The story that the housekeeper of the pastor in Hochheim told.[32] Ice-skating on the uneven acreage[33] in the moonlight, "what I earn during the day from my lyre."[34] — Ravaillac.[35]

11[12]

25. Wagner is an *organizer* of *masses*: of a great mass of myth, of great, long-winded scenes. Legislative for very large relationships. Therefore he can be *simple* as *no* dramatist has *ever* been. He thereby attains the highest effect. An eye for the great rhythm distinguishes him. With regard to the rhythm in small things, he is for what is lively, active, manifold; all music seems *stiff* after his;[36] he makes everything previous into an archaic art. It is as though there had never even been an orchestra either, before *his* resounded: the animated life of *every* instrument was not there at all before.

11[13]

26. What is *superfluous* in art: even goodness of a particular kind should exist for once. The *wealth* of art in the variety of forms and repetitions has the disadvantage of using up, deadening the form. Hence we should be very strict toward imitators. Greek tragedy was over with when the dilettantes pounced upon it. — The most beautiful thing is the *inimitability of Shakespeare* and *Wagner*. I.e., in many things, many means of effect, they are immediately and massively imitated, and there are no gifted composers who would not already have Wagner's imprint, in the songs, the harmony, the free, long melody, etc. The danger of such imitation is quite great even, as with Michelangelo. We must convince ourselves all the more strongly of the *intimate connection* of Wagnerian *means* and *ends*, in order to feel almost disgusted when the means are employed in isolation for completely different and small ends.

Wagner *must* have the effect upon musicians of making them into virtuosos of execution and into strict teachers; but he should *put* them *off* from insane composing.

27. The danger of *naturalism* is especially great, *according to* Wagner. What is terrifying, intoxicating, etc. pursued *for its own sake*. An immense abundance of means is there, indeed.[37]

11[14]

In order to be able to approach the inheritance of the past, we must also feel ourselves obliged to pay its debts. We must make up for what it has neglected and perpetrated: that is the reasonable thanks for us being allowed to have a part in what they have gained and achieved.

11[15][38]

24. Pre-Wagnerian music had an *epic-lyrical* character; a *mood*, e.g., a reverent, repentant, joyous, etc. one, wanted to express itself; a certain homogeneity of forms and a sustained duration eventually put the listeners in this mood. The total *form* of a mood-image received certain laws of beginning and end, avoidance of boredom and monotony determined the *length*. Then the *contrastive effects* of the *moods* succeeding one another came into use and later, too, in the same piece of music, the *contrast* of the *ethos*. Very frequently a masculine and a feminine motif. These are all still primitive stages of music. In so doing, it most often wants only to *entertain*, and at most, *to move*: the moods dare not be too deep, nor too strong, and the contrast can therefore also not be too bold. Gradually, however, one learned nonetheless to invent a multitude of symbolic forms for all sorts of moods. And now something *new* happened: one became sick of the arbitrary *contrasting* and of *mood* in general, the ἦθος[39] and its opposites; whereas one became on the other hand ever more refined in rare moods, in the depiction of abnormal characters (blasé, childlike, elderly, national). Beethoven *invented* the language of *passion*, no longer of mood:

and thereby the *form* of mood-music was impossible: it was no longer possible now to paint an idyllic lake. An inner dramatic event — for *every passion follows a dramatic course* — imposed its own form upon itself; the traditional theme of mood-music frequently had a blocking and disturbing effect, strangling passion like a rigid law. It was often a *contradiction*: *pathos that was supposed to express itself in the form of ethos*. For pathos, the great form is necessary in order to reproduce the great swinging arc[40] of every passion; the symphony became known for this due to Beethoven, yet still with reliance upon the contrasts of *circumstances*;[41] so that he often extracted three four *stages* from the complete course of a passion and left the *line* of the *entire* passion more to be intuited by sketching four points of its trajectory. From this, an alienation from music emerged for many listeners: they could not recognize the trajectory and the contrastive effects of the individual parts were also incomprehensible. And so there emerged among lesser musicians the pure *arbitrariness* of the parts and their succession; the connectedness of the whole was lacking, it was four pieces. (Just as Aeschylus extracted four points from life and myth and later the parts became independent.) Therefore: the invention of the great form of passion, not being understood, led back to the single movement with subjective content and the relationship of tension among the parts completely ceased; only that frequently one had recourse again to earlier contrastive effects. For one must *have* passion in order to learn how to represent it, to understand it: musicians like Schubert, Schumann Mendelssohn have only ethos, and therefore the post-Beethoven symphony is such a curious formation. In individual parts, they stammer Beethoven's language of pathos; that confuses the listener even more. Means are not suited to the intention and the intention is not at all clear. The long C-major symphony of Schubert is boring, because the individual movements only seem to have their justification in the whole, but in truth have it only in the small, individual things. The only thing that these musicians have accomplished is that they have made a multitude of forms of expression more accessible, more widespread, especially in the song, too. — An example in the *ninth* symphony of Beethoven: here the first movement gives the whole tone and direction of the passion and its course: it constantly roars ahead, the trip through woods chasms monsters: there in the distance the waterfall roars, there it plunges downward in powerful leaps, with an immense rhythm in its thunder.[42] *Peace while traveling* is the second movement (*self-reflection* of passion and *self-judgment*),[43] with the vision of an *eternal* peace that smiles down sorrowfully-blissfully upon all wandering and hunting. The third movement is a moment from the highest trajectory of passion: its course is beneath the stars, restless, comet-like, will-o'-wisp-like, ghostly-inhuman, a sort of deviation, the *restlessness*, inner flickering fire, exhausting, torturously being pulled forward, without hope and love: scornful bitter sometimes, as a spirit wanders about, never finding rest, over graves. And now the fourth movement: heart-rending shriek: the soul no longer bears its burden, it does not endure the restless frenzy, it throws away from itself even the vision of eternal peace that rises to the surface in it, it gnashes, it suffers terribly. Then it recognizes its curse: its *solitariness*, its detachment, even the eternity of the individual is only a curse for it. Then it, the solitary soul, hears a human voice[44] that speaks to it like to all individuals and speaks indeed as if to *friends* and summons to the joy of the multitude. That is its song. And now the song of *passion for what is human in general* storms in, with its own movement and flight: which, however, would never have been *so high* if the passion of the nightly onward-storming *isolated* individual had not been so great. It ties *compassion* to the *passion* of the individual, not as contrast, but instead as effect from that cause. —

Thus with Beethoven. Now Wagner *invents*, after Beethoven, the representation of *intermingled passions* and now needs the visible drama for elucidation, word and gesture. He sets *humans* opposite one another; he extricates himself from the subjective element of passion, he no longer represents *himself*: or rather, indeed himself, but as the resonance of many passionately behaving persons, whose soul-life lives on in him, in the *artful in- and beside-one-another*. The task is so high that obscurity is a great danger, and therefore Wagner's entire energy is directed toward clarity of the musical language.[45]

He has achieved what no one has ever yet achieved: the absolutely strongest and clearest language of feeling. All earlier music seems stiff, feeble, mannered, timid. The unbelievable *firmness* and *determination* of every *degree* of feeling is the only thing that matters to him: he has accomplished within music what the inventor of the free-standing figure did within sculpture:[46] on that rests his director's force in modifying the tempo;[47] he has before him, as it were, a more objective and hardened impression of the tenderest or wildest movements, which he *hits* with conclusive certainty, he always shoots, as a marksman, into the heart.[48] For him, everything is thus *individualized passion*; it has storm and fire, all of nature is full of life, never indefinite, never mood-like, but instead like something willing, desiring. — Drama is now for him the active life of many passions and their *history*, a bundle of energies and tongues of fire, as it were, which make each other clash, repel, flare up, die down.[49]

Through opera, many individual means of expressing passion were invented and made popularly understandable. For it is not only necessary to invent this symbolism, but also to train an understanding audience. This has occurred least in the concert; there the affectation of "higher art" and of higher taste rules. But in the failed dramatic nonform of the opera, much understanding for what is symbolic was smuggled in. Here one wanted the *effect* and was honest enough about it, far from the refined hypocrisy that defends the "worth of art without effects"; there one gradually received a complete grand sum of effects, i.e., of understandable symbolic forms: there now, a genius could arrive and assert control over them. For no form is so common that it could not be reinterpreted by the hand of the genius into an expression of what is highest and noblest. — The feeling for prolonged passion upon the stage was trained from the side of *Schiller* (and of Shakespeare): a higher degree of culture, since the people otherwise always want only piecework and give up completeness and duration. — All these partial preliminaries and preparations always brought their own measure of absurdity and learnedness along with them; and the aesthetic *expression*, the writing and reading *about it*, was completely disgusting. It required the eye of the genius so that *nevertheless* a *training* for the drama and music of passion was present there and that the only thing that counted was that now for once everything that originally belonged together, but, historically, had now come to be taught individually, be combined once again and the *attempt* hazarded as to whether one *would* now *understand* the *whole*. The first attempts of Wagner succeeded only moderately, indeed, he almost had to despair. The sticking to dogma, to what is traditional, that is usual in Germany objected to everything in the new species, that much of it was lacking from every *previously* existing species: one saw *bad* opera, bad symphonic music, bad Shakespearean drama in the work of Wagner. *Individuals* felt the effect, and these were now the *public* for Wagner. He taught them not to be concerned about the previous aesthetics. While setting his listeners and spectators free, he more and more set his own energy free from all acquired learning. The divine feeling of having found his kingdom, where he was ruler, came over him more and more. There runs through *Tristan* a feeling of well-being from *newly attained* mastery, of recklessly speaking what he *can* and wants, that has indeed its equal in no work of the world. Now for the first time he has found the *great form* (the prolonged passion, the many-headed passion);[50] the fear of being misunderstood that forced him up to that point still always to raise up and to isolate the individual part too much (e.g., in *Lohengrin*), to entice the public, as it were, by approximation to the accustomed form, in short, the wish to entice, that has now left him. Nothing is more unbearable for him than to lose his listeners, in this he is a genuine artist who wants to speak *understandably* of the blissful world of his being; a work of art that does not let itself be understood is a contradiction. For art is precisely the power to really *communicate* what one has experienced, nothing more! — Now he recognized the *weaknesses* in communicability of the *word-drama* as *music* for itself. The former has to work through thoughts word gesture upon feeling, therefore belongs within *rhetoric*. But passion is not always *eloquent*; here it *must* be, and indeed at length. The word is a used-up and worn-out way to communicate, and so the word-poet must *color* language and thoughts in uncustomary ways, in order thus to find the expression of passion, but thereby falls easily into *incomprehensibility*; on the other hand, he must raise up the whole through a depth of thoughts and formulations and thus falls into *untruth*, i.e., passion does *not really* express itself thus and therefore does not communicate itself either. Through the connection of music and language and gesture, Wagner attains, above all, the power to represent directly the *basic movements of what is within*, which can only be expressed through word and gesture; and now word and gesture become easily understandable. Now the dramatic actor can be *natural* once again (the earlier ones had to be affected, to speak formulaically etc.). The entire performative domain of the drama could be *simpler*, the idealizing element was not to be created first through the great complexity of the structure etc., the force of music was able to raise everything up at every moment. *Language* converted itself from a language of thoughts into a language of *feeling*, became more compact, threw away the unsingable auxiliary verbs etc. With this new *light*-apparatus, he had it in his power to give a *conviction*[51] to the inner life such as no artist had ever been able to attain: he could obtain a momentary belief in the miraculous.[52] *Hence* he could also represent *processes* that have *little* action in the banal sense, but instead play ⟨themselves⟩ out almost entirely inwardly and yet call up with the highest *understandability* the *participation* of the listeners, e.g., in *Tristan*. From this now follows an *ennobling of the passionate gesture, of the plastic element*, in general the music, because it *stretches out* sensation, as it were (for sung passion is longer than spoken),[53] brings with it an *overcoming* of the unplastic *excitation*, of *what is all too active*, from which the word-drama suffers. — After the artist knew all this as his field of power, he reached for the *material* that was great enough to show that here was a power such as no artist in the world has possessed — for *the tragedy of the gods and of heroes in general.* "The history of religion as tragedy."

11[16][54]

Instrumentation: he first trained the wind instruments for great effects, all earlier ones are dilettantes compared to him, even Beethoven.

11[17][55]

The dramatic actor now has a *model* in music. It came to be through a submergence in the alien entity, Wagner does not cheat like the poets with dragons, toads etc.:[56] the range of what he has experienced and can represent is unlimited.

Self-control of the artist, who reins in a triple-powered ruling imagination like three horses, toward the highest goal.

No symphonic excess.[57]

11[18]

23. A word about the *poet* Wagner. *Thinking in visible and palpable processes*, not in ideas is what is *really poetic*: this shows itself in myth; at the basis of which lies not an idea, as one generally thinks, but which is instead itself a kind of thinking, but not in concepts, I mean a worldview that cannot be encompassed in words, but instead in processes. As music appears for a deaf person, who only sees the Chladni sand-figures,[58] so is myth for the *nonthinker*, the common people; and for them the poet composes, who in this regard belongs himself to the common people, I mean to the nonthinkers. *The Ring of the Nibelung* is an immense *thought system without the conceptual form of thought*. Perhaps a philosopher would be able to create something completely equivalent to it, wholly without image and action: then we would have two disparate spheres. From

the one, we could not access the other: in order to reach the one, one would have to be a pure thinker, in order to reach the other, a pure poet. The thoughts that the heroes of poetry express are not the ideas of the poet as poet: he thinks in processes, the sequence of scenes, and that which occurs is his thinking.[59] Only the many semi-poets produce confusion: i.e., the artists who are not completely poets. — Now, if Wagner sometimes takes Christian-Germanic myth, sometimes sailor legends, sometimes Buddhist, sometimes heathen-German myths, sometimes Protestant bourgeois society, it is clear that he stands *freely* above the *religious* significance of these myths and demands this of his listeners, too; just as the Greek dramatists stood freely above it, and already Homer. Aeschylus, too, changed his representations as he pleased, even of Zeus. A poet is never *pious*.[60] There is no cult, no fear and anxiety ⟨and⟩ flattery[61] before these gods, one *does not believe in them*. The Greek who in a superstitious way saw the god in the stage-hero was not the spectator that Aeschylus wanted. The religiosity of the idols and fetishes must be done with if someone is to think as freely in processes as poets. Wagner encountered a tremendous point in time: when all religion of all *earlier ages wavers in its dogmatic idol- and fetish-effect*: he is the tragic poet at the end of all religion, the "twilight of the gods." So he made the whole of history serviceable for himself, he lays claim upon *history* as his field of thought: so uncommon is his creating that he is not stifled by all *that has been*, but which can instead only express itself in him. — In what light, now, does he see all that has been and has passed away? — The amazing significance of *death* is foregrounded here: death is *judgment*, but freely chosen, greatly desired judgment, full of awful charms as if it were more than a portal into nothingness. (With every strong step of life upon the stage, *death* resonates dully.)[62] Death is the seal upon every great passion and heroism, without it existence is worth nothing. To be ripe for it is the highest thing that can be attained, but also the hardest and earned by heroic struggles and suffering. Every such death is a gospel of *love*; and the entire music is a sort of metaphysics of love; it is a striving and wanting in a realm that seems to the ordinary gaze like the realm of not-wanting, a bathing in the sea of forgetfulness, a touching shadow play of a past passion.

11[19][63]

22. Wagner's art belongs not to *contemporary* art: he is far *ahead* or *beyond.* We should not give credit to our age for his existence, especially since it has done everything in order to hinder his existence. *Count up* what Wagner has *furthered* — in places where he was not blocked, but instead supported (Meyerbeer[64] to be presented as antithesis there, who put his transitory success on scene in the most artificial way — Wagner has always done the opposite, so that his "friends" in particular were always in a bad way, he never allowed them to rest, suddenly he was at them with something new outside of their horizon, they stood with yearning like the disciples in *Faust*[65] and looked upward). Just as little should the Leipzigers be allowed to honor him as their native son: instead their behavior toward Wagner calls to mind their behavior toward the Lutheran Reformation. My view of Wagner as "unfashionable" remains justified. For all other art and science, musicians and music teachers besides, wanted to block his way. — What concerns me is not to speak of Wagner's opponents; for I would have to speak of everyman. Who has not sinned? By shallowly not-wanting-to-hear or halfway-hearing etc. Yet I keep silent: as I understand how to do, but let the title show that I call this observation unfashionable.

11[20][66]

21. How unjustly one would behave to assume that for Wagner it was a matter of art alone and that he would consider it as the bandage for all other miserable circumstances! It is for him only the consolation vis-à-vis ἀνάγκη,[67] but where is the limit of ἀνάγκη, if we gaze upon the breadth of human life! For the individual it remains the primary consolation *vis-à-vis his personal* ἀνάγκη; but at the same time it steels the individual

so that he takes up the struggle for what is universal. It is precisely Wagner's drama that shows the fight to the finish of the individual with what is considered to be ἀνάγκη, law, tradition, contract, power, money; the individual cannot live in a more beautiful way than by ripening into death and sacrificing himself in this struggle.[68] The inexhaustible life of the species confronts the dying individual; *what* can the former not overcome! — Still, art is for an *interval of quiet* in the struggle, not for the struggle itself; for those moments when, looking backward and ahead, we understand everything symbolically, when a mild fatigue comes over us. Art is the dream for the sleep of the fighter, the refreshing dream for the refreshing sleep of the fighter. The day dawns once again, the sacred shadows disperse, and then art is far away. But its *comfort* accompanies us the entire day.[69] So it is the highest of the world's benefactors, even though its happiness is like a shadow. So art is a higher stage of religion, without its basic ordinary motives, begging among the gods and buying something,[70] without the vulgar craving for profit. And so art also appears historically when religions are dying out; admittedly, religions are then generally still conserved by art, through temples festival processions ritual, dramatic spectacles; besides the inherited gratitude toward the mythical figures that benefit art. A condition of humans that could do without art and religion[71] is perhaps not an impossibility, but we cannot even imagine it yet. Both of the greatest sufferings — 1) the uncertainty of *knowledge*, the noncommonality of it among all human beings and 2) the disparity of *abilities* — these sufferings are *in need of* art. We cannot be happy as long as everything around us is suffering: we cannot be moral as long as the course of things is determined by power and violence and injustice;[72] we cannot even be wise as long as all of humanity has not entered into the competition for wisdom. Everywhere the individual finds his *dissatisfaction*: how is he supposed to be able to endure it without at the same time recognizing something *sublime* and *meaningful* in his struggle and striving and perishing? This is what tragedy shows him; it takes pleasure in the rhythm of passion and in its sacrifice; it holds the tragic disposition erect and shows it to be present amid all changing of customs and religions.[73] Better to die than be untrue to its most inner characteristic, its passion, of which we are the embodiment! Woe to humanity if this tragic sensibility were ever to vanish! Only art is *not a direct* teacher and educator for action; the objects for which the tragic heroes strive are not things self-evidently worth striving for. It is as in a dream; those things that, while under the enchantment of art, we take to be worth striving for, so that it is better to choose to die than to renounce them, they are not or are only rarely useful in life; art is instead for calmness and repose, for the sleep of the active one; its problems are *simplified*, lightened, they are nothing but *abbreviations* of the infinitely complicated equation of real life. But its greatness and indispensability lie precisely in the fact that it arouses the semblance of a *simpler* world, of a *more precise solution of its riddle*. No one can do without this semblance; the more complicated our knowledge of the laws of life becomes, the more ardently we desire that simplification, even if only for brief moments; so much the greater becomes the *tension* between knowledge and the individual; art exists, *so that the bow does not break*. But since this gap becomes ever greater and an ever-higher tension is demanded of the individual in the age of perishing religions, we come into *a period of art*, as it has never yet *been necessary* and never yet existed.

11[21]

Of theater and the mania for diversion. Humans take the conventional for what is right. Our whole life and being is really highly uncommon and worth reflecting upon — corrupt![74]

— Wagner an *Alexander in reverse*: not a diffuser of culture, but instead a concentrator, a concave mirror, an assembler of all possible cultural material, from breadth into narrowness, from dispersal together into a middle-point. His force shows itself in pulling upon the threads that have become so slack. The *astringent*.[75]

We cannot be happy, as long as — And yet even knowledge is a reproach, as long as we the workers — — —[76]

Wagner as a vessel sailing along the coast[77]

Fairy tale for children and women[78]

Bayreuth struggle with the elements

11[22][79]

20. The history of the development of culture since the Greeks is actually quite short, if we consider the actual true distance covered, not taking any account at all of periods of stagnation, regression, hesitation, straying. The Hellenization of the world and the Orientalizing of the Hellenic — the task of Alexander the Great — is still the last great event; the transmission of a foreign culture still the problem with which we are reckoning. Meanwhile *Alexandrianism* has come forth in ever greater force; leaving aside the stupefying interlude of Christianity — the rhythmic play of both factors against each other, from which the world had to suffer[80] — of course, the march of science has moved onward. But with the infinite dispersal of the Hellenic spirit, the real cultural effect of the Hellenic is always more threadbare and fainter, too; above all, any unity is lacking, it is a confused fluctuation. So, then, a line of counter-Alexanders has now become necessary, who have the enormous strength to consolidate and to connect, to pull together the most distant threads and to prevent the fabric from fraying. Not to cut the Gordian knot of Greek culture, so that its ends flutter in all the corners of the world, but instead to bind it back together after it has been cut — that is *now* the task.[81] I recognize in Wagner such a counter-Alexander. He has, to speak medically, something *astringent*, he confines and unifies what was isolated and weak, sluggish: to this extent he belongs to the very great forces of culture and is the first of a new line of human beings. He rules over the religions, the arts, the sciences of history and yet he is the opposite of a polyhistorian, a talent pulling things together, adding them up and ordering them (as Aristotle[82] was for nature). He is someone who helps shape and breathe life

into those things he has brought together, a *simplifier of the world*.[83] In doing so, he has so many stages of humanity within him that he can also think himself completely into an immediate, contemporary task; he connects not only the most distant points of the great sea, but he *can* also, when he wants, be a vessel sailing along the coast and show himself equal to the smaller, fashionable work.[84]

11[23][85]
19. *A reform of the theater* — it seems almost laughable for the superficial spectator. Good, suppose it were reformed, what then has thereby happened? he will say. Well, the modern human being would thereby be changed and reformed; so necessarily is everything connected here. It is absolutely impossible to establish the worth of art without *introducing innovation* everywhere, in mores and in government, with justice and love. Even just to comprehend the extent to which the position of art has degenerated, the extent to which our theaters are an affront — we must willingly learn everything anew and come to understand the ruling commonplaceness as something very unusual and complex. The strangest barbarity, most vulgar amusement, pedantic intentions, pomposity and playing at the earnestness of art, profit, vanity of society, exhausted senses — all of this comes together in the theater. We really only need to compare the *Greek* one in order to see how vulgar and, moreover, vulgar in a baroque way our arrangements are. Supposing that we knew nothing about the Greeks, our conditions would perhaps be wholly unassailable, and we would consider the objections to be utopian dreams. "Given how human beings are, such an art is appropriate — they have never been different": — someone might say. To see in one and the same place solemn emotion and composure, the high point of our happiness, the highest strengthening of the noblest human beings, the most devoted self-sacrifice of the artists, this drama of all dramas itself, the victorious creator of such a work — is it not magic to have brought this to pass? Wouldn't the human

beings who could experience that already have to have been transformed and rejuvenated? Haven't we found a haven in the desolate vastness of the sea, a tranquility upon the waters? If I look back from there, how barren and disgusting the modern way of interacting with art seems to me, how degrading the singing and musicianship in our concerts and social life, the reading and speaking in our learned circles! And how pitiable is the position of the modern state, which, moreover, lets itself be called "culture state"! I have only *one* wish at such a sight, never to have to return to this shallow world or to be defended as much as possible against it; while I would like to offer to all those really suffering the hope that there still exist humans who will fight *for* them *against* the oppressive elements of a luxurious drive. I prefer to live together with the artisan, peasant and worker than with the present-day "cultivated person," with the pious, simple man without learning rather than with the scholar, indeed, even with the undisguised[86] servant of egoism rather than with the masked one.

11[24]

18. Wagner manifests his *power* especially in how he subjugates those who are reluctant. There is no longer any talented musician who does not inwardly attend to him and find him more worthy to listen to than all ⟨the⟩ other music taken together. Many who desperately want to be of some significance struggle against precisely this inner allurement that threatens to overwhelm them, but where do we see one who could now still keep himself free? — they become pettier, seek out bad allies and friends, flatter the age and thus get spoiled: but especially when they feign the great form, they are no longer honest, but want instead to deceive. In the best case, they are very diligent and learn what is to be learned in music: trusting that the "cultivated ones" can't tell the difficult difference between original and copy, between what is learnable and what is unlearnable, they throw themselves into creating.[87] The *smallest form* should be recommended to all of them, if they absolutely want to

compose, something that I, with a loose expression, would like to call the musical epigram; the wit and shaping energy would perhaps suffice for that and they could be honest; excellent things can still emerge from this, as with the Greeks, who also threw themselves into the smallest form when the great ones were forestalled.

Wagner himself wants no composer-school.

There one attaches oneself to the earlier masters with anxious eagerness, keeps one's ears closed and prefers to play the role of Schubert or Handel or any other character than that of Wagner. Impossible![88] The same inescapability among the literary opponents; apart from the real straw and wooden and number-counting heads, every even moderately gifted one has now been overcome; and the envy and hatred or even the need for bread and money, the obligation that one enters into with regard to newspapers, the fear of the public, the question of decorum, how one would prepare for oneself an adept retreat, all of that now gives everything that has been said and written about Wagner such a disgusting character. Now and then genuine rage breaks out and one has gone so far as to label all that is diabolical in the arts of seduction intoxication with the name "Wagner." All of this as a new means to increase that power! Whether one speaks of art in Japan or in the American prairies, only a single stance comes into consideration, that toward Wagner. And perhaps all modern art history, the last centuries before and the next ones after, may concentrate itself around *this one name*.

11[25]

17. How well Wagner understands how *to conclude things* is indicated by his preoccupation with German mythology. All scholars have worked only for him; now that the work of resurrecting German myth has been completed, that scholar-species has become superfluous. And so *should* scholars let themselves be made superfluous! Truly, it is only with a view to such final elimination of their species by a genius that they do

their work! As the kind who hope for redemption, enchanted into underground, sunless, laborious work! — Who would now have much more to say about Aeschylus and Soph⟨ocles⟩! Something greater is here, the essence, too, of *their* art, and at the same time the highest justification for the respect that they have enjoyed, trusting almost blindly. Just as the history of religion is placed at a turning point, so is art history; we can throw away an enormous sum of knowledge now, after the redeeming word has been spoken; a good part of scholarliness and history (especially aesthetics) has grown old, become rubbish. How others do not understand how to conclude things is indicated, e.g., by the preoccupation with the German fairy tale; it was rediscovered by scholars and picked up from old women and children. Instead of now sensing the high degree of *degradation* that lies in the transformation of men's myth into old women's fairy tales and breaking its spell, one occupied oneself with foolish childishness with artificial elaboration of the fairy tale,[89] like Schwind, for example; and our blasé urbanites behaved like children! All of German Romanticism was a scholarly movement, one wanted to get back to the *naïve* and knew that one really was no longer that at all. Anyone now who is not heroic cannot get through to what is simple and naïve; but those ones believed they could arrive there through coddling, aging, old-maidishness and a sort of intentional "second childhood." We must be able not to model our singing on the popular song, but instead to *offer a model for* singing it aloud, in order to be a popular singer. And Wagner understands that, he is populist in every fiber.[90]

11[26]

16. Wagner's *diadochi*:[91] he bequeaths his kingdom, too, "to the strongest,"[92] but we are not talking here about post-Wagnerian *art*: we will have to be careful for a long time to come about creating music, showing off and dabbling are over with. He proves himself to be a very great power of culture precisely because one cannot even say *all the places where* his influence can still break

out. Not through concepts alone, but instead through *action*, he has placed a question mark in front of our culture that calls itself completely modern. It is not modern, but instead old and already completely decayed. Here is the place to conquer and to triumph thoroughly; the greatest realms stand open; who, for example, will recognize the realm of education as rotten and overthrow it? (If we could drive the quiet, discontented, deep scholars to open revolt and avowal, that would be the most severe blood-letting of the entire preceding educational system. There would remain all the politically infected among the scholars and the literary dilettantes of all sorts.)[93] He has divined and betrayed that much is *very weak*; and the resistance of the previous power-holders, e.g., of the scholars, would not be able to withstand many battles. With the name "Bayreuth," I designate one of the most profound defeats that cultivated Germans have suffered; they did not participate, they furiously opposed it, the contempt of those to come will strike them.[94]

11[27][95]
⟨15.⟩ The *fundamental moral nature* of Wagner unfolds itself ever more visibly. It, too, needs sunshine, i.e., success in striving. A great goal brings great dangers! and the inadequacy for that and consequently also the lack of insight into this inadequacy — sometimes lying in the circumstances? — makes one *angry*, one looks to others to find the causes for the failure, goes off on byways and secret paths, always believing in one's goal, and holds the whole world responsible, becomes, as it were, embittered and irritable, unjust; so it happens that good natures go wild on the path toward what is best. — Even among those who chase after moral purification, among monks and hermits, savage and repeatedly sickened human beings can be found.[96] — Wagner, hollowed out and consumed by failure, would be a fearsome nature; it would wrap him in the gloomy melancholy of a revolutionary demon.[97] We should speak about the unrevealable sacredness of what is within only with modest reticence: but can it not be felt, how at the basis of the *Rienzi*, the *Flying Dutchman*,

Tannhäuser, Lohengrin, Tristan, Hans Sachs, Wotan, Brünnhilde a unifying underground stream of moral nobility flows along, and how this stream flows ever purer and brighter? What artist offers us a similar picture? Perhaps Schiller. Yet the scale is greater with Wagner, the path much more extended, too. Music, not only myth, expresses this process of purification: and in *The Ring of the Nibelung* such a loftiness and sanctity of mood is achieved that we cannot help but think of the glowing of ice- and snow-peaks. Wagner started like a wild force of nature, dark and restless, stormily sought satisfaction where most find it, recoiled in disgust, attempted it anew, strove for power, intoxicating success ecstasy and once again renunciation, attempted to throw off his burden, to forget, to begin anew; the entire stream plunged at times into this, at times into that valley, crept into the darkest ravines, violently snatched up cliffs and forests, demolishing, raving — in the night of this half-subterranean raging, a star stood over him: fidelity, selfless *fidelity*. He stamped it upon ever-new images, Elisabeth to Tannhäuser, brother to sister in *Rienzi*, friend to friend, servant to master, Elsa to Lohengrin, Senta to the flying Dutchman, Brünnhilde to Wotan's most inner wish, Brünnhilde to Siegfried: why did precisely this word gleam more brightly for him and cause him to think ceaselessly and to compose in processes? This is Wagner's primal secret:[98] the relationship of the two innermost forces of his being to each other, will and intellect — that these remain loyal to each other is the great necessity, the one thing that is *necessary* for him, through which he remains *whole*; while he sees around him the most terrible dangers of infidelity, the temptations to it. Each of these drives strives to reach the immeasurable for itself, wants satisfaction, it is the most inner spiritual fear of Wagner that they remain faithful. His artistic talents are supposed to remain faithful to him as well, and yet the noblest kind of curiosity entices him aside, enticing, e.g., the temptation to the symphonic form: do you not feel it, how often Wagner subjects himself with cruel decisiveness to the dramatic whole that is as inexorable as a fate and how the musician does not race off to the place he desires so greatly?[99] — This fidelity to himself or to a higher self, of something feminine to something masculine, is Wagner's innermost problem; looking outward from here is how he understands the *world*. Just think only of the abundance of talents, all of which *want* their own way! With Wagner, *fidelity* is even the more universal concept, under which falls love, sexual, brotherly-sisterly, childish love. The whole theme of fidelity is exhausted by him; the most magnificent is certainly Brünnhilde, who *against* Wotan's command preserves fidelity to Wotan and thereby makes possible the redemption of the world — a mythic thought of the highest rank and completely suited to him. But there, too, the feeling of the *infidelity* suffered is the most terrible thing that any poet has ever imagined: the oath "by the point of the spear" of Brünnhilde[100] the most heart-rending thing that exists; passion falls upon us there as if with tiger claws. Wagner first *discovered* for art the many *tragic* possibilities that lie in fidelity. His own life[101] went through these possibilities and was thereby one of the hardest lives that can be lived. *Not-hoping* lies over the greatest half of his life; hence also not-despairing; but he may often have felt like a wanderer who passes through the night with a heavy burden, alone: a sudden death did not appear to him at this time as a horrifying, but rather as a seductive attractive apparition. Burden, path and night — all suddenly gone![102] *Fidelity* held him and struggled with the apparition.

11[28]

14. As *musician*, Wagner has something of *Demosthenes*, the terrible seriousness toward the object and the grip and the force of the grip, so that he always grasps the object; he places his hand around it, in an instant, and takes hold of it as if it were made of bronze. Like Demosthenes, he conceals his artistry, he makes us forgot it and yet he is, like him, the last and supreme manifestation of a whole line of powerful artistic spirits. He has nothing epideictic about him, unlike all previous

musicians, all of whom occasionally make their art into a game and put themselves on display: with Wagner, one thinks neither of what interests, nor of what delights, but instead merely feels what is *necessary*.[103] To this belonged a tremendous force of will and the highest artistic purity of character. No one has imposed such *stringent laws* upon himself as Wagner,[104] just consider the relationship of the singing voices to the unsung speech and, on the other hand, of the melody of the voices to the entire symphonic context of the music in order to see a true marvel! And isn't every score of Wagner a sort of proof that *before him* no real effort and work and conscientiousness at all went into it?[105] Diligence and inventiveness in the most individual things is actually an ideal. How does a poet then appear to someone! Like something very comfortable and carefree,[106] like a blessed human being with many idle hours who avoids work. With this, Wagner has raised all practicing musicians into prominence, they can all be in their performance with their soul, because their task demands a soul. The virtuosic craftsman of art is done away with by Wagner; he no longer attracts. Through his effort and burden and pressure Wagner has made it easier for those who practice art, he has protected them against the feeling of being dishonored. And thus Wagner has *helped* all of those who concern themselves with art; soon it will no longer be possible for the *frivolous* pursuit of art by our courts, state-theaters, concert societies, feeble friends of art and all sorts of "people given over to quiet drunkenness,"[107] who devote themselves to art in their cozy little rooms in feeble self-satisfaction,[108] to save itself from general *contempt*. We, those who know all that depends upon art being for once correctly conceived, what a mesh of duties — disdain in the deepest way at least all of the existing arrangements for the care of art. The *opposite* has admittedly burst forth into something immense! and it is possible that those to come are too weak to overcome it. With Demosthenes, it was finished. But there are still enough people here who are the fertile land upon which Wagner can sow — enough who understand at least how to fight and to work: Bayreuth proves it. There we have for the days to come beautiful work to get at the weeds with sickle and scythe. Through this *work* we ennoble ourselves; for up to now, it was in my eyes an almost contemptible thing to be called a "friend of art," and I esteemed the clearly recognizable enemies of art more; for with them the feeling nonetheless often betrayed itself that this would be an occupation for a pompous and egotistical class, far from the need of the people and basically a means to "distinguish" oneself precisely from the people. Down with art that does not push in itself for the revolution of society, for the renewal and unification of the people!

11[29][109]
13. The *improvisational.* To explain Shakespeare, Wagner has alluded to how he could be thought of as an improvising actor who had the presence of mind to freeze his improvis⟨ation⟩;[110] and he characterizes himself similarly as musician. "Self-renunciation"[111] as the essence of this art — entering into alien souls, pleasure in this exchange; now such an interchange of souls in the musician is a phenomenon of the highest kind: the nonsubjectivity of the musician something entirely new. Thus Wagner places the *Meistersinger* beside *Tristan* — the bitter-joyful mastery of *Tristan*, the thoroughly fermented, more brightly golden mastery of the *Meistersinger*:[112] the older musicians had no conception at all of such a possibility; if they did not want to express *their* mood, *their* passion, they were stiff or played with the traditional melodic types. We must attend especially to how the music sometimes stands decisively in opposition to Wagner's personal disposition: thus, Hagen as wedding-herald is one of Wagner's most audacious self-renunciations. Someone should just try to imitate that after first taking sides with his soul! The highest thing perhaps is mime. And then look at how, when miraculous deeds occur, how much the music there *believes* in this miracle, e.g., when Siegfried forges his sword: for which a power of renunciation[113] from time exists of which our "poets" have no inkling either.

If ⟨they⟩ produce this miracle, they are swindling; as our philosophasters are swindling when they immerse themselves in "mysticism." But that is the curse of contemporary philosophiers,[114] that they pretend with their brains empty of imagination, sober and at the same time confused, as if they were really capable of mysticism; for which reason it is advisable to remain six steps away from anyone who takes mystical turns, as from a dishonest companion; at least it is questionable, if it is only an embarrassed mysticism at the point where the understanding becomes uncertain, the eye grows dim, and the self-possessed person draws back — almost every thinker grazes against such limits. Wagner dives down and into alien minds, senses, ages and in no way deceives us. A giant, a cave-worm, Rhine maidens — all of that would be deceitfulness and foolish trifling for our "poets": they do not have the magic in their bodies to bring nature to life and to increase the animate part of the world! Even if it were only for a moment — but he *was* transformed in this moment and bore the impression of it: listen to how the *toad* crawls![115]

11[30]

Since for once a completely great human being has been granted to us not all too blessed humans of this age, we should rejoice at it in our hearts and also *show* that we are rejoicing; for joy that seeks no companions, but hides instead in its cozy little room is hateful. Perhaps we are able thus to increase somewhat the happiness in the world: and filled as we are, often enough to overflowing, with so much hate and ardor, we should least of all withhold our happiness from others: it is our return gift and I very much wish that a surplus of it thereby abides. If the truth is most often bitter and nonetheless is spoken, it would be cruel and malicious to consume the sweet truth for oneself in private and to permit nobody to have a share.

11[31][116]

12. *That art is not the fruit of the luxury of classes* or of individuals, but instead precisely belongs to and has to give thanks for its emergence to a *society freed from luxury* is the new idea. How such a society would have to be constituted, Wagner shows in mythical image in the *Nibelung*: where the gods are annihilated, power and gold have run their curse-laden path to the end, where the spirit of fidelity, love rules among human beings. Art up to now is the fruit of luxury (yet not the churchly kind); music, too, has had its part of that and maintained a playful character until it came to consciousness through Beethoven and was *purified* by Wagner. For he is the cathartic human being for art. It is really in the poor and in those who are not well off, also in those who are little instructed, that Wagner's art has its firmest refuge. — Wagner is completely right: where the politicians and the sages cease, there the artist begins, as seer and presager of the new ideas.[117] The next enormous sphere to be conquered is education:[118] and only when a sufficient mass of human beings feels itself in contradiction to all existing powers, will they also place their shoulders to the beams. It is a sectarian art and will be a sectarian education: but with the highest striving to get beyond the sect. It lies in its nature not to differentiate a boundary, a class, only through external force can it be a sect for a time. As long as humans still exist who are not newly educated, the newly educated have to suffer.

"We should all be *geniuses*" Wagner.[119]

11[32][120]

11. Wagner's *prose writings*, extraordinarily dense with ideas, are hard to understand, because he does not want to accentuate and because in the larger structure of sentences he does not weigh primary and secondary accents against one another; everything is as important for him as if everything were underlined. These writings will be found to be clearer by far when well read aloud: for they are written in the style of spoken discourse, not of written discourse. There is a restless rhythm in

them, an inequality of tempo, whereby they create confusion as prose; many times the dialectic is broken, carried forward by leaps of feeling and often with a sort of reluctance, hidden, as it were; as if the artist were ashamed of conceptual demonstration. The greatest difficulty for the uninitiated is the form of authoritative dignity that is wholly peculiar to him and difficult to describe: it seems to me as if Wagner were often speaking *in the presence of enemies*, as it were, with whom he may be unfamiliar and toward whom he shows himself to be not natural, but instead reserved, restrained. However, the sweeping passion often enough breaks through this deliberate draping; then the artificial, heavy periods, richly swollen[121] with superfluous words, break apart and sentences and complete pages escape from him that are among the most beautiful examples of German prose: especially so in the "Beethoven." On the whole, the reader was absent from him when he wrote prose; he was thinking of the common people and felt like the common people when he created as an artist; but as a prosaic explicator — toward whom did he direct himself then! indeed, is he supposed to have the "cultivated ones," the scholars, before his eyes? He almost had to do so: and hence the compulsion, self-compulsion. Necessity prompted his theoretical writings, he depicts it himself: he had taken away from him his most beautiful means of communicating, the example.[122] Nonetheless I would like to know what degree of confusion the discourse about Wagner and about music would have reached if he had not written: and a force that *strikes dumb* is present in certain writings like the "Beethoven," "Actor and Singer," "On Conducting," as must show itself ever more clearly in the progress of our culture. Here is someone completely great who speaks of what he has experienced: what would the small people who have experienced nothing, our aestheticians and art historians, still have to say! But even the noteworthy older aesthetic writings have sunk in value since then; we need Wagner's writings now more than Lessing's "Laocoön" and Schiller's prose writings.[123] Besides, they are richer, also easier to understand than Schiller's aesthetic writings, also much more fundamental; and deserve therefore much more than Schiller's to be read and explicated in the schools and universities. They are really the most important aesthetic writings that exist — too bad that after all we still have to say such things! Everything there — problem and solution — is experienced suffered and triumphantly achieved, no foolish canonization and swearing upon Aristotle comes between, as interferes even with Lessing. Moreover, they are an excellent means of training in one of the most beautiful lessons, to eavesdrop upon a great artist in his becoming, to see how he improves himself — even when he stumbles he still strikes sparks — [124] frees, clarifies and "clothed in content,"[125] he emerges from indeterminacy. These writings have nothing at all canonical, strict: instead the canonical lies in the works. They are attempts to conceive experience, to peel it in concepts. Let anyone who can, do it better; it was an unpleasant compulsion for Wagner to have to do it at all. After all, his whole life long, no one lifted a burden from him.

11[33][126]
For the *conclusion*.
10. *Great talent* is the most magnificent spectacle[127] in the world; where it appears, the earth becomes a summer garden and the rosebushes wish never to cease blooming.[128] Everything must turn out well for it, regardless of the difficulty of the trials through which it had to pass. It is nourished[129] upon poison and thereby becomes healthy and strong, even when someone else would have been ruined by it. Every risk makes it more courageous, every triumph makes it more self-possessed. It is stimulated and goaded by the ridicule of the surrounding world, it savors them like praise and balm: if it sleeps, "it sleeps only to put new energy in itself"; if it goes astray, it returns home from this error and straying with the most marvelous booty. It makes the body ever healthier and does not feed off life, the longer it lives; it rules over the human being like a winged passion and permits him to fly at precisely the moment when the foot

is exhausted by plodding through sand or chafed by treading on stones. It cannot help but impart, and everyone may partake of its scent; it is generous and compassionate without any reflection, it does not regard the person and is not stingy with its gifts. Rejected, it gives more lavishly, misused by those to whom it has given, it even adds to its gifts the precious treasure it possesses; and never were the recipients wholly worthy of the gift: so say both the oldest and the most recent experiences. In this way,[130] great talent is the most enigmatic thing, an abyss in which strength and goodness are united,[131] a bridge between self and nonself: who could name the *purpose* for which it exists at all? Could the greater really be present for the sake of the lesser, the supreme talent for the sake of the smallest, the great virtue and sanctity for the sake of the frail? If this were the case — only for an instant are we granted such a boundless possibility:[132] so this would be like a sunny beam of love, in which all earthly life goldenly gleamed.

11[34][133]

9. Through Wagner, it has been proven once again that the individual, during an ordinary human life,[134] can manifest something *completely new* that takes away the breath of one who swears by the canon of the gradualness of development. All talented human beings are very swift — I just want to see how long it takes until our not so swift contemporaries have followed behind; their faith in slowness and in the ant-work of many is no flattery of their own talent. There were no portents, no transitions, no intermediary stages that pointed to a work such as the *Nibelung*, an enterprise such as Bayreuth. No one but Wagner knew the long road to the goal and the goal itself; it is a circumnavigation of the world in the realm of art, whereby, so it seems, it was not only a new art, but *true* art itself that was discovered. All prior modern arts, either because isolated or as hermit- or luxury-arts, are thereby devalued;[135] the half-dead memories of the true art that we moderns inherited from the Greeks may now rest in peace. For many things, the final hour has come.[136] All

frivolous, enfeebled art is scared to death, all monkish-solitary, atrophied art redeemed. All of the talking and noise that modern cultivation has made about art will be felt to be shamelessly importunate now that every disciple of the newly arisen[137] art is dedicating himself to a five-year Pythagorean silence. He yearns for holier waters and for consecrations; for[138] who did not dirty his hands and heart on the repulsive idol-worship of the prior art! *Silence and purity* — to that he pledges himself.

11[35]

8. Prominent is Wagner's drive toward *communication* and his inventiveness in communicating.[139] A thought like his, conceived in the greatest vigor and born for beauty would seem condemned to remain a phantom if Wagner did not possess this flexible and insatiable communicability. He thinks his thoughts into the prevailing circumstances and times, and if the expression of it seems stunted, it has nonetheless itself remained pure and great in Wagner's head and heart. Wherever he remotely perceived a small or significant[140] opportunity to manifest his thought by means of examples, he was prepared; wherever a halfway receptive soul opened itself up to him, he cast in his seeds. He attaches hopes to situations at which the cold observer can only shrug his shoulders; he deceives himself a hundred times in order to prove just once to such an observer that he is right — and in order to be proven right after all in the long run to all of these skeptics.[141] The small and large orchestras that he directed, the individual musicians and actors to whom he uttered one word,[142] the cities that witnessed how seriously he took his activities, the princes and ladies who, half shyly, half lovingly, sought to snatch something of him,[143] the various European countries to which he belonged for a while, the most zealously repeated news that he gave of his plans (and off which for decades already the aesthetic reporters of the newspapers have almost lived), the writings with which he helped himself when he could not proceed to action, the students whom he trained — everywhere an echo of his thought, often intentionally distorted, but thousandfold;

and[144] we need not wait much longer for the overwhelming force of the mighty voice with which he called out to the world to be matched by the overwhelming force of the echo, too. Then it is no longer possible not to hear him.[145] While he passes thus through everyone, he does not become the slave of those to whom he communicates himself: he himself strides higher and does not remain under the spell of the once-expressed word, nor in general of any of his own past.[146] Just consider and tremble at this consideration: what was at stake if Wagner had never be able to display his thought through an example such as he now displays in Bayreuth!; and how great even was the probability that a thought[147] of which other humans did not let themselves dream would have remained only a dream, too, in the head of the one who conceived it and that in place of Bayreuth we would be speaking of a "utopia." It is indeed astonishing, all that comfortable humans term utopias:[148] but here the most uncomfortable and boldest humans would almost be right to speak of utopias. A higher degree of disgust and despair at human beings, a more obstinate selfishness of the discoverer would have sufficed: and basically, Wagner's contemporaries have also done everything in order to make him disgusted and to force him back into himself.[149] But he did not grow tired and remained gracious in his will to communicate.

He got over the incompetence and the prudish oppressiveness with which one now and then condescended to promote his art, as though the gathering crowd on the streets of Nürnberg at night (in the *Meistersinger*) could be represented by ballet dancers;[150] he tolerated it, although often with the bitterest restraint, that his work took possession of people under precisely the names and forms that he combated, in the distortion into "opera"; he even endured the most bitter thing — the great martyr — seeing his friends intoxicated by "successes" and "victories," when his singularly lofty idea was torn right down the middle and denied. As compensation for all these deepest necessities, he finally said: my great work is done, now you shall see it — there on the hill near Bayreuth. That was his revenge: he passed on his highest possessions, the accumulated treasure of twenty years of mastery! — [151] But the person to whom something is given must also be able to take: and great sensibility for giving demands a great sensibility for taking.[152] Here, however, the treasure is almost excessively great: in order to lift it, Wagner[153] had also *to transfer* his force, his confidence, his daring, his lightning-quick comprehension, his loyal conduct to us: and this demonic transferability of the entire Wagnerian nature is almost as amazing as his nature itself. In every orchestra that Wagner leads we can see an example: what he called "modification of the tempo" and was the first to practice is basically a transfer of the Wagnerian rhythm of the soul to the souls of the musicians he led; and as the souls of the musicians are thus redeemed and transfigured into the heights, the soul of music is also in turn redeemed from the iron grating of mathematically divided time and now for the first time speaks audibly to us. And so, as Wagner communicates himself to musicians, the spirit and rhythm of his Bayreuth work must communicate itself to viewers and listeners, so that their soul is stretched, their bows already tensed as never before: only then will the immensity be completely done, when it, too, works in an immense way and rips up after itself a furrow[154] that can never be filled in again. *Whither* this furrow is being ripped, in what direction, — who could guess completely? But one supposition, a single one among others, may already now become audible.

(With this, transition to the final chapter: ἀνάγκη, meaning of art, continuation, its place in the reestablished society, education.)

11[36]

Wagner is great, so that we all become great.

11[37]

7. We could also count Wagner's *friends* among his *dangers*; it is extremely wonderful how he has almost unconsciously over his entire life avoided every formation of factions, how on the

other hand a circle of followers forms during every phase of his art, apparently restricting him. He passes right through the midst of them and does not permit himself to be tied down. His path was too long for any individual to have been able very easily to accompany him from the beginning; and so unusual and steep — almost all of them at some time lost their breath. In almost all the periods of Wagner's life his friends would have liked to make him *dogmatic*, his enemies likewise; and if a lesser sort of lust to rule had been in him, he could have become the master of the German musical world much sooner.[155,156]

The unfortunate belief that a school of composers had to and would be modeled on him has, I suspect, never been Wagner's belief; what he as musician wanted to and did train people for is to be masterful directors and performing artists, truly dramatic singers. Otherwise it is indeed the moment in the development of music when a much higher energy and artistic morality reveal themselves in becoming a skilled master of performance and interpretation than in continuing to go on composing, i.e., diluting the effects of what is truly great by imitating it and multiplying its effects. The proper thing is to deal much more reverently with music and precisely for that reason to curtail the foolish drive to production; whereas the task of rendering the great art of Beethoven and Wagner has just been set for the first time and will demand unheard-of diligence and character in the most gifted talents.[157] And then to train the people to this height: which again, can only occur through what is best. Now, to be sure, the repugnant operation of our cultivated musical institutions has not hindered that greatest of scandals which the Germans have committed in art — that a great war found as its musical expression a "folk song" like "Watch on the Rhine";[158] such a mawkish and vulgar thing that any farmhand in a German army would previously have spat out. And then the encouragement of male choral music, where one hammers the glazed folk song into people's heads with sugary harmony and the arts of tempo! and celebrates German choral festivals, laughing in the face of our great music![159]

11[38][160]

5. *Idleness* and work in Wagner: there always exist rest stops and pauses for great cultural movements, and to them, to be sure, individual talents also correspond completely: thus, within the solemn and panting[161] Reformation movement, Montaigne is such an achieving of serenity with itself a peaceful being-for-itself and[162] exhalation; so Shakespeare certainly read him. I sometimes feel this benefit in Horace, and there are moods in which such sentences carry in them a magical mellowness.[163] So Wagner lingers in history; and there is no doubt that this mission falls to it today, to be able to exhale for once in the enormous struggle toward new goals and to feel itself detached, as it were.[164] If the Germans have devoted themselves to the study of history for[165] a century, then this demonstrates that they are the retarding obstructing inhibiting and pacifying force in the movement of the modern age: something that in the minds of some people might accrue to their credit.[166] On the whole it is a most dangerous indication when the spiritual struggle of a people is directed predominantly toward history, a mark[167] of enervation, of regression and weakness, of having grown weary: this is what our scholars of today represent in the history of the modern spirit, in contradistinction to all reform and revolutionary movements,[168] they have not set themselves the proudest task, but for that they have secured for themselves a certain kind of peaceful happiness.[169] To be sure, every freer, more manly step takes us beyond them, a creative[170] human being can stay among them only when he has grown weary.[171] Thus is Wagner related to history and philology; it is for him a tonic on the tempestuous voyage. History will perhaps for once be able to not be this, if as some day must happen, it is written in a more rigorous and deeper sensibility, and from out of a more powerful soul[172] than it has hitherto been done by the German scholars: all of their works have an aura of the prettified, submissive, and self-satisfied about them, and they are satisfied with the course of things. It already means a lot if one of them lets it be known that he is satisfied precisely because[173] things could have turned

out even worse, most of them believe instinctively that things are just fine the way they just happened to have turned out. If history were no longer a disguised Christian theodicy,[174] if it were written with more justice and ardent[175] sympathy, it would become a fearsome tool of revolution: whereas it has now served as an opiate against everything subversive. The situation is similar in the case of philosophy; all that most people want to learn from it is[176] a rough understanding of things so that they then can adapt themselves to them: and even in its most noble forms its tranquilizing and comforting power[177] is so strongly exaggerated[178] that those who are indolent and quietistic[179] are led to believe they are seeking the same thing philosophy[180] seeks. By contrast, it seems to me that the most important question[181] for all philosophies is the extent to which things possess an unalterable character: so that, once this question has been answered, we may with relentless courage set about the *improvement* of that *aspect* of the world *recognized as being alterable*. They also teach that themselves,[182] in that they worked at the improvement of the very alterable insight of human beings instead of keeping their wisdom to themselves; the true disciples of true philosophies also learn this: those who, like Wagner, know how to derive from them[183] only increased courage and decisiveness for[184] their path, but no sleeping potions.[185] Wagner is most like a philosopher where he is most energetic and heroic;[186] and there is perhaps no bolder symbolism for the heroic and philosophical[187] attitude toward the world than Siegfried's words to the Rhine maidens, as he throws the clods of earth over his head,[188] "thus I throw it far away from me."[189] This is the philosophy that annihilates the gods, on which Wotan's spear shatters.[190]

11[39][191]

6. How he as *a learner* then becomes master once again over what has been learned with regard to history. If Wagner then overcomes once again his formative force, then history has become something different for him; the past has balled itself up, as it were, solidified; he stands in relation to it as the Greek

to his myth, as to something that one forms and spins further with love and shy devotion; it has become more pliant more mutable than a reality and nonetheless bears more signs of the reality that once was than any past event. Where else has medieval chivalry taken on as much body and soul as in *Lohengrin*? And won't the *Meistersinger* tell future generations about the nature of the German spirit, indeed, more than tell about it:[192] won't it instead be one of the ripest fruits of this spirit that always[193] seeks to reform, not to revolutionize, and that in spite of the solid foundation of its contentment has not forgotten the noblest form of discontent, the *rejuvenating deed*?

It is to be recalled, how alone *in music generally what is completely scholarly* is *overcome* — it is the *highest* triumph of the modern spirit, and the first musician, Wagner, shows again *in nuce*[194] the same overcoming energy.

11[40][195]

4. *The language* of the poems. Wagner suffers from the degeneration and debilitation of our language, from the sins and wastefulness of earlier centuries, from the auxiliary verbs, the manifold losses and mutilations of the case-designations, from the cumbersome system of particles characteristic of our syntax: while he rejoices with deep pride in the age-old primitiveness and inexhaustibility, the resonant strength of its roots, in which he intuited, in contrast to the highly derivative and artificial-rhetorical Romance languages, a wonderful proximity to and disposition for music, for true music. Wagner's poetry is full of a love for the German language, a warmth and frankness in his dealings with it that, with the exception of Goethe, can be felt in no other German.[196] One should be able to sing every word, and gods and heroes should take it in their mouths: that was an enormous challenge that Wagner ⟨set⟩ for his linguistic imagination, at which anyone else would have had to despair: for our language is almost too aged and dilapidated; and yet when he struck the rock with his staff an abundant stream of water issued forth. Bold[197] terseness, concreteness of expression,

power and rhythmic variation, a remarkable wealth of strong and meaningful words, syntactic simplicity, an almost unique[198] inventiveness in the language of fluctuating feeling, of intuition, a populist and proverbial quality that occasionally bubbles up quite purely and freshly — these are among the qualities that would have to be enumerated, and even then the one that is most powerful and most worthy of admiration would still have been omitted. Anyone who reads one after the other two such compositions as *Tristan* and *Die Meistersinger* will feel a similar amazement for the verbal expression[199] as for the music: namely, how was it possible to have creative control over two worlds that are so different in color form figuration as in soul. This is the most powerful aspect of Wagner's talent, something at which only a great master will succeed:[200] to coin a distinctive language for every work and also give the new inwardness a new body, a new sound. In the face of such rarest of all[201] power, the criticism that focuses on sporadic excesses and oddities or on the frequent obscurities will always remain[202] merely petty and unfruitful; to be sure, those who until now have voiced their criticism most loudly have basically found not so much the language as the soul,[203] the manner of feeling and suffering, offensive, that is, completely and entirely inaccessible and scandalous. We will wait until these critics themselves have a different soul, for then they, too, will speak a different language: and then, it seems to me, the German language will on the whole be better off than it is today: something Wagnerian, that is, and not so much David Straussish!

11[41]

2. *The rhythmical sense in what is great.* The design of every Wagnerian drama is of a simplicity that is even greater than that of ancient tragedy; and thereby the dramatic tension is the highest. This lies in the effect of the great forms, their oppositions, their simple connections, that is the ancient element in the structure of these dramas. — Reflect upon the introductions to the three individual acts, the relationship of

the three acts to one another; there shows itself here a simple greatness of the architect, which has no equal anywhere in modern poetry. The tension rests upon the relationships among the high points of the passions, never upon the effect of the new and surprising spectacle. I wish I had the degree of rhythmical sight-ability to be able to survey the whole *Nibelung* work in the same way as I sometimes succeed in doing with the individual works: but I do still divine there a special species of rhythmical delights of the highest degree. The Rhine maidens' scene with Siegfried in the final act of the final drama and the Rhine maidens' scene with Alberich in the first act of the first drama, the loving jubilation of Siegfried and Brünnhilde when they find each other in the final act of *Siegfried* and the parting jubilation of the ones separating in the first act of the *Götterdämmerung* etc. Then again, the Norns' scene at the beginning of the first act (prelude) of the *Götterdämmerung*. In *Tristan* yearning for love (Act 2), yearning for death in the third act. The conclusion in the individual act is often (*Tristan* I, *Valkyrie* I, *Siegfried* I) a plunging into a stream that rushes ever faster, the increasing breadth and at the same time rapidity of sensation, with the highest certainty. Other acts have a catastrophe and afterwards a shock and *arresting* of sensation at the colossal things that have occurred: thus Mark in the second act of *Tristan*; the procession of men with Siegfried's corpse.

11[42]

3. A *violent will* that seeks out, as it were, all paths, crevices and ravines to bring itself to light, leaping, clambering, flying, fluttering and colliding wildly with the walls; a sudden elemental streaming that shoots forth unsatisfied toward all sides of the streambed; a sea-divinity restlessly resting upon hidden cliffs, grown sore and savage, who has more pleasure in the storm than in the smooth mirroring of the heavens — this is one side of Wagnerian nature, fertile and unpacified, tormenting itself and others (the Norn gave me the spirit that is forever "unsatisfied").[204] This will, tied to a narrow spirit and

gaining power by chance would have been a disaster. Only an entirely high and free spirit could direct this savage nature onto the path of goodness and helpfulness and preserve it from raging destructively against itself. This spirit, which settled upon Wagner and which showed the direction like a flame to the seafarer tossed back and forth amid storms, was the spirit of music; it led him, without having first put him in chains; as, for example, the spirit of politics would have done if it had wanted to join itself to such a nature. So he was allowed to remain free, for it was a spirit full of love, one whose mildly persuasive voice overflowed with kindness and tenderness, a spirit that hates violent acts and peremptory commands and wishes to see no one in fetters.[205] There were hours and times when doubt plagued him in a frightful way,[206] whether this spirit had still remained true to him; and if he then felt its nobly powerful wing-beat around him, a deep, warm gratitude and an abundance of unspoken vows rose upward to it: *fidelity toward the spirit of music* became his religion. — But *how* music spoke to Wagner's will, we halfway infer from how music speaks to us: but who could speak completely clearly about this? Enough that almost *all* other music to us — not simply to me: for truthfully I need not speak of me alone — that almost all other music sounds to us only like an alienated constrained unfree language, as though it should be played before those who were not worthy of seriousness or as though it should be used for purposes of instruction and demonstration for those who were not even worthy of the playing. There is in *all other* music only a few short hours[207] when suddenly that language presses toward us, which we *always* hear in Wagner's music: rare moments of forgetfulness that overcome the music, as it were, when the music speaks with itself and directs its gaze upward, like Raphael's Cecilia,[208] away from the listeners who demand from it distraction and amusement or erudition.[209] I would not have known upon what path I might ever have come to participate in the *purest* sunlit happiness other than through Wagner's music: and this, even though it is by no means always speaking of happiness, but instead of the frightening and uncanny underworldly forces of human drives, of the suffering in all happiness and of the finitude of our happiness; the happiness that streams forth from it must therefore lie in the way in which it speaks. — Just verify where Wagner has his real pleasure and delight, in what sort of scenes, conflicts, catastrophes — there we comprehend what he is and what music is for him. Wotan's relationship to Siegfried is something amazing, such as no poetry in the world has: the love and the forced enmity and the pleasure in annihilation.[210] This is highly symbolic for Wagner's nature: love for that whereby we will be redeemed judged and annihilated: but quite divinely felt!

11[43][211]

Amid streaming rain and darkened skies the cornerstone was laid. We were silent while driving back to the city and for a long time Wagner turned his gaze inward with a look that would be impossible to describe in words. On this day he began his sixtieth year. A hastening concentrating look.

Alexander, who offers a taste of Asia and Europe — his inner gaze — to see this!

I would like to follow along with this inward look: from there the Bayreuth work appears at its most wonderful.

Those who fall are supposed to see their entire lives fly past them with unbelievable speed. So, too, those who put the seal on their life's work in a specific event: the significance of the cornerstone. This *infinitely hastened inward looking of Wagner is* surely the highest spectacle.

Wagner describes how he looks upon his work in Bayreuth: the torment and apprehension from the first to the last moment, the poison[212] in the deformation of the basic ideas, there are so many things to weigh against one another!

Wagner's feeling as the cornerstone was laid. Anyone who can *concentrate* his feeling at the spectacle into that of Wagner has surely taken away with him what is highest.

11[44][213]

A great event is great only for the *great* observer. The Bayreuth event causes me concern: where are the eyes to see everything? Especially since the highest spectacle is perhaps Wagner himself, to be overseen only from a much higher standpoint. And yet, in order to be able to *rejoice* completely, we must see this Bayreuth fact not only from our perspective, but *from Wagner's*, to displace ourselves *into him*.

11[45][214]

1. The Germans are a *learning* people;[215] and if by exception a great talent appears for once among them, this talent also displays itself to them to an extent that is inconceivable for other peoples. Wagner's art and {his} will remain at present something immeasurable for non-Germans, just because they are not used to such a polyphony of the most varied kinds of knowledge in their artists and because in general they already feel themselves even more encumbered than amazed by the broad span of German knowledge. In order to become a master in music, almost every human life now is already too short: one is hardly done learning if one divides up the territory and, for example, seeks one's achievement in the art of performance. Wagner was a consummate master of music and of the stage and an innovator and contributor with regard to all fundamental technical matters. But he developed into much more: and in order to develop in this way, he was spared no more than anyone else acquiring the highest culture in the domain where he was supposed to create and innovate.[216] Wagner the renewer of the simple drama, the discoverer of the place of art in a true human society, the poetic[217] elucidator of past views of life, the philosopher, the historian, the aesthetician Wagner, the German mythologist who was the first to draw a circle around the marvelous ancient system and to carve into it the runes of his mind — what an abundance of knowledge he had to gather together and encompass in order to be able to become all this! And yet the sum of all this did not crush his will to act, nor did the attractions of the individual

aspects lead him astray;[218] in order to measure the enormity of such a character, take, for example, the great countermodel of Goethe, who appears like a river system with many branches, a system, however, whose entire energy[219] does not flow into the sea, but that loses and disperses just as much energy along its meandering course as it discharges in its delta. True, a being such as Goethe possesses and creates more peace of mind, he is surrounded by a mildness and noble wastefulness:[220] whereas Wagner's art and the force of his current can perhaps frighten people and frighten them off.[221] But let those who are so inclined be afraid: we others want only to become all the more courageous by seeing with our own eyes for once a hero who "has not learned to be afraid."[222,223] He not only passes through fire,[224] but also through the mist of knowledge and scholarship and finds his predetermined work.[225]

11[46][226]
Wagner in Bayreuth — a *spectacle at the spectacle*![227]
A. *What he is* and *how he developed into it*. Musician poet writer.
The improvisational. Ethical. Dangerous.[228]
B. **What he can do.**
1. *Power* (1 concluding 2 astringent 3 legislative
4 communicating).[229]
2. *Aftereffect* (the ninth symphony, the apparently reactionary, "the heroic sages," the ἀνάγκη).[230]
The philologist
the German element
self-education
the dramas
the language of the poetry[231]
the harmony
the plastic element.

Wagner's power 1) concluding
2) astringent
3) legislative, organizing in masses
4) communicating

11[47][232]

Introduction. From what point is the Bayreuth event to be viewed?[233]
Something new in *a* life — silence — being pure 9.[234] Wagner's gaze.[235]

Becoming. The fundamental moral nature 3: oppositions, *fidelity* 15. 32. spirit of music.[236]
The learner 1: history vanquished by the artist 6.[237]
Dangers 33. promoting 7. unfashionable 22.[238]

Being and expression of power (polyphony and unity of his expressions of power).
Polyphony of talent (*effect* of the Dionysian *will*, which everywhere wants to get out). The great *talent* as conclusion?[239]
The spectacular (if one wanted to explain everything from one defect).
The improvisational — self-renunciation 13.[240]
Development of the music of passion and of drama 24. 28. 29.[241]
The poet 23.[242] The dialogue.
The rhythmical sense in what is great 2.[243] No cloud formation, as it seems at first.[244]
The reposing one: historian and philosopher 5.[245]
Abundance of his characters, to which he is attached with deep inwardness!
The prose writer 11.[246]
The communicator 8.[247]
The Demosthenean 14.[248]
Language of poetry 4.[249]
Wagner at his most beautiful in the *repetitions* (love sce⟨nes⟩, questions etc., the same motives — funeral march).
The concluding 17.[250]
Counter-Alexander, the astringent 20. History vanquished 6.[251]
Organizer of masses 25.[252]

Populist 30. 31.[253]
The great talent 10.[254]

Future. Art and ἀνάγκη 21. 35.[255]
Reform of the theater — nothing insignificant. Society in Bayreuth and otherwise 19.[256]
Subjugating 18.[257]
Wagner's diadochi 16.[258]
Opprobrium toward modern art 36.[259]
No luxury art: reform of society 12.[260]
Dangerous after-effects. Naturalism 27.[261]
Composers' school.[262]
Superfluous elements in art 26.[263]
Apparently reactionary elements 34.[264]
Collection of great figures and scenes.
Ninth Symphony[265] and conclusion of the *Nibelung*.
He will be: the seer of a new order.
Think *how deeply moved* would be a society that has become *serious* about abolishing power and lying and now sees the work! Anyone who could look upon this *moment* would be *blinded* for everything contemporary.[266]

11[48][267]
3. The primitive mood of the dithyr⟨ambic⟩ dram⟨atist⟩.[268]
4. Word melody gesture.[269]
5. Rhythm in what is great.[270]
6. The poet.[271]
7. The musician.[272]
8. The concluding the astringent.[273]

11[49][274]
2. There is intentional *experimenting*: **derivation** of influence — whither everything:[275]

A) into the *purely* aesthetic and *insipid* (or *random*)	Depiction of the disciples Dangers of imitation

B) into what is *compromising* and dangerous	Political etc. Antiscientific Religious-restorative Immorally-caress[276]

11[50]

— against the arrogance of the knowledgeable and their foolishness (on the right to imagination, Eckermann, p. 251[277]), he takes the part of the *people*: he unites, he recalls the impossibility of a life lived in knowledge.

— I know about that a quarter-hour sooner than many; but when I am old, I will have something in common with all of them.[278]

11[51][279]

Anyone who is so happy as to be able to account for *what Wagner is*, he has also to a certain degree participated in the incomparable happiness that Wagner bears in himself: in the happiness of his talent. This is a growing forest, a shooting up of the most manifold energies, which hold themselves reciprocally within limits, so that they climb joyfully and straight upward and all together form a whole. To feel unity in variety in order to love the variety inwardly — that is his secret: his eye is directed by nature toward connections, not only toward the connection of the arts to one another, but also to the joining of state society and art: therefore a legislative capability may be attributed to him in the strongest degree. He surveys great relationships with a single glance and does not allow himself to be constrained by what is small.

As the inner visual world of the epic must precede that of the plastic arts, so, too, the inner *imitation*-world[280] of the music that of dramatic art.

A passionate yearning for luxury and splendor in Wagner: precisely from that place was he enabled to understand, to condemn this drive most inwardly within him. His external life is related to this tendency like a teasing[281] farce with its alternation of neediness and luxury. With the art of luxury, he criticized himself and saw through himself.

11[52][282]

As musician. The Demosthenean.[283]
As poet. Language.[284]
Prose writings.[285]
Effect in subjugating the opponents.[286]
To conclude, to make superfluous.[287]
The improvisational.[288]
Drive to communication.[289]

Wagner's friends.[290]
He bequeaths his kingdom to the *strongest.*[291]

11[53]

Communication to friends (without being subjugated), to enemies (subjugating).[292]

To conclude.[293]

And as his friends did not manage to subjugate him with their love, so his enemies did not manage to protect themselves through their enmity from being subjugated.

11[54]

Wagner as musician.[294]
As poet. Language.[295]
Rhythmist.[296]
Prose writer.[297]
Wagner to history and philosophy.[298]

11[55]

Musician[299]
Poet[300]
Communicator[301]
Writer[302]
for friends educator[303]

Diadochi.[304]

11[56][305]

What will Wagner be? —
the god wants power: contracts guilt unfreedom
he seeks a hero who would fight freely for him (against him), in order to assert his power
transformation of the will. —
afterward: only in order to get free of his guilt.
As Siegfried dies, Wotan is freed of his guilt and chooses to perish.[306]

11[57][307]

What the music already intuits, that is what the hero experiences only at the end of his road: his life, the most pitiable event in the world, the music, the most compassionate thing in the world, follows him at every step. *How is it capable of that?* — To comprehend this, we must seek to attain an insight into the nature of the dithyrambic dramatist. —

11[58][308]

§6. The improvisational.[309] The dithyrambic dramatist.
But the Beethovenian music had to come first: that of *impersonal* passion.[310]
§7. The musician. Demosthenean rhythm-sense.[311]
§8. Poet and writer. Communication in the form of retrospection.[312]
§9. Purifier of art, purifier of himself; the "friend of art" set aside.[313] The *great* talent.[314]
§10. Diadochi.[315] Misunderstandings dangerous: the apparently reactionary[316] — the apparently naturalistic.[317]
§11. *The Ring of the Nibelung.*[318]

11[59][319]

Luxury art. Employment of the means for untrue needs. Weakening of the true needs. Separation of people from one another. Overworking of many people, in order to satisfy sham needs, while the true needs are not satisfied. The social question is the *continued existence* of *luxury*, i.e., of what is unnecessary and superfluous and unsatisfying in the relationship of work to art. The practical countermeasure is the *cynicism* of simplicity on the one side (⟨1.⟩ negative: in proof that we do not need that sham satisfaction; 2. positive: the *drama* — — —

11[60][320]

1 As *learner* (fidelity).
2 The rhythmic sense in what is great.
3 Vehement will and spirit of music (fidelity).
4 *Language* of poetry.
5 Leisure and history and philosophy.
6 History vanquished by the artist (fidelity).
7 Wagner's friends as danger. No composers-school.
8 Talent for *communication* (transition to concluding chapter).
9 Something *new* in a short life. Being silent and being pure.
10 The great talent.
11 Prose writings.
12 No luxury art: reform of society.
13 Improvisational — self-renunciation.
14 The Demosthenean, contempt for the previous friends of art.
15 The ethical development, *fidelity* key concept.
16 Wagner's diadochi. Much very weak.
17 The *concluding one*, he makes many scholars superfluous.
18 Subduing of the reluctant.
19 Reform of the theater, to what extent nothing insignificant. The people in Bayreuth and their opposite otherwise.
20 Counter-Alexander, the astringent, simplifier of the world.
21 Art and ἀνάγκη.

22 Wagner not fashionable. What promoted him!
23 The poet at the end of religions.
24 Development of the music of passion and of drama. Conclusion with the content of the Nibelung *myth*.
25 Organizer of masses.
26 The superfluous in art.
27 Danger of naturalism after Wagner.
28 Long-winded passion.
29 Entwined passion, many-headed.
30 The populist (in prose).
31 Populist in relation to Goethe's *Faust*.
32 Love Empedoclean.
33 What is dangerous in Wagner.
34 Reactionary elements.
35 Struggle with ἀνάγκη.
36 Opprobrium toward modern art.

Dramatist — demonic communicability
two-sided 1 oneself to others
2 others to oneself (self-renunciation).
Musician.
Poet.
Actor.
Total organizer.

[12 = U II 10. Mp XIII 4, 13–46. Summer–End of September 1875]

12[1]

Influence of the *Oresteia*.[1] Predramatic part.[2]

The line of the highest kind of *completeness* in the form, up to the point of a game, as if with gentle *clouds*, in no composer.[3]

The uneasiness of people in official posts, the incompatibility of which he saw through.

The public has nonetheless judged Wagner quite differently than I thought.

12[2][4]

Wagner has opened up a great realm of inner nature historically, too, and made the whole emergence of art comprehensible.

In a world grown sober, he indicates the forces from which everything good and great even for this sobered world has grown.

He allows a new stream of such primal forces to stream over us and shows the inexhaustibility of the inner source of human nature.

12[3]

There exist, perhaps, a few completely inattentive people who even now know nothing at all about Bayreuth and the things that now attach themselves[5] to this name: and then countless others who know and relate much about it that is false. But even what is true and excellent about it that would remain to be reported, how faintly it lives in the sensations and words of those who are honest enough to acknowledge it: and on the other hand, how inexpressible it must seem even to the very same people who are completely inflamed by the fire of the spirit[6] that here for the first time wants to speak to humanity.[7] Between those sensing it weakly and the speechless, I myself stand in the middle: to confess this is neither presumptuous nor all too modest, but instead only painful:[8] why precisely that, no one needs to know. But indeed, I take from my middle position a feeling of duty[9] to speak and to say some things more clearly than has occurred up to now with regard to these events. I renounce out of necessity bringing into form and connection the quite various reflections to which I feel myself urged; one could, to be sure, present the impression of a whole and complete thing via some art of deception:[10] I want to remain honest and to say that I can now do no better than I do here, even though admittedly I do it badly enough.

12[4]

Future *of the Bayreuth summers*: unification of all truly living human beings: artists bring up their art, writers their works to be read aloud, reformers their new ideas. It shall be a general *spa for curing souls*: there the new genius awakes, there a kingdom of goodness is unfolded.

12[5]

Wagner's music gives the impression *of sublime work*, in comparison with the more superficial manner of the older ones.

The "*unbending-intractable*."

12[6][11]

Wagner's *aftereffect* — all of the dangers that he avoided as an artist we will fully recognize only when there might be imitators — is now *to be enumerated* here.

12[7]

First we believe in a philosopher. Then we say: "though he may be incorrect in the way in which he proves his principles, the principles are true." But finally: it does not matter how the principles go, the *nature* of the man stands in for a hundred systems for us. As a teacher he may be incorrect a hundred times: but his being itself is correct; we want to rely upon that. There is something in a philosopher that can never be in a philosophy: namely, the cause of many philosophies, the great human being.

12[8]

How through Wagner the aesthetic oppositions "subjective," "objective," romantic, classical, naïve, sentimental, are completely abolished; they do not *fit*.

12[9]

— — — to write:[12] in Goethe's age, completely different things ruled.

Degeneration: contemporary poets and literary writers, young Germany, Romanticism, Goethe.

Progeneration: Luther Goethe Schiller Schopenhauer Beethoven Wagner.

Propagation of the German essence *high above* everything (after-Luther).

What art is in our time. Mostly something degrading or hermitic-egotistical.

What is Bayreuth?

Nothing harmless.

Position of art toward ἀνάγκη.[13]

Perhaps our sensation exaggerates somewhat: we need to make up for needing *too much* through *one thing*, through Bayreuth.

Art has now become so powerful in the blood of some people that it can also determine their relationship to[14] the rest of the world.

It is a *revolution* that is now taking place in Bayreuth, the constitution of a new power that is far from feeling itself only to be aesthetic.

For the deeper gaze it is nothing revolutionary: but instead the *continuation* of the German spirit in its geniuses: in especially frightening, indeed bewildering illumination through political showing off with what is national (whereas what is respected in the national is considered precisely by us as almost inimical, or at least what is most dangerous).

The aesthetic phenomenon inquires: searches ahead: do there still exist *related* forces?

12[10][15]

It takes a long time before the drama, indeed the expos⟨ition⟩ begins.

Childhood — something old precocious — the youth of the human being, his naïveté much later in the moderns.

Leipzig — spiritual tasting, superficiality of sensation, pliable nature, bad prevailing tendencies of literature.

He seemed to dilettantize, to lust and leisure without pleasure.

Nobody should complain about a lack of experiences, but at most[16] about an excess.[17]

In *Tannhäuser*, the better nature can only suffer and beg for the other, they are separate.

In *Lohengrin*, desire from power to love, to questionable fidelity.

In *The Flying Dutchman*, the gloomy wandering that becomes a curse: the sorrow of homesickness.

Desire for power, ecstasy of the senses — shrinking away from disgusting morality and mendacity.

He landed in the world of theater, the frivolous, particularly empty one.

Restless, great indigence — always ready with a most extreme means.

He grew from no art school, without any teacher.

12[11][18]

To give up fidelity in favor of positions in life power influence (German master).

12[12]

what is dangerous — tendency toward pretense and trickery

dramatic — fidelity — artwork of the future

fidelity learning[19]

fidelity — deductions through life — resistance to professions (only so far as to feel oneself as master)[20]

fidelity — talents want to be individual.[21]

Bayreuth — goal.

12[13][22]

For whom am I creating? he looks through his listeners with the gaze ⟨of the⟩ dramatist. And then he is looking jealously upon others.

The image of the listeners, distrust toward them, despair (question whether musicians still — — —).

Success — stick to the stage.[23]

Friends

Symphonic.

How can true love reside in a creator?

12[14][24]

Common need.

Saga material.

He grew into the simple sublimity of myth.

The parched yearning of the popular soul.

He speaks first to the sense of the popular saga.

He investigates modern civilization.[25,26]

Finally he finds the forward-looking gaze, he transforms myth.

He wants himself to help to bring about political change: great *error*, he imagines the moment for producing the common people is at the *door*! Revolutionary on behalf of the theater![27]

Effect through writings, assisting! The effect is still always pursued as *immediate*. Even *as artist he* still *takes it* into consideration (*Tannhäuser*)!!

He propagated his faith as artist (also as writer), what affected and moved him most strongly, he collected into works of art. *Tannhäuser Lohengrin*. There was one *question*: do there exist *other* Wagners?

He inferred from the deepest effect that he felt, those that he would make. Works of art became *questions* — if you feel as I feel, then you will also *have* the same *needs*. He thereby discovered the *disparity* — *dreadful isolation*. He no longer had any wish for the existence of the political world.[28]

He exempted *music*.

Then, when a multitude suffers as he suffers — that would be a common people. Then it would also **have** the same **needs**. For his striving for power was also in accord with nature, with the common people. He saw his artwork more closely in front of him and believed the people to be *close* too. He found the *deepest effect* upon himself from popular belief and from the dramatic song.[29] These he joined together. What had an effect upon him would work at some point on the common people: it will be the ones that a *common need* ties together. He *multiplied himself into the common people*.[30]

Third Period: the age seems futile to him,[31] he retreated entirely into himself, the effect lies far from him, he completes one score after another,[32] renounces power: the future becomes very far away.[33] Fidelity. Schopenhauer. He becomes solitary.

Friends announce themselves, the precursors of changed times and sensibilities, giving shelter[34] — he finds out that he has already had the incomparable effect.[35]

Danger from the side of friends at the earlier stage.

He sees in the war a war against "civilization" and confidence in German bravery.

He comprehends: his art is the artwork of the future and a precursor, a stimulus to a new society. He understands his position in relation to those to come differently than at the earlier stage.

Fidelity.

12[15][36]

If a multitude suffered the same need that he was suffering — that would be a common people, he tells himself. Then their similar needs would also be similarly satisfied. Now if he looks at what most profoundly comforts him and brings him happiness in his need, he finds myth and music: here he receives the deepest gratification, therefore here, too, he must be most deeply in need, and necessary. Now music is an exceptional art, not useful for luxury, but emerged as something comforting for humble and simple people; he finds a magnificent correlation between both and feels[37] his energy for drama as a connective force between these spheres. His artwork, which now affects him so incomparably, he poses as a question: where are those upon whom it has a similar effect? These will also suffer and have the same need as I. A multitude of us is the common people for which we yearn. Now he experiences[38] a terrible deception, although he helps with his writings; everything is strange, one measures according to old standards, one criticizes in the old way, one does not feel the new question. He despairs, for the common people is not there, his need is not felt, his artwork is a communication to the deaf and blind, the prospect of effect and power is hopeless. He staggers and falters. The possibility of an overthrow of things stands as a hope before him, perhaps planting can come afterward. — In a short time, he is a political refugee and in misery. It is the second great crisis.

Alone, the age appears meaningless to him, he has retreated completely into himself, no hope anymore. He now lays aside all concern for effect, everything seductive and questionable, everything that eases understanding, and speaks only with himself. His gaze at the world turns toward the depths, he sees suffering in the foundation and purifies himself of all optimism. Longing to pass from the day into the night, *Tristan*. He rediscovers German Lutheran cheerfulness, which other nations do not comprehend, thoroughly fermented mastery of *Die M⟨eister⟩singer*. Friends approach; many almost dangerous, they want to make him dogmatic. He gets through untouched, it is no longer a matter of aesthetics and music for him. An immense work, the total expression of his insight and prospect, with an amazing metaphysical hesitation at the end. Power resigns out of love. He wants to display this work, the artwork of the future: whereas the present is not the *future* on which he counts. The war, symbolically understood, gives courage.

12[16]

Striving and wanting power have now become impersonal, are channeled purely into creation. His art of supreme perfection and expressive capability: he no longer thinks of an effect to *be experienced*. He wants to leave the work behind, completes one score after another.[39]

Overnight, it was suddenly different. He sympathized with the German war in a particular way, as was not the case elsewhere in Germany. He acquired faith in one thing, whereas he no longer had any with regard to the Germans, German courage connected to presence of mind and constancy, he saw something related to his creation and was overjoyed. Perhaps I am now finding — not the common people, but instead only so many friends and fellow-sufferers, to whom I can show the work as it is meant to be.[40] It was for him a question of the establishment of the *style*, of the tradition, for a very distant future.[41] — If we now see "the artwork of the future," we should nonetheless always say, it is not this time that Wagner meant by that "future"! What Wagner *will* be, that is still something completely different than what he now can be.[42]

12[17][43]

And now the ruling thought of his life stepped up to him, in ever-new splendor, almost transformed, yet almost still more powerful, more attractive. Effect, incomparable effect! — but how! over whom! No longer upon the public of the theater, as it is, no longer upon the modern human being in general, given how he relates to art. No longer, either, with the powers of the previous successes. At this point in time of the decisive "No longer," he grasped the nature of the *common people* and its opposite, the society of luxury.

12[18][44]

The past seems *foreshortened* in a dual way, first because it is seen only from a single visual angle, although an important and necessary one, and then because much is excluded from a world seen in this way, according to one standard. But not only is the past made more surveyable, as it were, through foreshortening: all of life, even that of the past and future, appears in a reduced standard and can thus be judged more easily. The degree to which humans have dealings with art, the depth or superficiality of the relations, the truth or vanity in this interaction, are used to judge ages and peoples: their need for art as a sign of their morality and wisdom. We can know quite a lot about a person if we know precisely whether he needs art in general, whether plastic or auditory, to which masters he is inclined, etc. If the artist himself takes up this appraisal, we cannot blame him if he believes that he has here a standard of values in general: in his observation of life, art is the solar system. Human beings without art are unthinkable for him, like humans without representations of space and time. He finds nothing in which art would not express itself: in the way in which a person thinks, dreams, walks, eats, converses, writes, reads, fights, worships, educates, divides up his days and his life, how he constructs the state, distinguishes among the classes: everywhere here one must differentiate between an external appearance and a disposition from which someone acts. In this external appearance,[45] as well as in this disposition is something that is *art*: a certain creative pressure toward the — — —

12[19][46]

6. Wagner's doubt: — Has the world become old, impoverished?[47]
   Through Beethoven's refutation of his doubt: innocence.[48]
   Pastoral — eternal humanity.[49]
   Music does not suffice. Strauß.[50]
   Against the absolute musician, the hermitic despiser of the world of appearance. Drama not a kind of art, not a branch of art.[51]
   Inspiration of the inner imagination.
   Stimulation of the symbolic motives for movement.
7. Changeable. Unchangeable.
   Drama as *prophecy* of a purer life (in opposition to backward-looking ancient drama).[52]
   Attempt to understand Wagner, too, as backward-looking: *restorative* tendencies. The *people*. Genius.
8. The generative point in *opera*.
   Schiller's presentiment.[53]
   The three difficulties — *word-melody* etc.
   Everywhere development out of what has degenerated to the core.
   Exemplary, it is apparently a reversion, still more a discarding of what is false nongenuine late.
9. *To purify* before and alongside the creating.[54]
   Writer.
10. The *poet*. Myth. Language. Goethe.
11. The musician.
12. *Die Nibelungen*: the world-foreshortener: his life and nature in tremendous reflexes.

12[20][55]

I said it would be possible that the redeemed art would speak to human beings and not be heard. David Strauß heard the Pastoral and heard nothing.

12[21][56]

What Thucydides thinks about the state.

Thucydides, Book III chap. 84 is genuine.[57] Supposedly it is unclear, and in style and thought displays the νεωτερισμός,[58] something revolutionary. I think we are frightened by the ideas of this chapter; in part, we have not even understood them well. And so we allow one of the few testimonies to escape where[59] Thucydides speaks of his most inner disposition, where he says what human nature is about!

The human being is envious, an enemy of what is distinguished, his envy wants *to do harm*; so he does not put up with a situation in which envy has a nonharmful force, the condition of laws.

They prefer revenge to justice, egoistical gain rather than a situation where one does them no harm (inflicts no injustice);[60] they prefer τὸ κερδαίνειν to μὴ ἀδικεῖν[61] (i.e., to not harming them, not doing them an injustice) — and yet they were in a situation where envy had no harmful character.

They were protected from one another and from an outbreak of their malevolence in envy; and now they exposed themselves to an unprotected condition — why? in order to take revenge upon others. They just could not master their affects.

Here Thucydides has given his theory of the *state*: and also said what must happen as soon as the state ceases — reciprocal laceration and releasing of all affects. There human nature manifests itself purely, it is held in check by the state. Moreover, the πόλις[62] does not appear here as a product of human beings, not as a clever protective arrangement of egoisms against one another. Thucydides believes humans were just not clever enough for that, but instead were ruled by affects, momentary. The state is for him indeed a *divine institution*. The highest respect for the νόμοι[63] shows through. Humans could not institute it according to their *φύσις*![64]

In the state, justice rules, not revenge, everyone is protected against injustice from the other, and grudges have no harmful character. Nevertheless, they overthrow it, they forget their own advantage: so blind are they in their passion!

For διὰ πάθους ἐπιθυμοῦντες, I read διὰ παντὸς ἐπιφθονοῦντες — (διὰ παντὸς[65] occurs three times elsewhere in Thucydides, v. index).

The nobility of disposition consists to a very great part in good nature (εὔηθες[66]): lack of distrust, harmlessness.

12[22][67]

On *Darwinism*.

The more sense of community, sympathetic affections, a human possessed, the more he held to his tribe; and the tribe preserved itself best where there were the most self-sacrificing individuals. Here good, sound customs *were strengthened*, here the subordination of the individual was learned and character given steadiness and reinforced by upbringing. — Yet here the danger of stability, of increasing stupidity, is great.

Unconstrained, much more uncertain and *weaker* individuals, who attempt new things and attempt many different things, are the ones on whom progress depends: countless individuals of this kind perish without effect, but in general they *loosen things up* and thus inflict from time to time a *weakening* upon the stable element, introduce something new in one spot or another that has grown weak. This new thing is gradually assimilated by the overall intact collective being.

Degenerating natures, the slight degenerations[68] are of the highest significance. Wherever progress is to ensue, a weakening must precede it.

The strongest natures possess the type firmly and maintain it. —

Degeneration is always mutilation: but one loss is seldom without an advantage in some other respect. A more sickly individual, e.g., becomes calmer and wiser; someone with one eye will have one stronger eye, a blind person sees more deeply within.

The important principle is not the struggle for existence! An increase in the stabilizing force through communal feeling in the individual, the possibility of attaining higher goals through degenerate natures and partial weakenings of the stabilizing force. The weaker nature, as the more noble or at least more free, makes any progress possible at all.

A people that has begun to weaken somewhere and to crumble, but is on the whole still strong: it can absorb and assimilate the infection of what is new.

Likewise the individual human: the *problem of education* is putting him so firmly and vigorously on track that he as a whole can no longer be diverted from his path. *But* then *the educator* has to inflict *wounds upon him*: and if pain, need have resulted from this, something new and refined can also be inoculated there. The whole force will now take it in and thus be improved.

The Germans were not only wounded, but almost bled to death, one took ⟨from them⟩ custom religion language freedom. They did not perish: but they have proven that they are a deeply *suffering* nation in that they discovered *music*; they have experienced the blessing of sickness. —

In opposition to this doctrine, Darwinism is a philosophy for butcher boys. And the place that they give to breeding, that they give to woman! Is it true, then, that women only have a taste and inclination for the strongest butcher boys! Not even among the animals is it so.

Moreover, I want to stand by my observation among human beings and to guard against drawing conclusions about animal development from laws about human improvement on the basis of weaker, degenerate natures. Whether it would be much more permissible to do this than to systematize humans, too, in bestial terms on the basis of bestiality and its laws: as Herr Häckel in Jena does, and those like him, like D. Strauß. —

12[23]

That the more ideal natures are not such good citizens —

12[24]

In order to explain what I understand to be Wagner's concentrating force, by the phrase, he is a simplifier of the world, I say this as preface. He found two new problems, that of music and that of drama: he found them where all great problems lie, in the street, at everyone's feet and yet concealed from every eye. What does it mean that in more recent times precisely an art such as that of music arises? Is this not a contradiction for everyone who visualizes the image of this age? Must he not say: music simply *could* not emerge from this age: but then what is its existence? A chance accident? But first, a single master could be accidental; however, the appearance of such a series of shining lights and suns truly shows that we should not be thinking of a comet's appearance. Now Wagner gives one answer: the existence of music is connected to the strength of the modern age, but this has brought with it tremendous weaknesses in other organs: and this diseased and exhausted condition is the one for which a remedy is growing in music.[69] First, it has a relationship to language, as a universally preverbal language to the completely plundered enfeebled rhetorically and poetically used-up language: the general sickening of all speakers, the incapacity to really still communicate with one another: if poetry is now already composing for everyone, so language now does the thinking for everyone, he is its slave and nobody has individuality anymore under this tremendous pressure. Raised up by music, we must feel ourselves for once placed so far distant that we perceive what is typically similar in everything that is spoken, is written: then it seems to us as if all individual[70] cultivation was *impossible*, because it attempts to base itself upon the word; and that now pulls everyone back into the old paths.[71] Secondly, Wagner felt the position of music in relation to the now visible world of appearances of modern life: it is imageless and therefore antagonistic to all created images. Now an unspeakable exhaustion likewise shows ⟨itself⟩ in everything into which humans now try to shape appearance: everything present there, everything more beautifully present there, even what is ugly is more sublimely present there. Walking, standing and moving oneself, the form of sociability, the manners of public speakers, the gestures of youths, the arts of women: everything, everything in which earlier times shaped the body and made it into the mirror of more beautiful or greater movements is completely decayed or late imitation: in the best case, all of it is Renaissance and, indeed, the aftergrowth of that (French civilization). If we here apprehend music as the antagonist of gymnastics, a point has been attained in it, in any case, from where modern life appears offensively barbaric. For the one who lives in the rhythmic flow of great music recognizes first in himself and from there in all others how incapable he generally is to set against this pure and heightened and yet powerfully agitated inner life of music something that would correspond to it as image, as appearance: while he generally has from this seeking only the painful impression that he is looking into a confusion of distortions and exaggerations. Now the impression of music is itself so strong that not only the rhythm of gymnastics has to give an account of itself before it: everything that has rhythmical properties to it, the whole life regimen of individuals, the politics of peoples, the behavior of commercial interests to one another, the struggle of classes, the opposition between a people and a nonpeople — involuntarily, the human being filled with music will measure and judge it according to music: he comprehends what it means to found a state upon music, which the Greeks had not only comprehended, but also expected.[72] And indeed, it is not even only what is rhythmical: the soulful honest element in impersonal passion, too, and the *peaceful* fire of music flowing up from inexhaustible depths — all of this becomes for him the judge of his modern world.[73]

Thus Wagner judges this world, because it does not correspond to the ideal that he carries in himself not as the image, but as the soul of music. He would have to deny and abolish it, if he were *only* a musician. And in fact, it is his deep contrast to all the other musicians of our age that they do not, as far as they are concerned, want this denial and abolition; he concludes from this that they do not have that fire in their bodies and consequently are not proper musicians. Either deny yourselves as musicians, cease to be such, or lift the world from its hinges by virtue of your inner energy — so he calls to them.

Now, this denial can be thought in various ways: revolutionary or ascetic. In the first case, the musician thinks first about creating an influential place for music, he will struggle against its stuntedness, its contemptible situation, its misuse for empty inconsequential entertainment: by consecrating individuals through his serious music and making them into tools of the revolutionary power of music, he will be able to hope to carry his influence everywhere: who could doubt, e.g., that a society that has taken the true spirit of Beethovenian music into itself would look very little like our contemporary society, in the form of the state, education, etc.! Second, that denial of contemporary appearance can easily lead to a still-further stage of denial. Anyone who, like Schopenhauer, sees in music a world behind this world, which has not yet entered into the form of individuation, and who on the other hand derives the frail, deeply hopeless character of life from the dividing power of indiv⟨iduation⟩, must make in music the conception, even if concept- and imageless, of a better world, an innocent, loving, serene-pensive one.

Retreating completely into this world, the musician then stands, as Wagner depicted it in Beethoven, almost in the sphere of blessedness: the incompar⟨able⟩ purity agitation glow the childlike immediacy, the complete lack of deception, the absence of convention that is characteristic of music, not of the other arts, which stand as copies too close to the world of appearances.

With this, it could now appear that a coexistence of music and the world of appearances would have to be a monstrosity, that their *incompatibility* would be quite settled. Here, now, Wagner made his second discovery, he found the problem of the *drama* once again. The human being who has taken the soul of music into himself and gazes from this fullness upon universal nature and the fate of human beings in all ages, does this not with disgust, with hatred: but instead, as Beethoven sees nature in the Pastoral, with love, with an all-understanding compassion.[74] In the greater images of human volition he sees before himself the type of his own volition, only with illusion and deceitful goals, so that he can foresee the tragic result of this individual volition. He grasps precisely love as the soul of music:[75] and precisely what he sees through the most in the hopelessness of his striving, he must love the most. On the other hand, the great musician is, as a copy of the universal will, in a natural sympathy with the individual that in the expansion of his volition comes close to the universal will; the fire that leads him through life, he recognizes as related to the fire of the music that holds sway in him: only that the will that appears in music is purer more innocent and more guileless and already, as a will that has become impersonal, comes close to[76] the entrance to self-denial and the condition of blessedness, from which the struggling hero is still far away: to be sure, perhaps not so far, since precisely because of the vehemence of his struggling he can suddenly be surprised sometime by the insight into the lack of success.[77]

12[25][78]

poetry as literature

the French rhetoric of style

to expect a change through the plastic arts is foolish[79]

the completely modern human being through and through still empty of music, not yet formed by it

lack of music in education, as dance a distorted image is related to the orchestrics, so the semblance to Greek appearance: the French style to the Greek; gymnastic art lamentable piecework.[80]

12[26][81,82]

The habitual thoughtlessness — or is it perhaps the foolish presumptuousness of modern humans? — brings along with it that Plato's deeply perceptive objections to art, tracing the richest experience, are no longer given a hearing; but anyone who is still teachable must perceive quite distinctly that the ruling sway of a powerful art also brings a host of dangers along with it and precisely the greatest artists have had an effect[83] that must instill[84] fear into more apprehensive thinkers at almost every new appearance of such powers. It seems all too easily as if art itself would have to establish the goals of active life, and the artist is then, with the most dangerous misunderstanding, understood as the immediate educator. If, in contrast, his amazing task is conceived correctly, that he has *to consecrate* for the struggling and goal-setting life, then we are just as correct to imagine him as himself cut off in the sharpest way from life itself, and to direct his effects into a riverbed that does not cross and determine the course of life. We would[85] hit the mark of Plato's opinion if we would hold firmly with some rigor to the idea that it is a matter of indifference what an artist thinks in a social and political regard: that, e.g., it must have carried no weight for the Athenians whether Aeschylus declared himself for or against limiting the size[86] of the Areopagus; indeed, I even believe that it is only by respecting precisely something supratemporal in the artist that we will be able to protect ourselves against the dangerous element lying in his direct effect upon the age. I want in this connection to draw attention to the fact that it is extremely natural and therefore[87] dangerous[88] *not* to understand Wagner *as* an artist, or to express it differently: to want to infer from his artworks specific hints for the shaping of life. This is so natural because Wagner himself made the attempt at various periods to find more specific answers for the question about the connection of his art with life. There are essays by him that are flooded with the magical light of one of his artworks — and every artwork has a light distinctively colored by him.

12[27]

Love and disdain.[89]

Conclusion: in what way does he simplify the world?[90]

Next chapter: the historical development of music.[91]

Wagner as purifier of art, of its position toward life — even as writer (to write what I suffer).[92,93]

12[28]

5.

After the break,[94] further. The simplifier of the world, as in philosophy.

He sees it from one single yet necessary visual angle: what about art? There he *foreshortens* history considerably.[95]

He *purifies*: he banishes the conception that the world has become organically *old*.

The source of nature still just as fresh, human beings still unexhausted.

We must banish only conceptual clouds, false anxieties, as though human beings were already *impoverished*.

Hatred toward the feeble friends of art.

The essence of *music* gives him the light; it stands in opposition to our conceptual and literary world (the world of *semblance* unfruitful, Hillebrand with his hopes ridiculous). Wagner develops the inner imagination.[96,97,98]

Schopenhauer conceives of it as something metaphysical, Wagner asks: is there a *life* that will at some time correspond to music? (The Greeks founded their states upon music)[99]

That *such a world* must *exist*, he perceives as *dramatist* (drama is not a *kind* of art, not a *branch* of literature).[100]

He sees phenomena in front of him in three dimensions, as it were — audible visible conceivable.

Where did he first see this phenomenon? In *opera*.

Schiller's presentiment.[101]

The modern artist always has to *purify* first, before he can create — most often the purification will first be a personal one.[102]

5.(b)

Wagner's struggle in the artwork.[103]

6.

Wagner in the opera. The public. Path to Beethoven.
The seemingly *reactionary-romantic*. Opposite of *civilization*.[104]

7.

The seemingly *desperate*. Opposite of the world of *appearance*.[105]
So he appears almost as a *restorative type*?
Logical laziness.
To feel. To surmise. The unconsciousness, instinctiveness. — But all this is only to be taken as *semblance*: its *character* is *progressive*.

12[29]

Wagner's struggle in the artwork.
Rienzi — opposite of "order," the reformer.
The Flying Dutchman — the mythical against the historical.
Tannhäuser Lohengrin — the Catholic against the Protestant (the Romantic against the Enlightenment).
Meistersinger — opposite of civilization, the German against the French.
Tristan — opposite of appearance. The metaphysical against life.
Nibelungen — voluntary renunciation of previous world powers: opposites of world periods — with transformation of the direction and the goals.

12[30]

Goethe calls all his works symbolic.[106]

So, too, one can understand the course of Wagner's life symbolically.

He begins in a spoiled art and, to be sure, discovering the only point where energy exists.

From there, he purifies his conception of this art and of himself.[107]

12[31][108]

— — — He goes not only through the fire, but also through the mist of knowledge and scholarship — — — with that *fidelity* toward a higher self or, more accurately, through the fidelity of a higher self toward him, which led him again and again out of his most serious dangers. This higher self required of him only *totalized deeds* of his polyphonic nature and bid him suffer and learn in order to be able to perform those deeds, it led him past ever more difficult tasks to testing and strengthening. The higher dangers and tests, however, approached him not as someone personally unsatisfied and suffering, not as someone learning, they grew out of a connection of suffering and learning, out of the vehement drive to set a saving idea against his own suffering, which he felt in ever higher generalization and for the understanding of which he had to take up history and philosophy: it is the dangers of the *intentions* through which the artist thwarted the purity of his becoming; his art was supposed to serve these intentions, it was supposed to accomplish more and accomplish more immediately than an art, moreover a new art struggling darkly toward the light, can manage; by defining it as the remedy successively for himself, for modern human beings and finally for life in general, he fell into the most severe sickness into which an artist can fall, into that of having definite intentions.[109] At first, he desired from it everything that his personal destiny did not offer him: disappointed here, he demanded from it a satisfaction and substitute for those tremendous lacks from which modern humanity and every individual in it suffer: disappointed here, too, and condemned to hopelessness, he discerned religion in his art, the comfort for existence in general. And here for the first time was the intentional element in his volition raised into something so unlimited that his art and everything unintentional in his nature could proceed fully free and unconstrained. —

12[32]

4.

To reflect upon *what Wagner is*, to review meditatively all of the life- and power-expressions of his much-divided-unitary nature: that will be the cure and recovery that everyone must desire who has thought about and suffered over how Wagner developed.[110] Such a truly great, truly liberated ability and authority is the most magnificent spectacle in the world; where such a talent appears, the earth, for the observer at least, becomes a summer-like garden. Out of pleasure from this spectacle, he can hardly do otherwise than himself put a transfiguring and almost justifying purposefulness into that painful becoming: to consider how everything must turn into good fortune and profit for the great nature, regardless of the difficulty of the trials through which it had to pass: how it nourishes itself upon poison and thereby becomes healthy and strong, how every danger has made it more courageous, every victory more reflective.[111] — — —

12[33][112]

There is nothing more hopeless than to speak to others about such complicated and rare states of the soul when they themselves cannot meet the speaker halfway through recollection of their own similar, even if many times weaker states and through a contemplative search into their inwardness. Presupposing such prepared listeners, however, I hold it definitely possible gradually to stamp the entire characteristic and single impression of a great talent so clearly upon sensation that we involuntarily infer backward from the decisive certainty of this impression to the state in which the artist feels himself forced into creating, i.e., feels the impression of the world upon himself as the call of his most characteristic force. But it all depends upon a *cognizance of this state*, and all pursuit of art can have only this goal for the nonartist, to discover in the end an entrance into those otherwise concealed mysteries of the soul in which the artwork is born. The artist is only an artist precisely as communicator concerning these mysteries; through his manner of speaking and communicating, he wants to make us into fellow initiates; he wants to direct us with his work toward something that is before the work, behind the work. "Nature is inwardly so much richer, more powerful, more blissful, more terrible, you do not know it, as you generally live!," the artist calls to us, "now follow me and leave behind you for once that dimly illuminated bit of nature and of life that is all you seem to know as real. I will lead you into a kingdom that is just as real: you yourselves shall decide, when you return from my cave to your day, which life is *more real*!"[113]

If this is, up to a certain point, the voice to us of every great artist, then it is above all surely the voice of Wagner. What it invites us to is a return to nature; and in this connection we ought to be least afraid of arousing misunderstandings with such a word. It is truly not a matter of comfortably resolving to behave naturally for once and to go for a stroll in an idyllic simplicity: so harmlessly was that challenge not intended. The artist knows quite well that all of us will never find the entrance into the still-unknown primal world of nature if he does not show us the way. For the burden that lies upon us is overpowering; a film woven of cold and artificial concepts and dogmas covers our eye; our feeling scarcely moves against the habit of the most entangled and harshest conformities or moves to a false beat, we have forgotten the language of feeling, too: so we are much too weak and cannot get far enough with our own energies to find nature. But the hand of our exhorter and liberator is overpowering, too: he leads us, without our seeing, where we are going: until suddenly we feel and hear and all at once know with all of our senses where we stand — *in free nature*, and ourselves transformed into *naturally free beings*.[114]

The significance of music. Liberation of music. The improvisational. Wagner subjugated. The Demosthenean. Wagner as poet, as prose writer. The astringent.

[13 = D 10a (PmN). Summer–Autumn 1875]

13[1][1]

——— Did the true music have to resound because human beings deserved it the least, but needed it the most? Just let yourself be absorbed for once into the rapturous wonder of this possibility: if we look from there back upon life, it gleams, however dreary and clouded it may previously have seemed; it becomes itself the image and likeness of Beethoven's music and speaks in the form of the appearance of salvation and regained innocence. "Never has any art in the world created something as brightly serene as these Symphonies in A-major and F-major, with all of the tonal works of the master from the divine time of his complete deafness so inwardly related to them. The effect of this upon the listener is liberation from all guilt — the effect here of the serenity immediately transcends all satisfaction from the beautiful. Here every obstinacy of a reason proud of its knowledge is immediately broken upon the magic of the overpowering of our entire nature; knowledge flees with the avowal of its error, and the tremendous delight of this avowal is what we shout for joy from our deepest soul, however seriously the wholly enchained demeanor of the auditor betrays to us his astonishment at the incapacity of our seeing and thinking vis-à-vis this truest of worlds. — All of the pain of existence is broken upon this prodigious ease in playing with it; the creator of worlds, Brahma, laughs at himself, since he recognizes the illusion about himself; regained innocence plays in jest with the thorn of expiated guilt, liberated conscience teases itself with the torment it has endured. — Now, too, he threw his glance upon appearance, which, illuminated by *his* inner light, communicated itself again in wondrous reflection to his inwardness. Now, once again, only the essence of things speaks to him and shows them to him in the calm light of beauty. Now he understands the woods, the stream, the meadow, the blue ether, the cheerful crowd, the loving pair, the song of the birds, the drift of the clouds, the roar of the storm, the delight of the blissfully moved calmness. There all of his seeing and shaping are permeated by the amazing serenity that, first through him, has become characteristic of music. Even lamentation, so inwardly inherent to all sounds, is soothed into smiling: the world regains the innocence of a child. 'May you be with me today in Paradise'[2] — who did not hear this word of the redeemer called out to him when he listened to the Pastoral Symphony?"[3]

7.

— — —

[14 = Mp XIII 4, 9–12. Autumn 1875–Spring 1876]

14[1][1]

1. Wotan strives for *power*, becomes unfree, entangled in guilt and curse: he *needs* the *free one.*
2. Must resist what is dearest, annihilate it — must punish the truest love (and Brünnhilde).
3. *Disgust* at *power* seizes him.
4. *Love* for the magnificent, *free* Siegfried turns him around, he shows him the world, *renounces.*
5. He sees the curse let loose on what is dearest, too, and suffers terribly, he *yearns* for *not-being.*
6. The *death* of the free one first *redeems* the world and the gods from the *curse*: justice is satisfied — the god can *die.*

14[2][2]

— The god becomes ever greater, the more he withdraws.

— Siegfried, the free fearless one, emerges from the alliance against law and custom, his procreators perish.

— He, the freest one, becomes unfree and faithless out of forgetfulness; the freedom of human beings is forfeited through forgetting the past: evil and the curse, through forgetting comes the curse.

— Brünnhilde loses through love her personal knowledge and falls into the deepest sorrow, out of which she cannot help herself. But takes from her fate a supreme knowledge of all "deepest suffering of grieving love opened my eyes."[3]

— An age that has not only fought for the freedom of thought, but sought to release itself from all of the past in the struggle with necessity: that will become the *people* for whom the artwork of the future (begotten in contradiction to all that is past) is destined.

14[3][4]

His writings not populist.

But his art, to be sure: it overcomes the opposition of the people and those who are cultivated.

That separates it from all Renaissance culture (Goethe as laggard, philologist-poet — also "Faust").[5]

Already thereby he seems to point toward a future — according to Schiller's saying.[6]

14[4][7]

Only insofar as he cares about the *safeguarding* of his art does he turn to existing powers, to the cultivated people, to the national — he thinks of living on in union with the most powerful people, that of the Reformation, to whom he assigns the mission of "channeling the sea of revolution into the bed of the placidly flowing stream of humanity."[8]

But the idea of his artwork is, like the idea of every good German, *supra-German* and not national: like his Reformation.

14[5]

Schiller's call.[9]

In contrast, the seemingly reactionary.[10]

14[6]

He stands before religion as detached as Aeschylus before various Zeuses.

Essentially unreligious.[11]

Future of a society of Wagner's — insofar as he is a completely modern human being, it is also art of the present.

14[7][12]

What will he become?

The one who gazes back into a past and interprets it — he has anticipated this past.

Individual phases in Wotan: for power — disgust — abandoning it — dedicating it to the *free human being.*

Conclusion — Wagner's words: where political wisdom and art etc.[13]

Schiller's words.[14]

The simplifier of the world — the interpreter of its history.[15]

14[8][16]

The great event. In order to understand it completely, the Wagnerian view of himself is necessary — how he came to be, what he is, what he will become. (1)

I. How he came to be.

<table>
<tr><td rowspan="2">Dangers of nature and of talents.</td><td>Childhood, youth scattered, without naïveté
then the most dangerous splitting of his being:
significance of fidelity.</td><td>(2)</td></tr>
<tr><td>Discord and dissatisfaction of the external life.
Danger of the powerful drive to learn.
Fidelity triumphs, his being remains whole.</td><td>(3)</td></tr>
</table>

What *task* does he have to fulfill?

Dangers, laid in his task and mission.

Most general task of art in the modern age. (4)

Special task of music:
with regard to language (5)

to the world of appearance
to incorrect sensation. (6)

General disposition and constitution of Wagner's soul as a creative artist fulfilling his task
(represented in the dispositions that his art elicits in the listener). (7)

More specific dispositions as a result of his development. (8)

II. What he is:

as poet
sculptor
musician
and on the whole (9)

III. What he will become.

As artist of the future he strives to found a style-tradition

His means to this goal:
Exemplary examples
Written works
he seeks shelter for his artworks among the existing powers
but he *creates* solely for humans of a specific future (10)

Whose nature can be guessed from his artworks, insofar as the need can be inferred backward from the satisfaction.
The motives of his art.
Incompatibility of that with the character of contemporary humanity.
Not so much seer of a future, but interpreter and transfigurer of a past. (11)

14[9]

Art-capacity of communication
Highest capacity to *communicate* by virtue of the highest *clarity*[17]
Poet
intermingled passion
flow of an act
much wider circle of circumstances
great rhythmic sense in constraining of passion, highest artistic unity in passionate human beings[18]
the dangerous qualities
fate of art *his* fate
talent of communication
without ⟨being⟩ subjugated by friends
but, to be sure, communicating himself to the friend
otherwise through example
only difficulties with the "cultivated person"
— Writings. Populism (Faust)[19,20]

14[10][21]

9. The artist
10. the daemonic communicability
11. What not communicable for contemporary humans:
Artwork of the future
Idea of *Die Nibelungen*

14[11]

Siegfried, from an alliance against all morality
the free human being, without fear
becomes unfree, faithless, through forgetfulness
still, in his death he redeems the world from the curse
Wotan — — —

[15 = U II 11. Spring 1876]

15[1]

Hypothetical propositions in German. "If" originally expresses a *wish*; propositions in this form, "if this is so, then from that" contain in the antecedent clause a *question* or a *doubt*. Therefore this latter form should not be completely confused with the former, still less is it alone somehow correct (as *W⟨agner⟩* seems to think, who employs it almost exclusively).

15[2]

Long periods should be avoided: or, in case they are necessary, should be judged purely logically; I want people to hear the logical scaffolding clearly clanging: for the periods should serve to make thinking easier; clarity is the first requirement: what do beauty and numbers in the periods matter to us (Germans!)!

15[3]

It is the *right time* finally for us to attend artistically to the German language. For its corporeality is fully developed; if we let go of it, it will suddenly degenerate. We must come to its aid with knowledge and diligence and direct toward it the effort that the Greek rhetoricians directed toward theirs — when it was also too late to still hope for a new youth. Now all the pots of paint, including Luther's German style, stand ready for use — it is only necessary that the right painter and colorist arrive. A craft must emerge so that from it an art will come to be. Even our classics were naturalists of style.

15[4]

1. Preparation and education. 2. Architect's plan. 3. Building material.

15[5][1]

Addendum to David Strauss.

p. 106 "we have long known that God, being 'omnipresent,' does not need any particular residence"

p. 44[2] "so Schleiermacher in his way brings forth once again a god-human"

p. 287 "boldly encompassing class of society"

p. 238 "from our standpoint, moral action is so inseparable from its reflex into feeling, that it can never have its value as beatitude annulled."

p. 49 "the Christian cultus, this garment tailored for an incarnate God, fits loosely and shapelessly as soon as it is placed upon a mere human being."

15[6][3]

Lichtenberg: "I know that there are famous writers, who were, however, basically shallow-minded — traits easily found together in Germany — who for all of their self-conceit, were taken by the best minds from whom I could inquire, to be shallow-minded."

15[7][4]

The newest Testament of all bequeaths its wisdom to those who are "poor in spirit,"[5] because they have learned either nothing or too much or nothing correctly and have read bad books, e.g., only their own.

15[8][6]

Wasn't it Aristotle's opinion[7] that we should kill the products of old men — because they are not fully capable of life?

15[9][8]

Otto Jahn, to whom the Beethovenian Ode to Joy did not seem cheerful enough.

15[10][9]

The effects of Hegel and Heine upon German style! The latter destroys the scarcely finished work of our great language-artists, that is, the hardly attained feeling for unified color of style; he loves the many-colored fool's jacket. His ideas, his images, his observations, his *sentiments,*[10] his words do not fit together, he masters as virtuoso every kind of style, but makes use of this mastery only in order to jumble all of them together. With Hegel everything is worthless gray, with Heine an electric play of colors, which, however, attacks the eyes just as frightfully as that gray deadens them. Hegel as stylist is a factor, Heine a farceur.[11]

15[11][12]

The new faith can move no mountains, but, to be sure, words. —

15[12][13]

Empedocles[14] said of the Agrigentians: they indulged in their pleasures as though they expected to die the next day, and they built as if they would never die. Strauss builds as though his book were going to die tomorrow and behaves as if it were never, ever to die. —

15[13][15]

Not the Straussian book, only its success is the event that forces us to speak. There is no idea in it that would be worth noting as good and new. —

15[14][16]

Well-washed rags do clothe cleanly, to be sure, yet in any case still in rags.

15[15][17,18]

The south German dialects have long since lost the individual forms of past tense.

Rückert places imperfect, present and perfect tenses beside one another in a pernicious way, e.g.,

> As he now at the border toll
> Did not want to declare what he is bringing,
> And has to open up his boxes,
> The customs agent *has tracked down* his find.

Such a *perfect tense in narrative* is completely blameworthy.

15[16]

Leaving out the participle: "The mail is sent, the brother is with, the song is out, the sun is down, the door is open, the guest is away, the money is gone, the fortress is over." "He has a scarf around, he has the thing away, he has the riddle out."

15[17][19]

Perfect {tense} with "to have" as auxiliary verb. Originally "he has build*ed* a house," "I have boughted a dress," therefore apposition of the accusative as with "he *shoots the hare* dead" ("deaded" old).

15[18]

The subjunctive form has developed from the imperfect. The representation of the past recast into the no-longer-present: "he lived" contains "he no longer lives." Now the subjunctive expresses the denial of the nonpresent, taken from the "no-longer-present." In older German, "I would speak" for every nonfulfillment in time, now we differentiate "I would speak" (not yet fulfilled) and "I would have spoken" (never fulfilled). "It would go well," but it has not gone well.

15[19]

The *present subjunctive* is differentiated from the indicative in that the indicative expresses a knowing, the subjunctive a believing. From that, indirect speech develops: we deny definite knowing, yet express the belief that something is true. Indirect speech formerly only in the form of the imperfect-subjunctive, and still occurs in this way. Old "I could speak" (conditional); new "I would speak." Old "he could speak" (in indirect speech), new "he would speak" (present subjunctive). — In Switzerland one says "the Russians were to have crossed the Balkans" for "were supposed to have." It is good and worth imitating.

15[20]

1. We must strive to limit *the existence of auxiliary verbs*!
2. The *embedding* of *prepositions* to be avoided!
3. Be careful with "must" "permitted to, want to, supposed to, would like to, could"!
4. *The formation* {of clauses} with "that" has also become excessive.
5. *Production of the subjunctive and the imperfect!*
6. *The genitive of the thing should be conserved*, instead of the hypertropic prepositions, e.g., to praise the hero's actions, to ask about the foreigner's origins, to heal the sick person's wounds. To be maintained in "to accuse, to blame, to fault, to calm, to charge, to cross, to transfer, to redeem, to release (from custody), to settle, to release, to lift, to dismiss, to rob, to banish (from the country), to expose, to unload, to dismiss, to remove, to deem worthy, to make sure, to free, to teach (someone better, the future)." With the reflexive pronoun we are much more conservative: "to praise one's actions, to rejoice in one's long life" "to interest oneself in a man" "to consider a thing for oneself, to make use of one's opportunity, to defend one's life, to fear one's death" perhaps "to get angry at one's treatment, to worry about one's fate, to take fright at one's danger."

15[21]

Quite correct are both "mich dünkt" and "mir dünkt,"[20] "es friert mich" "mir friert."[21] "Ich schlage dir ins Gesicht, ich schlage dich ins Gesicht."[22]

Dative or accusative with to seem, to disgust, to cause pain, to have a presentiment of.

15[22]

The *genitive* is now formal with the verb "the sparkling wine was poured by the Bohemian," but still completely ordinary, e.g., where people enjoy playing with words and make *them* up themselves. To enjoy the bread, to be astonished at what is heard, to mock the cripple, to watch out for danger, to forget his mother. To imagine a better future, to fear the approaching misfortune, to be filled with the most joyous life, to give voice to the liveliest song (of the woods, e.g.,), to cure a child.

15[23][23]

The *preposition* "*von*" has *suppressed* the genitive. Not with "sated with, tired of, full of, quits with, empty of, free from, without, able to, skillful in, partaking of, get hold of, sick of, intent upon, aware of, in need of, conscious of, authorized for, in memory of, faded, joyful, worth, catch sight of." The common dialects hardly recognize the genitive at all anymore: "the garden of the neighbor" (yet also the neighbor's garden).

15[24]

Magistrate's is *genitive* (in the sense of magistrate's people). *Dative plural* everywhere with place-names on -houses, -huts, -mountains, -valleys, -fields, -woods, -lindens, -oaks. To bathe is "to go to the baths," to moor a boat "to the boat's mooring." Thus in Roth*en*stein, Altenberg. *To* left out.

15[25]

Task: a simple extract from Overbeck's book *Christlichkeit der Theologie*.[24] From my *Birth of Tragedy*.

15[26]

Warning against combinations like "research-assistance." "Culture-war."

Likewise against confidence in the capacity of *a single* word, as, e.g., "the view of the performance capability of modern photography *in* connection with the printing press."

15[27]

The various kinds of style:

A. Style of the intellect (unmetrical) or the "style without feeling."

B. Style of the will (either prose or poetry — metrical or half-rhythmical) or

1. the ἦθος[25] 2. the πάθος[26] "the style of indistinct thinking."[27]

The style of the intellect emerges late, always on the basis of the ethical style. But at first mostly poetic (the image of the individual determines it, the priest, the prophet with ἦθος), later simple-everyday (after the image of the eminent man, who speaks simply and selectively). The sobering of the way of thinking must manifest itself everywhere now, likewise the hatred for indistinct thinking.

Written language does without *emphasis* and thereby without an exceptional means for attaining understanding. It must therefore make an effort to *replace* this: here is a major difference between written and spoken discourse. The latter can rely upon emphasis: written language must be more distinct, briefer, less ambiguous, but its greatest difficulty is to allow the passions to sympathize more or less with the emphasis. Question: how do we emphasize a word without getting assistance from tone (since we have no signs for tone)? Second: how do we emphasize one clause of a sentence? Often things must be written differently than spoken. Clarity is union of light and shadow.

To read to read aloud to lecture stipulate three kinds of style. Here reading aloud is the kind in which the voice must be managed most artfully, since it ⟨has⟩ to replace the lack of gesticulation, reading the kind where the style has to be most perfected, because here voice and gesticulation are omitted as means of expression. We could call the species of reading-aloud the *natural* species, if the gestures really were superfluous here, thus would not need to be replaced (to read behind a curtain): by someone completely motionless, where the body would remain still, e.g., the history of Herodotus. The sort of reading that is *natural* would be where there was no consideration at all of modulation of the voice and gestures, e.g., in mathematics.

[16 = N II 1. 1876]

16[1]

I aesthetics II on ethics and the doctrine of happiness

16[2]

Nobody clever — wedding — ruins — maiden happiness

16[3][1]

People who have the talent for representation see only what is representable in things. There is much they do not comprehend. So, too, writers and teachers. All of them basically think only of their talent: whether they otherwise become better or worse does not matter to them.[2]

As human being, musician, philologist, writer, philosopher — in everything I now notice how it is for me — the same, everywhere the same! If I were ambitious, perhaps there would be no reason at all to despair: but since I have so little of that, there is *almost* reason to despair. Written near Chillon Castle, about 6 in the evening.

16[4]

Liberation.
Philologist.
Marriage.
Age.
Religion.
Wagner.
etc.

16[5]

Leopardi — Chamfort — Larochefoucault — Vauvenargues — Coleridge Table Talk.

To translate.

History of literature.

On philology.

Book: Free teachers.

1. path to liberation.
2. the school of educators.
3. the wanderer.
4. Hail to death!

16[6][3]

Asceticism under the general consideration of suicide, likewise the unegoistical sacrifice.

16[7][4]

Every human being has his *recipes* for putting up with[5] life (in part to easily sustain it, in part to make it easy, if it has ever shown itself to be hard), even the criminal. This art of life, applied everywhere, is to be summarized. To be explained, what the recipes of *religion* really accomplish.

Not to *make* life easy, but to take it easily.

Many want to *make it hard,* in order to offer *their highest recipes* afterward (art asceticism etc.).

16[8]

"*the easy life*"

(ῥεῖα ζώοντες)[6]

"*path to spiritual* freedom"

the Greeks

teacher

marriage

property and work.

16[9][7]

The easy life.
Path to freedom.
Death of the old culture.
Teacher.
Woman and child.
Property and work.

16[10][8]

Unfashionable Observations.

1. The Cultivated Philistines (Counterfeiting of cultivation).
2 History.
3. The Philosopher.
4. The Artist.
5. The Teacher.
6. Woman and Child.
7. Property and Work.
8. Greeks.
9. Religion.
10. Liberation.
11. State.
12. Nature.
13. Sociability.

16[11]

1. Nature 1883
2. Woman and Child 1878
3. Property and Work 1881
4. The Teacher 1882
5. Sociability 1884
6. Those Who Live Easily 1880
7. Greeks 1879
8. Free Spirit 1877
9. State 1885

16[12]

Seven unfashionable observations — 1873–78.

For every Observation addendum in aphorisms.

Later: Addenda to the unfashionable observations (aphoristic).

16[13][9]

To provide a joy every day — "friend."[10]

16[14][11]

to make a necessity out of virtue

16[15]

To eat nothing 1 day every week.

Evenings only milk and tea.

4 hours daily out walking. (with notebook)

Collection: on the German language.[12]

Maxims.

Unfashionable Observations 29th–37th year of life.

38th–48th.

49th–58th.

16[16][13]

There are various steps toward freedom. If someone cannot mount this one (e.g., if his temperament is stubborn) then perhaps another. One form of energy will then be abnormally strongly developed, e.g., the sense for independence, which can just as well lead to freedom as dependence can to love.

16[17][14]

A maternal element is in every form of love: but not a paternal one.

16[18][15]

Signs of an inconsiderate superiority on the part of people who are friends are very painful and go deeply into the heart.

16[19][16]

Consilia juventutis plus divinitatis habent.[17] Bacon.

16[20]

My style has a certain voluptuous conciseness.

16[21][18]

The poet must first see a thing *precisely* and afterward see it again imprecisely: intentionally veil it over. Many attempt this directly; but that is not successful (as with Schiller). Nature must gleam through the garment.

16[22]

The one who leaves things out is an artist: the one who adds, a slanderer.

16[23]

The etymologies in Wagner are genuinely artistic, albeit unscientific: that is the proper relationship to nature.

16[24][19]

delirium tremens of the ascetic

16[25][20]

The powerful afterlife of the free spirit — he considers himself as a teaching that is burned into humanity.

Free spirit out of self-defensiveness, out of a desire for power.

16[26]

revenge often for *impotence* (Isocrates)[21]

16[27][22]

The *nadir* of German culture with Strauss's book after the war — corresponding to the common pleasure-seeking disposition — the *low-water mark* in the stream of German culture.

16[28][23]

A freethinking human being goes through the development of entire generations in advance.

16[29][24]

People who, like Hillebrandt, are only a few years ahead of public opinion: who likewise have only a public opinion.

16[30][25]

We can take pride in an unbroken line of *good* ancestors down through our father: it is a legitimation of our own self to ourselves. But a *single* break in the chain destroys the nobility. Do you have nobody violent avaricious licentious malicious cruel among your ancestors? we should ask everyone. — To this extent, I am noble to the 4th degree: further back I cannot see.

16[31][26]

Many men are not at all indignant for themselves about the adultery of their spouses, presupposing that they thereby get rid of them without loss.

16[32][27]

The disobedience of sons toward their fathers always goes precisely as far as possible, i.e., the obedience displays itself as precisely the minimum still permitted. But it lies wholly in the fathers' hands to set the limits, because they have the education and thus the habituation in their hands.

16[33][28]

Goal: to attune a reader so elastically that he gets up on tiptoes.

16[34][29]

Free-spiritedness fairy tales lasciviousness lift humans on tiptoes.

16[35][30]

To allow ourselves time for thinking: the source waters must flow together again.

16[36][31]

The illusion of the sexual drive has the strange character of periodically being incurable: it catches in its nets again and again, even though periods of complete disillusionment lie in between.

16[37][32]

If we have no luck, we should provide our own luck.

16[38][33]

Inactivity among "active people." They do not know the reason why they work, they lose *vitam*[34] senselessly: they lack the mode of higher activity, the *individual* mode, they think like officials businesspeople, but are inactive as humans of a unique kind.

16[39][35]

The higher ambition in the *vita umbratica*:[36] to distinguish oneself in a fundamental way!

16[40][37]

It is the misfortune of active people that their activity is always a bit irrational: they roll along as unconsciously as the stone falls.

16[41]

Perhaps we serve the general welfare more by having things go badly and go to ruin for us than if we were to triumph.

16[42][38]

Everyone has his own opinion about everything, because he is his own being — yet he must reflect a great deal!

Things are divisible into those about which knowing and those about which opinions are possible.

16[43][39]

It is the same with freedom as with health: it is individual.

16[44][40]

The free spirit will grasp only a tip of an event, but does not want to have it in its complete breadth (e.g., war — Bayreuth).

16[45][41]

Modern cloisters — foundations for such free spirits — something easy with our great wealth.

16[46]

Dialogue of the free spirits: how several climb a steep mountain, not fighting with one another and squabbling over the ground — the detestable disputing.

16[47][42]

How does the free spirit finally stand with regard to the active life? Lightly tied — no slave of his actions.

16[48][43]

The scholar has lost honor, he is in competition with the *active* people who take their pleasures hurriedly.

16[49][44]

To reach his external goal in a timely way, a small official position, a property that just provides sustenance. To live so that an overturning of everything cannot shake us very much.

16[50][45]

Sunlight glitters in the bottom and shows what the waves flow over: rough stone.

16[51][46]

Esteem for the contemplative life *has decreased.* Once they were opposites, the priest and the *esprit fort*:[47] a sort of new birth of both in a single person now possible.

16[52][48]

It is a matter of how much breath you have, to be able to dive into this element: if you have a lot, you will be able to see to the very bottom.

16[53][49]

In order to see a thing *completely*, a human being must have two eyes, one of love and one of hatred.

16[54][50]

Productive people rarely become free spirits; the poets remain religiously backward. The politicians — — —

16[55]

The image of the free spirit remained incomplete in the previous century: they negated too little and had *themselves* left over.

[17 = U II 5b. Summer 1876]

17[1][1]

On the aesthetic: some blunt things.

Leaving things out a primary technique of idealism. One is not allowed to look so closely, one *forces* the *spectator back* a *great distance, so that he observes from there* (as in decorative painting). How important is the start of the distancing of the observer! Here the creative artist dare not falter. Precisely here is shown how scrupulously he must proceed from the strongest feeling of *his* auditor.

Meter lays *a gauze over* reality; a bit more artificial speech conceals and elevates something; the "muffled." The final means with which art works, to sympathize quite naïvely! Is very rare! They are rather foolish things that come from this. It is likewise with religion.

The great value of *indistinct thinking* for art.

Love and mockery belong *together* with imitation, as in Archilochus. Is indeed the most fertile condition of the human soul!

17[2][2]

The *illogical* belongs to the unconquerable *necessity* of human existence: from that comes much that is *very good*! It is so firmly fixed in language, in art, in the affects, religion, in everything that lends value to life! Naïve people, who want to transform human nature into a logical one! There certainly exist degrees of approximation, but how much gets lost there! From time to time, a person requires nature once again, i.e., his illogical *primeval position* toward things. From that arise his best drives.

17[3][3]

The *two worlds behind each other*: Siegfried's life, in the background the fate of the gods. Most metaphysically felt.

17[4]

It has for the Germans come to pass *once again* as after the **Reformation**; they have likewise now completely lost Schiller and Goethe's Reformation, the high spirit from which they worked; everything that is praised now is a complete opposite to that, and so there has developed among those who are honest a sort of contempt for that spirit. It is absolutely a matter of whether human beings are great; what goes along with that is not to be assessed too quickly; but the national, as it is understood now, actually demands *narrowness* as dogma. How the petty hagglers feel themselves to be beyond Schiller!

17[5]

On Darwinism.
Common feeling with humanity.
On the state.
On religion.

17[6][4]

Heart-felt compassion with himself is the highest feeling that a human being can attain.

17[7][5]

Enough, that one is thereby temporarily put to sleep and that a human being no longer thinks then about his suffering. It is the best thing in the world that there exist sleep and forgetfulness for its madness: all ethical systems count upon this best of traits in the worst of worlds.

17[8][6]

Life is not worth it, given all the bother.

17[9]

Many people are not afraid of death, but of having the dying spin out far too long, e.g., through sickness, and prefer life to this condition.

17[10]

And so someone says: "that author shall not come close to me; he says so many bad things about human beings, he must be quite bad himself." Answer: but then you yourself must be even worse, for you say bad and, moreover, untrue things about the best people who exist, those who speak truly and do not spare themselves!

17[11][7]

The sick person is often healthier in his soul than the healthy person.

17[12]

Religious contemplation of the world without sharpness and depth of intellect makes religion into the most disgusting thing in the world.

17[13][8]

There are women who, wherever we may dig, have nothing inside, but are instead wholly masks: almost spectral beings, blood-sucking, never satisfying.

17[14][9]

We fear the hostile disposition of our neighbor because we know that this disposition will enable him to penetrate our secrets and teach him to disdain us, as we disdain ourselves.

17[15][10]

How does it happen that we suffer more from the contempt of others than from our own? It is more damaging to us.

17[16][11]

The genial state of a human being is where he finds himself simultaneously in a state of love and mockery toward one and the same thing.

17[17]

The purpose of the state should never be the state, but instead always the individual.

17[18][12]

Anyone who wants to embellish things for his conception must do as the poet does who wants to embellish an idea: he stretches it out into meter and lays the web of rhythm over it: for that, he must *worsen* the idea a little, so that it fits into the verse. The *worsening of knowledge*, in order then to bend the things of art: a secret of those who take pleasure in life.

17[19][13]

The subtlest trick of Christianity was to speak of love: as it was also of Plato. There is something so ambiguous concentrating recollective in it and the lowest intelligence still senses the shimmering of this word: the oldest woman and the most rational man thank love for the noblest, least selfish moments of their lives.

17[20][14]

That the Jews are the worst people on earth accords well with the fact that it was precisely among Jews that the Christian teaching of the entire sinfulness and contemptibility of human beings emerged — and that they rejected it.

17[21]

Path to spiritual freedom.

Steps of education.

Parents. Kin neighbors. Friends. Public schools. Teachers. History of peoples. Nature. Mathematics. Geography. Travels. Antiquity. Age of life, associating with elders. Civil service. Public service. Arrangement into religious denominations. Marriage. Women. Children. Solitary. Unmarried. Occupation. Honor. Those without property. Those without honesty. The press. Immortality. Associating with the dead. Benefit of death, being ripe. Too early insight into the lack of purpose and utility.

17[22][15]

Unfashionable observations. I have connected and collected what makes individuals great and self-reliant, and also the viewpoints toward which they can ally themselves. I see, we are in *ascendance*: we will in a short time be the refuge of the entire culture. All other movements are inimical to culture (the socialist just like that of the great state, that of monetary powers, even that of the sciences).

I want to give peace back to human beings, without which no culture can come to be and persist. Likewise *simplicity.*

17[23]

What matters to me are only the *motives* of humans: the *objective existence* of *knowledge* is an abomination to me. The highest knowledge will be washed away if humans become worse.

17[24][16]

I look back upon childhood and youthful years with sorrow and feel from day to day more liberated. Transition from inhibition into uninhibitedness.

17[25]

Tension of feeling at the emergence of the first *Unfashionable Observation*. Fear for the genius and his work and at the same time the sight of Straussian complacency. What is *falsified* in all spiritual nourishment! The *enervation* of all knowers! The faltering morality in right and wrong, and the unconstrained pursuit of pleasure in vulgar things! The deceitful form of happiness!

17[26]

Calm simplicity and grandeur![17]

In style, too, an image of this striving, as result of the most concentrated energy of my nature.

"*The path to yourself.*"

17[27]

As knowledge can ignite the will, so can partial knowledge cloud it over and make it unhealthy: so that it no longer feels hunger and thirst in the right way and cannot even be redeemed. *Production* of the *individual*, in order then to really know what it requires!

17[28]

The purpose of bearing children is to put *freer* humans than we are into the world. No consideration is as important as the one concerning the inheritability of qualities.

17[29][18]

Nature directs a man toward multiple marriages in succession: first, an older girl. Transition of this later into the maternal.

"Alcestis wants to die for her spouse," bestows motherly love upon him: she wants to allow a second marriage. She is fetched back from Hades.

17[30][19]

I am astonished by people who sigh so for their youth, e.g., for their student years: it is a sign that they have become *less free* and felt themselves to be better off back then. I feel precisely the reverse and know nothing less desirable than childhood and youth: I feel myself now younger and freer than ever.

17[31][20,21]

A wanderer passes through the night
At a steady pace;
And takes along with him
The curved valley and lengthy heights.
The night is beautiful —
He strides along and does not stand still,
Does not know where his path will take him. —

Then a bird sings out in the night. —
— "Ah, bird, what have you done?
How you check my sense and foot
And pour sweet chagrin
Over me, so that I must now stand still,
And must attend,
To read your tone and greeting?" —

The good bird goes silent and speaks:
No, wanderer, no! I do not greet you
With this noise;
I sing because the night is so beautiful.
Yet you shall keep going ever farther on
And never understand my song.
Just pass on by
And when your step sounds from far away
I'll raise my nighttime song again
As well as I can. —
Farewell, you poor wayfarer! —

17[32][22]

The artist needs infidelity of memory in order to not transcribe nature, but reshape it.

17[33]

"Above Things." — Whoever has fully comprehended the preposition "above" has comprehended the extent of human pride and misery. Anyone who is *above* things is not *in* things — therefore not even *in* himself! He can take pride in the latter.[23]

17[34][24]

Failure and being despised are good means to become free. We set our contempt against that: you add nothing for me to that! So am I, then, as I am.

17[35][25]

People make themselves, in becoming older, *superfluous*.

17[36]

Here and there in the *Unfashionable Observations*, I have still left *sally ports* for myself.

17[37]

In Catholic countries, celibacy has almost done away with the children of priests: mild, halfway-self-denying human beings.

17[38]

People toss and turn, now to this side, now ⟨to⟩ that, the pain is great.

17[39][26]

Glittering sunshine of knowledge sinks through the river of things to its bottom.

17[40][27]

In the individual species, just as in individual cultural periods, the will strives to become faint and good and to die out.

17[41][28]

Esteem for the *contemplative* life has decreased. — Therefore my viewpoint is unfashionable. Once the priest and the *esprit fort*[29] were opposites, both within the contemplative life.

17[42][30]

How does the free spirit stand with regard to the active life? Lightly tied to it, no slave of it.

17[43]

Active people make use only of ideas and remedies found by the contemplative ones.

17[44]

The free spirit lives for the future of human beings in such a way that he discovers new possibilities of life and weighs the old ones.

17[45]

Epicurus's *Canon*[31] to be utilized.

17[46][32]

Restoration of calm and quiet for the realm of the intellect, setting aside of modern noise.

A desire for calming and a deepening such as has never yet existed must come over human beings, if they ever become tired of the modern rush.

17[47][33]

Those horrible people who see in everyone a patron and a superior or a bridge to some advantage and who thoroughly flatter themselves about this are not suited to be free spirits and to be their friends. More likely to become free spirits are those who see something tyrannical in everyone, even in friends, benefactors, teachers, who decisively decline great favors.

17[48][34]

Even the *ambitious one* can become a free spirit, for he has here a means to distinguish himself in a fundamental way.

17[49][35]

What is the goal of all *linguistics* if not to find some day a *universal language*? Then the European universal human being would exist. To what end, then, would there still be that awful learning of *languages*!

17[50][36]

Anyone who wants to employ his money well as a free spirit should found institutions in the form of cloisters, in order to make possible friendly cohabitation in the greatest simplicity for people who want otherwise no longer to have anything to do with the world.

17[51][37]

The modern sickness is: an excess of *experiences*. Therefore everyone should take themselves home early in order not to lose themselves in the experiences.

17[52]

It is an evil symptom that we make such ado about love of the fatherland and politics. It seems that there is nothing higher that we can praise.

17[53][38]

Modern agitation has become so great that all the great results of culture thereby vanish, gradually there is lacking the sensibility appropriate to them. So civilization is heading into a new barbarism. But humanity dare not be led into this single stream of the "active ones." I have hopes for the counterweight, the contemplative element in the Russian peasant and in the Asian. This will at some point correct in larger measure the character of humanity.

17[54][39]

As we go westward, the craze for movement becomes ever greater, so that all Europeans already appear to Americans to be comfortable and pleasure-loving.

Where both streams meet and blend together, humanity reaches its goal: the highest knowledge about the value of existence (not possible in one place because the activity of thinking is too slight, not possible in the other because this activity is directed differently).

17[55][40]

I imagine future thinkers in whom the European-American restlessness is united with the hundred-times inherited Asiatic contemplativeness: such a combination brings a solution to the world riddle. Meanwhile the observant free spirits have their mission: they remove all the barriers that stand in the way of a blending of human beings: religions states monarchical instincts, illusions of wealth and poverty, prejudices about health and races — etc.

17[56][41]

Everyone who speaks mysteriously about his plans appears to us foolish and pompous. It will not be that much of a thing. To want not to speak of a thing seems like unjustified self-esteem and is considered pedantic.

17[57][42]

The restlessness of soul that I deplore is perhaps precisely the condition that drives me to production. The pious ones who yearn for complete peace uproot their best activities.

17[58]

The free spirit is "envious like the gods" of the stupid contentedness of human beings. νεμεσσητικόν[43] is envy of the gods.

17[59]

The simple *appearance* of the *truth*.

17[60]

Constraints necessary in order to produce genius.

17[61][44]

To find a *middle* line among three talents — my problem.

17[62]

To make every hobby central and to weave it into the available talents.

17[63]

Vices have given much occasion for free-spiritedness. Likewise the fear of eternal punishment: one shook off these burdensome ideas and thereby got rid of religion.

17[64][45]

We can easily wean ourselves from religious opinions, if only we begin early enough.

17[65]

Primary error of present-day instruction is that it is given by the hour and with everything all mixed up.

17[66][46]

Long live the noble betrayers!

17[67]

Democratic, honest states have to furnish the *highest* education *to everyone*, whatever the cost.

17[68]

That art depicts what is *true about nature* is the illusion that it arouses, not the philosophical reality.

17[69]

Holy envy.

17[70][47]

To heighten cleanliness into purity: perhaps even into the concept of beauty among the Greeks.

17[71][48]

We pass on general views through habituation, so that we can turn all of our energy to personal advantage within the given circle. It protects against wasting personal energy.

17[72][49]

Human and all too human.
Path to liberation of the spirit.
The easing of life.
Woman and child.
State and society.

17[73]

Five[50] small acts of freedom have more effect than all freethinking.

17[74][51]

We can live like the easy-living gods if we have the lively delight in the truth.

17[75]

1. The constrained spirits.
2. The type of higher development, necessity of free-spiritedness.
3. Emergence of the free spirit — development, nonhabituation.
4. Partial free spirits.

17[76][52]

States marriages etc. rest upon faith, not upon knowledge. But that is a *pudendum*:[53] it was insolent of Christianity to proclaim the secret and to demand faith and to reject knowledge.

Religion everywhere rests upon faith.

The state *exists*, therefore its principle is right. The monarchical principle must be true, for monarchy exists.

17[77][54]

That Christ is supposed to have redeemed the world is audacious.

17[78][55]

It is a part of *purity* that in the course of life we seek refuge less and less in the metaphysical.

17[79][56]

Impure thinking and style.

17[80][57]

To judge art according to its effects and according to its causes — two aesthetics!

17[81]

The ascetic a bad and irregular brain.

Ecstasy voluptuousness of the intellect.

17[82][58]

Leisure and idleness are being lost! slandered again!

17[83][59]

§ How successes are made: see spiritual freedom.

§ Idleness.

17[84][60]

It is open to all eyes that after the last war between the Germans and the French, just about every German became one degree more dishonest avid for pleasure avaricious thoughtless: the general admiration for Strauss was the memorial monument that was placed to commemorate the lowest point of the stream of German culture: a freethinking aged theologian became the herald of public complacency.

17[85][61]

To conclude: the free spirits are the *easy-living* gods.

17[86]

We spoil our heads with religion — *not* to reflect at all.

17[87][62]

You should not educate to yourself, but instead beyond yourself.

No great man points toward himself, but instead always above himself.

17[88]

Since I do not yet have the misfortune, the burden, to be counted among the famous men — out of my modest obscurity[63] — — —

17[89][64]

Humans attach the same predicates to causes as to effects.

17[90]

Lack of character can be the sign of a preponderance of spirit.

17[91]

If everyone becomes a free spirit, the foundation becomes weak: such a culture eventually decays or evaporates like dew and mist.

17[92][65]

That at the beginning of all vices we nonetheless still find ourselves very much in proximity to virtue.

17[93][66]

The free spirit does not take much action: hence uncertainty with regard to anyone full of character.

He strays in thought, too: easily skepticism.

17[94][67]

A people that begins to engage in politics must be very rich in order not to perish by it.

17[95][68]

A primordially Catholic France and a Greek Catholic Russia will never go into a single yoke — hence the German statesman has promoted the German movement.

17[96][69]

With the same means with which one has shattered the small state, one shatters the great state.

17[97][70]

Free-traders are criminals statesmen etc.

17[98][71]

Constrained thinking required as morality: killing cats a crime among the Egyptians. We punish the action, not the disposition: not in order to deter, but in order to buy off a god and avert *general destruction*.

17[99]

False analogy to the Swiss movement[72] — they demand the small state. Their cantons were not small states.

17[100][73]

No *ethics* can be based upon the pure knowledge of things: there we must be like nature, neither good nor evil.

17[101][74]

I would like the definition of the *scoundrel*. It is not the robber, the murderer, the thief.

17[102][75]

In the Catholic Church an ear is created (through confession) into which we can speak our secret, without consequences. What a relief! Also good is the idea of making up for an injustice by a *good deed* (even if rendered to different people). That is the true "punishment."

17[103][76]

If someone has satisfied his needs, boredom comes over him; how can he get rid of this? Only by creating new passions for himself, in order then to satisfy these, too. We produce a need by causing ourselves distress: which through habit gradually loses its painful character and becomes pleasure. Think of tobacco-smoking.

17[104][77]

Free and constrained spirits.
Woman and child.
Professions and occupations.
Easing of life.
Human and all too human.[78]

17[105][79]

The Plowshare.

Guidance toward spiritual liberation.

First chapter:	Free and constrained spirits.
Second	The easing of life.[80]
Third	Professions and occupations.[81]
Fourth	Woman and child.[82]
Fifth	Society.[83]
Sixth	By oneself alone.
Seventh	The school of the educators.

[18 = M I 1. September 1876]

The Plowshare.

18[1][1]

"If you want to follow me, till with the plow!, then many will enjoy what is yours, certainly the poor man and the rich one will enjoy what is yours, the wolf and the eagle and absolutely all creatures will enjoy what is yours."

Der Meier Helmbrecht.

Paths to spiritual freedom.

18[2]

1.2. All public schools are set up for middling natures, therefore for those whose fruits are not much worth considering, if they do become ripe. To them are sacrificed the higher spirits and temperaments, upon whose ripening and bearing of fruit everything really depends. In this, too, we show ourselves as belonging to an age whose culture is perishing from the methods of culture. Admittedly, a talented nature knows how to help itself: its inventive energy shows itself especially in how it, despite the bad ground in which it is placed, despite the bad surroundings to which one wishes to adapt it, despite the bad nourishment on which it is fattened, knows how to maintain its energies. But herein lies no justification for the stupidity of those who place it in this situation.

18[3]
3. Detachment from uncomprehending surroundings: — A deep injury and offense arises when people with whom we have for a long time associated intimately and to whom we gave the best that we had, have occasion to let us notice their low opinion of us. Anyone who associates carefully with people and does not offend them, in order not to be offended, generally experiences to his dismay that people have not even noticed his carefulness or even that they do notice it and treat it lightly in order to make fun of it.

18[4]
4. Method of distancing people from ourselves: — We cannot annoy somebody and turn him against us more than if we want to force him to think of things that he wants most forcibly to dismiss from his awareness, e.g., theologians on the honesty in confession, philologists on the educating force of antiquity, statesmen on the purpose of the state, businesspeople on the sense of all monetary acquisition, women on the randomness and frailty of their inclinations and alliances.

18[5]
8. It is useful to demand more: — Anyone who wants to attain something must quite emphatically demand even more; we then concede to him the lesser amount of his demand and are content that he is content.

18[6][2]
12. Value of a depressed mood: — People who live under an inner pressure tend to excesses — even of thought. Cruelty is often a sign of a discordant inner disposition that desires numbing: just like a certain cruel inconsiderateness of thought.

18[7]
24. If we travel on from place to place and ask everywhere which persons are most highly valued in every location, we find out

how rare superior intelligences are. We would like to have the least to do over the long run with precisely those intelligences who are respected and influential, for we notice with them that they are valued only as leaders of advantageous views, that their usefulness for many gives them their reputation. A country of many millions of persons shrinks under such a view, and everything that is valued becomes suspect for us.[3]

Among protectionists and free-traders,[4] what is at stake is the advantage of private persons who have mendaciously trimmed themselves with science and patriotism.[5]

18[8][6]

27. Without productivity, life is unworthy and unbearable: but supposing that you had no productivity or only a weak one, then consider liberation from life, by which I mean not so much suicide as that ever fuller liberation from the illusions of life — until you finally like an overripe[7] apple fall from the tree. If the free spirit has reached the heights, all the motives of the will no longer have an effect upon him, even if his will would still like to bite: it no longer can, for it has lost all of its teeth.

18[9]

31. We should lose our belief in God, freedom and immortality like our first teeth, only then does the proper bite grow in.

18[10]

32. Perhaps the only means of deliverance from the fear of death is: to teach of an eternal life: another, more certain[8] one, in any case, to instill a longing for death.

18[11][9]

33. We get habituated to religious opinions in the first fifteen years of our lives, and in the next fifteen years we get dehabituated once again; the tenth year of life is when a human being is now generally the most religious. — Even if it were useful at first to lay a human being upon the breast of the nurse religion

and to allow him to drink the milk of faith, so that later and gradually he becomes accustomed to the bread and meat of knowledge: the time still seems to me too long, considering the brevity of human life. The present economy would perhaps be correct if a human being first entered the blossoming of his energy and reason at the age of sixty. But actually, he now becomes wise and powerless at the same time. —

18[12][10]

38. It is the sign of either a very anxious or a very proud disposition to see in everyone, even in friends, benefactors, teachers, the danger of a tyrannical superiority and to be on guard in receiving large favors. But no free spirit will exist who would not have this disposition.

Human and All Too Human.

18[13]

51. People with whom it is unpleasant for us to associate do us a favor if they give us cause to separate ourselves from them. Afterwards we are much more ready to do a good turn for them from a distance or not to begrudge them.

18[14]

52. We think of the moral difference between an honest man and a rogue as much too large; on the other hand, the intellectual difference usually is large. The laws against thieves and murderers are made for the benefit of those who are cultivated and rich.

18[15]

55. There is much more contentment than discontentedness in the world. Practically speaking, *optimism* is in control; — theoretical pessimism emerges from the observation: how bad and absurd the basis for our contentment is; it is amazed at the slight amount of prudence and reason in this contentment; it would find continual discontent comprehensible.

18[16][11]
57. The restlessness of soul that philosophical people deplore in themselves is perhaps precisely the condition from which their higher productivity flows. If they were to attain that complete peace, they would probably have uprooted their best activity and thereby made themselves useless and superfluous.

18[17][12]
58. Everyone who speaks mysteriously about his intention or lets it be noticed that he does not speak about it at all attunes his fellow human beings to irony.

18[18][13]
60. The good tendency in us often collects its source-water from vices and bad moods, in order then to burst forth more strongly. When virtue has slept, it will rise refreshed.

18[19][14]
62. What can be the motive for the closing off of nations from one another that is demanded now, whereas everything else points toward their blending? I believe dynastic interests and business interests go hand in hand there. So then all the liberal parties make use of national seclusion as a roundabout way to shape social life more freely. While one is constructing great nation-states, one gets rid of smaller rulers and influence of individual oppressive castes;[15] whereby it is self-evident that the same power that now has to shatter the small state will at some point have to shatter the great state. It is, on the other hand, a blind prejudice that it is races and differences of lineage that now transform nations into great states.

18[20][16]
64. Concerning industriousness, scholars produce many beautiful words; the main thing is that without their industriousness they would bore themselves to death.

18[21][17]

65. Christianity and La Rochefoucauld are useful when they cast suspicion on the motives of human action: for the assumption of the fundamental injustice of every action, of every judgment has great influence upon whether a human being frees himself from the all too vehement will.

18[22][18]

66. Young people often complain that they have not had any experiences, whereas they suffer precisely from having had too many: it is the apex of modern thoughtlessness.

18[23]

67. Philosophers of the second rank are divided into *aside-thinkers* and *opposed-thinkers*, that is, into those who execute a side-wing for an existing structure according to the given ground plan (for which the virtue of a capable builder suffices), and those who are led so far into continual resistance and contradiction that they finally establish a different system opposed to an already existing one. All other philosophers are *over*-thinkers, historians of what has been thought, of those who have thought: apart from those few who stand for themselves, grow forth from themselves and alone deserve to be called "thinkers." These think day and night and no longer even notice it, like those who live in a smithy no longer hear the noise of the anvil: for them, it is like it was for Newton (who was once asked how he had ever managed to come up with his discoveries and who simply replied: "by always thinking about them.")

18[24][19]

68. The public is impolite in a double way toward a writer: It praises one of his works at the price of another by the same author and then: if the author has written one time, it continually demands new texts — as if thereby, in having been given a gift, it had acquired ascendancy over the giver.

18[25][20]

71. Signs of an inconsiderate superiority on the part of persons who are friends or are obliged to us by gratitude are very painful and cut deeply into the heart.

18[26]

77. People complain about the lack of breeding of the masses; if this were proven, the reproach would fall heavily upon the cultivated people; the masses are precisely as good and evil as cultivated people are. They show themselves to be evil and ill-bred to the same extent as cultivated people show themselves to be ill-bred; live as one may, one precedes them as leader; one elevates or spoils them according to whether one elevates or spoils oneself.

18[27]

90. Almost every good writer writes only a single book. All of the rest are only prefaces, preliminary attempts, explanations, appendices to it; indeed, many a very good writer has never written *his* book, for example Lessing, whose intellectual significance rises high above every one of his texts, every one of his poetic attempts.[21]

18[28][22]

91. I differentiate *great* writers, especially the ones who give shape to language — those whose handling of the language lets it live on or be revived — and *classic* writers. The latter are called classic with regard to their imitability and exemplarity, whereas the great writers are not to be imitated. With classic writers, language and word are dead; the animal no longer lives in the mussel and so they string together mussel after mussel. But with Goethe, it lives on.

18[29]

92. How does it happen that someone in love feels the effect of tragedy and of every art more strongly, whereas the complete

silencing of the will is nonetheless described as the real contemplative condition? It seems instead as if the will must first be plowed up, as it were, in order to take into itself the seeds of art.

The easy life.

18[30][23]

101. Every human being has his own recipes for how life is to be endured and, indeed, how it is to be easily sustained or to be made easy after it has shown itself to be hard.

18[31]

104. If life is supposed to be felt ever more heavily over the course of history, we can no doubt ask whether the inventiveness of humans is in the end sufficient, too, for the highest degrees of this increase in difficulty.

18[32]

112. The person who does not have this Christian-like comfort[24] and to whom, on the other hand, philosophy did not give the return gift of complete irresponsibility, is badly off: he knows himself only too well and despises himself because he is measuring his nature in an erroneous way as guilty; therefore he looks upon his fellow human beings with anxiety, lest they penetrate his secrets. He takes his fellow human beings either to really be better than himself, because he knows them less well, or he pretends as if he took them for better in order to win them over and to dispose them to feel the same toward himself. The vanity and ambition of humans most often rest upon the feeling of their own contempt: they want others to deceive themselves about them; they rejoice in every judgment of their fellow human beings when it sounds favorable to them, even when they know that it is false; their effort is to prevent the whole truth about themselves from coming to light.

18[33][25]

113. The remedies against pain that people employ are frequently only narcotics. All such remedies, however, belong to a lower level of the healing art. We find narcotics working via mental representations in the religions and arts, which belong to this extent within the history of the healing art. Religions understand particularly well how to use suppositions to shift the cause of suffering out of sight, for example, by saying to parents whose child has died, he (or she) has not died, and adding, with regard to the dead body, your child even lives on as a more beautiful one.

18[34][26]

115. It is well known that love and reverence cannot easily be felt together with regard to the same person. The hardest and rarest thing, however, would be this, that the highest love and the lowest degree of respect would be found next to each other; thus, contempt as the judgment of the head and love as the drive of the heart. And nevertheless, this situation is possible and is demonstrated by history. The one who could love himself with the purest form of love would be the one who had at the same time contempt for himself, and who would say to himself: despise nobody except for yourself, because you can know only yourself. This is perhaps the position of the founder of the Christian religion toward the world. Self-love out of pity for oneself and one's complete contemptibility is the kernel of Christianity without any of its shell and mythology. The feeling of this contemptibility springs from self-knowledge and this, in turn, from a need for revenge. If someone has suffered enough from himself, injured himself enough through sinfulness of every kind, he begins to feel the feeling of revenge toward himself. Penetrating self-observation and eventually self-contempt are the natural consequences, for many people even asceticism, i.e., revenge upon oneself in a violent act of antipathy and hatred. And in that a human being expects more effort and haste from himself, the same

propensity toward revenge manifests itself. That amid all of this a human being still loves himself seems then like a miracle, and we generally attribute such a refined and incomprehensible love to a god, but it is the human being himself who is capable of such a love, in a sort of self-forgiveness, for he cannot stop loving himself, since his love can never be a thing of the head. In this situation, love becomes master over the feeling of revenge, the human being is able to act once again and to live on; admittedly he does not think very highly of this action and of all earthly striving, it is almost purposeless, but he cannot do otherwise than to act; as the Christian of the first era comforts himself with the prospect of the downfall of the world and hopes then to be done finally with his contemptible nature driving him to act, so every human being can now know that it will in any case someday be over for humanity and with that, the expression of purposelessness must be placed upon all human striving; for that purpose, he will find out more and more about the fundamental errors in all exertion and bring them to light; impure thinking lies at the basis of all of them. He will, for example, perceive that all parents procreate their child without responsibility and educate without knowledge the one to be educated, so that they inevitably do things wrong and violate an alien sphere. This is part of the wretchedness of existence, and so human beings eventually feel full of dissatisfaction with everything that they do and the highest that they can attain will be: to have compassion for themselves; love and compassion for oneself are reserved for the highest stages of the difficulty of life, as the strongest means of relief.

Woman and Child.

18[35][27]

116. To the awkward question, whence do you come, human being? I answer: from father and mother, and let's leave it at that.

18[36]

118. If I find everywhere a degradation of the Germans, I assume the cause of this to be that for four decades a more vulgar spirit has governed the making of marriages, for example, in the middle classes the pure pandering for money and rank; the daughters are supposed to be taken care of and the men want to marry for property or advantage; hence we see in the children, too, the vulgar origin of these marriages.

18[37][28]

119. The best part of marriage is friendship. If this is great enough, it may itself, by moderation, look beyond and overcome the aphrodisiac element. Without friendship, marriage makes both parties vulgar in thinking and contemptible.

18[38][29]

123. The living together of spouses is the primary means for making a good marriage rare, for even the best friendships only rarely tolerate this.[30]

18[39]

124. Among the most affecting aspects of a good marriage is the mutually shared knowledge of the disgusting secret from which the new child is begotten and born. Especially in procreation do we feel the degradation of what is most beloved, out of love.

18[40]

125. No son needs to be grateful to his father for his existence, he should perhaps even be angry with him because of certain inherited traits (an inclination to violent temper, lasciviousness). Fathers have a great deal to do in order to make up for having had sons.[31]

18[41]

126. Fathers who quite sincerely feel their own inadequacy and continually yearn for the heights of intellect and heart[32] have a

right to beget children. If they ever impart this inclination, this desire, then they are already sharing with the child many a large hint about what is truly worth striving for, and for such hints alone does the adult tend to be truly thankful to his parents.

18[42][33]

130. Humans are destined to be either father or mother, in one sense or another. Without productivity, life is horrible, hence youth means nothing to me, for in it, it is not possible or not reasonable to produce.

18[43]

131. If women were as intent upon the beauty of men, men would as a rule eventually become beautiful and vain — as is now the rule for women. It shows the excessive enthusiasm and perhaps the higher cast of mind of the man that he wants the woman to be beautiful. It shows the greater understanding and the sobriety of women (perhaps also their lack of aesthetic feeling) that women also accept ugly men; they look more to the basic facts, which here means: protection, maintenance;[34] men more to the beautiful appearance, to the transfiguration of existence, even if this were thereby to become more arduous.

18[44]

135. It puts love[35] far below friendship that it demands exclusive possession, whereas one person can have several good friends, and these friends become one another's friends.[36]

18[45]

140. Women who especially love their sons are most often vain and conceited. Women who do not make a great deal of their sons are most often right in this, but give it to be understood that no better child was to be expected from such a father: thus their vanity manifests itself.

On the Greeks.

18[46][37]

143. If we think of the Greeks as tribes small in numbers on densely populated soil, of how they found the inner parts of the mainland covered with a race of Mongolian descent, found the coast trimmed with a Semitic stripe and Thracians settled in between, thus we see the necessity above all of holding on to and always reproducing the superiority of quality; with that, they practiced their magic upon the masses. The feeling of holding on all alone as higher beings among a hostile majority forced them continuously toward the highest spiritual tension.

18[47][38]

146. The Platonic Socrates is in the real sense a caricature; for he is overloaded with qualities that can never come together in a single person. Plato is not enough of a dramatist to hold the image of Socrates steady even in one dialogue. It is therefore in fact a fluid caricature. On the other hand, the *Memorabilia* of Xenophon gives a really true image, which is precisely as clever as the object of the image was; but we must understand how to read this book. The philologists basically think that Socrates has nothing to say to them and are therefore bored with it. Other people feel that this book both stings and cheers.

18[48][39]

153. The gods make a human being even worse when they do not wish him well; that is not only Greek, that is human nature. If someone does not love another, he wishes privately that he become worse and thus justify, as it were, his aversion. This is part of the dismal philosophy of hatred, which has not yet been written.

Continuation of
"Human and All Too Human."

18[49]
154. A stupid prince who is lucky is perhaps the happiest creature under the sun, for the propriety of the court lets him seem precisely as wise as he luckily needs to be. A stupid prince who is unlucky still always lives tolerably, for he can give vent to his ill humor and discontent upon others. A clever prince who is lucky is generally a gleaming predator; a clever prince who is unlucky, in contrast, a very irritable predator that one should lock in a cage; he does not deceive himself about his failures and that makes him so angry. A clever prince, who is at the same time good, is most often quite unhappy, for he must do many things for which he is too good or too clever.

18[50][40]
155. We basically take the aspiration and intentions of a human being, however dangerous and strange they may be, as pardoned or at least as excusable, if he stakes his life upon them. In no other way, perhaps, can humans so clearly express how highly they take the value of life.[41]

18[51][42]
156. Our crimes against criminals consist in treating them like scoundrels. I would wish to hear for once the definition of a scoundrel. The core of the scoundrel seems to be unrecognizable to the eye of justice and therefore its arm does not reach him.

18[52][43]
157. The meaning of the oldest punishments is not: to deter from the misdeed, but instead *first*: an attempt to make up for the damage, for example, through a fine paid to the relatives of someone who has been slain; *second*, there belong here the measures that concern the community, in order to secure itself as a *whole* against the wrath of an offended deity, hence the

murderer in Homer must become a fugitive from his homeland; there is not a moral, but indeed a religious stain that lies upon him: he endangers the community to which he belongs. This type of rule is superfluous for us.

18[53][44]

158. The fundamental idea for a new, more humane penal law would have to be: to set aside an injustice to the extent that the damage can be made good; and then to compensate the evil deed by a good deed. This good deed would not have to be rendered to the one who was damaged and offended, but toward anyone at all; one has, in fact, rarely committed the crime against an individual, but generally against a member of human society — one thereby owes society a good deed. This is not to be understood so coarsely, as if a theft were to be made good through a gift; rather, the one who has demonstrated his ill will should now demonstrate his good will.

18[54]

162. We can doubt whether the good human being who thirsts for knowledge is well served by becoming ever better. A little more sin on occasion probably makes him wiser. Everyone will know from his own experience in what condition he had the most deeply understanding sympathy with the uncertainty of society and of marriage.[45]

18[55][46]

163. The thief, once punished, really has a claim upon compensation, inasmuch as he has lost his reputation due to administration of justice. What he suffers from this, that he is from now on considered a thief, goes far beyond atoning for a one-time debt.

18[56][47]

164. The Catholic Church has, through the institution of confession, created an ear into which we can divulge our secret

without dangerous consequences. This was a great easing of life, for we forget our guilt from the moment when we have related it to others, but generally others do not forget it.

18[57][48]
165. Anyone who really places nonexistence higher than existence should in relation to his neighbor rather promote the latter's nonexistence than his existence; because the moralists want to avoid this demand, they invent principles such as that everyone can release only himself into nonexistence.[49]

18[58][50]
167. No previous ethics lets itself be based upon the pure knowledge of things; from that, there follows only this, that we, like nature, must be neither good nor evil. The demand to be good arises out of impure knowing.

18[59]
168. Injustice sometimes leaves behind a wound in the one who does it, yet not often. The bites of conscience[51] are more the exception than the rule. To offend someone who is repugnant to us so that we are freed from associating with him even produces a blessed sigh of relief at the freedom attained. But perhaps doing injustice is self-defense here.

18[60][52]
169. The statesman must be able to project a good conscience about his undertakings and needs for this enthusiastic honest people and, even more, those who are able to seem to be so.

18[61][53]
173. Anyone who also has the drive toward cleanliness in spiritual matters will[54] put up with religions only for a short time and then flee into a metaphysics; later he will also divest himself of metaphysics, step by step. It is probable that the drive toward cleanliness in moral matters will more likely adopt an

opposite path; this drive is always tied instead to impurity of thinking and makes this perhaps ever more impure.

18[62][55]

176. The plowshare cuts into hard and soft earth, it passes over what is high and what is low, and brings it near. This book is for one who is good and one who is evil, for the lowly and the powerful. Someone evil who reads it will become better, someone good worse, the lesser stronger, the stronger less.

[19 = U II 5c. October–December 1876]

Bex,[1] from 3 October on

19[1][2]
1. Philology is the art of learning and teaching how to read, in an age that reads too much. Only the philologist reads slowly and reflects upon six lines for half an hour. Not his result, but instead this training is his achievement.

19[2][3]
2. The history of philology is the history of a species of diligent, but untalented humans. Hence the senseless fighting and subsequent overestimation of a few sharp-witted and richer natures who *fell in* among *the philologists*.

19[3]
3. That the philologists are qualified (more so, e.g., than the physicians) to educate the youth is a prejudice that is, in addition, proved daily by experience to be a lie. We therefore do here as with street-sweepers, whom nobody tests either as to whether they understand best how to sweep the streets; it is enough that they have the will to do this unclean business. Likewise, every class turns down the business of educating the youth and is content that the philologists — do not do it.

19[4]

4. Antiquity has been discovered in all essentials by artists statesmen and philosophers, not by philologists: and this up to the present day.

19[5]

5. That one understands a Sophoclean tragedy wrongly in 100 places and simply passes over many corrupt passages, yet can still understand and explain the tragedy better than the most painstaking philologist, is what the philologists do not want to believe.

Anyone who reads a clever author and believes at the end that he has understood everything, exc.[4] — he is lucky.[5]

19[6]

6. I believe that I understand Shakespeare[6] better than teachers of modern English, even though I make many mistakes. Generally, in fact, everyone will understand an old author better than the philological language teacher: why is this so? — Because philologists are nothing other than aged high schoolers.

19[7]

8. Subtler minds are exposed to pressure from those who are always telling tales at which one should *laugh*: where it does not suffice to smile.

19[8]

12. A master will choose to associate with masters of other arts and be among **his** pupils, but not with colleagues and definitely not with those who are only professionals and not masters.

19[9][7]

14. Those who can rejoice with us stand higher and nearer to us than those who suffer with us. Shared joy makes the "friend" (the one with whom we rejoice),[8] shared suffering the companion in suffering. — An ethic of compassion needs supplementation by the still-higher ethic of friendship.

19[10][9]
15. People become Protestants Catholics Turks according to their homeland, as someone born in a country producing wine becomes a drinker of wine.

19[11][10]
17. Whoever on the whole denies himself many things will readily allow himself to indulge in small things. So there has perhaps existed no professional class that understood the erotic so exclusively as debauchery as the Catholic priestly class that renounced *love*. In exchange, it allowed itself the occasional *lust*.

19[12][11]
18. Someone can *speak very much to the point* and yet in such a way that everyone in the world cries out about the opposite. Thus Socrates spoke very much to the point, but in front of a world-historical forum: his judges judged in the opposite sense. — Masters talk down to their listeners.[12]

19[13][13]
19. If someone does not have a good father, he should provide himself with one. That a son adopts a father for himself is more reasonable than the opposite: because he knows much more precisely what he needs.

19[14]
20. The prestige of doctors rests upon the ignorance of those who are healthy and sick: and this ignorance rests in turn upon the prestige of doctors.

19[15]
21. The best doctor will be able to have only a single patient; every human being is a medical history.[14]

19[16]
23. To guess at and to expose an author who does not name himself means treating him as if one were dealing with a

disguised criminal or a mischievous beauty, which may be permitted often enough: but there are cases where we have to honor his reticence at least as much as that of a prince traveling incognito.

19[17][15]

The estimation of qualities can only be comparative, our own interest wants the *highest* estimation.

Competition or annihilation.

19[18][16]

24. The illusion of the sexual drive is a net that, when it is torn, always knits itself back together.[17]

19[19]

27. In order to derive the benefit from a dangerous speculation in money, we must do as with a cold bath — quickly in, quickly out.

19[20]

28. The dramatic musician must have not only ears, but also eyes in his ears.

19[21][18]

32. Workers complain that they are overworked. But the same overworking is found everywhere, among businesspeople scholars public officials soldiers: among the rich classes, overworking appears as the inner drive of an all too great activity, among workers it is imposed from without, that is the difference.[19] A moderation of this drive would indirectly benefit the worker, too. He would prefer not to believe that the present-day banker lives with richer pleasures or with more dignity than he does.

19[22][20]

35. Most writers write badly because they communicate to us not their thoughts, but instead the thinking of the thoughts. It

is often vanity that makes the sentences so full, it is the accompanying cackle of the hen that wants to make us notice the egg, namely a small thought standing in the middle of a full sentence.[21]

19[23]

36. A human being is furthest away from the animal as a child, his intellect at its most human. With the fifteenth year and puberty, he comes one step closer to the animal, with the possessive sensibility of his thirties (the middle line between laziness and covetous desire) one additional step. In his sixties he frequently loses even his shame; then the seventy-year-old steps before us as an unveiled beast: just look out for eyes and teeth.

19[24][22]

38. Disobedience and independence, especially inward, of the sons toward the fathers generally goes precisely as far as possible, i.e., as the father in any way still puts up with; from which it results that it is much more uncomfortable to be a father than a son.

19[25][23]

Irony is ignoble.

19[26]

41. As soon as we have grasped that a prince is no longer of any account, when political changes have occurred in his country,[24] and is still of interest only for the courtiers and country people, we should get out of his way, since we dare not deal with him as a private individual.[25]

19[27]

42. The active person wants to distract himself with art, the artist demands the greatest concentration. In consequence, they have to be dissatisfied with each other and set upon each other. Art does not really exist for these active people at all,

but instead for those who have a surplus of leisure time and can therefore bestow their highest seriousness[26] once in a while upon the artist: those active people (whether they be workers or bankers or public officials) have to provide for the existence of this class of idle Olympians with their excess labor.[27] If[28] the existence of this class is a bad thing, then art is a bad thing, too.

Art the activity of idle people.

Pleasures form the leisure of active people.

19[28]

43. In 50 years every energetic man in Europe will be an expert in weapons and military maneuvers, the better qualified one even in tactics. From then on, anyone who brings opinions to power can know that he has gained an experienced[29] army for his opinions. That will determine the history of opinions.

19[29][30]

45. Three-fourths of all lies have come into the world by antithesis.

19[30][31]

Tone of youth too loud.

19[31][32]

The vain person and the lover imagine that they are vain or in love because of another person.

19[32][33]

50. The best author is ashamed of being a writer, he is too rich in thoughts and too noble not to be ashamed to allow his wealth to be seen other than occasionally.[34]

19[33]

51. To bring a grape and a talent to ripeness, one needs as many days of rain as of sun.

19[34]
52. We underestimate the value of an evil act if we do not take into account how many tongues it sets in motion, how much energy it unleashes and for how many people it serves as matter for reflection or elevation.

19[35]
53. The eclipse of Europe can depend upon whether five or six freer spirits remain true to themselves or not.

19[36][35]
54. No one is responsible for their actions, no one for their nature: judging is the same as being unjust. This holds equally true when an individual judges himself. — The principle is as clear as daylight and yet here everyone prefers to go back into shadows and into untruth: from fear of losing their power of sight completely, therefore because of the supposed consequences.

19[37]
55. Morality becomes widespread only when what illuminates the intellect makes known to us the greatest possible number of new and higher possibilities for action and thereby offers for selection a host of new motives for action, so that we are given opportunities. A human being is very often seized by a lower motive only because he did not know a higher one, and he remains mediocre and lowly in his actions because no opportunity was offered to him to show his greater and purer instincts. — Many people wait their entire lives for the opportunity to be good in *their* way.[36]

19[38][37]
56. In the choice between a bodily and spiritual posterity, we have to weigh in favor of the latter that here we are father and mother in a single person and that the child, when it is born, requires no further education, but instead only its introduction into the world.

19[39][38]

59. Philosophy can gradually deliver us from two bad sensations: first, from the fear upon the deathbed, because there is nothing to be afraid of there, second, from the regret and pangs of conscience after an action, because every action was completely unavoidable. With regard to everything in the past, a cold fatalism is the philosophical disposition.

The uneasiness after an action, however, may not be less if I perceive that it was necessity: it is a pain that cannot be ameliorated by reproach revenge etc. For its entire nature, its *esse*[39] in accusing the action is only one new step in the same irrationality that wants to make us responsible for every individual action. Because the uneasiness exists, so must responsibility exist, somewhere therefore, a freedom: thus did Schopenhauer come upon the concept of intelligible freedom. But the fact of the uneasiness does not prove the rational reasonableness of this uneasiness: and only if it were so would we be able to draw the further conclusion in the Schopenhauerian way. — The uneasiness, moreover, certainly does exist now, but the habit can perhaps be broken.

But if a bad clumsy action does not have any uneasiness as a result, this cold disposition to which one would have become accustomed with regard to the past, would also have uprooted the joy in what was done. Now the behavior of humans, however, is determined by anticipation of the pleasure or displeasure to be gained from it: if this is lost, no feeling would restrain them any longer from a bad action and nothing would draw them any longer toward a good action. They would be just as cold with regard to what is to come as with regard to what is in the past. Now would commence the cold deliberation as to whether living or not-living is to be preferred: and suicide resulting from presence of mind would be the consequence. In knowing or intimating this state of affairs, every human being and every ethics as well resists the abolition of freedom: the latter wrongly, since philosophy should have absolutely no regard for the consequences of truth, but only for truth. — [40] That life as a whole should not result in any feeling (pleasure or displeasure) is warded off for the same reason (hence the significance that is ascribed to the deathbed).

19[40]
65. "Become the one, who you are":[41] that is the call that is *always* allowed to only a few people, but is superfluous for the fewest of these few.

19[41][42]
66. The ethics of every pessimistic religion consists of evasions of suicide.

19[42][43]
70. And what came to the assistance of her virtue? The voice of conscience? — Oh no, the voice of the neighbor.

19[43][44]
71. Self-sufficient people sometimes show themselves to be vain out of good-naturedness: e.g., in order not to cast shame on the vanity of specific classes.

19[44][45]
72. The self-sufficient person becomes vain when he senses the higher self-sufficiency of someone else, which, however, rarely occurs.

19[45][46]
73. No conclusion can be drawn about talent, as to whether someone is predominantly vain or self-sufficient: the greatest genius is sometimes vain as a young girl and would be in a position to color his hair. This vanity is perhaps a habit left over and magnified since the time when he still had no right to believe in himself and first had to beg for the small change of this belief from other people.

19[46]
79. We frequently escape our pursuers better by going more slowly than by going more quickly; that holds true especially for literary pursuers.

19[47][47]
Kotzebue — "in him we live and move and have our being."[48]
Shakespeare, accident in the history of the theater.
Schiller is a better theater-poet.

19[48]
84. The pious person feels himself superior to the impious person: I will believe in Christian humility when I see that the pious person humbles himself before the impious person.

19[49][49]
I change many rhythms of the lines on account of the reader.

19[50]
90. We prefer to bestow upon someone all of our heart rather than all of our money. — How does that come about? — We bestow our heart and have it still, but the money we no longer have.

19[51]
93. No writer up until now has had enough spirit to be permitted to write rhetorically.

19[52]
96. A beautiful woman really does have something in common with the truth (whatever the slanderers might say!): both make us happier when they are desired than when they are possessed.

19[53]
99. An alliance is firmer if the allies believe in one another than if they know about one another: for which reason among lovers the alliance is firmer before the marital union than after it.

19[54][50]

100. No prince who wants to wage war was ever at a loss for a *casus belli.*[51] But all motives that we acknowledge publicly show that all of us are never at a loss for a *casus belli*. Every action is done from motives and from a presumed[52] motive.

19[55]

103. A statesman divides human beings into two kinds, first tools, second enemies. Therefore there is really only a single kind of human being for him: enemies.

19[56][53]

108. Either we make our outer lives hard and our internal lives easy for ourselves with the help of a religion or the reverse: the first is the case with Christianity, the latter with the perishing of religions. From this it results that a religion comes into being in order to unburden the heart and perishes when it no longer has anything here to unburden.[54]

19[57]

110. "A spirit is precisely as deep as he is high," someone said. Now, with the expression "high spirit" one thinks of the force and energy of the upswing, of flight, with the expression "deep spirit" of the remoteness of the goal toward which the spirit has made its way. The proposition therefore means to say: a spirit gets just as far as he can fly. But this is not true: rarely does a spirit get as far as he was really able to fly. Therefore the proposition must go: rarely is a spirit as deep as he is high.

19[58]

111. If formerly smallpox put the strength and health of a bodily constitution to the test and the people who did not come through it became deadly:[55] so now we can perhaps consider the religious infection as such a test for the strength and health of the spiritual constitution. Either we overcome it or we perish spiritually from it.

19[59]

Elements of Cultivation

1) Errors.
2) False conclusions.
3) Passions.
4) The constrained spirits.
5) Forgetfulness.
6) The human being as a thing.
7) The degenerated natures.
8) The emergence of the sense for truth.
9) Future of culture.

19[60]

113. The treaties of European states are now effective exactly as long as the pressure that created them is still there. That is therefore a situation in which force (in the physical sense) decides and leads to its consequence. This is the following one: the great states swallow up the small states, the monster state swallows up the great state — and the monster state bursts apart because eventually it lacks the belt that could encompass its body: the hostility of neighbors. Splitting into atomic state-structures is the most distant still-plausible perspective for European politics. Battle of society within itself carries on the habit of war.

19[61][56]

114. There are no educators anymore; under this name we are always only buying people who are themselves not educated. — There are teachers, but no educators, stablemen, but no riders.

19[62][57]

116. From time to time, a party attempts to clean off some tatters of dirtied Christianity and to clothe itself with them — the effect is slight: for freshly washed rags clothe cleanly, to be sure, but still only in rags.

19[63][58]

117. At the sight of the countless churches that Christianity built once upon a time, we have to say to ourselves: there is not religion enough at present to clear away these buildings. Likewise: there is lacking now religion enough even to destroy religion.

19[64][59]

112. Public opinions come from private laziness. But what comes from private opinions? — Public passions.

19[65]

118) *we live in a culture that is perishing from the means to culture.*[60]

Abolition of nations — the European human being.
Abstention from politics.
Drawing aside of talents.
Contempt for the press.
Religion and art only as remedies.
Simple life.
Disdain for social differences.
Higher tribunal for the sciences.
Liberation of women.
Friendships — intertwined circles.
Organization of the economy of the spirit.
Institutions follow opinions automatically.

19[66][61]

Greeting to the Moralists.

Absence of moralists.[62]
The active people.[63]
Those who want to become free.[64]
Free spirit.[65]
Wounding.[66]
Impossible without productivity — therefore free spirit.[67]
Sigh over earlier youth.[68]
Father or mother.[69]

Production of genius.[70] Middle of the way.[71]
Poets as *easers*.[72]
Aesthetics.[73]
Poets. Writers. Philologists.[74]
Art — active people.[75]
Society.[76]
Woman and child.[77]
State (Greeks).[78]
Religious matters.[79]
Higher moral propositions (good and Evil) (vanity).[80]
Highest easing of life.[81]
fatum tristissimum.[82,83]

19[67]

Voice of history.[84]
Everything general first:
Free-spirited stroll:[85] in order to detach human beings from what is traditional.
1. By oneself alone.
2. Woman and child.
3. Society.
4. Art — poets — aesthetics.
5. State.
6. Religious matters.
7. Easing of life.

19[68]

Homo liber de nulla re minus quam de morte cogitate et ejus sapientia non mortis sed vitae meditatio est.[86] Spinoza.

19[69]

Anyone who thinks more acutely does not like the images of poets, too many unlike things are brought into memory all at once; as someone who hears acutely hears the overtones of a tone as discordance.

19[70]

c. 4. the free spirit and the philosopher.
5. within a culture: examples.
6. contemporary position.
7. future.

19[71]

The compassionate person feels himself to be the stronger one, which leads to the desire to be ready to intervene, if only he could help. Pain like the aesthetic[87] an after-echo.

19[72]

Themes:

On maxims.
On the novella.
Against the poets.
The philosopher out of pleasure, who does indeed think about precursors, but not about successors (pleasure in what?).
Difference between free spirit and philosopher.
Thucydides as ideal of the free spirit–sophist.
Origin of compassion.
Suicide in the religions.
The sick person.
Vanities of scholars.

19[73]

We attempt to bring into *connection* with one another the things that call forth a similar sensation in us e.g., spring love beauty nature, divinity etc. This interweaving of things corresponds *in no way at all* to the real causal linkage. Poets and philosophers love to arrange things thus; art and morality come together.

19[74]

They call the unification of the German governments into a single state a "great idea." It is the same sort of people who will one day become enthusiastic about the united states of Europe: it is the still "greater idea."

19[75][88]

The diversity of languages is what prevents us the most from seeing what is basically taking place — the vanishing of what is national and the creation of the European human being.

19[76]

All of the foundations of culture have decayed: therefore culture must perish.

19[77]

The 10 Commandments of the Free Spirit.

Thou shalt neither love nor hate peoples.
Thou shalt not engage in politics.
Thou shalt not be rich and not a beggar.
Thou shalt avoid those who are famous and influential.
Thou shalt take thy wife from a different people than thine own.
Thou shalt let thy children be educated by thy friends.
Thou shalt subject thyself to no ceremony of the church.
Thou shalt not regret an offense, but for its sake do one good deed more.
Thou shalt prefer exile in order to be able to speak the truth.
Thou shalt let the world be against thyself and thyself against the world.[89]

19[78]

Chap. II. The Free Spirit in the Present Time.
Chap. III. Goals of the Free Spirit: Future of Humanity.
Chap. IV. Emergence of the Free Spirit.

19[79]

Future in a few centuries. Economy of the earth, allowing bad races to die out, breeding of better ones, one language. Wholly new conditions for humans, even for a higher being? It is now the business class that prevents a complete sinking back into barbarism (telegraphy, geography, industr⟨ial⟩ invention, etc.).

19[80][90]

To speak the truth when untruth rules is mingled with so much pleasure that a human being chooses exile, in fact even worse things, for its sake.

19[81]

Il maudit les savants et ne voulut plus vivre qu'en bonne compagnie.[91] Voltaire (Zadig)

19[82]

Philologists.

Why are high school students becoming more stupid? Due to the example of teachers who make everything seem stupid, the authors etc.

Why are philologists so zealous about corrupt passages? From vanity: the ancients mean nothing[92] to them, but they mean a great deal to themselves.

Is there an intellectually stimulating edition for schools?

19[83]

Because humans do not find much of value in the world to the extent that it is explicable, they think that what is true and important would have to lie in what is inexplicable; they tie their highest sensations and presentiments to what is dark inexplicable. Now, nothing at all essential needs to lie in this unilluminated realm, it *could* be empty: the same thing, moreover, would result for a human being if he had only one dark place in his knowledge: from that he then conjures forth what he needs[93] and populates the dark passage with ghosts and presentiments.

19[84]

If humans accustom themselves to hold strictly to the truth and to be on guard against everything metaphysical unilluminated, the pleasure from poetic fictions might someday be connected to the feeling of doing something forbidden: it would be a sweet pleasure, but without pangs of conscience afterward and along with it.

19[85]

The so-called metaphysical need proves nothing about a reality corresponding to this need: on the contrary, because we are needy here, we hear the language of the will, not that of the intellect and go astray if we believe this voice. A god would have to be presumed if he were provable, *without* a need letting him seem necessary to us.

19[86]

Themes.

Of the free spirit.
The inexplicable and the explicable.
Downfall of the old culture.
Causes of art.
Suicide.
Vanity of scholars.
Maxims.
The writer.
The sick person.
The perfectibility of humans.
On the novella.
Association.
The intellect of women.
Friendship.
Phases of morality.
On power.
Simplicity o⟨f the⟩ good.
Hope.

Nobility.
Battle against fate.
Good and evil.
Replacement for religious motives.
Promising.
Intellect and morality.
Boredom — idleness.
Punishment and regret.
Philologists as teachers.
Thucydides type of the Sophist⟨ic⟩ free sense.

19[87]

The judgments of the jury are wrong for the same reason for which the grading of a pupil by a teaching staff is wrong: they result from a negotiation among various judgments that have been made: presuming the most favorable case, that *one* of the jurors has judged correctly, the composite result is in the middle between the correct and several wrong judgments i.e., in any case wrong.

19[88]

A poet must not have so specific a concept of his public in his soul as the painter does of a specific distance from which the picture is supposed be viewed correctly and which demands a specific visual acuity from the viewer. More recent poetic creations are only partially enjoyed by us, everyone picks what to each of them tastes good; we do not stand in the necessary relationship to these works of art. The poets themselves are uncertain[94] and have now this, now that audience in mind; they do not themselves believe that we grasp their entire intention and attempt to please through details or through the subject matter. How everything that now makes a storyteller good is lost upon the contemporary public: which wants only the subject matter of the story and would like to be interested carried away overpowered: through facts, which criminal acts, e.g., embody the best, not through the art of the storyteller.[95]

19[89][96]

Prehistoric ages are determined for immeasurable periods of time by tradition, nothing occurs. In historical time, the fact is every time a loosening from tradition, a difference of opinion, it is *free-spiritedness* that makes history. The more quickly the turnaround of opinions ensues, the more quickly the world runs, the chronicle transforms itself into the journal, and finally the telegraph confirms how within hours the opinions of humans have changed.

19[90]

A beautiful woman must have many good qualities in marriage, in order to help make up for the fact that she is beautiful.

19[91]

Communicability of truth, of opinions in general.

19[92]

What does an opinion *accomplish*? — asks the statesman. Is it a force?

19[93][97]

Humans become *accustomed to appraising* an *unfamiliar opinion more highly* than their own.

19[94][98]

Pious people ask: does this opinion make you happy? — that counts as proof for and against the truth. Now, if a crazy person believes he is God and is happy in this — as does happen — it is proven in consequence that a god exists.

19[95]

In a tragedy, the eloquence that will necessarily prevail is precisely the one practiced and highly esteemed in a given age. So with the Greeks, so with the French, so too with Shakespeare. In him, the Spanish influence that prevailed in Elizabeth's court is unmistakable: the profusion of images, their far-fetchedness is not generally human, but Spanish. In the Italian novella as in Le Sage, the refined rhetorical culture of the nobility and the Renaissance prevails. — We have no courtly eloquence, nor any public one, like the Greeks: therefore there is nothing to be done with speech in drama, it is naturalizing. Goethe in *Tasso* has recourse to the model of the Renaissance. Schiller depends upon the French. Wagner gives up completely the art of speech.

19[96]

Humans have a tendency, when they seek for reasons for what is traditional, always to assign the deepest reasons. For they sense the tremendous beneficent consequences, so they seek for a deep wisdom-filled intention in the soul of those who implanted tradition. — But the case is the reverse: the emergence of God, of marriage is shallow and stupid, the foundation of tradition must be placed very low intellectually.

19[97]

If we throw off a *belief*, we do not throw off the *consequences* that have grown out of it. These live on thanks to tradition: tradition closes our eyes concerning the bond between belief and consequence. The consequence seems to exist on its own account. The consequence denies its father.

19[98]

What is the *reaction of opinions*? If an opinion ceases to be interesting, we seek to lend charm to it by holding it up against the opposite opinion. But the opposite opinion generally leads us astray and makes new followers: it has in the meantime become more interesting.

19[99]

Aristotle thinks that through tragedy the excess of compassion and fear is purged, the audience member returns home *colder*. Plato, on the contrary, thinks that he is more susceptible to emotion and fear than ever. — Plato's question about the moral significance of art has not yet been posed again.[99] The artist needs the unleashing of passion. We scarcely allow ourselves to take pleasure anymore in the passions that the Athenian comic dramatist wants to purge from his audience: lust slanderousness indecency etc. Actually, Athens became soft. Art cannot be considered as a replacement for religion: because for someone who has finished, it is superfluous, for someone who is struggling, no replacement for religion, but at most a secondary assistance for religion. — Perhaps its place is as Mainländer takes it to be, a secondary assistance for knowledge, it allows us to see peace and the great success of knowledge from far away, like blue mountains. The replacement for religion is not art, but knowledge.[100]

19[100][101]

Religions do not express any truths whatsoever *sensu allegorico*,[102] but *no* truths *at all* — that is to be objected against Schopenhauer. The *consensus gentium*[103] in religious views is instead more of a counterargument against any underlying truth. Not an age-old priestly wisdom, but instead the fear of what is inexplicable is the origin of religion: what there is of reason in it has entered into it by underhanded ways.

19[101]

The study of psychology belonged to ancient rhetoric. How far behind we are! The party press really does have a smidgen of psychology, also of diplomacy — all as practice. Modern psychology is indispensable for the reformer.

19[102]

The modern reformer takes human beings to be like clay. With time and institutions, anything can be made out of them, we can make them into animals and into angels. There is little solid there. "Reforming of humanity!"

19[103][104]

It is all to be conceded, what religion has done for humans that is useful: directly lending happiness and comfort. If we cannot unite truth with utility, its case is lost. Why should humanity sacrifice itself for truth? Indeed, it cannot really do so. All striving for truth up until now has utility in mind: the distant usefulness of mathematics was what the father was attending to in his studying son. One would have taken as idiotic a person who occupied himself with something from which nothing, or even injury, resulted. One took as generally dangerous anyone who pollutes the air that humans breathe. If religion is necessary in order to live, then the one who unsettles it is generally dangerous: if the lie is necessary, it should not be unsettled. Therefore — is truth possible in connection with life? —

19[104][105]

We care for ourselves — and then also for our sons: the latter concern prevents a human being from living completely individually and carelessly. He wants institutions that benefit his son. The continuation of humanity depends upon this: if people had no children, everything would fall apart. Caring for the child involves caring for possessions and a secure position: for property and order in society. Greed and ambition are the drives that are perhaps connected with this concern about one's brood: they are very large as a result of inheritance, even if in special cases the brood is lacking: when striving has its purpose, its head cut off: the body nonetheless still moves.

19[105]

A good educator can have it happen that he deeply offends the pupil simply in order to stifle in the germ a stupid thing that he wants to say.

19[106][106]

The martyr against his will and the honorable person who is disdained, as a coward etc., whereas he is only as he *can* be.

19[107][107]

It is the way of constrained spirits to prefer *any explanation whatsoever* to none; in this they are undemanding. High culture demands that we allow many things to stand peacefully unexplained. ἐπέχω.[108]

19[108][109]

The *obscure thing* counts as more important more dangerous than the clear one. Fear lives in the most inward part of human fantasy. The final form of religion consists of really conceding dark inexplicable regions; within them, however, we think the world riddle must be hiding.

19[109]

Through houses built on stilts[110] etc. is proven that there has been a *step forward* for humanity. But whether this assumption is permitted on the basis of the last 4000 ⟨years⟩ of humanity is doubtful. But science has made progress: with that, the highest form of the preceding culture has been annihilated and can never emerge again.

19[110][111]

Instinct is like a worm whose head we have cut off and which nonetheless moves farther in the same direction.

19[111]

Love is not at all explained by Schopenhauer. Just sexuality.[112] Then a special inclination out of aesthetic co-judgments, which have become very strong by inheritance. The black man wants the black woman and disdains the white one. With the "genius of the species" nothing at all has been gained.[113]

19[112]

Not in order to be immortal, nor with regard to propagation do humans *fall in love*: against Plato.[114] Instead, for the sake of pleasure. They would do it even if women were infertile; properly then, for the first time! Greek pederasty is not unnatural, the *causa finalis* of which, according to Plato, is supposed to be "to engender beautiful speeches."[115]

19[113][116]

Every human being takes the greatest interest in himself, but is accustomed to respecting the judgment of others more highly than his own: belief in authority, inherited and bred in, foundation of society morality etc. From these two premises *vanity* results: a human being confirms for himself his own value through the judgment of others.

19[114]

Everything moral has at some time been not yet "moral," but compulsion. Only since tradition exists do good actions exist.

19[115]

To trace *unegoistical* impulses back to egoistical ones is methodologically imperative. The social instinct goes back to the individual who comprehends that he will be preserved only if he incorporates himself into an association. Esteem for what is social will then be inherited and, since the most useful members are also the most honored, continually further strengthened. Now a bright flame exists, to suffer anything for the fatherland (also for every similar organization, e.g., science). The egoistical purpose is forgotten. The "good" emerges when we forget the origin. — The parental instinct is first bred to maturity in society, we need descendants, so we take marriage under our protection and honor it. — Unegoistical love, too (between the sexes), is certainly at first a compulsory thing, *compelled* by society. Only later customary and inherited and finally like an original impulse. At first, the drive goes only toward satisfaction, without concern for the other individual, cruel. — Are all parental instincts of animals also to be traced back to society? —

19[116][117]

Here begin the "thoughts and drafts" from fall and winter 1876.

22 December 1876 I wrote this last page.

19[117][118]

Introduction.

In memory of Goethe "if someone speaks he should speak positively."

19[118]

Human and All Too Human.
Sociable Sayings.

19[119][119]

The maxim as theme of sociability.

19[120]

The Old Culture.

1. Impure thinking in the foundation of culture.[120]
2. Morality.
3. Religion.
4. Art (language).
5. The free spirits.
6. Women.
7. Saints.
8. The estimation of life.
9. Law.
10. Peoples.
11. Science.
12. Vanishing of the old culture.

[20 = Mp XIV 1a (Brenner). Winter 1876–1877]

20[1][1]
14. There is a double aesthetic. The one proceeds from the effects of art and draws conclusions about the corresponding causes; by proceeding thus, it stands under the magic of art and is itself a sort of poetry and intoxication: a resounding of art into the strings of science. The other aesthetic proceeds from the frequently absurd and childish beginnings of art: it is not capable of deriving the actual effects from this and will therefore attempt to limit the feeling about art in general and to cast suspicion upon those effects in every way, as though they were made up or sickly. From which it becomes clear which aesthetic is useful to art, which not and to what extent neither can be a science.

20[2][2]
16. — — — In fact, these consequences are questionable. If a bad, clumsy action at some point no longer has any uneasiness as a result, this cold disposition, to which we would have become accustomed with regard to what is past, would have also uprooted the joy in what was done. Now the behavior of humans, however, is determined by the anticipation of the pleasure or displeasure to be gained from them: if this is lost with regard to so-called moral pleasure or displeasure, then no feeling restrains

them any longer from a bad action, and nothing would draw them any longer toward a good action: except perhaps the regard for what is useful or harmful; morality would give way to a doctrine of utility. Humans would be just as cold and shrewd with regard to what is to come as with regard to what is past. Then they would be ripe for cold deliberation about what value their present lives have, which could still be painful enough, along with the consideration as to whether nonexistence is to be preferred to existence. In recognizing or sniffing out this state of affairs, every human being and every philosophical ethic as well, resists the abolition of responsibility: the latter wrongly, since philosophy should have absolutely no regard for the consequences of truth, but only for truth itself. — That the life of a human being as a whole should not result in any feeling of pleasure or displeasure, but instead finish with annihilation and complete lack of sensation, is generally rejected for the same reason: we are afraid of weakening the faith in the value of life and encouraging the pleasure of suicide. The will to life defends itself against the conclusions of reason and attempts to obscure them; hence the significance that we ascribe to the final moments of life upon the deathbed, as if there were still something there to fear or to hope for.

20[3]

1. A maxim is one link out of a chain of ideas; it requires that the reader reconstruct this chain with his own devices: that means it requires a great deal. A maxim is a presumption. — Or it is a warning: as Heraclitus knew. In order to be enjoyable, a maxim must first be stirred up and mingled with other materials (example, experiences, stories). Most people do not understand this and one can therefore express objectionable things unobjectionably in maxims.

20[4]
12. We get into an intense affective state of love more easily from a state of being smitten with another person than from one of complete coldness and freedom of disposition.

20[5]
20. How much more goodness and happiness there would be among humans if henceforth they would give to one another what of time, energy, wealth, overcoming of the heart, selflessness, love, they have up to now given to God. How much more? — Perhaps not so very much.

20[6][3]
21. Many people want to convince or persuade themselves of their own worth through the praise, amazement, envy of others; this matters much more to them than everything else and they make use of every means, even those of outwitting or intoxicating themselves. Indeed, they prefer a hundred times more to admire themselves than to be useful for themselves, and love themselves much more than is advantageous for them. In them, vanity is only the means to self-satisfaction. They want not so much to be prominent as to feel prominent, no matter whether they are.

20[7][4]
25. Where does envy of the gods originate? It seems that the Greeks did not believe in a peaceful and calm, but instead only in an arrogant and wanton happiness; it embittered them to see a happy person. They must on the whole have felt dispirited; for their souls were all too easily wounded by the sight of happiness. Wherever there was a distinguished talent, the throng of jealous people was exceptionally large. If he encountered misfortune, they said: it was necessary, too, he was far too arrogant; and yet everyone would have behaved the same, that is, arrogantly, if they had had the same talent; just as, when given the opportunity, everyone liked to play the god who sends misfortune upon talent.

20[8][5]

30. Vanity has two sources, either in the feeling of weakness or in that of power. A human being, as soon as he perceives his helplessness as an individual and the measure of his energies and possessions, thinks about exchange with his neighbors. The higher they assess his energies and possessions, so much the more can he gain for himself through this exchange. Now he knows only too precisely the weak sides of all that he possesses. Therefore he conceals these and turns the light upon the strong, dazzling qualities. This is one form of vanity; in addition, there exists the other one, which wants to awaken the appearance of dazzling qualities that in truth are not there: both together form the clear-sighted vanity (which is dissimulation). The person who is vain in this way wants to produce coveting toward himself and thereby a higher assessment. Envy emerges when someone is covetous, but has no or hardly any prospect of satisfying his coveting through exchange. We are all covetous toward others' possessions. First, because we know too well the weaknesses of our own possessions and their merits have become unattractive to us out of habit, and then because the other has placed his possessions in the most favorable light. We seem to be more in love with our own possessions, in order to let them appear more desirable. In an exchange,[6] everyone believes he has had an advantage over the others and has the higher gain for himself. The barterer takes himself to be clever; clear-sighted vanity increases in people the belief in their cleverness. The barterer believes he is the deceiver, but the one with whom he is exchanging believes the same of himself. — We cherish being envied because others who do not envy us, but can offer an exchange, are forced by the heightened coveting of envious people to a higher assessment of our goods. — The feeling of power, inherited, engenders blind vanity (whereas the other one was the open-eyed kind, looking for advantage); power does not discuss and compare, it takes itself for the highest power, it makes the highest claims;[7] if others offer their talents and energies with the same claims, there remains only war: the justice of these claims will be decided either through competition or

through annihilation of one of the competitors, at least of his outstanding capacity; jealousy[8] is the irritated state of someone powerful in relation to a powerful competitor; envy, the hopeless state of not being able to gain precedence over him: therefore when he is defeated in war. The envy of open-eyed vanity emerges from unsatisfied coveting; the envy of blind vanity is the consequence of a defeat.

20[9]

35. Resignation consists of a human being giving up the strong exertion of all the sinews of his thinking and feeling and placing himself back into a condition where his thinking and feeling become habitual and mechanical. This slackening is connected to a pleasure and the mechanical movement is at least without displeasure.

20[10][9]

38. We can suppress the greatest talent and spiritual inventiveness if we are insatiable in producing and allow the source waters no time to collect themselves.

20[11][10]

17. — — — To take the example of an excessive and almost unsuccessful inoculation; the Germans, originally having the exceptional tenacity and soundness that Tacitus, the greatest admirer of their health, portrays, were by the inoculation of Roman culture not only wounded, but almost bled to death: one took from them as much as one could of custom, religion, freedom, language; they did not perish, but they have proven through their soulful relationship to music that they are a deeply suffering nation. No people has as many wounded places as the Germans, and for precisely this reason they have a greater talent for every form of free-spiritedness. — I want with this observation intentionally to remain with human beings and to guard against drawing conclusions about animal natures and their laws from the laws concerning human improvement on

the basis of weaker and degenerate natures. — From this entire observation, the free spirit can take the proof that he is useful for the constrained spirits, too: for he helps so that the productions of the constrained spirits, their state, their culture, their morality do not become fixed and die out; he permits the invigorating sap of rejuvenation to flow ever anew into stem and branches.

20[12][11]
22. It is perhaps the most important goal for humanity that the value of life be measured and the reason why humanity exists be correctly determined. It therefore awaits the appearance of the highest intellect; for only this can definitively stipulate the value or nonvalue of life. Under what conditions, however, will this highest intellect emerge? It appears that those who promote human welfare overall still set themselves at present completely different goals than engendering this highest, value-determining intellect. One desires to produce a good life for as many people as possible and understands this good life, moreover, superficially enough.

20[13]
4. We often love a place, a person and go out of their way in the future; so great is the curiosity of the heart.

20[14][12]
31. One must be very shallow to return home from the usual social gatherings without pangs of conscience.

20[15][13]
34. It is practical when associating with friends and spouses to have much trust, but little intimacy, when associating with the rest of the world, in contrast, little trust and much intimacy.

20[16]
79. A free spirit's conscience will bite him more if he began his marriage with church ceremonies than if he seduced a young

woman; although the latter is blameworthy and punishable, the former is not.

20[17][14]
108. Anyone who praises his health has one sickness more.

20[18][15]

Education into being a free spirit.

First stage:	under the dominion of personal usefulness.
Second stage:	under the dominion of tradition.
Third stage:	under the dominion of religion.
Fourth stage:	under the dominion of art.
Fifth stage:	under the dominion of a metaphysical philosophy.
Sixth stage:	under the viewpoint of general usefulness.
Seventh stage:	under the dominating intent for knowledge.

January to mid-February
Sorrento 1877

20[19]
operetta[16]
positivism completely necessary
fate
refined heroism[17]
a statesman philanthropist[18]

20[20]
We love rough consistency — Overbeck

20[21]
Melody of the European human being: from which it results that there is still something to be done with this human being.

What is now the reigning melody in Europa, *l'idée fixe musicale*?[19] An operetta melody[20] (naturally, excluding the deaf or[21] W⟨agner⟩).

[21 = N II 3. End of 1876–Summer 1877]

21[1][1]
glacier little stone little flower

21[2][2]
All writers *experience* things too consciously, too uncertainly.

21[3]
Comb, necklace, earrings brooch — *a single* style it is[3] filigree.[4]

21[4]
"respectable criminal"[5]
"the vanity of scholars"
"friendship"
"praise of error"
"the European human being"

21[5]
Vanity is consistent with self-contempt — higher viewpoint[6] upon suicide.

21[6][7]
Periods of grand mot⟨ives⟩ [— — —] the personal not the impersonal.

21[7]

Openness concealment — as starting points for the virtues of a lower population.

Noble — vulgar for the higher caste.

21[8][8]

We do not enjoy hearing about actions of which the narrator does not think us capable: or they must go completely into something astonishing and exceptional.

21[9]

the free spirit
marriage
the easy life
psychological observations

21[10]

The lively leaping movements of a whale cause joy as if they were indicating play and pleasure: meanwhile, it is the torment that nature[9] is causing inside him. Thus we admire the liveliness of great statesmen.

21[11]

Humanity, a machine with tremendous energies, functioning in a disorderly way.

21[12]

On volcanic soil everything flourishes.

21[13]

Schopenhauer to the world like a blind man[10] to writing.

21[14][11]

The foreboding intuitive-illogical element in *German* nature is a sign that it has remained backward, still determined by the Middle Ages — many privileges lie therein, as in all things.

21[15][12]

The German future is not that of the German purse.

21[16][13]

Cultivation of the eye more important than of the ear.

21[17]

Path from freethinking does not go toward acting freely (individually) but instead toward administrative reorganizing of institutions.

21[18]

Mammal engendering-animal[14]

21[19]

Eleventh finger — thimble

21[20][15]

It is wounding to be under obligation to those who are highly respected.

21[21][16]

Dream of the toad.

21[22]

Ambitious people condemned by sickness to inactivity become their own worst enemies. Active ambition is a dermatological sickness of the soul, it drives everything harmful outward.

21[23][17]

Anyone who permits himself to speak publicly is obligated to contradict himself publicly, too, as soon as he changes his opinions.

21[24]

There are only reasons against individual suicide. Strong medicine. Moral reasons not at all.

21[25][18]

We must not wish to be too much in the right, but not too little either.

21[26][19]

The friend the most moral human being. Aristotle.[20]

21[27][21]

Everything depends upon the *action* — utility.

21[28]

For contemporary European culture, characteristic are slow intoxication and standing still at a certain limit.

21[29][22]

We never think of a female friend or beloved[23] as much as when the friendship or love affair stands in its final quarter.

21[30][24]

Anyone who first tries tasting pleasures carefully will afterward have scarcely a mouthful of pleasantn⟨ess⟩ left over.

21[31][25]

What is egoistical is considered as *evil*, in most cases wrongly; for that it *does harm* does not give it this character. It wants to preserve itself, character of self-defense (even to have emotion of the nerves can be a need). To do harm without need and with intention is senseless.

21[32][26]

People complain that socialist workers have the same acquisitive bourgeois sensibility, as soon as they attain the goal.

False: That is what is right. Views from the position: nobody is a protectionist if — — —

21[33]

All social eating and drinking, offensive.

21[34]

To listen to music smoking eating and drinking — out of ponderous Lutheran good-naturedness.

21[35]

Against intoxication.

21[36][27]

Utility in the essence of morality — the border dweller as murderer.

21[37]

Inconsistency of principle, caught up in, grown into, growing further into the movement, sometimes giving the principle a different direction.

21[38][28]

Bell chimes — golden light through the window. Dream. Cause imaginatively imposed into this a posteriori as in sensations of the eye.

21[39][29]

Eduard Leuchtenberg Roon
Plowshare.
1 Maxims.
2 On the knowledge of human beings.
3 General orientation.
4 Religion.
5 Art.
6 Morality.

21[40][30]
Love and hatred idiotic one-eyed, likewise "will."

21[41][31]
The explanation of nature corresponding to our highest moods is metaphysical.

21[42][32]
Passage in Tristram on barbarity.
C. Desmoulins
Executioner[33]
Cynicism refreshes execution.

21[43][34]
Socialism is based upon the *decision* to posit humans as being *equal* and to be just toward each one: it is the highest morality.

21[44][35]
The charm of science still arises *now* through contrast.

21[45]
Anyone who can, follow me in justice toward various cultures.

21[46][36]
Philosophy is the fata morgana[37] that pretends to offer the solution to the exhausted disciples of the sciences.

21[47][38]
People of substance have an ebb and flow, an inclination and disinclination, in relation to the same things. We must each of these various currents — — —

21[48][39]
Truth here stands completely on its head, a state of things that is particularly unbecoming for truth.

21[49][40]

Funeral hearse in the carnival once historical as the other floats are now.

21[50]

Tristan: Up- and over-swing of passion.

21[51][41]

Certain bits of knowledge protect themselves: we do not understand them.

21[52][42]

Faith in truth
Anyone who humbles himself
Compassion keeps silent

21[53][43]

Science causes pleasure in the one who advances it: *very little* in the one who receives the results.

But otherwise with art religion etc. We[44] must hold the kingdom of untruth within us: this is the tragedy.

21[54]

Violet (more red than blue) carpets curtains calming for the *nerves*, an American doctor has cured insanity with these.

21[55][45]

Even if someone has broken the habit of a religion, he still believes a proposition has been better proven if its disposition seems religious to us e.g., "a completely confident gospel."

21[56][46]

A. Conditions of educators.

1. contemplativeness
2. having lived through several cultures
3. a science.

⟨B.⟩ Themes:

C. Recuperations — — —

Centers of culture necessary, otherwise superficiality: why are the courts, the universities, the large cities not this?

21[57]

Plowman.

Judges at the same ⟨time⟩ pastors.

Preface afterward.

21[58]

Contrast of deeply suffering observation, its requirements for consolation and for scientific culture.

21[59][47]

Estimable judgment of a metaphysician like Schopenhauer as testimony for humans (but an unscientific one).

21[60][48]

What if human beings had *immediately* been endowed with *insight* into the truth, had not gone through the school of error?

21[61][49]

Effect of burning at the stake, the cruelty as source of strength for those at hand.

21[62]

The truth without influence like the setting sun.

21[63][50]

Beginning: our educators are themselves not educated.

Conclusion: to scare away *death* as long as possible. Eternity.

21[64][51]

Resurrection every[52] 300 years.[53]

21[65]

Q⟨uestion⟩. When we take something do we have it?
Yes.
But virginity?

21[66][54]

If we have begun to think publicly, we must then allow ourselves to contradict ourselves publicly.

21[67]

Goethe's favorite problem in *Wilhelm Meister*.

21[68][55]

To separate spiritual phases consciously, sign of culture.

21[69][56]

women marrying wedding

21[70][57]

Optim⟨ism⟩ pessim⟨ism⟩ nothing [—]

21[71]

Gray-green *outer garments* and bright blue *under*garments [—] with white lace

21[72][58]

Evil actions based upon errors e.g., revenge upon the belief in responsibility, likewise cruelty, insofar triumph of power.

21[73][59]

All evil qualities go back to the drive for preservation of the individual, who nonetheless is certainly not evil. *Displeasure* in hunger, if someone else — — —

21[74][60]

From a metaphysical age into a realistic one [+] is a deadly l⟨eap⟩ transitions [+]

21[75][61]

Against Aristotle, ghost stories — through art the sympathy of humans increased, after that morality, likewise through religion.

21[76][62]

What would the genius of culture be?

21[77][63]

Entry of science into the world upon byways not effectual.

21[78][64]

Why do we still hesitate and trouble ourselves with our joys — it does not matter — but anyone who wants [— —] to give us a shameful [— — —] otherwise we do not need to be ashamed.

21[79]

Girl-ape.

21[80][65]

Whatever we love, we should all the good sides of it — — —
Now we love ourselves — — —

21[81][66]

We esteem ourselves either on the basis of our own judgment or on authority.

Comparison a primary means for pleasure in ourselves.

21[82]

I On the history of culture.
II Human, All too human.

III Book of maxims.
IV Emergence of Greek literature.
V Writer and book.
VI Philologica.

21[83]

Morality often ⟨de⟩pends upon success.

21[84][67]

Concluding *vow* with regard to science. If you can do it, you will have to do it.

[22 = N II 2. Spring–Summer 1877]

22[1]

Window with green netting

22[2]

Greeting and dedication to friends.

22[3][1]

⟨*The infinite melo*⟩*dy* — one abandons the shore, gives oneself up to the waves.

22[4][2]

Crudeness that gives itself out to be force — art.

22[5][3]

To act such that humanity etc.: There we would have to be able to overlook what is advantageous. Who says that *one* way of acting is generally beneficial for the whole? history says the opposite. We are much more obligated to egoism.

22[6][4]

Ignorant people who have become familiar with one philosophy have the impression that they are now superior to all the other sciences and that they could have a say in everything — nothing more mistaken.

22[7]

Fire seriousness and happiness, how rarely in the eye and expression of a youth.

22[8][5]

1. Philology.
2. The style of famous German writers.
3. On the aesthetics of music.
4. On morality.
5. Emergence of Greek literature (emergence of a book therein).
6. The age "against metaphysics."
7. Dangers of music in the future.

22[9]

That world concealed from us much more empty of meaning than the known one. We involuntarily assume the opposite. But need as mother, error as father[6] have created the belief.

22[10][7]

Preface on philology. Everything as *practice.*
Homer's and Hesiod's contest.
Athena as goddess of love.
Solon's elegy a collection.
The prologue to the *Choephorae.*
Example of artistic response.
Life ⟨of⟩ Democritus.
Skeptical views on metrics.
Conjectanea[8] as appendix.

22[11][9]

Introduction into the philosophy of the present.
1 General viewpoints (philosophers).
2 On religion.
3 On music.
4 On art.
5 Science and progress.

22[12][10]

From the standpoint of utility, the maintaining of religion is by all means to be wished for, utility taken even in the highest sense (morality) (especially the tutelary state).

But it cannot be maintained, because no *sincere teachers* exist any longer.

Should, therefore, the educational system be overthrown? according to the intent of the Catholic Church? But all of the other advantages of life are based upon science.

Conflict not to *be aggravated* — English practice. Humans are not consistent.

The ceasing of this faith unleashes *energy*, held back up until now through metaphysical consolations. Therefore not to be underestimated.

These energies are hostile to the existing orders.

Is revolution necessary? — For now, a small fraction of European humanity is to be considered.

To recommend to governments *the freest* treatment, to repress nothing, rather to place themselves *at the forefront* in *spiritual* liberation: the more spiritual one makes the mass, the more *orderly* the paths it seeks.

From the side of private persons — founding of an association whose m⟨embers⟩ refrain from all religious forms. Propaganda in the whole world. With that, reconciliation of nations (opposite to Catholic reconciliation).

22[13]

Even wine, even art (festivals) belong among these consolations. Away with them! Associations against spiritual drinks very much in the service of the free spirits.

22[14]

The national idea and wars excellent antidotes against revolution.

Enflaming of religious interests (point of the culture war) as well.

A temporary brutalization not to be shunned (through dominance of natural scie⟨nce⟩ mechanics).

22[15][11]

Whether life experiences represented in the form of maxims have usefulness for others, I do not know, for the one who makes them, they are a benefit: they belong to the means for easing life.

And we can still gather maxims from the least satisfying thorniest events or stretches of life (and have from this a mouthful of gratification) and thus feel somewhat better.

22[16][12]

The state has to represent science, not religion, astronomy, not astrology. The latter are left to the private man.

22[17][13]

There are shorter and longer arcs in cultural development. To the height of the Enlightenment corresponds the height of the Counter-Enlightenment in Schopenhauer and Wagner.

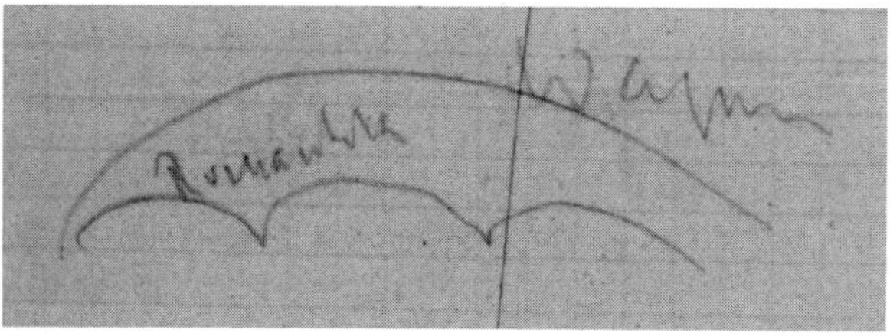

The high points of the small arcs come closest to the large arc — Romanticism.

22[18]

Our goal must be: **one** *form* of school for cultivating the entire people — and technical schools besides.

22[19]

Key to human action.
A different key.

22[20][14]

How is it possible that someone has contempt for himself in everything (knows himself to be "sinful" through and through) and yet still loves himself? The scientific explanation is completely different from the one the religious human being gives himself. That love he attributes to God: if he puts into all possible experiences the signs of a kind compassionate disposition, understands every consoled mood as an effect of that, therefore ascribes all better sensations to a being outside himself as the effective author, then the love with which he basically loves himself takes on the appearance of a divine love. This is unmerited, the human being further deduces, is grace.

Presupposition is that the human being feels himself free-willed and bad: this only through a false unscientific interpretation of his actions and sensations. He puts into one part of his actions the concept of sin, into the other part the concept of divinely merciful operations. False psychology, fantasy in the interpretation of motives is the essence of Christianity.

22[21][15]

— — — for whom the state is the rule of the devil.

22[22]

The publisher *thinks*, but the book-printer *directs*.[16]

22[23]

Dreary gray eye of earliest morning, damp sharp wind.

22[24][17]

Whatever is to live eternally in song must perish in life[18] (*restoration*-artificial blossoms).

22[25][19]

Modi⟨fied⟩ tempos. — We honor the great artist of the past less through that unproductive timidity that leaves every note to lie as it was placed than through active love and those efforts to awaken him ever newly to life, to keep him alive.

22[26][20]

Free spirit. Psychological. Morality. Art. Religion. Metaphysics.

Transition from religion to art with "impure thinking," "illogical stance toward the world."

Then the "poet."

Palliative. Means for easing life. Art etc.

22[27]

Morality
Religion
Art
finally: to become wise[21]

22[28][22]

Metaphysics: a few rungs backward, only the knowing human being should always be looking over the ladder, we are as complete humans not *only* knowledge.

22[29]

As the fog allows a mountain to seem lower, so psychic moodiness.

22[30]

I wish that we would eat in order to become full and not only because it tastes good — reason for why science.[23]

22[31]

Attila the *Hun* "human thundercloud."

22[32][24]

It teaches, if not modesty, at least caution. Schopenhauer Goethe.

22[33][25]

Appearance. It lies among our errors, which extend into the constitution of our intellect, that thing and appearance do not coincide.

22[34]

If you have eyes to see, use your mouth as well to say: "I saw it differently" so that — — —

Cave of Salamanca[26]

22[35][27]

— if we thereby think of the unconscious remedies and similar things — — —

22[36][28]

All art turns aside the thought of becoming. All want to seem like *improvisation*, instantaneous miracle (temple as work of the gods, statue as magical transformation of a soul into stone). So, too, all music. In certain kinds of music, this intended effect is suggested by artistic means (disorder).

22[37]

Necessary to absorb into myself the entirety of pessimism, and yet still to be bearer of idealism (preface).

22[38]

Independ⟨ent⟩ life. Book 9.

22[39][29]

Music of the beautiful soul

22[40][30]
Miscalculation in anarchy

22[41][31]
To die for someone is a slim proof of love.

22[42]
Poet-wisdom.

22[43][32]
Love as impartial as the rain that in certain circumstances soaks the sinner to the skin.

22[44][33]
hanging clouds of affliction, of moodiness

22[45][34]
Childlike and dreadful and sorrowful
the tune of time[35] often sounded to me:
see now[36] if I am singing her song?
listen for whether the earnest chimes
do not change into serious bells[37]
or whether it sounds
from high to low as from the tower in Genoa
Childlike and yet, ah, dreadful
Dreadful and sorrowful.

22[46]
School should teach the greatest freedom in rel⟨igious matters⟩, the most sober rigorous thinking. Unclarity and habitual inclinations will set very wide limits.

22[47][38]
Spirit of youthfulness, which has the privilege even of some bad habits, — I lack this now.

22[48][39]

This work, which under the provocative collective title *Unfashionable Observations* was handed over to the public in four sequential parts and which was completed essentially between Easter 1873 and August 1876 — — —

Heart first poured out in *Unfashionable Observations.* But wind and weather, which direct life even more than our star and which ⟨were⟩ not exactly favorable to me, were nonetheless perhaps still favorable in that[40] — — —

22[49][41]

— even if this would be a mocking misleading of German credulity[42] — — —

22[50]

Hunt in the *book.*

Mighty boar and also delicate deer certainly.

22[51]

The[43] character of dramatic music, which is just as distant from the German nature as the character of Bismarckian politics.

22[52]

Willing is in every case a self-deception. We[44] can think it only in opposition to must, as free will: and this is an error.

22[53][45]

— German youth — irony — good-humoredness laughing smiling worm-damage giving oneself airs

22[54]

Anyone who religion and art — Goethe — — — [46]

Manfred: Eckermann Riemer — — — [47]

22[55][48]

To play the flutes of time so that its dance goes more swiftly and whirls around — later the great calm, where everything appears creepy eerie as in the later hours after midnight. I myself am in time, it in me — self-experienced, self-*orgiasmus*.

22[56]

Will. From the quality of this feeling, of willing, nothing at all is immediately known to us about what to strive toward.

22[57][49]

One person says: I have sensation, but all creatures have sensation, from the beginning on. The other: I can never explain how sensation is supposed to have emerged at a particular point of historical development: therefore it was always there.

22[58][50]

Because I encounter sensation within me as something final indissoluble, this must likewise be the case in all creatures.

But that sensation in creatures without a brain (or thinking) really would be what we call sensation and not a simply mechanical process, which is only interpreted by us as sensation —

that sensation comes to pass with the assistance of the intellect.

Memory preformation really a process of the brain.

22[59][51]

the exultation of the know⟨ing⟩ human being

22[60][52]

Duel. Blood wipes away a hasty word, blood gives even to an ambiguous action afterward the respect of an honest one. — Suicide, for Ajax to satisfy the overwrought feeling of honor.

22[61][53,54]

Is nothing left hanging of Sorrento's scent?
Is everything wild, cool[55] mountain-nature,
Scarcely autumnally sun-warmed and without love?
Thus there is only one part of me in the book:
The better part, I bring it to the altar
For her, who was friend mother doctor to me.[56]

22[62][57]

We not only think within the dream, but the dream itself is the result of a[58] process of thinking.

22[63][59]

I find the lack of a sense of justice among women *disgraceful.* How they with their dagger-sharp intelligence are suspicious etc.

22[64][60]

The earlier writings were paintings, for which I took the colors from the materials that I was representing, as a chemist would, and used like an artist.

22[65]

The author, the girl, the soldier, the mother is that unegoistical?

22[66]

Primordial problems.
Language.
Writer.
Style.
High s⟨chool⟩.
Education.
Free spirit.

22[67]

Just as there exist no absolutely human gestures for humans, but instead they must always be adapted to the symbolism of a particular cultural stage, a people, a class, so there exists in no art an absolute form. "To break the forms" means only to bring to power a new symbolism. All form, however, is convention or compulsion.

22[68]

Friends.

You believe me to be alone — now receive the companions of the solitary one.

22[69][61]

I surely have a right to recall this poem here. What I myself was not capable of saying, but what, like many drops of light, fell upon my soul now and then — that is what it spoke, throwing the drops of light further [—]

My supplement: that is,[62] as a broken piece of arm and leg is related to a whole image.

22[70]

Good artists should not *listen*.

22[71]

Not earned — pride.

22[72][63]

— long-famous person Hutten Voltaire.

Among the 7 famous Schwabians[64] Strauss ahead courage.

22[73][65]

My good opinion of myself I first learned from others and continually subtract from it, with brooding, when I am sick.

A peaceful joyful solitude with me, in[66] good thoughts and[67] laughing — as I am, too —

22[74][68]

When language first counted as science — depiction of the further *promoters* of language. **Manuscript Basel**

22[75][69]

May reason lift up those who are reasonable
The artist should digest only art
And yet an artist *wrote* this book!
It was not his reason that did it, it was his *love.*

22[76]

We no doubt hear the hammering of the telegraph but do not understand it.

22[77][70]

Characters:
as the painted shoe of the painter is related to the shoe of the shoemaker,
as the painter's knowledge of the shoe to the shoemaker's knowledge of the shoe,
so characters sketched by poets to real characters.

22[78][71]

Lipiner. The most beautiful success, when it forces one to set down the book, to catch one's breath; tears of profound ecstasy, drunken swimming in melodious s⟨ound⟩[72] that makes the eyes close, as if one were diving in the blue depths of the southern sea; sorrowful emotion, when we look away from ourselves ashamed.

22[79][73]

If knowledge and again always knowledge is supposed to compensate for many other deprivations, and now its organ the head even there still pain and contradiction —

22[80][74]

In the Bavarian woods it began
Basel added something to that
In Sorrento it first spread itself large and wide
And Rosenlaui gave it space and freedom
The mountains labored, at beginning middle and end!
Terrible for the one who knows the proverb!
Thirteen months until the mother delivered the child —
Has an elephant then come to be?
Or even a ridiculous mouse? —
So worries the father. Just laugh and mock him!

22[81][75]

Jacob Burckhardt.

Since this book grew up in me, desire and shame[76] hold on
to me
Until such growth one day[77] blooms[78] a hundred times
more richly for you.
Already now I taste the happiness that I am following the
greater one,[79]
When he rejoices in the golden yield of his own planting.[80]

22[82][81]

The form of a work of art always has something careless. The sculptor can add or deduct many small features — likewise the piano player. We must position it so that it is effective: i.e., so that life has an effect upon life. As if someone is telling a story from his own life. Fall asleep —

22[83]

Blessed island
Robinson

22[84]

Strauss — Wagner

22[85][82]
Confirmation that youth [— — —] Prometheus

22[86]
Beethoven — that noble sweet dream, which presses from the heart into the spirit and calls it to peer into the red-encircled twilight toward what lies far away: hunger of a solitary soul.

22[87][83]
The exceptional pleasure that we owe to *morality* (in stories) and to art.[84]

22[88]
Ch⟨ained⟩ Prom⟨etheus⟩ as rainbow-bridge suspended across the last millennia, the highest culture-poem.

22[89][85]
Friend! The one who dared to tear you away from faith in the cross,
sends you this book: yet he himself makes the sign of the cross before the book.

22[90][86]
As Buddhism with its mild rice-eater morality worked against wars, India was stricken from the history of cultural powers.

22[91]
One person has unclear writing because his eye is weak: so he reads himself with difficulty. The other sees much more sharply and also reads the other's handwriting better than he — — —[87]

22[92][88,89]
A greeting offered with joyful spirit
To the master and the mistress,

Made happy by a new child,
From Basel free-spirited Friedrich.
He hopes that they in a heart-felt way
Will place their hands upon the child, testing
To see whether it is like the father
— Who knows? perhaps even a moustache —
And whether it will, on twos and fours
Romp around the world's territory.
In the mountains it would like to hatch into the light
To frisk about like a new-born goat
And like it to seek its own way,
Its own joy, good will and rank
Or perhaps choose the hermit's cell
And forest animal?
Whatever may be decided for it
As to its pilgrimage on earth: it does not want
To please many: fifteen in number
Of others become its cross and torment,
Only may it be that the devoted eye of the master,
To ward off the worst danger, looks on in blessing!
Only that the wise good will of the mistress
Directs its way toward its first voyage!

22[93][90,91]

This is autumn.
The sun creeps toward the mountain
And climbs upward
and rests with every step.
On weary, taut strings the wind
Plays its song:
Hope flees,
The wind echoes after it.
O fruit of the tree,
You tremble, fall!
What a secret did the night
Show to you,

So that an icy shiver veiled
Your cheek, the crimson one? —[92]
I am not beautiful,
So speaks the starflower,
Yet I love humans,
And I comfort humans,
They should still see flowers now,
Bend down toward me,
Ah! and break me off —[93]
In their eyes then gleams
Remembrance of *more beautiful ones*
And happiness.
I see it and then die,
And gladly die.
This is autumn. —

22[94][94,95]

At midday, when
Young summer climbs into the mountains,
Then it speaks, too,
Yet we only see its speaking:
Its breath flows like that of a wanderer
In winter frost:
The icy peaks and forest and spring
Answer it, too,
Yet we only see the answer.
For there more quickly leaps downward from the cliff
The cascade, as if in greeting,
And stands there like a white column, listening.
And darker still and truer gazes the forest
Than otherwise it gazes.
And between ice and dead gray stone
Lights suddenly look upward:
Who interprets it for you?
In the dead man's eye
Someday surely there will be light:

His child embraced him, filled with grief,
Kissed him.
Then the gleaming of the eye says
"I love you"
And snowy mountains and brook and forest
They, too, say
To the summer's boy just
This single word:
We love you!
We love you!
And he — he kisses them, filled with grief,
Ever more fervently,
And does not wish to leave:
He blows his word just like a veil
From his mouth — an awful word. —
Then round-about it listens
And scarcely breathes:
Then nature all around
Overflows, shuddering like
A glittering on the mountain:
She thinks and keeps silent. —
It was at midday

My greeting is a taking leave
I die young. — [96]

22[95][97]

If thinking is your fate, honor this fate with divine respect and sacrifice to it what is best, what is dearest.

So all discord, all conflict run together in concord and harmony.[98]

22[96][99]

Oath of the one who dedicates himself to knowledge.

22[97][100]

A human being who is spoiled by praise and blame — a tree that is spoiled by sunshine and rain — both are already spoiled and everything becomes a cause for their perishing.

22[98][101]

Poets will then learn to pray formally for misery and disorder.

22[99][102]

I am certainly not ungrateful, but I see no obligation to strangle myself with the cord of gratitude.

22[100][103]

"The most beautiful poem that a youth has ever composed"

22[101][104]

To become nature!

22[102]

Women who resemble those of Holbein not just externally and perhaps carry nothing essentially different in their heads and hearts.

22[103][105]

Irony vulgar — ironic culinary art:[106] to present oneself as ignorant — in order to allow our knowledge to step forth all the more distinctly.

Opposite of modesty: to feel oneself ignorant, where the other person admires our knowledge and ability.

22[104]

Everyone is fond of swear words, but nobody has ever believed that one justifiably came his way.

22[105][107]

Prudence demands that one also *pretend* to be that which *one is considered to be*, or maybe something less.

22[106][108]

I have never yet seen a distinguished person who has become spoiled by praise. — But it is a reliable measure when someone becomes lazy[109] by being praised: he is undistinguished.

22[107][110]

The error of almost every philosophy is a lack of knowledge about human beings, an imprecise psychological analysis. To that extent, the moralists advance knowledge more when they do not content themselves with the already available analyses of human actions.

The philosopher spreads his knowledge of nature around false psychological facts and wraps everything in metaphysical needs.

22[108][111]

We will find humans and the world to be much more harmless.

22[109][112]

"You should love God above all things."

22[110][113]

The development of song in opera gives an ever-new future to absolute music (through an increase of symbolism).

22[111]

How one and the same Christianity paints upon one person that sad-eyed poor-sinner demeanor, upon the face of the other a joyful benevolence.

22[112]

An experienced eye, in order to be able to read the past clearly from the multiply overwritten manuscript of human features and gestures.

22[113][114]

Conscious sensation is sensation about sensation, likewise conscious judging contains the judgment that something is being judged. The intellect is unknown to us without this doubling, naturally. But we can show that its activity is the much richer one. (It follows that "sensation" is without sensation in the first stage. First with the doubling is the name suitable. With the doubling, memory is operative.) To feel without it having gone through the brain: what is that? — pleasure and pain extend only as far as there is brain.

22[114][115]

It pleases us to name middle terms: it was the **degenerate** exemplars that could not maintain themselves in this way.

22[115]

If someone is *harsh* at the sight of those suffering and dying, how do we want to find fault with this?

22[116]

Everything that persists grabs on, causes desire — so much do we confuse what persists and what is good.

22[117]

Energy lives in a particular object, is connected to a locality. If we destroy the object, so, too, the energy or the life. The object itself is called "death" or "life" — "my death is in the egg" "here is your death" — especially *Russian* — recalls the metaphysicians who also separate "energy" from[116] "will."

22[118]

"Cultivated philistines." But it is not good to preach into the wind, so that they do not blow dust in our face — they move, however, where they must.

22[119][117,118]

Now I see more than you
Want to tell it to you

22[120][119]

a blind [—], yet in shoes and coat
[—] that is, [— — —]
[— —] as nanny and billy goat

22[121][120]

Now, however, it is clear as daylight
A human being has body and soul, a pair

22[122][121]

I know what shadow is and light
What body and soul — you do not know it

22[123][122]

Goat after goat without hesitation
Pushes past my knee
Licks my hand seems to ask
What I would be, blind and alone.

22[124][123]

Therein, to be sure, the little soul is hiding
It spares itself traveling, that is the point

22[125][124]

Yet behind his very worthy form
Everyone has a bundle strapped on
There is where he hides the soul
He spares it while traveling, I suppose

22[126][125]

How the body throws a shadow
The soul throws light
They have shadows every one
But not souls

22[127]

The blind young boy on the mountain path.

22[128]

I think I have through my critique increased the value of religion art metaphysics: sources of energy more than ever.

22[129][126]

He comes home then and unpacks his little soul
The same [— — —]

22[130][127]

If I sit thus upon the path
Until the shadow grows colder,
Until the herds of goats go past my knees without fear

22[131][128]

I must have blueberry bushes and forest around me and in front of me a glacier.

22[132][129]

Sit on the path the entire day
Until the shadow grows colder,
And into a deeper enclosure
Downward draws hearth and herdsman
All the goats push familiar⟨ly⟩ past
Lick my hand
that I may be blind and alone

22[133]

To divest ⟨oneself⟩ of all moral phrases (sacrifice duty), not to play along at all with the great comedy of hypocrisy (for by these threads they lead you, the ones who have seen through hypocrisy, toward *their* goals: because they take you to be too cowardly and stupid). *To be true* — may that once again be "moral" for you.

22[134]

Two young boys sat
in the blueberry bush
and looked at the large
green beetle,
on its back
a drop of sun
glittered:
it fell from out of
cool forest shadow
downward.

22[135][130]

Ecce ecce homunculus[131]

[23 = Mp XIV 1b. End of 1876–Summer 1877]

23[1]

The skillful movements of the foot while slipping stumbling climbing[1] are not the results of a blindly functioning, yet purposeful intellect, but were at some time learned, like the movements of the fingers while playing the piano. Nowadays, a great deal of this dexterity is immediately inherited.

23[2]

Humans set down what is similar as being the same, e.g., the priest occasionally as the god; the part the same as the whole e.g., in magic.

23[3][2]

We cannot explain what sensation is: but I believe it is not very much when we know it and certainly does not hide some riddle of the universe behind it.

23[4]

The same manner of thinking that even now determines the great masses, indeed, even the cultivated individual unless he is extremely self-aware, has served as foundation for the collective phenomena of culture. This *partie honteuse*[3] has brought about the most tremendous and marvelous consequences; culture, too, has a *pudendum*[4] as womb, just like a human being.

23[5]

Aristotle[5] thinks the sage σοφός[6] is the one who occupies himself solely with what is important amazing divine. The mistake there lies in the entire direction of thought. Precisely what is small weak human illogical defective is overlooked and yet we can become *wise* only through the most careful study of those very same things. The sage has to lay aside a great deal of pride, he should not raise his eyebrows so high, in the end he is the one who gives himself pleasure by disturbing the pleasure of human beings.

23[6]

If the sensation for something i.e., property kingship has once been aroused, it continues to grow the more we forget the origin. In the end, we speak about such things being "mysteries," because we are conscious of an exuberant strength of sensation, but, taken precisely, can provide no proper reason for it. Sobriety is necessary here, too, but admittedly a tremendous source of power dries up.

23[7]

Epicurus's position on style is typical for many circumstances. He believed he was turning back to nature because he wrote whatever occurred to him. In truth, so much care about expression had been inherited by him and grown up in him that he simply let himself go and still was not fully free and unconstrained. The "nature" that he attained was the instinct for style that had been cultivated by habituation. We call this naturalizing; we bend the bow somewhat more loosely e.g., Wagner in his approach to music, to the art of song. The Stoics and Rousseau are in the same sense naturalists: mythology of nature!

23[8]

Art hindering science among the Greeks.

23[9]

Why assume a *drive for preservation* at all?[7] Among countless purposeless forms, those more capable of life, more capable of *continued* life, came to the fore;[8] adaptations of the individual human organs over millions of years were necessary until finally the present body could regularly come into being and until there could regularly appear those facts that we generally ascribe to the drive for preserv⟨ation⟩. Basically, this now occurs just as[9] necessarily, according to chemical laws, as mechanically, as with a waterfall. The finger of the piano player has no "drive" to strike the correct keys, but instead only the habit. The word "drive" is really only a convenience and is applied everywhere that regular effects in organisms have not yet been traced back to their chemical and mechanical laws.[10]

23[10][11]

All goals and purposes that humans have were once conscious, too, in their ancestors; but they have been forgotten. Humans depend in their directions very much upon the past: Platon⟨ic⟩ ἀνάμνησις.[12] The head of the worm is cut off, but it moves in the same direction.

23[11][13]

People have also honored and religiously idealized obscure diseases, too, e.g., insanity St. Vitus's dance. By doing so, the expressions of these became ever more beautiful and grand. The same course of events with the intense affect of love, which people conceived as god, and so idealized not only for the representation, but in reality.

23[12][14]

It was a very lucky find by Schopenhauer when he spoke of the "will to life": we do not want to allow this expression to be taken from us again and are grateful to its originator in the name of the German language. But that should not keep us from perceiving that the concept will to life has not yet won its civil rights in the eyes of science, just as little as the concepts "soul" "god" life-force etc. Nor does Mainländer's reduction of this concept to many individual "wills to life" bring us any further — we obtain thereby, instead of a universal life force (which is supposed to be thought simultaneously as outside, above and within things!) individual life forces, against which the same objection can be made as against the universal one. For before a human being exists, his individual will does not yet exist either: or what should this then be? In life itself, but expressing itself — does the will to life then even exist? However, at least a will to remain *in* life, therefore, to select the better-known expression,[15] drive to preservation. Is it true that, when a human being looks within, he perceives himself as a *drive to preservation*? Instead, he perceives only that he is continually feeling, more precisely, that he has in one organ or another one or another generally completely insignificant sensation of pleasure or displeasure: the movement of the blood of the stomach of the intestines presses somehow upon the nerves, he is continually feeling and this feeling is continually changing.[16] Dreams betray this continuous inner transformation of feeling and interpret it fancifully. The positions that the limbs take up while sleeping make a rearrangement of the muscles necessary and influence the nerves and these, in turn, the brain. Our optic nerve our ear our sense of touch is always aroused in some way. But this fact of a continual arousal and perceptibility of feeling has nothing in common with the drive to preservation. The drive to preservation or love of life is either something completely conscious or only an unclear misleading word for something else: that we want to avoid *displeasure* in every possible way, and on the hand, to strive for pleasure. This universal fact of every animated thing is, however, in any case no first original fact, as Schopenhauer assumes about the will to life: — to flee displeasure, to seek pleasure presupposes the existence of experience and this, in turn, the intellect.[17] — The strength of the sensual pleasure does not prove the will to life, but the will to pleasure. The great fear of death, with which

Schopenhauer likewise argues in favor of his assumption of the will, has been trained for a long period of time by individual religions, which look at death as the decisive hour; it has thus *become* so great here and there. Should it be observed independently from that, however,[18] it is no longer as fear of *dying* i.e., of the untested and perhaps too greatly imagined *pain*, rather than the losses that come about in dying. It is not true that we want existence at any price,[19] e.g., not as animals, to which Schopenhauer so readily refers in order to establish the tremendous power of the general will to life.[20]

23[13][21]

Scholars like Paul de Lagarde[22] think that we would have to hold on to the facts of religious consciousness by means of science. But we can no doubt verify, describe, explain scientifically: but then, for the individual, it is all over with those facts. For the good faith in them is destroyed once we have grasped how erroneously human it appears in their essence. Science is the death of all religions, perhaps at some point of the arts as well.

23[14]

The sage knows *no morality* anymore except for the one that takes its laws from him, himself; indeed, the word "morality" already suits him no longer. For he has become fully immoral insofar as he acknowledges no morals no tradition, instead nothing except new life-questions and the answers to them. He moves forward upon untraveled paths, his energy grows the more he wanders. He is like a great conflagration that brings its own wind along with it, and is increased by it and carried farther along.[23]

23[15][24]

For dedicating our knowledge to culture, we are at the *happiest* imaginable point of time: every freedom of knowledge has been conquered and wrested away and yet we still stand close to all of the fundamental sensations upon which the old culture rests. It may be possible that the latter will be lacking a few generations later! —

23[16]

The moment in which airship flight is discovered and introduced is favorable for socialism, since it changes all concepts of landownership. Human beings are everywhere and nowhere, they are uprooted. We must secure ourselves through strictly reciprocal obligations and *exclusion of all those not obligated.* Otherwise, if he cannot pay, cannot fulfill obligations everything goes up in the air and settles down somewhere else.

23[17]

People who have no *scientific* culture *speak foolishly* when they talk about serious and difficult topics and do so with presumption. Socrates is right. The pomposity of humans is nearly as bad as complete madness. Admittedly, for action, for the building of culture, this zeal this sort of insanity for opinions is quite essential. Without frenzy nothing comes to pass. Nevertheless: since the knowledge of truths really does exist and affords pleasure, we want to hold its banner high, if without any grimace of pathos.[25]

23[18]

Even among the freest of thinkers mythology sneaks in when they speak of *nature.* Since nature is supposed to have provided for, to have striven for, to rejoice in this and that, or else: "human nature would have to be a botched job, if it — ." Will, nature are leftovers from the old belief in gods.

23[19][26]

All of those who make maxims fall easily into the mistake of expressing something general about humans, which is valid for ages or classes of society; but all philosophers who have written about humans have done the same — history in connection with animal history first lets it be recognized how great was the lack of presence of mind. Thus Schopenhauer, in order to show that the life of humans has a moral metaphysical purpose, refers to how at the end of life we become conscious of our moral qualities — as if such a feeling, even if it really did generally exist *now*, could prove anything other than that humans have accustomed themselves through certain opinions and dogmas to think when near death about their sins: that is to say: a fact such as the one Schopenhauer establishes proves that certain metaphysical representations exist and have existed, but not that they are true. Added to which, that chronologically it is a very limited fact and that e.g., in antiquity one very often died without thinking about sins. And even if it were a completely general observation, valid for all periods of humanity and for every human being, no proof of the truth of the proposition asserted by Schopenhauer is provided thereby.

23[20]

If men with strong spiritual needs think about the connection with women, there comes over them the feeling of approaching a net that is being drawn ever more tightly, and they suspect an everlasting pressure, and even, in the end, when it is a matter of educating children, a battle ever flaring up anew.

23[21][27]

If we seek for an explanation of nature and of humans that corresponds to our highest and strongest moods, we will come across only a metaphysical one. How humans would appear without all of these lofty errors — I believe, *animalistic*. If we were to imagine an animal endowed with the knowledge of a rigorous natural history, it would not thereby become a human being, but instead live on essentially as an animal, only that in its many idle hours, e.g., like a horse in front of a hayrack, it would read good books that would make it fully conceivable to it that *truth* and the *animal* get along together nicely.

23[22]

With almost all *philosophers*, the use of the predecessor and the struggle against him are not rigorous, and unjust. They have not learned *to read in an orderly way* and to interpret, the philosophers underestimate the difficulty of really understanding what someone has said and do not turn their carefulness in that direction. Thus Schopenhauer completely misunderstood Kant just as much as Plato. Artists, too, tend to read badly, they are inclined to allegorical and pneumatic explaining.

23[23]

God, just as well as the devil, can say to humans with complete justification: "Just disdain reason and science — and so we have you unconditionally."[28] In this point, they are allies. Moreover, we thereby see that there is not much significance in that "unconditionally."

23[24]

Humans originally look upon all changes in nature not as following laws, but as expressions of free will i.e., of blind inclinations aversions affects frenzy etc.: nature is a human being, only so much more overpowering and incalculable than ordinary human beings, a tyrant sleeping veiled in his tent; all things are action like him, not only his weapons tools are thought of as alive. Linguistics helps to prove that human beings completely misunderstood nature and named it falsely: we are, however, the heirs of these designations of things, the human spirit has grown up in these errors, has been nourished by and grown powerful from them.

23[25][29]

We reproach socialism with overlooking the actual inequality of humans; but that is no reproach, instead a characterization, because socialism *decides* to overlook that inequality and to treat humans as equal i.e., to allow the relationship of justice to go into effect among all of them, which rests upon the assumption that all are equally powerful, equally valuable; similar to how Christianity took humans as equal with regard to sinful depravity and need of salvation. The actual differences (between a good and a bad way of life) seem so small to it that one does not take it into account in the total reckoning; thus socialism also takes humans as predominantly equal, the difference between good and evil, intelligent and stupid, as insignificant or changeable: in which respect, moreover, it is in any case correct with regard to the image of human beings that distant lake-dweller ages[30] provide: we humans of this age *are* ess⟨entially⟩ equal. In that *decision*, to look beyond the differences, lies its inspirational energy.

23[26]

More and more, as humans become more developed, do they perceive the movement, the restlessness, what has taken place. To those less developed, most things seem to be stable, not only opinions, morals, but also boundaries, land and sea mountains etc. The eye only gradually decides in favor of what is in motion. Tremendous amounts of time were needed in order to grasp what stays the same, seemingly enduring, that was its first task, the plants perhaps already learned of this. Therefore did the faith in "things" become so unshakeably firm for human beings, just like the one in matter. But there are no things, instead everything flows — so judges insight, but instinct contradicts it at every moment.

23[27]

Schopenhauer conceives the world as an enormous human being, whose actions we see and whose character is completely unalterable: this we can deduce from its actions. To that extent, it is pantheism or perhaps pandiabolism, for he has no interest in reinterpreting all that he perceives into something good and perfect. But this entire difference between actions as effects and a self-subsistent character as cause is already false with respect to a human being, even more so with regard to the world. Something such as character has no existence in itself, but is instead an easing abstraction. And this is the value of metaphysicians such as Schopenhauer: they attempt a world-picture: only it is too bad that it changes the world into a human being: one would like to say, the world is Schopenhauer writ large. That is just[31] not true.

23[28][32]

The bitterest sufferings are those that do not bring any *great* agitation with them — for high passion, whatever sort it may be, has its happiness in itself — but instead those that gnaw, burrow and sting: therefore, especially those that are inflicted upon us by inconsiderate people who make use of their kind of superiority; for instance, in the aggravating circumstances when they make use of an intimate familiarity with us through a betrayal of friendship. The only great feeling that would let us fly away from such sufferings would be hatred with the prospect of revenge, of annihilation of the other. But a better person generally tells himself that the wrongdoer was not nearly as malicious as he seems to us and that many merits speak in his favor: so he represses the thought of retaliation, but does not thereby become happy; he is reliant on time, to the weakening of all memories. —

23[29][33]

Two things are harmful: the gnawing *annoyance* at an injury, with its hundredfold rumination spitting-out of what was experienced, then faint imaginary satisfactions of revenge — a real revenge and a quick one, even if its consequences weigh us down with pain, is much healthier. Second, life in *erotic* representations, which sully the imagination and gradually gain a supremacy from which health suffers. — Self-education has to be preventive here: both drives must be complied with in a natural way and the representation kept pure. Revenge forgone and love forgone make a human being sick, weak and bad.

23[30]

Beware of rings! (Rings are winding snakes that present themselves as being harmless.) these golden winding snakes certainly present themselves as being harmless —

23[31][34]

In what poem is there as much *crying* as in the *Odyssey*? — And most probably the poem also worked in the same way upon the Greeks listening in ancient times; everyone took pleasure in tears at the memory of all that had been suffered and lost. Every older man had a number of experiences in common with Odysseus, he felt everything along with the patient sufferer. — I am often moved to tears by what is not at all moving, but instead the simple plain reliable in Homer and likewise in *Hermann und Dorothea*,[35] e.g., Telemachus in the first song.

23[32][36]

The *unegoistical* drive is perhaps a late development of the *social* drive: in any case, not the reverse. The social drive emerges from the compulsion that is exerted to interest ourselves in another being (the slave in his master, the soldier in his leader) or from fear, with its insight that we must work together in order not to perish individually. This sensation, inherited, emerges later, without the original motive entering into consciousness along with it; it has become a need that looks around for the opportunity to engage itself. To interest oneself in others, in a community, in a thing (like science) *seems* then to be unegoistical, but fundamentally it was not. —

23[33]

Those thoroughly informed about North Americans say that "the ruling opinion in the United States declares itself against everyone who refrains from striving for the *highest* that is attainable for him. *To stay behind from free will* is actually considered a disgrace, as a sort of crime against society."[37]

23[34][38]

The world without eros. — Consider that by virtue of eros, two humans have mutual pleasure in each other: how completely different would this world of envy of fear and of discord appear without this!

23[35]

Tragic youths. — In the inclination of young people for tragedy, in their manner of prophesying woeful fates for themselves, of thinking badly of humans, is concealed something of the pleasure that becomes active in them when someone calls out: "How wise he is for his age: how he already knows the ways of the world!"

23[36]

It is a magnificent spectacle: from local interests, from personae who are tied to the smallest fatherlands, from works of art that were made for one day, for the festival, from nothing in short but points in space and time, there gradually grows an enduring culture bridging nations and peoples; the local takes on universal significance, the momentary monumental significance. We must look into this process in history; admittedly, our breath falters sometimes, so spun out is the yarn, so close to tearing are the knots that connected what is farthest away with what is recent! — Homer, first for all Hellenes, then for the whole Hellenic cultural world and now for everybody — is a fact over which one can weep.

23[37][39]

Schopenhauer rightly says: "The insight into the strict necessity of human actions is the dividing line that separates philosophical minds from the rest."[40] Falsely, however: "the ultimate and true revelation concerning the inner essence of the entirety of things must necessarily cohere tightly with that concerning the ethical meaning of human acting."[41] Likewise false: "all are capable of inferring, few of judging."[42]

23[38][43]

Even if someone endures martyrdom and death for his belief, he proves nothing about the *truth*, but only about the *strength of the belief* in what he takes to be true. (Christianity admittedly proceeds from the illicit idea: "whatever is strongly believed is true." "Whatever is strongly believed makes one blessed, courageous, etc.") The pathos of "truth" is in itself not beneficial for it insofar as this works against renewed examination and investigation. There is a sort of blindness connected with it, one even becomes, with this pathos, a fool: as Winkler puts it.[44] We must live through skeptical periods from time to time if indeed we want to have a right to call ourselves scientific personalities. Schopenhauer has multiply fortified his position with curses and oaths and almost everywhere with pathos; without these expedients, his philosophy would perhaps have become less well known (e.g., when he calls it the real perversity of disposition "to believe in no metaphysics").[45]

23[39]

Anyone who writes about the inner motives of humans cannot simply point them out coldly; for he cannot make his conclusions believable in this way. He must be able to awaken the memory of this and that passion, mood, and must therefore be an artist of representation. For this, in turn, it is necessary that he be familiar with all of these affects from experience; for otherwise he will offend through coldness and the appearance of disparaging what has so *deeply* moved and shaken other people. Hence he must have gone through the most important stages of humanity and be capable of placing himself upon them: he must have *been* religious, artistic, lascivious, ambitious, evil and good, patriotic and cosmopolitan, aristocratic and plebeian and have retained the force of representing them. For it is not the same with his theme as with mathematics, where there exist fully precise means of expression, numbers and lines, which are completely unambiguous. Every word about the motives of human beings is imprecise and suggestive, but we must understand how to suggest *strongly* in order to represent a strong feeling.

23[40][46]

There are *trickling* thinkers and *flowing* ones, just as springs differ from one another. Lichtenberg holds his glass diligently beneath and eventually fills it full; but he did not have the time to pass the full glass along to us; his relatives[47] have measured out the drops to us. There we easily become unfair. In himself, the flowing thinker awakens the appearance of *complete energy*, but this can also simply be deception.

23[41][48]

Not only the faith in God, also the faith in virtuous humans, actions, the esteem for "unegoistical" drives, therefore also errors in the field of psychology have helped humanity forward. It makes a great difference whether someone imitates Plutarch's heroes with enthusiasm or analyzes doubtfully. The faith in the good has made humans better: as a conviction about the opposite makes humans weaker more distrustful etc. This is the effect of La Rochefoucauld and of the author of the *Psychological Observations*:[49] these sharpshooting marksmen always hit the bull's-eye, but in the interest of human welfare we might wish that they did not have this sense of diminishment and suspicion.

23[42][50]

The *charm* of many writings e.g., of *Tristram Shandy* is based, among other things, on how the inherited and cultivated[51] shyness of not seeing, not admitting to oneself many things, is resisted in them, and thus how a mischievous game is played with a certain "chastity of the soul."[52] If we were to imagine this shyness no longer being inherited, that charm would disappear. To this extent, the value of the most excellent writings is highly dependent upon the seemingly changeable constitution of the inner human being; the strengthening of one feeling, the weakening of another, allows this and that writer of the first rank to become boring: as e.g., the Spanish honor and devotion in the dramatists, the medieval-symbolic element in Dante is sometimes unbearable and does harm to their representatives in our feelings.

23[43][53]

The exceptional *uncertainty* of all *systems of instruction* has its basis in the fact that no generally acknowledged foundation any longer exists, and that now neither Christianity nor antiquity nor the natural sciences nor philosophy has overruling and prevailing power. We move unsteadily[54] among quite various demands: in the end, the national state still wants a "national" culture, thereby bringing the lack of clarity to its peak — for national and culture are contradictions.[55] Even in the universities, the fortresses of science, there are people who, with the secretiveness of traitors, acknowledge religion or metaphysics as still-higher powers *above* science.

23[44]

Teachers of entire classes set for themselves a false ambition, to treat their pupils individually differently. Now, it is, however, probable to the highest degree that the teacher, with his slight and one-sided relationship to the pupils, does not know them exactly and makes some gross mistakes in his judgment of one or another character (which, moreover, is still flexible in young people and should not be treated as completed fact). The disadvantage that the knowledge of the class brings with it, that some pupils will fundamentally always be treated erroneously, outweighs all possible advantages of an individualizing education, indeed, outweighs them by far. In general, all teachers' judgments about an individual are false and premature: and no proof of scientific care and caution. One should always simply try to maintain an equivalence and equal estimation of all pupils and take the level to be fairly high, indeed, one should treat all grading with obviously low regard and limit oneself to making the subject of instruction interesting, so much so that the teacher attributes it *to himself, in front of* the class, if a pupil shows himself to be conspicuously uninterested — : it is a guaranteed recipe and leaves the conscience of the teacher quieter besides. — It is self-evident, moreover, that education in classes is really only a makeshift for when the individual person absolutely cannot be educated by an individual teacher and consequently the individual character and the talent must be left to go their own way: which is admittedly dangerous. But is the individual educator not likewise a danger? —

23[45][56]

Astonishment of naïve people that the state does not support education and schooling in a completely nonpartisan way: why else would it have taken it in hand with all that effort! The means to have control over spirits. (Candidature of all teachers for positions! thus one *has* them.)

23[46]

We gain a new pleasure when *metaphysical representations* seem humorous to us and the solemn demeanor, the emotion at the supposed disclosure, the mysterious shuddering seem to us like an old ghost story. Let us not be mistrustful toward ourselves! Yet we do have the results of a long dominion of metaphysics in us, certain complex moods and sensations that belong to the highest attainments of human nature; in no way do we give these up with that innocent mockery. — But why should we not laugh when Schopenhauer wants to explain the aversion toward the toad to us metaphysically,[57] when the parents become opportunistic causes for the genius of the species[58] etc.?

23[47][59]

Rée to be described as a sharpshooting marksman who always hits the bull's-eye.

23[48][60]

Moral *self-observation* is not at all sufficient now, history and the knowledge of backward peoples are part of coming to know the entangled motives of our behavior. In them, the entire history of humanity plays ⟨itself⟩ out, all of their great errors and false representations are woven into it; because we no longer share these, we no longer seek them either in the motives of our act⟨ions⟩, but they resound along with them as mood coloring overtone. We think that we really have enumerated all motives when we have classified the motives of humans according to the *necessary* satisfaction of their claims. But there were countless almost unbelievable, indeed insane needs that would not now be so easy to guess: these are all still working together.

23[49][61]

Sometimes we are overcome by indignation if we hear a naturalistic historical explanation when we are, for instance, most deeply moved by a death breach of faith courtship. But such sensations *prove* nothing, they are, in turn, simply to be explained. The sensations have *become* deep, but were not always so; and there is no real basis corresponding to that highest intensification, they are imaginations.

23[50]

If geniuses[62] have unpleasant, even bad qualities, we must be all the more grateful for their good qualities, that they could still bring these fruits to ripeness in such soil, with these neighbors, amid such a climate, such worm-damage.

23[51]

Many things in the restored Catholicism[63] are judged falsely by us, because southern expressions of religiousness are present here. It looks to us superficial, fanciful untrue-exaggerated: but Protestantism, too, is comprehensible only for northern natures.

23[52][64]

Music only gradually became so symbolic, humans have learned more and more to understand spiritual processes along with certain turns of phrase and figures. These do not lie in it from the beginning. Music is not an immediate expression of the will, but can only *seem* so to us in the fullness of art.

23[53]

Music has as a total art no character at all, it can be holy and ordinary, and is both of these things first when it has become symbolic through and through. Those sublimated glorifications of music in general, as they are to be found e.g., in Bettina, are descriptions of the effects of *a specific* music upon quite specific individuals, all of whom have those sublimated states within themselves and now approach the music *through* them, too.

23[54]

We originally praise what is unegoistical because it is useful, ⟨we find fault with⟩[65] what is egoistical because it is harmful. But what if this were an *error*! If what is egoistical were useful in a much higher degree, to other humans as well, than what is unegoistical! What if we had, in finding fault with what is egoistical, always been thinking only of the *stupid* egoism! Basically we were praising cleverness? — Admittedly, goodness and stupidity go together, too, *un bon homme*[66] etc.

23[55]

To judge according to the novella "On Malanger Fjord," Th. Mügge[67] is the only German narrative talent in the Scottish style; he is absolutely masterfully reliable.

23[56]

Praise of Epicurus. — Wisdom has not gotten a single step beyond *Epicurus* — and often many thousands of steps behind him.

23[57]

If I arrange things according to the degree of pleasure that they arouse, there stands at the top: musical improvisation in a good hour, then hearing individual things of Wagner and Beethoven, then having good ideas occur to me while walking before midday, then sensuality etc.

23[58]

The pleasure in art depends upon knowledge (practice); even with the most popular art. There is no immediate effect upon the hearer, a reaching beyond the limits of the intellect. Many people do not enjoy Wagnerian music because they have not, through the highest musical education, become capable of finding pleasure in it.

23[59][68]

People who detach themselves in a prominent way from inherited morality are "conscience"-less, can only become this in the same way that abortions emerge; the growing and forming of oneself continue even after the birth, in consequence of inherited habits and energies. So we could in that case expand the concept of the abortion and speak, for instance, of *monsters.* The rest of humanity has the same rights against them as against abortions and monsters: it is allowed to destroy them in order not to promote the propagation of backward miscarried creatures. E.G., the *murderer* is a miscarriage. —

23[60]

One[69] *usual experience*: it went badly, but much better than I believed.

23[61][70]

Happiness and unhappiness. — In many people, happiness shows itself to be more moving than their unhappiness. — Who can without tears hear cheerful music coming out of an insane asylum?

23[62]

When walking along a forest stream, the melody that lies in our senses seems to become audible in strong trembling tones; indeed, it sometimes seems that the melody that we are following runs one tone ahead of the inner image of the melody and attains its own independence, which, however, is only illusion.

23[63]

The primary element of ambition is to come to the *feeling* of our *power*. The joy in power is not to be traced back to the fact that we rejoice in standing admired in the opinion of others. Praise and blame, love and hate are all the same for the ambitious person who wants power.

Fear (negative) and will to power[71] (positive) explain our strong regard for the opinions of people.

Pleasure in power. — The pleasure in power is explained from the hundredfold experienced displeasure of dependence, of impotence. If this experience does not exist, the pleasure is lacking as well.

23[64][72]

Signs of higher natures. — The metaphysical representations of a human being are evidence of his higher nature, nobler needs: to this extent, we should always speak of them in the most respectful tone.

23[65][73]

Utility and liability of all martyrdom. — The many deaths of martyrs have become sources of energy for humans on the side of conviction-stubbornness, not on the side of stringent truth-testing. Cruelties do harm to the truth, but benefit the will (which manifests itself in belief).

23[66][74]

To what extent does it comfort an unfortunate person not to have deserved a punishment? He will at best have profited humanity as a means of deterrence: but had he not deserved to be considered as a means? But as soon as we perceive that nobody earns anything, that point of view no longer comforts us at all either. Moreover, we should rejoice under any circumstances in serving as a means for the improvement of humans.

23[67][75]

Usual form of suspicion. — We are unjustly suspicious toward books whose results displease us — and the reverse. In any one party, the principles of the party struggle are never seriously examined: only the opposition parties and their interests produce a strong critique.

23[68][76]

Many people hit the nail, but not on the head, they make the problem hopelessly crooked. It would be better if they had completely missed the thing.

23[69][77]

Replacement of what is accidental by what is necessary. — At the stage of higher spiritual liberation, we should replace everything accidental-natural that we have connected to life with what is chosen-necessary. Anyone who has inadequate friends from before should detach himself; we should under certain circumstances choose a new father, new children.

23[70]

Large effects falsely deduced. — To trace large effects back to large causes is a very common false conclusion. In the first place, there can be small causes, which, however, work for a long time. And then the object being affected can be like a magnifying mirror: a bad poet can have a large effect because the public is precisely homogeneous with him, e.g., Uhland among his fellow Schwabians.

23[71]

Seek solitude in order to be able best to benefit many or all[78] (multitude): if you seek in a different way, it will make you weak sick and into a withering limb.

23[72][79]

Not the absence of love, but the absence of friendship makes the unhappy marriage.

23[73]

The expression "wages" has spread into our age from the time when someone of humble birth unfree always felt himself to be happy blessed if one gave or granted him anything, when he was encouraged like an animal, now with the whip now with temptations, but never "earned" anything. If that person does what he must do, there is no merit therein: if he is rewarded nonetheless, this is a surplus favor, kindness.

23[74][80]

Contemporary dramatists often proceed from a false conception of drama and are *drasticists*: whatever the price, there has to be screaming crying fighting shooting killing for them. But "drama" means "event" *factum*, in opposition to *fictum*.[81] Nor does even the historical derivation of the Greek word-concept prove them right. Even less so the history of drama; for the Greeks outright avoided the representation of drastic things.

23[75]

The former proof of miracles. — If someone dips his hand into glowing molten metal and pulls it out unhurt, it still always creates astonishment, but formerly[82] people certainly believed they were seeing a miracle: the one who did this himself believed in a mysterious force and supernatural assistance. Even someone now who does not know[83] the explanation of the fact[84] nonetheless believes it occurs naturally and that he would be just as successful as the other. Formerly, one could have *proven* any assertion in this way and everyone would have believed such proof.

23[76]

The scientific methods *unburden* the world of great pathos, they show how for no reason we have worked ourselves up into this height of feeling. We now laugh and are amazed at a quarrel that enrages two enemies and gradually entire families, and finally determines the fate of peoples, while the cause has perhaps long been forgotten: but such a course of events is the symbol of all large affects and passions in the world, which are always ridiculously small in their origin. Now humans stand amazed above all at the *height* of their feeling and the *humbleness* of the origin; in the long run, this opposition is moderated, for the embarrassing feeling of ridiculousness works quietly on a human being who has here, for once, begun to know. — There are demanding virtues that can assert their height only under metaphysical presuppositions e.g., virginity; whereas it does not mean much in itself, like a pale unproductive half-virtue that makes us inclined, moreover, to pass sentence of heresy upon our fellow humans.

23[77][85]

If we differentiate stages of morality, I would name as the first: subordination under tradition, *respect* and *piety* toward tradition and its *representatives* (the elders) as second stage. Constraint of the intellect, limitation of its reaching about and experimenting, *enhancement of feeling* within the delimited field of permitted representations. — In contrast, the demand for unegoistical impersonal behavior, in which we generally see the origin of morality, belongs to the pessimistic religions insofar as these proceed from the reprehensibility of the ego, the person,[86] hence the metaphysical significance of the "radical-evil" that they placed beforehand within humans. From pessimistic religion is where Kant took radical-evil as well as the belief that what is unegoistical is the sign of what is moral. Now, this exists, however, as Schopenhauer correctly saw, only in giving in to certain sensations, e.g., compassion benevolence. But we *cannot demand*, command sensations. But morality has always demanded, it will consequently not let "being compassionate and benevolent" (being unegoistical) count as the decisive sign[87] of the "moral human being": as one actually often speaks about "immoral people," who are, however, very good-natured and compassionate.

23[78][88]

The false presupposition of all morality is the error that humans act freely and are responsible. Every law, every regulation (in the state, society, school) presupposes this belief, we are so accustomed to it that we praise and blame, even *after* the insight into irresponsibility has been acquired: whereas, however, we do not blame and praise nature. To demand unegoistical actions, as the pessimistic religions do, to demand love: that presupposes the same fundamental error.

23[79][89]

To explain monogamy and its great force, we should really guard against solemn hypotheses, to which the aforementioned shame[90] before a mystery misleads us. In the first place, a moral origin is not to be thought of at all; even[91] animals have it in many cases. Everywhere that the female is rarer than the male or requires effort by the male to be located, the desire emerges to defend possession of her against new claims of other males. The male does not let go of the female, once obtained, because he knows how hard a new one is to find once she has been lost. Monogamy is not voluntary limitation to *a single* woman while one has the choice among many, but instead the assertion of possession in female-poor circumstances. Hence jealousy swelled up to its present strength and has been inherited by us from the animal kingdom over extremely long periods of time. In political states, the tradition of monogamy has in many cases become sanctioned for various considerations of utility, above all, for the well-being of the family, which must be organized in the most secure way possible. The estimation of women also increased in them, too, so that they later *themselves* preferred the relationship of monogamy to all others. — If women really were a piece of property in the mode of a house-slave,[92] there nonetheless came to be, with the cohabitation of two human beings, with common joys and sorrows, and because women could also refuse obedience in many things and serve as representative of the man in many things, a higher position for the married woman. — Today, when the women in civilized states really are in the majority, monogamy is still protected only by the gradually overwhelming sanction of tradition; the natural basis no longer exists. For precisely this reason, there really continues to exist, behind the back of solemnly treated and venerated monogamy, a form of polygamy.[93]

23[80]

When Schopenhauer confers primacy upon the will and lets the intellect be added, the whole mind, as it is now known to us, can no longer be used for demonstration. For it has become intellectual through and through (just as our sensation of tones in music became intellectual). I mean: we can no longer think pleasure and pain and desire as separated at all from the intellect. The height variety delicacy of the mind has been bred to maturity by countless processes of thought; as poetry is related to contemporary music as the teacher of all symbolism, so thought to the contemporary mind. These thoughts have frequently been errors; e.g., the mood of piety rests completely upon error. Pleasure and pain have been cultivated like an *art*, through precisely the same means as an art. The real motives of actions now behave like the melodies of contemporary music; we can no longer say at all where melody, where accompaniment harmony is; thus is everything artificially woven together in the motives of action, several motives are in motion alongside one another and give to one another reciprocally harmony color expression mood. With certain moods, we may well think we have separated the will from the intellect, it is a deception; they are a result. Every emotion has become intellectual; what someone e.g., feels in love is the result of all the reflecting about it, of all the metaphysics ever connected to it, of all the related *neighboring moods ringing along with it.*

23[81]

In considering the *origin of art,* we should not proceed from aesthetic states and the like; those are late results, just like the artist. Instead, humans like animals seek pleasure and are inventive in this. Morality emerges when they seek what is useful i.e., what does not afford pleasure immediately or even at all, but guarantees *painlessness,* especially in the interest of multiple people. The beautiful and art originate in the direct production of the most numerous and most varied *pleasures.* Humans have overleaped the animal limit of a mating season; that shows them on the path of inventing pleasures. They have inherited many sensual pleasures from the animals (the attraction of coloring in peacocks, pleasure in song with songbirds). Humans invented work without effort, *play,* activity without rational purpose. The roaming of the imagination, dreaming up what is impossible, even nonsensical, causes joy because it is activity without sense and purpose. To move oneself with arms and legs is an embryo of the aesthetic drive. Dance is movement without purpose; flight from boredom is the mother of all arts. Everything *sudden* gives pleasure, if it does not *do harm,* thus wit, brilliance, loudness (light, the noise of drumming). For a tension is relaxed in that it excites and yet does no harm. One strives for emotion in itself, crying, fright (in horror stories) tension: everything that excites is pleasant, therefore displeasure is felt in opposition to boredom as pleasure.

23[82][94]

If someone advances science to the detriment of humanity (— that is, there is no preestablished harmony between the advancement of science and of humanity),[95] we can say to him:

if you want for your satisfaction to sacrifice humanity to your knowledge, so do we want to sacrifice you to the general well-being, here the good purpose sanctifies the means. Anyone who would want to poison humanity for the sake of an experiment would be tied in bonds by us as a completely dangerous subject; we demand: the welfare of humanity must be the limiting standpoint in the domain of investigating truth (not the guiding thought, but the one that sets certain limits). Admittedly, the inquisition lies near at hand there; for the welfare of all was the standpoint from which one persecuted heretics. In a certain sense, therefore, an *inquisition-censorship* is necessary, admittedly[96] the means will become more and more humane.

23[83][97]

An old city, moonlight in the alleyways, a solitary male voice — that affects us as if the past appeared embodied and wanted to speak to us[98] — the dreadfulness of life, the purposelessness of all striving, the gleam of rays round about, the deep happiness in all desiring and regretting: that is its theme.[99]

23[84][100]

We overestimate in artists the continual *improvisation* that, precisely with the most original artists, does not exist, but does, to be sure, with semi-reproductive imitators. Beethoven seeks out his melodies in many pieces, collected with much seeking. But the artists themselves wish that what is instinctive "divine" unconscious in them be assessed most highly and do not depict the facts of the matter accurately when they speak about it. The imagination (as e.g., with actors) puts forward many forms *without choosing*, the higher culture of the artist's *taste* makes the selection among these births and kills off the others with the harshness of a Lycurgean wet nurse.[101]

23[85][102]

The distinctive merit of our culture is *comparison*. We bring together the most various products of older cultures and appraise them; to do *this* well is our task. Our strength shall show itself in how we *choose*; we should be judges.

23[86]

In conclusion: *reason* and *science*, "the *highest* of *all* human *energies*!"[103]

23[87][104]

We call someone *moral* who subordinates himself with regard to a law recognized by him and acts in accordance with it, whether this be a law of the state, or the voice of God in the form of religious commandments, or even simply conscience, or philosophical "duty." Whether someone believes in such laws correctly or incorrectly makes no difference: for morality, it is important only that he be guided by them. — Within the various spheres of egoism, there is a difference between higher and lower: to place oneself here, on the side of the higher more purified egoism, we likewise call moral. — We do not yet call a moral way of behaving *good* without something further. Goodness of soul is attributed to a person who readily displays compassion mutual joy self-sacrifice according to inner drives, not with regard to a law. Thus morality has become instinct, bound up with pleasure in its exercise, as tends to happen after lengthy inheritance and habituation: that is what we call being good.[105]

23[88]

We speak of extenuating circumstances: they are supposed to diminish the *guilt* and accordingly the punishment should fall more lightly. But if we look into the genesis of the guilt, we gradually mitigate the guilt completely, and then there ought to be no punishment at all. For with unfreedom of the will there basically is no guilt. If we allow punishment to have validity as deterrence, there should *not* be *any* extenuating circumstances related to the emergence of the guilt. Once the act has been verified, the punishment follows inexorably; a human being is a means to the well-being of all. Even Christianity says: Judge not![106] admittedly with regard to personal disadvantage. Christ: "God shall judge." But this is an error.

23[89]

Philosophers find the *will to life* proven especially by the fact that they see into what is terrible and useless about life and yet do not have recourse to *suicide* — but their *portrayal* of life could be *false*! —

23[90]

However the question of the critique of the faculty of knowledge might now be answered, the investigation is so difficult, the self-examination of one's own thoughts so subtle, that its result has nothing at all to do with the results of previously existing religion art and morality. These do not owe their results to such scientific procedures, but instead to highly unscientific ones. The need for them is without any consequences for the "truth," reality of their assumptions.

23[91]

A good artistic work of *narrative* will unfold the primary motif as a plant grows, shaping itself forth ever more clearly until the blossom finally opens up as new, and yet foreseen. The art of the novelist is especially that of allowing the theme to be a prelude, anticipating it symbolically several times, preparing the mood in which we anticipate the outbreak of the storm, making tones adjacent to the primary melody sound and thus exciting in every way the inventive capacity of the reader, as if he were supposed to guess a riddle; but then *solve* this in a way that nonetheless still surprises the reader. — As the boy plays, so will the man work, an event at school can allow all characters involved to already recognize clearly a politically great course of events. — Perhaps a *philosophy*, too, *is to be represented* such that one places the real assertion only at the end and, to be sure, with tremendous emphasis.[107]

23[92][108]

It is a sign of *greatness* to be able to produce great happiness with *the slightest of gifts*.

23[93][109]

The *philosophy* of great human beings generally corresponds to the *age* at which the *conception* of it was made. Thus, for someone who knows intimately Schopenhauer's twenties, the entire philosophy of Schopenhauer can be clearly worked out, *prophesied*.

23[94][110]

Every human being is *educated* by the circumstances, companions, parents, siblings, events of the time, of the place: but all of this is education by chance and frequently suited to develop him quite unhappily. But humanity as a whole has not yet gotten beyond this *education by chance*: hindered by the metaphysical representation (upon which even Lessing's acute spirit became dulled) that a god has taken in hand the education of humanity and that we cannot fully comprehend his ways. Henceforth, education has to set ecumenical goals for itself and to exclude chance even in the fate of peoples: — the task is so great that a wholly new kind of educators, a new system of doctors teachers priests natural scientists artists of the old culture[111] — — —

23[95]

The prudence of the ancient poets is shown in the way that they raise *feeling from one step to the next* and thus increase it to a very high level. Modern ones like to attempt it with a sudden onslaught; or: they pull right away upon the bell-rope of passion with all their might. But if they are not successful at this at the start, they are also lost.[112] A good book should, as a whole, resemble a ladder of feeling, it would have to have access only from one side, the reader would have to feel confused if he attempted to make his way on his own. Every good book would thus protect itself; who likes to drag along behind himself a rope strung with words that he does not understand in the first place? Spoken as an allegory: when someone read aloud to me Calderon's the steadfast Prince in the translation of Schlegel,[113] I felt like this: I pulled my rope along for a while and finally let go of it with discontent, made a new attempt and once again pulled a string full of words behind me, but rarely did the clarifying redeeming word arrive: agony annoyance, like with a picture on which all of the drawing is faded and one thing can mean many things.

23[96][114]

The mistake of the moralists consists in how they set egoistical and unegoistical like immoral and moral opposite each other in order to explain what is moral, i.e., how they take the final goal of moral development, our present-day sensibility, as the starting point. But this final phase of development is conditioned by countless stages, by influences from philosophy and metaphysics, from Christianity, and really not to be used in order to explain the origin of what is moral. Moreover, it is possible that unegoistical behavior is indeed a concept common with us, but not a real fact, instead only a seeming one; the derivation of compassion e.g., is perhaps to be traced to egoism, just as there probably exist no acts of malice in itself, of doing harm without a personal reason etc. The realm of morality has been above all the realm of custom, but one really did not in every age call the one who had the custom of *un*egoistical actions, of compassion and the like, the "good human being," but rather the one who in general followed *custom*. Opposite him stood the evil human being, the one without custom (the indecent one).[115]

23[97]

Sympathy with the neighbor is a *late* result of culture: how far the imagination must be developed in order to feel with others as with ourselves (only when we have learned first to feel with our own *non*-present pains and joys through recollection and to feel them like present ones). Art certainly has a large part, when it teaches us to have compassion even with represented feelings of unreal persons.

23[98]

The good *review* of a scientific book consists in having *better solved* the problem it sets up; it would be in accord with this if the critique of a work of art were to consist in someone better representing the motif to be represented by the work of art, e.g., a musician were to show in action that someone else has not known how to make enough of his theme; likewise with a sculptor, a writer of novels. All good critique means making better; hence *being able to make better* is an indispensable condition for the critic. — But look now at the ordinary critics of art and philosophy! They say: "we don't like it"; but by what means do they want to prove that their taste stands[116] more developed, higher, if not through the act?

23[99][117]

We speak of *presentiments* as if e.g., religion were to have anticipatory awareness of certain knowledge, albeit obscurely. Such a relationship between religion and science does not exist. What we call presentiment is established upon completely different motives than scientific ones, grounded upon completely different methods, not even on semi-scientific method. It is *accidental* if the one looks similar to the other. All religions together are supposed to contain obscurely certain common "truths," we believe that we are saying something favorable about a philosophy if we bring religious fantasy onto its side: but it is the reverse. Science and religion will *not* be able to look *at all* similar in their results.

23[100][118]

There are, living on beside one another at the same time, humans of the most various stages of culture, even in the highly developed nations. In German and Switzerland everything that ruled over souls from the Reformation still persists somewhere, it is possible to wander backward through several centuries and to speak to people from these ages. Indeed, the very richly developed human being (like Goethe) lives great stretches of time, complete centuries in advance, in the various phases of his nature.

23[101][119]

Artists are the *advocates of passion*, for it is full of effect and gives the artist ten times more opportunity to show off his art. Thus emerges the appearance of the passions being something glorious, desirable, for the poets take the most beautiful words into their mouths; but really, they glorify passion because they want to glorify *themselves* the most. In part, they are themselves also of a passionate tendency and to that extent their own advocates. But now they establish what is worth glorifying in the world, they are the born eulogists of things — they have really altered the position of humans toward passion i.e., *even subtilized, ennobled this*: e.g., love. It is their accomplishment.

23[102][120]

Mme de Staël: the age of insight has its innocence just as much as the golden age.

23[103][121]

Value of the pangs of conscience for spiritual liberation. — There is no doubt that the pangs of conscience have contributed essentially to the increase of spiritual freedom in the world. They frequently excite a critique of representations that, on the basis of earlier actions, had such painful effects; and one discovered that there was not much in them except for habit and the general opinion within the society in which one lived. If someone was able to free himself from both of these, the pangs of conscience were also softened.

23[104]

Artists could be the happiest human beings, for it is permitted to them to produce what is perfect as *a whole* and, indeed, often; whereas the others are always working only on small parts of a whole. But the artists spoil themselves with the sight of what is perfect and whole and demand it everywhere else, too, they make higher claims, are envious, have not accustomed themselves to governing themselves, are arrogant in judgment; and sometimes their creating lacks the enjoying and praising recipient.

23[105]

Pathos belongs in art. — Who does not become poisonously and inwardly enraged[122] when he hears someone who takes his life far too pathetically and speaks of "Golgotha" and "Gethsemane"! — We put up with what is pathetic only in art; the living human being should be modest and not too loud.

23[106][123]

To want what the other wants and, indeed, for his sake, not for our own, that makes the friend, says Aristotle.[124] Here, the unegoistical action is described; if we find ourselves constantly in such a state of mind toward certain persons, this is friendship. According to the now usual conception of morality, the relation of friendship is the most moral one that exists.

23[107]

We must have lived for a time in the metaphysical atmosphere, in order simply to experience how good it feels to see all things in sober morning freshness and to draw deep breaths of pure air.

23[108]

To read correctly. — The art of reading correctly is so rare that almost everyone must first have a document a law a contract interpreted for him; in particular, much has been spoiled by the Christian preachers who from the pulpit continually afflict the Bible with the most desperate art of interpretation[125] and awaken respect far and wide for such an artificially casuistic manner, indeed, even imitation of it.

23[109]

If morality is to be traced back to the viewpoint of the common utility and harm, it is consistent to measure the moral component of an action not according to the intentions of the individual, but instead according to the act and its success. Splitting the soul and diagnostics[126] belong to a concept of ethics in which it is not at all a matter of utility and harm. One demands the action and does not trouble oneself so anxiously about the motives (the entanglement of which, moreover, is far too great for us not to be always going somewhat astray with *every* psychological analysis of an action).

23[110][127]

Spiritual transition climates. — We have set ourselves free from many representations — God eternal life requiting other-worldly and this-worldly justice, sin savior need for salvation — ; a sort of provisional sickness demands a replacement in the empty places, the skin shudders a bit at the frost, because previously it had been clothed here. There are philosophies that represent *transition climates*, as it were, for those who cannot yet directly endure the fresh air of the heights. — Compare how the Greek philosophical sects serve as transition climates: the old polis and its cultivation still continue to have an effect in them: but *for what purpose* should there be transitioning? — it has perhaps not been found. Or was it the *sophist*, the full free spirit?[128]

23[111][129]

We should no longer pay any attention when people complain about the lost folk traditions (in costume customs legal concepts dialects forms of poetry etc.). At precisely this price do we raise ourselves to what is supranational, to the universal goals of humanity, to thorough knowledge, to understanding and enjoyment of what is past, not native. — In short, precisely thereby do we cease to be barbarians.

23[112][130]

The sublime[131] works as stimulant and pepper upon those who are fatigued, the beautiful brings calming for those who have been stimulated — that is a primary difference. Someone who is stimulated shies away from the sublime, someone who is fatigued is bored with the beautiful. Moreover, the sublime, if it is disjoined from the beautiful, is identical to the ugly (i.e., to everything not beautiful); and as there exists an art of the beautiful soul, so too an art of the ugly soul.

23[113][132]

Self-contempt. — That vehement inclination toward self-examination and -contempt that we perceive among sinners penitents and saints is often to be traced back to a general exhaustion of their will to live (or nerves), against which they apply even the most painful stimuli.

23[114][133]

Consider how the errors of great philosophies generally have their starting point in a false explanation of particular human actions and sensations, how upon the basis of an erroneous analysis e.g., of the so-called unegoistical actions a false ethic is built, for the sake of which then, in turn, religion and mythological confusion are put to use and finally the shadows of these dismal spirits fall even upon physics and the total worldview; if we consider all of this, we see how improper the usual underestimation of psychological observation is: whereas it is precisely the superficiality of psychological observation, therefore the result of that underestimation, that has laid the most dangerous traps for human thinking and judging and constantly lays them anew. Whence, now, this disrespect? For instance, because such remarks are also occasionally successful with the empty and vain riffraff of society, male or female gender, because one tended at certain times to toss moral maxims around in the carnival of witty coquettishness like a type of confetti? — But the difference is exceptional precisely when a rigorously weighing thinker expresses the same psychological proposition that has at some time been discovered in those circles, too, and equips it with the imprint and portrait of *his* authority. Perhaps nothing is as necessary now as groundwork for all future philosophizing as piling up psychological work stone upon stone, pebble upon pebble and courageously resisting all disregard for this sort of work. To what discoveries will a later generation come, thanks to such material! — Admittedly, that dishonest spirit must be kept far away from this region, in which e.g., Schleiermacher called upon his pupils to investigate the psychological facts of religious consciousness: for here it was aimed from the start at maintaining religion and perpetuating theology (to which he wanted to assign a new task).[134] — As there are no purposes in nature and nevertheless it creates things of the highest purposefulness, so, too, will the genuine science work without purposes (utility welfare of human beings), but instead become a piece of nature,[135] i.e., attain here and there what is purposeful (useful), without having wanted to do so.

23[115]

Among the peculiarities of the Indo-Germanic languages that set them in contrast against the original mother tongue, we have to recognize the leftover traces of the lost languages that those peoples originally had who were attacked and conquered by nomadic Indo-Germanic tribes: so that the language of the conquerors likewise became victorious and passed over to those who had been subjugated. Perhaps the old habits lingered on, in the accent and such things, and passed over to the newly learned language.

23[116]

Thankful for consequences. — Many metaphysical and historical hypotheses are defended so strongly only because we are so grateful for their consequences.

23[117][136]

Delight in nature. — In a critique of the delight in nature, there is much that is to be subtracted that is not at all to be traced back to aesthetic stimulation, e.g., in climbing a high mountain the effect of the thin light air, the consciousness of the conquered difficulty, the resting, the geographical interest, the intention of finding to be beautiful the same thing that other people found beautiful, the anticipated delight in sometime telling about it.

23[118]

There are places in the side passage of the allegretto of the A-major symphony[137] where life creeps along as pleasantly as the minutes at a rose-hedge on summer evenings.

23[119]

Hope[138] is the rainbow over the steeply downward-plunging stream of life, swallowed up a hundred times by the spray and always piecing itself back together again, and with gentle beautiful boldness leaping over it where it roars most wildly and dangerously.

23[120]

Let us not underestimate even the shallower merry jovial women, they are there to amuse, there is much too much seriousness in the world. Even the deceptions in this area have their virgin honey. — If women become more capable substantial, there will no longer be any safe places in the world for harmless foolishness. Love affairs belong to the harmless things of existence.

23[121]

A Socratic means. — Socrates is right: we should, in order not to be completely subjugated by Eros, get involved with the less beautiful women.

23[122][139]

When someone has accustomed himself to making books, he pulls his perhaps completely lucid ideas apart in such a way that they become unwieldy and obscure. Thus, even Kant allowed himself to be determined by the scholarly manner of making books (which is even considered by the traditional judgment as an academic obligation) into that verbose kind of communication, which is doubly lamentable with him because he was always lacking for time (because of his academic duties): during the writing he frequently had first to think himself back into his train of thought. Had he been satisfied, in Hume's way, to communicate in the shortest form what he had established *prior to* the writing (perhaps on a walk), the entire conflict about the correct understanding of Kant, which still lives on today, would have been superfluous.

23[123]

Premature eloquence grinds down all ideas for immediate effective use and is therefore easily a hindrance to deep comprehension and in general a thorough immersion in self-contemplation. — Hence democratic states foster eloquence in the schools. —

23[124]

Experienced people return reluctantly to regions, to people that they have at one time loved a great deal. Happiness and separation should be tied together at their ends: thus we carry the treasure along with us.

23[125][140]

While Schopenhauer says about the world of appearance that it lets the essence of the thing in itself be recognized in its written characters, more rigorous logicians[141] have denied every connection between the unconditioned, the metaphysical world, and the world known to us: so that in the appearance the thing in itself does not appear at all. Both sides seem to me to overlook that there are various erroneous basic conceptions of the intellect that provide the reason why thing in itself and appearance seem to stand in irremediable opposition: we have entangled the appearance in so many errors, indeed, woven so many of them into it, that nobody can any longer think the world of appearances separated from them. Therefore: the bad illogical habits of the intellect, passed down from the beginning, first tore open the whole gulf between thing in itself and appearance; this gulf persists only insofar as our intellect and its errors persist. Schopenhauer, on the other hand, has brought together all of the characteristic traits of our world of appearance — i.e., of the representation of the world spun out of intellectual errors and inherited by us — and instead of indicting the intellect as the guilty party, accused the essence of things of being the cause of this factual character of the world. — A history of the emergence of thought will dispense decisively with both conceptions: the results of which might perhaps boil down to this proposition: what we now call the world is the result of a host of errors that emerged during the overall development of organic beings, merged together as they grew and are now passed on to us as the accumulated treasure of the entire past. Rigorous science can really free us only to a small extent from this world as representation, insofar as it cannot break the force of age-old habits: but it can shed light upon the history of the emergence of this world as representation.

23[126][142]

It is true, never has there been as much philosophizing in Germany as at present: even at the time of Hegel's highest power over German minds, not nearly so many philosophical writings appeared as in the last 15 years. But am I mistaken? Or am I right to suppose that a great danger lies in this sign? The *type* of philosophizing beloved now is such that it seems like a symptom of an *aversion* getting the upper hand against exact rigorous methodical studies. It is an enjoyable, under certain circumstances witty tossing around of philosophical idea-balls, which have now become catchable for almost every understanding; such a game looks better than tiresomely poring over difficult individual problems of science and in fact gives a certain cultivation to the social and public making of effects. — I wish that I were mistaken.

23[127][143]

Anyone who speaks of the attractiveness of danger knows the pleasure in the emotion of fear in itself.[144]

23[128]

Women in colonies. — The respect and courtesy that the Americans render to women is inherited from the time in which the latter were significantly in the minority: it is a peculiarity of colonial states. Many things among the Greeks can be explained from this. An exceptional case: where the colonists encounter many women, there generally emerges a decline in the estimation of women.

23[129]

The highly developed human being simply sets aside the natural things of existence that earlier stages of culture love, like eating drinking etc., without much talking and false embellishment. This is precisely where sociability, marriage belong as well; there no longer falls upon all such things the strong emphasis that other ages have for them. Good, it may be "more formless," less beautiful to see, the religious impression is withdrawn from these things and much "poetry" along with it. However, these losses are richly compensated, above all much energy saved, time saved (as with our clothing) and the entire sensibility not directed toward these superficialities. Someone who wants to achieve mastery in something raises himself to a noble sort of being through his goal. — Just as in the arts we have carried a lot of ugly things into the realm of art through spiritualization, so, too, in life; we must feel what pulses in these at first glance unbeautiful forms of life, what *new* and *higher* powers, then a higher beauty opens itself to our sight.

23[130]

It belongs among the oddities of metaphysical philosophizing, to intensify a problem and to establish it as unsolvable, unless we see a miracle as a solution, e.g., to see the essence of the actor in self-renunciation[145] and outright transformation: whereas the real problem, however, is *by what means of illusion* the actor manages to make it *seem* as if he were transformed.

23[131]

The thinking spirit among musicians is generally fresh, they are more often ingenious than the scholars; for they have in the exercise of their art the means to obtain nearly complete peace, a sort of sleep-life for reflective thought; hence it arises so cheerfully and morning-fresh[146] when the musician ceases to make music. — We sometimes deceive ourselves about this because the cultivation of the musician is often slight and he does not have enough material *upon* which he could demonstrate spirit. It is the same with ⟨the⟩ thinking spirit of women.[147]

23[132]

Anyone who fashions maxims in the German language has the difficulty that precisely at the end they cannot be sharply and strictly finished off, instead that auxiliary verbs tumble along afterward like debris and rubbish after a rolling stone. — Even the subtlest mind is not capable of properly appreciating the art of polishing maxims if he has not himself competed[148] in this area. Without this practical instruction, we take it to be easier than it is, we do not have a sharp enough feel for what is successful; hence the readers of maxims get a relatively slight satisfaction from them, just like the ordinary observer of cameos.[149] Only in competition do we learn to know what is good: so we should, for the sake of the pleasure of knowledge, at least really practice a science an art, and perhaps work out a novel, a philosophical observation, a speech from time to time; — [150] through reflection upon our own experiences, we then also comprehend the related areas bordering upon these experiences — and achieve access to many of the best sensations of pleasure.[151]

23[133][152]

We are also unjust when we find great men to be *too great* and the things in the world to be too profound. Anyone who wants to give the deepest meaning to life entangles the world in fables; we are all still deeply tangled up in it, however free-minded we may seem to ourselves. There is a strong tendency, age-old and innate, to exaggerate the distances, to apply the colors too strongly, to take what glitters as more probable. Energy manifests itself above all in this all too sharp accentuation; but the energy in moderation is the higher one, justice is harder than devotion and love. — If a murderer does not want to acknowledge the evil of his action and claims the right to call something good that the whole world calls evil, he dissociates himself from the development of human beings: do we have to concede this right to him? If someone were to justify so-called bad actions by separation from traditional judgments and an assertion of irresponsibility, are we permitted to say: "he is allowed to assert something like that only purely theoretically, but not to act practically in accordance with it"? Or: "as a thinker he is right, but he is not allowed to do evil." To what extent is the individual permitted to free himself from his past? As far as he can? And when he recognizes that false judgments, considerations and rough utility were at work in this past? That the halo around goodness, the gleam of brimstone around evil were thereby to vanish? If the strongest motives, taken from the honor and shame of our fellow human being, are no longer effective, because he can oppose the truth to this judgment?

23[134]

Why do people not invent entire *histories of peoples*, of revolutions, of political parties? Why does the author of the novel not enter into rivalry with the historian? I see here a future for the art of fiction.

23[135]

Formerly, one made definitions because one believed that within every word concept there dwelled a sum of predicates that one only needed to draw forth. But there is placed within words only a very uncertain hint of things: one only defines reasonably in order to say what one wants a word to mean, and leaves it to everyone else to delimit anew the sense of a word: it is not binding.

23[136][153]

The *school* of *educators* emerges on the basis of the insight: that our educators themselves have not been educated, that the need for them becomes ever greater, the quality ever less, that the sciences can scarcely impede barbarism in the individual through the natural separation of the fields of work, that there is no tribunal of culture that could take into consideration the spiritual welfare of the entire human species apart from national interests: an international ministry of education.

23[137]

It is to the disadvantage of a maxim when it stands by itself; in a book, on the other hand, it has in its surroundings a springboard from which we can raise ourselves up to it. We must understand how to place less significant ideas around significant ones, how to enclose the latter within them, thus the precious stone with material of lesser value. If maxims follow after one another, we involuntarily take the one as the setting for the others, push this one back in order to make another prominent, i.e., we make ourselves a surrogate of a book.

23[138][154]

Since *art* is becoming *ever more soulful*, the later masters notice that the artworks of the earlier age do not suit them and this causes them to help things along there and to believe that it is only the technical conditions that the old masters were lacking at that time. Thus Wagner[155] thinks that Beethoven *would* have written his scores better i.e., more soulfully if the instruments had been better; especially, though, in the modification of the tempo, he thinks that Beethoven, like all earlier ones, was insufficient only in markings. In truth, however, the soul was not yet so tenderly moved, so lively at each moment. All older art was rigid, stiff; in Greece as with us. Mathematics, symmetry, strict time ruled. — Should we give modern musicians the right to *animate* older works more? — Yes; for only by giving our soul to them do they still live on. Anyone who is acquainted with dramatic soulful music will perform Bach completely differently, involuntarily. If he hears it performed differently, he no longer understands it. Is a historical performance really *possible*?[156]

23[139]

The inventors of the Indo-German language probably belonged to the highest caste and made use of the available lesser languages. A high philosophical and poetic cultivation spoke out of them and formed a corresponding language; this is a conscious product of art; musical poetic genius was part of it. Then it became a language of poets and sages, later spread itself across the nearest castes and emigrated along with the warrior tribes. It was the most valuable legacy of the homeland, which one held on to tenaciously.

23[140][157]

The poets, in accordance with their nature, which is simply that of artists i.e., of rare exceptional humans, do not always praise what deserves to be praised by all people, but give preference to precisely what seems to them good as artists. Likewise, they rarely attack with success[158] when they are satirists. Cervantes could have fought against the Inquisition, but he preferred to make its victims i.e., heretics and idealists[159] of every kind, ridiculous in addition. After a life full of accidents and missed turns he was nonetheless still inclined to launch a literary assault upon a false direction of taste in Spanish readers; he fought against the chivalric novels. Imperceptibly,[160] this attack became in his hands the most general ironizing of all higher aspirations: he made all of Spain, including all the idiots, laugh and seem wise to themselves: it is a fact that no book has been so much laughed at as *Don Quixote*. With such a success, he belongs to the decadence of Spanish culture, he is a national misfortune. I think that he was contemptuous of human beings and did not exclude himself; or isn't he just making fun when he recounts how they played tricks on the sick man at the baron's court? Is he really supposed not to have laughed at the heretic being burned at the stake? Yes, he does not even spare his hero from that frightful dawning of awareness about his own condition at the end of life: if it is not cruelty, it is coldness, hard-heartedness that bade him create this sort of final scene, contempt toward the readers, who, as he knew, would not have been disturbed in their laughter by this conclusion.[161]

23[141]

All orig⟨inally⟩ stiff, painful sensation gradually becomes pleasant. From compulsion comes habit, from that custom, finally virtue is connected with pleasure. But the humans who have reached this final stage do not want to know anything about how their distant ancestors began the path.

23[142]

A human being sometimes strives for an emotion in itself, and uses humans only as a means. Most strongly in cruelty. But in the pleasure from what is tragic, too, there is something of this (Goethe found this sense for what is cruel in Schiller).[162] In the dramatic art in general, a human being wants emotions, e.g., of compassion, without having to help. Think of tightrope walkers, jugglers. — The passions habituate humans to them: that is why very passionate peoples e.g., Greeks and Italians have such delight in the art of passion, of emotion in itself; without it, they are bored.

23[143]

Sensation cannot remain steady and at a single level, it must grow or diminish. The reverence for the Greek polis added up to an infinite sum, finally the individual was no longer able to bear this burden.

23[144][163]

It is the way of unscientific people to prefer any explanation whatsoever of something to none, they want to hear nothing about abstinence.

23[145][164]

A highly capable human being experiences the state of *ripeness* several times insofar as he lives through various cultures and attains a high point in his understanding and comprehension of every individual one of them: and so a human being can feel in himself in advance the content of entire centuries: because the route that he takes through the various cultures is the same one that several generations take after one another. — Thus he also has several times the state of *unripeness*, of perfect blooming, of over-ripeness: he passes through this entire series of steps first perhaps as a religious, then again as an artistic and finally a scientific human being.[165]

23[146][166]

We are always newly amazed at how *Shakespeare* was able to have his heroes speak so appropriately, so thoughtfully each time, so that they utter maxims that are meaningful in themselves and yet also, in turn, sound suitable for their character? There we may well suppose, in order to explain it, that such speeches are a mosaic of *opportunistically discovered individual sentences*. I would like to counter this supposition, that there is a continual habit with the dramatist of inventing every remark only in accord with the character of a particular person, in relation to a situation: a habit that really is completely different from ours: to make the remark for the sake of its truth, completely[167] apart from person and situation. But we, too, sometimes ask ourselves: "what would you say *if* you were experiencing this?" The dramatist is accustomed to this *hypothetical speech*, it has become his nature always to invent his ideas under such presuppositions.

23[147][168]

Just as old richly meaningful religious ceremonies finally remain behind as superstitious not-understood procedures, so history in general, when it lives on only habitually, becomes similar to magical nonsense or carnivalistic disguise. The sun that is supposed to shine upon the Pope at the proclamation of infallibility, the dove that is supposed to fly as well, now seem like dubious little tricks that aim only at deception; but the old culture is full of this, and the entire distinction as to where illusion begins was not even made. Now, a showy Catholic funeral hearse was moving along with its retinue in one of the side alleys of Naples, while a short distance away the carnival was raging: all the colorful floats that imitated the costumes and the pomp of earlier cultures. But that funeral hearse, too, becomes at one time this sort of historical carnival procession; the colorful shell remains and delights, the kernel has flown away or it has hidden itself as the deceitful intent is hidden inside the tricks of the priest in order to awaken belief.

23[148][169]

Antiquity is on the whole the age of the talent for *rejoicing in festivals*. The thousand causes for rejoicing were not devised without astuteness and great reflection; a good part of the mental activity that is now directed toward the invention of machines, toward the solution of scientific problems, was at that time directed toward increasing the sources of joy: the sensation, the effect was supposed to be bent into something pleasant, we alter the causes of sorrow, we are prophylactic, they were palliative. — Our festivals are in fairness culture-festivals and on the whole rare.

23[149]

We take pleasure in a small act of malice because it does us so little harm e.g., in *sarcasm*; indeed, when we feel ourselves fully protected, even a large act of malice (for instance, in the poisonous venom of a pamphlet) serves to provide comfort; for it does not harm us and thereby approaches the effect of the comic — it surprises, frightens a little, and yet does not cause any damage.

23[150]

Art does not belong to nature, instead only to human beings.[170] — In nature there is no *tone*, it is silent; no color. Also no form, for this is the result of a reflection of the surface in the eye, but in itself there is no above and below, inner and outer. If we could see differently than by dint of reflection, we would not speak of forms, but instead perhaps see into the inside, so that the gaze would gradually cut through a thing.[171] Nature, from which we take our subject, is something quite indifferent, uninteresting, no mysterious primal ground, no uncovered world-riddle; we may indeed often be capable through science of getting beyond sensory perception, e.g., to conceive tone as a trembling movement; the more we dehumanize nature, the emptier more meaningless it becomes for us. — Art is based totally upon humanized nature, upon a nature entangled and woven through with errors and illusions that no art can disregard; ⟨it⟩[172] does not grasp the essence of things because it is completely tied to the eye and the ear. Only inferential understanding leads to the essence. It teaches us e.g., ⟨that⟩[173] matter itself is an age-old ingrained prejudice, stemming from the way that the eye sees reflective surfaces and the human organ of touch is very dull: that is, where we feel points of resistance, we involuntarily construct continuous resisting *planes* (which, however, only exist in our representation), under the habitual illusion of the reflecting eye, which is itself also basically only a coarse organ of touch. A ball of electric currents that revolve around a specific point would be felt like something material, like a solid thing: and the chemical atom is indeed such a figure, which is circumscribed by the end points of various movements. We are now accustomed to dividing what is moved and the movement; but in this we stand under the impression of age-old false conclusions: the moved thing is invented, imagined in, since our organs are not fine enough to perceive the movement everywhere and present us with something persistent: whereas there fundamentally exists no "thing," nothing abiding.[174]

23[151]

Since the modern education of human beings demands much greater mental activity, humanity must struggle much more energetically toward *health* in order not to have nervously overstimulated, indeed, crazy descendants (for otherwise a posterity of crazy and overstrained people would be quite possible — as the overripe individuals of late Athens sometimes flirt with insanity): therefore, through pairing up of healthy parents, the right strengthening of women, gymnastic exercises that must be as usual and as much desired as daily bread, prophylaxis of illnesses, rational nourishment, housing, in general through knowledge of anatomy etc.

23[152][175]

Christianity says "there are no virtues, but instead sins." With this, all human behavior is slandered and poisoned, also the confidence in humans shaken. Now philosophy in the manner of La Rochefoucauld still seconds this, it traces the celebrated human virtues back to petty and ignoble motives. So it is a true deliverance to learn that there are neither good nor bad actions in themselves, that in the same sense as the proposition of Christianity, the opposed one of antiquity can also be established "there are no sins, instead only virtues" i.e., actions according to the viewpoint of the good (only that the judgment about good varies). Everyone behaves in accordance with what is advantageous for him, nobody is voluntarily evil i.e., self-harming. It is a great step forward to learn that everything moral has nothing to do with the thing in itself, but is instead "opinion," belongs in the realm of the quite variable intellect.[176] Admittedly: as our ear has created the sense for music (which also does not exist in itself), so do we have the moral sense as a high result of previous humanity. But it is not grounded upon logical laws of thought and upon rigorous observation of nature, but instead, like the sense for the arts, upon many false judgments and wrong inferences. Science cannot keep from uncovering this illogical foundation of morality, as it does with art. Perhaps in the long run it thereby weakens this sense somewhat: but the *sense for truth* is itself one of the highest and most powerful *efflorescences of this moral sense*. Here lies the compensation.

23[153]

Barbarizing effect of abstraction and sublimation on the occasion of Aristotelian⟨ism⟩[177] in science.

23[154][178]

If we are thinking about higher utility, about ecumenical purposes with the word morality, there is more morality contained in *trade* than in life according to that Kantian demand, "do as you want to be done unto"[179] or in the Christian turn toward the rule of conduct of the saying: "love your neighbor for the sake of God."[180] Kant's proposition yields a petty bourgeois private respectability of custom and stands in opposition to economic purposes: of which he does not even have any idea. How little any obligatory love really does signify, but especially a love of this indirect kind, like Christian love of the neighbor, that has been demonstrated by the history of Christianity: which, in contrast to the results of Buddhistic, rice-eating morality is thoroughly violent and bloody. And what does it actually mean: "I love my fellow humans for the sake of God!" Is it more than if someone says: "I love all police for the sake of justice" or what a little girl might say: "I love Schopenhauer because grandfather likes him: he knew him"?

23[155]

The pathos of feeling has come into the world through certain views about things,[181] not through things themselves:[182] e.g., everything that *Faust* in the first scene indicates as cause for his suffering[183] is erroneous, that is, has become so heavy with meaning on the basis of metaphysical fabrications: if he could perceive this, the pathos would be lacking in his mood.[184]

23[156]

(From the Preface)

After I have learned more from year to year about how difficult it is to find the truth, I have become distrustful toward the belief in having found the truth: it is a primary obstacle to the truth. Yet if all those who thought so highly of their convictions, made sacrifices of all kinds to them, indeed, spared neither honor body nor life in their service, had devoted merely half of their strength to investigating by what right they adhered to this or that conviction or the way in which they had come to it: how peaceful would human history then appear! How much more knowledge would there be! We would have been spared all the cruel scenes, the persecution of heretics, for two reasons: first because the inquisitors would have inquired above all into themselves and would have gotten beyond the presumption that they were defending the absolute truth; and then because the heretics themselves would not have given any further credence to propositions as badly grounded as the propositions of all religious true believers and heretics are, once they had thoroughly investigated them.[185]

Now I have before me this time a theme that is perhaps the most important one for humanity — for what has not emerged, become strong, good and bad through education? — in addition, it lets itself be dealt with in large measure only after disbelief has become the ruling disposition. So I would now like to warn especially the fiery youths who are thirsty for conviction not immediately to consider my teachings as a rule of conduct for life, but instead as theses to be well considered, which humanity may wait to introduce in practice for as long as they have not been sufficiently protected against doubt and reasons. Moreover, truth did not fall to me from heaven, for I am no "genius," have no intuitive insight through a hole in the cloak of appearance. Schopenhauer may be the warning example: he is, in all the points on which he takes himself to be a "genius," wrong.

23[157][186]

Life becomes easy and pleasant through a reckless liberation of the spirit, which experimentally calls into question all the representations that burden life so much, make it so unbearable: so that we, in order to have the joy of this disburdening, prefer the simplest life that this joy makes possible for us.

23[158]

Paul Winkler[187] 1685 "human beings are wise as long as they seek the truth; but if they think they have found it, they become a fool."

23[159][188]

I want to declare explicitly to readers of my earlier writings that I have given up the metaphysical-artistic views that essentially predominated in them: they are pleasant, but untenable. Anyone who prematurely allows himself to speak publicly is generally soon forced to contradict himself in public about that.

23[160][189]

In *Conclusion.*

I want to become *wise* by my sixtieth year and recognize this as a goal for many. A great deal of science is to be acquired successively and blended into myself. It is the good fortune of our age that we can for a time grow up in a religion and, in music, have a completely genuine mode of access to art; for later ages, that will no longer be so easily available. With the help of these personal experiences we can first understand tremendous stretches of humanity: which is important because all of our culture rests upon these stretches. We *must* understand religion and art — otherwise we cannot become wise. But we must be able to see beyond them; if we remain within them, we do not *understand* them. Likewise, metaphysics is a stage upon which we must have stood. Likewise history and relativism. We must, as individuals, follow the course of humanity in great steps and get beyond what has been the goal up to now.

Anyone who wants to become *wise* has an *individual goal* into which everything experienced, good fortune bad fortune injustice etc., is dissolved as means and aid. Moreover, human life comes into the right form then, for the *old* human being attains the goal most easily in accord with his entire nature. Life proceeds interestingly, too, the theme is quite large and not to be exhausted too early. — Knowledge itself has no further goal.

23[161][190]

The moral purity of humans has been advanced more through some false representations than the truth would have been capable of doing. That a God wants what is good, that the body is to be conquered in order to make the soul free, that responsibility for all actions and thoughts exists, that has elevated and refined humanity. Even just establishing "what is good"!

23[162]

In the preliterary age the higher intelligence must have presented itself differently than in the literary one: the individual, connected with earlier sages and reminded of the limited nature of knowing by no written tradition, may have taken itself for almost suprahuman. The sage loses more and more of his eminence.

23[163]

Once *words* exist, humans believe something must correspond to them e.g., soul God will fate etc.

23[164]

The so-called metaphysical need is a counterauthority against the truth of any metaphysics whatsoever. The will commands.

23[165]

The advantage that the pure human being brings to his fellow humans lies in the example that he gives: he thereby rescues them from their wild demon, even if only for a few moments. — A great deal depends upon the moments.

23[166]

The nobler motives are the complicated ones; all simple motives stand fairly low. It is like with simple and complicated organisms. The length and difficulty of the entire path throws the appearance of something great and high upon the one who walks it.

23[167][191]

If humans had not built houses for gods, architecture would still lie in the cradle. The tasks that humans set for themselves on the basis of false assumptions (e.g., soul detachable from the body), have given rise to the highest forms of culture. "Truths" are not capable of providing such motives.

23[168][192]

If we want to have experiences about *art*, we should make some works of art, there is no other path to aesthetic judgment. Most artists are themselves useful only in that they acquire, hold on to and exaggerate[193] the consciousness of the great masters: therefore, like heat-conducting media,[194] as it were. Some novellas, a novel, a tragedy — that we can make without suffering shipwreck in our primary occupations; we should also by no means put such things into print. In general, we should learn to be manifoldly *productive*: it is the main trick in order to become wise in many things.

23[169][195]

It is one stage of culture to esteem what is great and extreme, the great human being, the strongest productivity, the warmest heart. But in order to comprehend the world, we must come to a higher stage, that what is small and unpretentious is more important in its effects e.g., the constrained spirits etc.

23[170]

The most favorable point in time for a people to take over leadership in scientific matters is the one in which enough force tenacity rigor is inherited by the individual in order to make possible for him a triumphant joyous isolation from public opinions: this point in time has now arrived again in England, which is unmistakably ahead of all peoples at present in philosophy natural science history, in the field of discoveries and the diffusion of culture. The leading figures in science there deliberate with one another like kings who, to be sure, all regard themselves as relatives,[196] but presuppose acknowledgment of their independence. In Germany, on the contrary, they believe they will attain everything through education methods schools:[197] as a sign for the fact that they lack the personalities and[198] path-breaking natures who have at all times gone their own way. They breed those useful workers who work in time with one another and to whom the *pensum*[199] has already been prescribed from those ages when Germany, by virtue of its original spirits, held the spiritual leadership of Europe: therefore around the turn of the previous century.

23[171]

The defects of style sometimes give it its charm. — Alexander von Humboldt's style. The ideas have something uncertain insofar as it is not a matter of communication of facts. Besides, everything is raised into the heights and covered with a sheen by selected beautiful words: the long sentences stretch it out. So this style as a whole produces a mood, a thirst, we make our eyes small because we would all too gladly like to see something clear, everything swims attractively transfigured off in the distance: like one of those wave-like mirages that seem to be (to lead before the senses) a sea an oasis a forest to someone who is exhausted[200] thirsty.

23[172]

A new portrayal of the *doctrine of art* must begin with the fact that a human being rejoices in all *mental stimulations*, precisely as emotions, even the painful ones: he wants intoxication. Art stimulates him in a playful way to pain tears anger desire, but without all the bad practical consequences: yet there are also humans who accept those consequences simply in order to have the emotion (a cruel person).

23[173][201]

Schopenhauer unfortunately smuggled the worst mysticism into the concept "intuitive knowledge," as though we were to have, by virtue of this, an immediate vision into the essence of the world, through a hole in the cloak of appearance, as it were, and as if there were privileged people who were capable of communicating something definitive and decisive about the world by means of this miraculous prophetic vision, without the toil and rigor of science. Such people do not exist: and henceforth miracles will no longer find any believers for the field of knowledge either.

23[174]

The silkworm that has hatched still drags the empty pupa behind it for a while; image.[202]

23[175]

Inclination and disinclination irrational. — Once inclination or disinclination has bitten down, it is hard to get free, as when a turtle has bitten stubbornly into a stick. Love, hate and the turtle are stupid.

23[176]

With the unegoistical drive, the inclination toward a person is what is decisive (when it is not the pleasure in compassion and just as little the warding off of displeasure that we feel at the sight of suffering). But does the inclination for all of that make such an occurrence nonmoral? Is then all being interested in something lying outside of us moral? — Also all objective interest (with art and science) belong in the field of what is unegoistical — but also of what is moral?

23[177]

Philosophy not to be conceived religiously. — To grasp a philosophy with religious needs means to misunderstand it completely. We seek a new faith, a new authority — but anyone who wants faith and authority has it more comfortably and more securely in the traditional religions.

23[178]

It was evening, the scent of pines streamed out, one looked across to gray mountains, above the snow was shimmering.

Calm blue sky gathered above. — We *never* see something like this as it is in itself, but instead are always laying a delicate membrane of the soul over it — this, then, is what we see. Inherited feelings, our own moods are awakened amid these[203] things of nature. We see something of ourselves — to that extent, this world, too, is our representation. Forest mountains, yes, that is not only concept, it is our experience and history, a piece of us.[204]

23[179]

Superstition. — People who are greatly excited are the most superstitious. The restoration of religions lies in periods of great disruption and uncertainty. Where everything gives way, we grab for the tapestry of illusions of what is beyond.

23[180]

The dying child. — We give to a child who must die whatever he wants, sweets — and so what if it spoils the stomach? — And aren't we all in the situation of such a child? —

23[181][205]

A procession on the feast of Corpus Christi, children and old men brought me to tears. Why? — Evening piano-playing from out of an insane asylum.

23[182]

Might not many who are *ambitious* basically be seeking only the *emotion* that is connected with ambitious aspirations? We can hinder suffocate or make such a feeling grow large; the latter is what the emotionally needy do. Many even seek to annoy themselves — so far does that need for emotion go.

23[183]

Consideration for different opinions is most often to be explained by *fear*; a good part of politeness (the wish not to displease) belongs here. Thus is the *goodness* of humans, with the assistance of inheritance, brought up through fear.

23[184][206]

Utility of b⟨ackward⟩ p⟨oints of view⟩. — Backward points of view (political social, or entire types among artists, metaphysicians) are just as necessary as progressive movements: they produce the necessary friction and are sources of energy for new aspirations.

23[185][207]

Faith moves mountains.[208] — It is an interesting superstition that *faith* could move mountains, that a certain high degree of taking something to be true can reshape things according to this faith, that error becomes truth if only there is no grain of doubt in it: i.e., the strength of the faith supplements the lack of knowledge; the world becomes such as we represent it to ourselves.

23[186][209]

Love and hate not original forces. — Behind *hating* lies *fearing*, behind *loving* needing. Behind fearing and need lie experience (judging[210] and memory). The intellect seems to be older than feeling.[211]

23[187][212]

Enlargement of experience. — There are cases where *dreams* really enrich the circle of our experience: who would know, without dreams, how someone feels *when floating on air*?

23[188][213]

Yearning for death. — As someone who is seasick peers out from the boat toward the coast in the first gray of morning, so we often yearn for death — we know that we cannot change the course and the direction of our boat.

23[189][214]

Sorrow and sensual pleasure. — Why is a person in a state of sorrow more inclined to abandon himself blindly to sensory pleasures? Is it what is anesthetizing in them that he desires? Or need for emotion at any price? — Sancho Panza says "if a person abandons himself too much to sorrow, he becomes an animal."[215]

23[190][216]

When Richard Wagner performs Beethoven, it is self-evident that Wagner's soul will sound through Beethoven and that tempo dynamics interpretation of individual phrases dramatization of the whole is Wagnerian and not Beethovenian. Anyone who wants to get annoyed at this is permitted to do so: Beethoven himself, however, would have said "it is I and you, but it sounds good together; so should it always be." On the contrary, when a second-grade master performs Beethoven, Beethoven will take on something of the soul of the small master — for the scent of the soul immediately attaches itself to the music and does not let itself be blown away from it. — I fear Beethoven would have had no joy in this and would say "this is I and not-I, to the devil with it!"

23[191][217]

The philologist is the one who can read and write, the poet the one who had "*to dictate*"[218] following the clear derivation of the words and according to history, since he cannot read and write. We can derive many important things from this opposition of the scholar of reading/writing and the poet.

23[192][219]

Not only in the behavior of the state that punishes in order to deter, but in the behavior of every individual who praises or blames, the principle "the end justifies the means" is being followed: for blaming likewise only makes sense as a means to deter and henceforth to work as a motive; praising wants to urge on, to challenge to imitation: but insofar as both are done *as if* they applied to an action that had taken place, lying and pretense are not to be avoided in any praising and blaming;

they are precisely the means that are sanctified by the higher end. Assuming, admittedly, that everyone, the ones blaming as well as the ones being blamed, are convinced by the doctrine of complete irresponsibility and blamelessness, then the blame no longer works unless habit, especially the habit of vanity and ambition, remains stronger than all of the convictions instilled by doctrines.

23[193]

Ah, if mediocre people only had any idea of how surely their accomplishments are felt by the *oligarchs of the spirit* — who live in every age — to be mediocre! Not even the greatest success with the masses would comfort them.

23[194][220]

Motto:
Dance of ideas, one of the Graces
is leading you:
o how you delight my senses! —
Woe! What do I see! Falling from
the leader, her mask and veil,
and ahead of the dance
strides cruel necessity.[221]

Rosenlauibad
June 1877
August 1877

23[195][222]

And if the author of this book asks himself for[223] whose benefit he wishes to have made his[224] notes, he is immodest enough to name right away that thinker who as author of that text on the origin of moral sensations acquired for himself[225] a right of ownership to the regions adjacent to his scientific district and who set forth in his investigations those decisive ideas that also had a govern⟨ing⟩ effect upon this book.[226] This proposition, made hard and cutting by the hammer-blows of historical knowledge, can perhaps someday serve as the ax that gets laid to the root of the "metaphysical need of human beings": and to that extent it would belong to the most consequential propositions of human knowledge.

23[196]

Travel book
to be read while underway.

Preface — — —[227]

People who work a lot within one specific profession keep their general views about the things of the world almost unchanged: these become ever harder, ever more tyrannical in their heads. Hence those times in which humans are required to abandon their work are so important, because then for the first time new concepts and sensations may once again push their way up, and their energy is not already used by the daily claims of duty and habit. We modern people must all travel a lot for the sake of our spiritual health: and we will travel more and more, the more work is done. To travelers, therefore, must turn those who work for the transformation of general views.

From this specific consideration, however, there results a specific form of communication: for those long-spun-out systems of thought that show themselves accessible only to the most patient attentiveness and demand weeks-long stillness, the most withdrawn solitude, are opposed to the winged and restless nature of travel.[228] There must be books that we do not read through, but frequently open up: we remain with one or another sentence today, attach ourselves to a different one tomorrow, and reflect once again from the depths of our heart: for and against, within and out beyond, however the spirit moves us, so long as every time we thereby become cheerful and clear-headed. Gradually there emerges from this sort of animated — genuine, because not forced — reflection a certain general remodulation of views: and with it that general feeling of spiritual recuperation, as if the bow were again strung with new string and could be drawn more strongly than ever. We have traveled usefully.

If now, after such preliminary remarks and with regard to this book, one essential question still remains, I am not the one who can answer it. The preface is the author's right; the reader's, however — the afterword.[229]

Friedrich Nietzsche

Rosenlaui-Bad, on 26 July
Summer equinox 1877
(Midsummer equinox?)

23[197]

1 *New Year's Eve*: the phantom sound escapes
my ear itself[230]
Cold — the stars glitter
O you
Mockery-filled mask of the universe
— old and new time — *before* the new year.
2 the fountain in the moonlight
beautiful bored malicious
wants to overflow coldly
3 Mornings on the boat. Where to? we do not risk death[231]
4 The blind man on the path. The soul gives no gleam[232]
5 *Ecce homunculus*[233] — chimes[234]
6 Alpa Alpa[235]
7 Campo Santo
8 Mountain crystal

[24 = Mp XIV 1c. Autumn 1877]

24[1][1]

On the Doctrine of Art.

1 The real and supposed sufferings of the genius
2 The excellence of a work of art proven, if it is moving?
3 Seriousness formerly in spinning out forms and symbols: now in something else
4 Rejection of inspiration; the selecting power of judgment
5 Drasticists, not dramatists
6 Damming up of productive energy: explanation of improvisation
7 what is incomplete made use of
8 the thinking spirit of the musician fresh, but uncultivated.
9 weaker morality of artists with regard to knowing truth
10 art conserves, connects earlier and contemporary views
11 artists are permitted to deny progress.
12 soulful music in restored Catholicism
13 how could Shakespeare come to such characteristic speeches for all personae without a miracle?
14 our vanity demands the cult of genius and of inspiration
15 ambition gives wings to the Greek artists
16 bad writers always necessary — need of the unripe age
17 art proceeds from natural ignorance about humans, it is not for physicists and philosophers. The "characters" not created.
18 art takes over the feelings heightened by religion.

19 art ever more soulful, false conclusion about older art
20 the poets extol what is interesting to the *artist* e.g., Cervantes.
21 value of ideas that have not been finished.
22 art, tied to eye and ear, has nothing to do with the essence of things
23 the vanishing of good manners and the prospect
24 art draws the artist back to older views.
25 music is as the heir of poetry so meaningful, symbolic
26 overestimation of improvisation
27 the church prepares all the moods of art.
28 the artists as advocates for the passions
29 passionate peoples take pleasure in the art of passion.
30 conspicuous greatness overestimated
31 houses for gods — otherwise architecture in the cradle: therefore the error
32 in order to become experienced in art, we should produce it
33 Plato is right about the immoral effect of tragedy
34 Schopenhauer as thinker *above* the passions
35 the shuddering of genius at itself. The piece of insanity in genius
36 the noblest form of beauty
37 music as the dying refrain of a culture. Wagner
38 the ancients raise feeling gradually, the moderns try for a sudden attack
39 original artists can make completely empty stuff
40 perhaps we will soon stand in a relation of memory to art
41 origin of art
42 among the metaphysical presuppositions art has higher value
43 joy in nonsense

24[2][2]

Introduction: Reasoning backward from effect to cause.

I or IV the origin of art 7 15 19 21 25 41 43 the aesthetic state — silencing of the will false. There we are cold.

III the artist as genius 1 4 6 13 14 26 30 35 39
IV or I estimation of art 2 17 16 22 29 36 37 42
V disadvantageous consequences of art 5 9 10 20 24 28 33
VI the future of art 3 8 11 23 32 38 40 34
II reliance upon religion 12 18 27 31 in addition "on music"

for III: the belief in genius falsifies the representation of the emergence of the work of art 4 6 13 26, from the life of the artist, also with the artist himself 1 35

explanation of faith. Everything great overestimated. 30
our vanity 14
survival[3] of begodded human beings.
difference among "originals" still only relative 39

difference between objective and nonobjective, the artistic geniuses are nonobjective, they want an effective form of the world — "intuitive knowledge" the world more objective, purer, clearer in their heads.

24[3][4]

Friendship.[5] Woman and child.[6] Education.[7] Easing of life. Progress. The writer.[8] Death. Society. Thoughts of discontent.[9]

Manners. Health.

Tricks. Experience. Thinkers. Necessity. On his age. Youth. War. Punishment. Interesting. Cleanliness. Revenge. Duel. Festivals. Free spirit, unpleasant character. Individual affects and states. Morality. Religion. Science. Philosophy. Writers. Art. State and society. Emergence of culture. Easing of life. Thoughts of solitary discontent. Profession. Society. Friendship. Woman and child. Questions of education.

Praise. To promote more. Loyalty. Justice. Modesty. Hate. Fear. Ambition. Love. Passion. Brutality. Fortune misfortune. Impolite. Vanity. Suspicion. Shame. Integrity. Criminals. Contempt. Spirit. Half-knowers. Courage. Speaking. Boredom. Maliciousness. Danger. Greatness. Death. Comfort. Laziness. Disguise. Humanity. General progress.

Dishonesty. Degeneration. Hope. Envy. Corruption. Polemic. Work. Gratitude. Deep human beings. Masters. Arrogance.

Diligence. Virtue. Evil will. Students. Diplomats. Blame. Resignation. Flattery. Talent. Reputation. Merit. Laughing. Distinction. Denying oneself. Party. Memory. Habit. Trust. Youth. Moment. Nobility. Power.

24[4][10]

1 Conviction and truth (faith moves mountains) (loyalty)
2 Responsibility.
3 Justice. (Praise and blame private.)
4 Mysteries (marriage — kingdom, future) shame
5 Culture-flexibility. Melancholy
6 Origin of morality. Tradition. Habit. Benevolence. Relations with people.
7 Asceticism and holiness.
8 Consciousness of sins.

24[5][11]

Metaphys⟨ics⟩
Politics press party society
Education school instruction
Culture
Morality
Music
Young people
Surroundings relations
Author
Art. Genius.

24[6]

The political illness of a nation is generally the cause of its spiritual rejuvenation and power.

24[7][12]

The parents are not, as the metaphysical philosopher thinks, the acciden⟨tal-⟩cau⟨ses⟩ of the children — rather, the children are the opportunistic effects of the parents;[13] the latter basically want pleasure and occasionally happen thereby to have children.

24[8][14]

So that hero — dragon.

24[9]

All little poets believe healthy human understanding is cheap, and that they would have it as soon as they wanted it. — And they do not suspect that they must remain little poets for precisely this reason, because they will *never* have it.

24[10]

Epilogue. — I greet you all, my readers, who do not intentionally look into this book with false and crossed eyes, you who are capable of recognizing more in it than a fool's hut in which a distorted and grotesque image of spiritual freedom has been hung for worship. You know what I gave and how I gave: what I could and how much more I wanted — namely, to stretch an electric cord across a century, from out of a death-room into the birthing room of new freedoms of the spirit. May you now practice a beautiful requital for everything good and bad that I have said and done! There are those among you who shall[15] requite something small with something great and what was wished for with what was possible: — the feeling with which I think of every one of these shall be expressed here at the end of this book, as a rhythmical greeting:

Since this book grew up in me, desire and shame torment me,
Until such growth one day blooms more richly and more beautifully for you.
Already now I taste the happiness that I am following after someone greater,
When he rejoices in the golden yield of his own harvest.[16,17]

[25 = Mp XIV 1d. (Gast). Autumn 1877]

25[1][1]

Socialism.

First: As on-lookers, we deceive ourselves concerning the sufferings and privations of the lower strata of the people, because we involuntarily measure according to the standard of our own sensation, as if we ourselves were to be transferred into their situation with our highly sensitive and susceptible brain. In truth, sufferings and privations increase with the growth of the culture of the individual; the lower strata are the dullest, to improve their situation means: to make them more susceptible to suffering.

Second: If we contemplate not the well-being of the individual, but instead the goals of humanity, it is very questionable whether under the ordered circumstances that socialism demands the results of humanity that *could* ensue would be as great as those that *have* ensued from the disordered circumstances of the past. The great human being and the great work probably grow only in the freedom of the wilderness. Humanity has no other goals than great human beings and great works.

Third: Because a great deal of hard and rough work must be done, people must also be maintained who submit to that, insofar, that is, as machines cannot spare them from this work. If the need and the refinement of higher cultivation penetrates the worker class, it can no longer do that work without suffering disproportionately. A worker developed this far strives for leisure and demands not lightening of the work, but liberation from it, that is: he wants to burden someone else. We could perhaps think of satisfying his wishes and introducing on a large scale barbarian peoples from Asia and Africa, so that the civilized world would continually be making the uncivilized world serviceable for itself, and in this way nonculture would be considered as an obligation to compulsory service. In fact, in the states of Europe the culture of the worker and of the employer have often gotten so close that the extended expectation of grinding mechanical labor evokes the feeling of indignation.

Fourth: If we have grasped how the sense of fairness and justice has emerged, we must contradict the socialists when they make justice into their principle. In the state of nature, the principle does not hold that: "what is right for one is fair for the other," but instead, power decides there. Insofar as the socialists want the complete overthrow of society, they are calling upon power. Only when the representatives of the future order stand opposite the old orders in battle and both powers find themselves equal or similarly strong are agreements possible and on the basis of the agreements, a justice *emerges* afterward. — Human rights do not exist.[2]

Fifth: If a lowly worker says to the rich manufacturer: "You do not *deserve* your good fortune," he is right, but his inferences from this are false: nobody deserves his good fortune, nobody his misfortune.

Sixth: Happiness on the earth will not be increased by the transformation of institutions, but by us making the gloomy, sickly, brooding, bilious temperament die out. The external situation adds or subtracts little. Insofar as the socialists mostly have that bad sort of temperament, they diminish under all circumstances happiness on earth, even if they should succeed in founding a new order.

Seventh: Only within tradition, stable customs, limitation is there contentment in the world; the socialists are connected to all the powers that destroy tradition, custom, limitation; new constitutive capacities have not yet become manifest among them.

Eighth: The best that socialism brings with it is the stimulation that it communicates to the widest circles: it *entertains* humans and brings to the lowest strata a sort of practical-philosophical discourse. To this extent it is a source of energy for the spirit.

25[2][3]

Preface.

If it happens that even the author, placed in front of his own book, looks into its face with surprise and the question crosses his lips: am I this? am I not this? — how much more must readers of his earlier writings have such a feeling, especially when they do not personally know the author of them and he stands before their souls only as the spirit and character of those writings. To these readers, those who at all times have been present, loyal, unafraid inciters and defenders of my higher self — I therefore owe an explanation, not about what the book is, but instead what it means for them, for me: the same explanation that I give to myself when I, as I said, occasionally look into the eyes of my own child with amazement and find it at times a little uncanny, at times all too harmless.

Every one of us, the most notable human beings of this age, carries that inner free-spirited agitation around with him, which to a degree inaccessible to all earlier ages makes us sensitive and resistant to the lightest pressure of any authority whatsoever. It is an accident that none of us has up to now wholly become the type of the free spirit of the present, whereas we do perceive the start of it and the sketched outline, as it were, of its nature, as if its eyes were upon all of us. Now, while the author of this book has for a considerable time been tracking those great typical human beings who are growing out of this age and beyond it, in order to be at some point the supports of a future culture, that lack of an essential type did not escape him; he sought to help himself by attempting to see the image of the free spirit of the present according to that inner indication and gradually painting it. By paying careful attention to the hours in which that spirit spoke out of him, by finding the law of the hours, the inner connection of that spiritual speech, for him, a spirit became a person, and a person almost a form. In the end he could no longer bring himself simply to paint this form publicly as the type of the free spirit of the present; he preferred the bolder step of allowing the spirit to speak, indeed of imputing a book to it. May anyone hearing this speech feel his nearness with confidence, may he feel how that almost nervous free-spirited irritability, that resistance toward the last remains of compulsion and commanded restraint are tied to a secured, mild and almost joyful soul, toward which nobody needs to be on guard against tricks and sudden outbreaks! This free companion particularly lacks the grumbling tone and sullenness, the qualities of old dogs and people who have lain for a long time on the chain; the modern free spirit is not, like his ancestors, born from battle, rather from the *peace of the dissolution* into which he sees that all the spiritual powers of the old constrained world have entered. After this greatest revolution in history has occurred, his soul can be without envy and almost without need, he does not strive for much for himself, not much more; he is satisfied that the free fearless floating above humans, customs, laws and the traditional estimations of things is the most desirable state. He gladly shares the joy in this state; anyone who wants more from him, he refers, with a little mockery upon his lips, with benevolent shaking of the head, to his brother, the free human being of action: the circumstances of whose "freedom" are admittedly peculiar, about which many a story could be told. —

After the author — I almost said: the poet — has said in such a way the prologue on behalf of his play and hero, let the latter himself now take the stage and begin his monological play. Is it tragedy? Or comedy, or tragicomedy? The word may be lacking that would fully suffice for description here: so may a verse come to our aid to prepare the listener:

Play of ideas, one of the Graces
is leading you:
O how you delight my senses! —
Woe! What do I see! Falling from
the leader, her mask and veil,
and ahead of the dance
strides cruel necessity.[4,5]

25[3][6]

I Philosophy of Culture.[7]
II On the History of the Moral Sensations.
III The Religious Life.
IV From the Soul of Artists and Writers.
V Of the First and Last Things.[8]
VI In Relations with Others.
VII Woman and Child.
VIII A Glance at the State.
IX By Oneself Alone.

[26 = D 11. Winter 1876–1877]

26[1][1]

Passion for belittling as useful. — It is not only a few people who find it thoroughly necessary, in order to maintain their self-esteem and a certain proficiency in action, to disparage and to belittle for themselves all the people they have known. In that we all have the advantage of that proficiency, we must for better or worse approve of the necessary tool for it, the envy and passion for belittling.

Reference Matter

Notes

The following symbols are used throughout the text and notes:

[ ]	Deletion by Nietzsche
| |	Addition by Nietzsche
{ }	Addition by the translator or editors
⟨ ⟩	Addition by the editors (Colli and Montinari)
[?]	Uncertain word
— — —	Unfinished or incomplete sentence or thought
Italics	Underlined once by Nietzsche
Bold	Underlined twice or more by Nietzsche
NL	Books in Nietzsche's personal library

Variants and editions of Nietzsche's works are referred to by the following abbreviations:

CW	*The Complete Works of Friedrich Nietzsche*
KGB	*Briefwechsel: Kritische Gesamtausgabe*
KGW	*Kritische Gesamtausgabe*
KSA	*Kritische Studienausgabe*
Cp	Correction in the proofs
Fe	First edition
Le	Twenty-volume 1894 Leipzig edition of Nietzsche's works (*Großoktav-Ausgabe*)

Le[2]	*Großoktav-Ausgabe*, second edition (1897, edited by Fritz Koegel)
Ms	Manuscript
Pd	Preliminary draft
Pm	Printer's manuscript (clean final copy of handwritten MS)
PmG	Change made by Gast in the printer's manuscript
PmN	Change made by Nietzsche in the printer's manuscript
Pp	Page proofs
Sd	Second draft
Se	Subsequent emendation
Up	Uncorrected proofs

Titles of Nietzsche's works are referred to by the following abbreviations:

AC	*The Antichrist*
BGE	*Beyond Good and Evil*
BT	*The Birth of Tragedy*
D	*Dawn*
DD	*Dionysus Dithyrambs*
DS	*David Strauss the Confessor and the Writer*
EH	*Ecce Homo*
GM	*On the Genealogy of Morality*
HAH	*Human, All Too Human*
HL	*On the Utility and Liability of History for Life*
JS	*The Joyful Science*
MM	*Mixed Opinions and Maxims*
NCW	*Nietzsche Contra Wagner*
SE	*Schopenhauer as Educator*
TI	*Twilight of the Idols*
UO	*Unfashionable Observations*
WA	*The Case of Wagner*
WB	*Richard Wagner in Bayreuth*
WP	*The Will to Power*

WS	*The Wanderer and His Shadow*
Z	*Thus Spoke Zarathustra*

Citations from Schopenhauer's works will provide the page number from the German edition Nietzsche used followed by the page number from the following English translations and use these abbreviated titles:

Ethics	*The Two Fundamental Problems of Ethics*. Translated by Christopher Janaway. Cambridge: Cambridge University Press, 2009.
Manuscript	*Manuscript Remains in Four Volumes*. Edited by Arthur Hübscher. Translated by E. F. J. Payne. Oxford: Berg, 1988–90.
Parerga 1	*Parerga and Paralipomena*. Volume 1. Translated and edited by Sabine Roehr and Christopher Janaway. Cambridge: Cambridge University Press, 2014.
Parerga 2	*Parerga and Paralipomena*. Volume 2. Translated and edited by Adrian Del Caro and Christopher Janaway. Cambridge: Cambridge University Press, 2015.
World 1	*The World as Will and Representation*. Volume 1. Translated by Judith Norman, Alistair Welchman, and Christopher Janaway. Cambridge: Cambridge University Press, 2010.
World 2	*The World as Will and Representation*. Volume 2. Translated and edited by Judith Norman, Alistair Welchman, and Christopher Janaway. Cambridge: Cambridge University Press, 2017.

Editorial Note to Volume 12

Unless another volume in *CW* is cited, all cross-references to fragments in the notes are references to fragments in this volume.

[1 = N I 4. Winter–Spring 1875]

1. Heinrich Romundt, a friend of N from the Leipzig years, had been an unsalaried lecturer in philosophy in Basel since the summer semester of 1873, and lived starting in the summer of 1874 with Franz Overbeck and N in a house they nicknamed the "Baumannshöhle" {"Baumann's Cave" is an actual cave in the town of Rübeland, about 150 km northwest of Leipzig. It is the oldest show cave in Germany, open to guided visits since 1649.}, Schützengraben 45.

2. Plan for ten new *Unfashionable Observations*; cf. N to Hans von Bülow: "I have arranged the next 5 years in order to complete within that time the remaining 10 Unfashionables . . ." (2 January 1875) {*KGB* II:5, 3}.

3. Plan for a "Collected Edition" of the *Unfashionables*, with a few chronological and content changes for the ten still to be written, by comparison with 1[3].

4. *Cultivated Philistine] Bildungsphilister* {For the translation of *Bildung*, see note 20 to 3[7] below.}

5. *DS.*

6. *HL.*

7. *SE.*

8. The uncompleted *Unfashionable* "We Philologists."

9. *WB.*

10. A start on this is perhaps 5[166].

[2 = U II 8a. Up to the beginning of March 1875]

The following introductory note appears in *KGW* IV:4, 93:

"We Philologists"

On the basis of the incidental notes contained in it, a small notebook, **N I 4** {a detailed description of each individual manuscript can be found in the "Overview of Nietzsche's Manuscripts 1875–1877," pp. 549–52}, can be dated to the time from January to May 1875, and therefore constitutes the beginning of the posthumous fragments of this section.

Approximately twenty months (October 1874–July 1876) lie between the appearance of the third and fourth *Unfashionable*

Observations; during this time there takes place one of N's most significant inner transformations, the phases of which allow themselves to be traced by indications in the letters (see the Chronicle on N's life in *CW* 19), but much more precisely in the fragments. N begins to plan the continuation of his *Unfashionable Observations*: he intends to write ten more of them — this stays the same in the plans from N I 4 (1[2] and 1[3]); the anticipated length of publication time (five years, according to the letter of 25 October 1874 to Malwida von Meysenbug {*KGB* II:3, 268}) is compressed to three years: one *Observation* is supposed to be finished every three months up to Easter 1878. Since October, "the content of No. 4 has more or less come to" N (to Rohde, 7 October 1874 {*KGB* II:3, 263}). But "the heavy commitment of this winter, reading Greek literary history, makes it seem unlikely to me that I will soon be able to take it in hand again," it says in the draft of a letter to R. Wagner (10 October {*KGB* II:3, 265}), and one month later: "On the contrary, there will be no new Unfashionable this winter, it cannot be forced" (to Rohde, 15 November {*KGB* II:3, 275}). After the start in autumn 1874, N has to give up working on the fourth *Unfashionable* in order to concentrate on his lectures on Greek literary history, hence "to yoke himself like a horse," who can "scarcely look right or left" (to his mother and sister, 3 December {*KGB* II:3, 278}). During the Christmas holidays, he announces from Naumburg: "I have now covered the history of the Greek epic in my collegium . . . In return, I want to be spared from all literature in these holidays, but have instead piled all the compositions of my youth around me; something ought to get brewed from them . . . Much has gone through my head in the last months, and I have repeatedly been unfashionably fructified once again, yet when will I find time?" (to Gersdorff, 24 December {1874; *KGB* II:3, 285}). During these holidays, the "Hymn to Friendship" is finished. Only after his return to Basel (beginning of January 1875) does N again take in hand "No. 4," that is, the still-unfinished *Observation* "We Philologists."

Notebook U II 8 is for the greatest part dedicated to studies for "We Philologists," specifically from pages 238/239 to 108. (Note: As in almost all of the larger notebooks, N wrote on the pages first from the back to the front.) These pages can be divided into two strata. The first stratum (238–200) contains notes that were transferred almost entirely to a copy that was prepared by N's friend Carl von Gersdorff during his stay in Basel (March 1875): **Mp XIII 6b**. The fragments are for the greatest part transcribed without changes, according to a five-part structure (that originates with N) and supplemented often with additions or sometimes with new fragments in N's hand. These fragments are published here according to the structure and the revised text of Mp XIII 6b; in doing so, the corresponding text in U II 8 has been utilized to eliminate Gersdorff's errors in reading or hearing. (Note: It cannot be determined whether N dictated to Gersdorff or Gersdorff transcribed the notes instead. Judging by Gersdorff's errors, both seem to have occurred.) Those fragments of the first stratum not transcribed are published before those of the copy: **U II 8a**. According to a remark by N cited at the beginning, we have to ask which of the notes in U II 8, 238–200, go back to autumn 1874. A *terminus post quem* {"earliest possible date"} is the borrowing of the second volume of F. A. Wolf's *Kleinen Schriften* {"Brief writings"} from the Basel University Library on 19 February 1875. N's excerpts from Wolf — that is, a considerable part of these fragments — begin in U II 8 with page 214. The dating of Mp XIII 6b, however, is firm: March 1875. As a result, only the eight fragments from U II 8a require a closer chronological specification: of these, 2[1] was transcribed by Gersdorff as a motto (only the second paragraph of this fragment is in N's hand), and 2[4–8] are found after page 214 of U II 8 and therefore originated after 19 February 1875. Only the dating of 2[2] and 2[3] remains uncertain, for which reason this stratum was dated "Up to the beginning of March 1875."

The second stratum — **U II 8b** — includes pages 198 to 108. The even-numbered pages 196–146 were numbered by N himself from 1–25; — as already on the preceding pages — all the fragments up to page 148 are supplied with numbers 1–5, which refer to the already completed five-part structure in Mp XIII 6b. After page 146, fragments belonging to the circle of ideas of the *Observation* on philologists become less and less frequent. N was probably referring to pages 198–146 when he wrote on 8 May 1875 to Gersdorff {*KGB* II:5, 48}: "[T]hings are going badly with the fourth Observation: to be sure, I have approximately 40 pages more of notes such as those you wrote up. But free flow and courage for the whole are still lacking." The dating of this stratum to spring-summer 1875 seems acceptable according to what has been said, so much the more since fragments 5[72–84] let us infer a renewed reading of Schopenhauer and N acquired the Frauenstädt edition of the philosopher on 25 June 1875. (Note: According to the invoice issued by the bookseller. A certain contradiction with N's words to Gersdorff cited above seems to arise as a result, in that these fragments already begin with page 176; yet the issuance of an invoice does not have to occur at the same time as the possession of the relevant book.)

In between Mp XIII 6b and U II 8b, we can insert a smaller stratum from N I 3, a notebook that N had already used in 1872 and then later, in summer of 1879, took in hand once again. This stratum is designated as **N I 3b**.

After having begun by using the back sides of the pages from U II 8 from back to front, N entered notes about the pre-Platonic philosophers in the first pages of this notebook ("Science and wisdom in conflict, as represented in earlier Greek philosophers"). According to the handwriting, these notes belong to the year 1875, perhaps in part even to the same period as the fragments of the back part of U II 8. A chronological reference pointing to summer 1875 is offered by the concealed citation from Schopenhauer in 6[14]. On the other hand, it is not probable — contrary to the interpretation that Ernst Holzer gave to a later remark of N's sister (cf. the Naumann-Kröner *Großoktav-Ausgabe* 10:508) — that N, considering the revision of the fall and the worsening of his health toward the end of 1875, wrote these pages later than September 1875. Nevertheless, the dating to the summer is not completely certain. This stratum is designated as **U II 8c**.

A final attempt at carrying out "We Philologists" is presented by the pages of **Mp XIII 6a**, which likewise cannot be dated with certainty; preliminary drafts of the two longer fragments 7[6] and 7[7] exist in U II 8, 184–87, hence these are to be inserted after U II 8b; however, the first five less extensive fragments (7[1–5]) could be older; according to the handwriting they belong to the year 1875 (perhaps end of 1874?).

1. Later insertion at the beginning of the *Ms*, as motto.

2. Handwriting by Carl von Gersdorff; cf. Otto Böthlingk, *Indische Sprüche: Sanskrit und Deutsch* {"Indian maxims: Sanskrit and German"}, 3 vols. (St. Petersburg{: Commissionäre der Kaiserlichen Akademie der Wissenschaften,} 1870–73){, I, 61.} *NL*. Gersdorff, who had this book with him during his visit to Basel in March 1875, gave it to N at the end of the year; cf. Gersdorff to N, 10 December 1875 {*KGB* II:6, 1, 255,} and N to Gersdorff, 13 December 1875 {*KGB* II:5, 127ff.}.

3. *Mihi scribere.]* "To write for myself." {Underlined by N.} Cf. *MM* 167 and corresponding note {*CW* 4, 463n208}.

4. *Wolf's]* Friedrich August Wolf (1759–1824). N borrowed these books of his from the Basel University Library on {18} February 1875: *Kleine Schriften in lateinischer und deutscher Sprache* {"Brief texts in Latin and German"}, vol. II: *Deutsche Aufsätze* {"German essays"}, ed. Gottfried Bernhardy (Halle{: Verlag der Buchhandlung des Waisenhauses,} 1869); the two volumes are numbered continuously (vol. II = pp. 593–1200); cited henceforth as Wolf, *KS*.

5. *"Quid . . . fustibus."]* "What, you donkey, am I to teach you your letters? A donkey doesn't need words: he needs a whipping." {Cicero, *Against Piso*} Cf. Wolf, *KS* 1046n.

6. Cf. 3[4].

7. Cf. Friedrich Maximilian Klinger, *Betrachtungen und Gedanken über verschiedene Gegenstände der Welt und der Literatur* {"Observations and thoughts about various objects in the world and in literature"} (*Werke*, vol. XII {Königsberg: Nicolovius,} 1809), no. 581{, p. 138}.

[3 = Mp XIII 6b. (U II 8, 239–200). March 1875]

1. Cf. *HAH* 607; handwriting by N. {Cf. Friedrich Max Müller, *Einleitung in die Vergleichende Religionswissenschaft* ("Introduction to the comparative science of religion") (Strassburg: Karl J. Trübner, 1874), 26.}

2. Handwriting by N. Cf. Johann Friedrich Julius Arnoldt, *Friedrich August Wolf in seinem Verhältnisse zum Schulwesen und*

zur Paedagokik dargestellt {"Friedrich August Wolf depicted in his relationship with schooling and pedagogy"} (Braunschweig{: Schwetschke,} 1861–62), 2 vols. (borrowed by N from the Basel University Library on 9 May 1871), I:26; "on 8 April, the Prorector at that time, the famed medical doctor Ernst Gottfried Baldinger, finally, though not without resistance — for 'anyone who would like to apply to that sort of *doctrinas philosophicae facultatis* {"teachings of the philosophical faculty"} must be enrolled as a theology student' — nonetheless allowed {Wolf} to matriculate as *Philologiae studiosus* {"student of philology"}, a momentous event for his future position in his scholarly field, which bestowed upon him the foremost honor of becoming the *archegete* {leader or founder of a city in ancient Greece} of future philological study in Germany."

3. Cf. 7[6]. Handwriting by N. N's note: Beginning p. 11 p. 6 ⟨i.e., U II 8, 174, 186, where fragments 5[55] and 5[31] are to be found⟩.

4. Reworked by N.

5. *from prejudices]* Added by N.

6. On this by N: see next page ⟨i.e., Mp XIII 6b, 5⟩.

7. *humanitarian humanity] Humanitäts-Menschheit* {A similar phrase occurs in 3[6], "*Humanitäts*"*-Studien*, where the context strongly suggests a translation such as "the humanities" or "humanistic studies." See also 3[12]. The choice of "humanitarian" here is meant to indicate the link across these entries, while also conveying a sense of the mocking disparagement that is part of N's critique here of the discipline of philology. See also note 18, which quotes a passage from Wolf that includes the term *Humanitäts-Studien*, and notes 35 and 36 below.}

8. On this by N: see next page, see page after that, see p. 18, p. 15 ⟨i.e., Mp XIII 6b, 5, 6 and U II 8, 160, 166⟩; further note by N on this: human⟨ism⟩ relig⟨ious⟩ ration⟨alism⟩ optimism p. 7 ⟨i.e., U II 8, 184 (5[33])⟩.

9. On this by N: see p. 19 ⟨i.e., U II 8, 158 (5[99])⟩.

10. *the Romans]* From: antiquity

11. On this by N: see p. 20, 13 ⟨i.e., U II 8, 156 (5[107]), 170 (5[60])⟩.

12. *or in support of it]* Added by N.

13. On this by N: see p. 10, p. 17, p. 9, p. 7 6a ⟨i.e., U II 8, 176, 162, 178, 184, 187 (5[51, 88, 43, 35, 32])⟩.

14. *sophrosyne]* "moderation"

15. On this by N: see p. 9 ⟨i.e., U II 8, 178 (5[45])⟩.

16. *race]* Followed by a crossed-out copy of 2[5] "There remains . . . victorious language"

17. Wolf, *KS* 844.

18. Cf. Wolf, *KS* 814: "Sometimes we call it philology, sometimes classical learning, sometimes old literature, sometimes humanistic studies, at times even by a completely modern name that is completely foreign to it, beautiful sciences." Note to this: "The last name will now, it seems, be used less by the nation itself that apparently brought it into fashion. We more often hear *littérature* than *belles lettres*. But when, as sometimes, a scholar writing in Latin used, or perhaps even said *litteras bellas*, the intent was clearly to make a joke. For our circle of knowledge the designation is not at all appropriate: it has, moreover, sides that attract in all sorts of other ways than by *beauté*."

19. {See note 7 to 3[4].}

20. *cultivation] Bildung* {*Bildung* is an untranslatable German word, a concept with a long history in German philosophy and culture, and an idea central to N's work in this early period. Both "cultivation" and "education" can be appropriate in specific contexts; both English terms leave out nuances of complex meaning conveyed by the German word. N also has the alternative German word, *Erziehung*, which is typically translated as "education," as I have also done. For reasons that he articulates fully in his afterword to *CW* 11, 477–79, Richard Gray consistently chose "cultivation" as the appropriate term for *Bildung* in the *UO*. I am in agreement with the logic of his preference and have followed this practice throughout *HAH* and its related notebooks (given their close relation to the *UO*). N also notes a nuance of meaning in a related word by spelling "culture" with either a German *K* (*Kultur*), where it can have a dismissive tone, or a French *C* (*cultur*), where that negative element is absent. Nonetheless, on occasion *Bildung* is used by N to refer to something clearly like "education"

(as in his reference to a system of "classical education" in 5[132], where I have rendered it in that way.}

21. *"not at all . . . spiritual culture."]* Cf. Wolf, *KS* 817.

22. On this by N: cf. p. 23 ⟨i.e., U II 8, 150 (5[122])⟩.

23. *"in an auspiciously . . . external life"]* Cf. Wolf, *KS* 818.

24. *"similar to . . . higher enlightenment"]* Cf. Wolf, *KS* 818n.

25. *"with the Greeks . . . spiritual refinement"]* Cf. Wolf, *KS* 818n.

26. Cf. Wolf, *KS* 1110. Added in pencil at U II 8, 213: On the sinister {aspects} of philology.

27. *so many]* many (in Wolf)

28. Cf. Wolf, *KS* 735–36.

29. *corpus juris]* "juridical corpus"

30. *Wolf one time recalled]* Cf. Wolf, *KS* 1175.

31. *severioribus]* "more severe"; Mp XIII 6b: *deterioribus* ("worse") (listening error by Gersdorff).

32. *Horatii . . . ostendat."]* {Horace's *Odes* "in order, above all, to show what they can produce *in higher studies*." The phrase "*in severioribus studiis*" underlined by N.}

33. Cf. Wolf, *KS* 1065n.

34. *book of comedies]* Terence

35. *humanness] das Menschliche*

36. *humaneness] dem Humanen*

37. On this by N: cf. p. 5, p. 3 ⟨i.e., U II 8, 188, 192 (5[29, 18]); cf. 10[10], 11[22]; *WB* 4 {*CW* 2, 273, lines 18–20}⟩. Later entry in U II 8, 217: Obscurity in the amalgamation of antiquity and of Christianity.

38. *philologist-poets]* Cf. 5[17, 107, 109]; 14[3]; on the "poet-philologists" of the Italian Renaissance, cf. Jacob Burckhardt, *Die Cultur der Renaissance in Italien* {*The Civilization of the Renaissance in Italy*, trans. S. G. C. Middlemore (London: Penguin Books, 1990)} (Leipzig{: Seemann}, 1869), 114, 119–20, 161. *NL.*

39. *Schiller).]* U II 8: Schiller). Judging is the most difficult thing. Cf. 3[17].

40. *falsified?]* Added afterward by N: cf. p. 21 now a purer knowledge of the ancients {is} possible: whether less effective?; cf. p. 10 ⟨i.e., U II 8, 154, 176 (5[109, 53])⟩.

41. *hard]* Cf. note 39 to 3[15] above; added afterward by N: transition to the act. Conclusion p. 9 ⟨i.e., U II 8, 178 (perhaps 5[47])⟩.

42. Handwriting by N.

43. *what we term]* U II 8, 238, lacking in Mp XIII 6b.

44. *the disposition thereto]* written above: manifestly not-having-been-called

45. *bene navigavi cum naufragium feci]* "I had a good voyage, even though I was shipwrecked." {Cf. *WA* 4, *CW* 9, 12; *CW* 18, 16[44].}

46. *and]* U II 8, 239: or (correction by Gersdorff of his previous transcription error of "or" for "and" at Mp XIII 6b)

47. *many will . . . providence."]* N is playing upon the following passage in Schopenhauer, "Transcendent speculation on the apparent deliberateness in the fate of the individual": "For the data provided merely by *cognition* might be ascribed to the fact that chance, which plays us a hundred cruel tricks that seem intentional in their maliciousness, once in a while turns out to be particularly favorable, or indirectly provides very well for us. In all such cases we recognize the hand of providence in chance, and the most distinctly when, against our own insight, indeed in ways abhorred by us, it has led us to an exhilarating goal, where we then say *tunc bene navigavi, cum naufragium feci* ["Back then I had a good voyage, even though I was shipwrecked"]." (*Parerga 1*, 216{/177–78}). {Cf. the tale of Zeno being shipwrecked in Diogenes Laërtius, "Life of Zeno," *Lives of Eminent Philosophers* VII, 2.}

48. *yet]* Lacking in Mp XIII 6b.

49. For U II 8, 238, the words "duty, service to the state" are inserted on p. 239. Crossed out at the end of U II 8, 236: This also concerns the genesis of the *contemporary philologist*: skeptical-melancholic stance. But how *else* have philologists emerged?

50. *This may well . . . philologists]* U II 8, 238: But if we look away from the salvation of the individual

51. *a]* your (reading error by Gast at Mp XIII 6b)

52. *Romans!]* U II 8, Mp XIII 6b: Romans?

53. *to act . . . individual]* U II 8, 228, from: to count as [pass for] an individual

54. *lesser]* U II 8, Mp XIII 6b: little

55. *Bergk's literary history]* Theodor Bergk's *Griechische Literaturgeschichte* {"Greek literary history"} (Berlin{: Weidmannsche

Buchhandlung,} 1872), vol. 1, was borrowed multiple times by N from the Basel University Library between {May} 1873 and April 1876.

56. Cf. Wolf, *KS* 1043n.

57. *Bentley]* In a letter to T. Hemsterhuys, 1708. {Cf. *The Correspondence of Richard Bentley*, vol. 1, ed. C. Wordsworth (London: John Murray, 1842), 270.}

58. *"non tam . . . exigam."]* "I am not accustomed to stipulate so great a price for my little emendations that I expect or require therefrom any exceptional thanks."

59. *admiration]* U II 8, Mp XIII 6b: significance

60. Cf. Wolf, *KS* 1051: the praise of Horace by Bentley grew "as the highest new model of refined perceptions, many-sided reading and penetrating acuteness"; cf. 5[106]; 19[2].

61. *It is now . . . critic.]* Cf. 7[5].

62. Cf. Wolf, *KS* 1077n.

63. Cf. Wolf, *KS* 1087.

64. *litterator]* {teacher of reading, writing, and grammar}

65. *Wolf . . . styles.]* Cf. Wolf, *KS* 740.

66. *Winckelmann]* Name lacking at Mp XIII 6b, since Gersdorff could not decipher the word.

67. *Wolf concedes . . . uninitiated."]* Cf. Wolf, *KS* 739. "In any case, the laws of historical investigations, like philological critique, which is their basis, demand a rare mixture of spiritual coldness and a petty, restless concern for a hundred things trivial in themselves, with an all-inspiriting, particularity-devouring fire and a talent for divination that is an annoyance to the uninitiated. Our Winckelmann, we must admit, lacked that more common talent, or rather, it did not come into operation correctly given the lack of complete preparation for his history of art . . ."

68. Cf. Wolf, *KS* 833n.

69. *divination]* Cf. Wolf, *KS* 832.

70. *Lachmann]* As examples for this, Ernst Howald, *FN und die klassische Philologie* {"FN and classical philology"} (Gotha{: F. A. Perthes,} 1920), cites in note 3: *De choricis systematis tragicorum Graecorum* {"Concerning the choral odes of Greek tragedy"} (Berlin{: Berolini,} 1819); *De mensura tragoediarum* {"Concerning the meters of tragedies"} (Berlin{: Berolini,} 1822).

71. Handwriting by N.

72. Cf. 5[46].

73. *actually]* Word missing at Mp XIII 6b.

74. Cf. Wolf, *KS* 1117.

75. Cf. Wolf, *KS* 833.

76. Cf. Wolf, *KS* 834–35n.

77. *τέχναι and artes]* "techniques and arts"

78. *brontology]* "science of thunder"

79. Cf. Wolf, *KS* 849.

80. *make use]* made use (Wolf)

81. Cf. Goethe, "Winckelmann" {in *Goethe's Sämmtliche Werke in vierzig Bänden* ("Goethe's collected works in forty volumes"), vol. 30 (Stuttgart; Augsburg; Tübingen: J. G. Cotta, 1857). *NL.*}

82. N cites from Friedrich Maximilian Klinger, *Betrachtungen und Gedanken über verschiedene Gegenstände der Welt und der Literatur* {"Observations and thoughts about various objects in the world and in literature"}, no. 94 (*Werke*, vol. XI {[Königsberg: Nicolovius,} 1809], {82}).

83. *their]* U II 8, Mp XIII 6b: the

84. *Dubito.]* "I doubt it."

85. *it is . . . day-laborer]* According to the words of Achilles in *Odyssey*, bk. 11, lines 489–91.

86. *lifeless]* U II 8; *Le*: bloodless; but since "bloodless" can be read quite clearly in U II 8, it is difficult to presume a reading error of Gersdorff, more likely a revision of N while dictating; the variants 10 and 14 also allow a dictation of N in this case to seem probable.

87. *(To sacrifice many sheep.)]* Mp XIII 6b; in U II 8, added by N on the neighboring page in ink and without parentheses. {Odysseus needed to sacrifice sheep in order to be able to speak to the dead.}

88. *in a state of the soul]* Mp XIII 6b, U II 8: of the state of the soul

89. Cf. 5[166], 17[19]; *MM* 95.

90. Cf. Wolf, *KS* 1033–34n; 5[110]. {*A Confutation of Atheism* was a series of eight sermons Bentley delivered as the inaugural Boyle lecture in 1692.}

91. Cf. Wolf, *KS* 1077n.

92. Cf. Wolf, *KS* 820–21.

93. *or]* "and" in Wolf.

94. Cf. Wolf, *KS* 836.

95. *skeptical-melancholic]* Cf. the deletion at U II 8, 236 after 3[21].

96. *classical] Ms*: Classical

97. *classical] Ms*: Classical

98. Cf. 3[69].

99. *saint]* Mp XIII 6b, *Le*, *Le*[2]: as saint

100. *quisquilia]* "trifling matters"

101. Cf. 3[63].

102. *Danaïds]* {In one version of their story, the daughters of Danaus were condemned to an afterlife in Tartarus of endlessly attempting to fill a leaking tub with water, this as punishment for having slain their husbands at their father's command.}

103. *that philology has encountered] Le*, *Ms*: that philology has fallen upon

104. *The greatest . . . discovered.]* Cf. *WB* 4 {*CW* 2, 273, lines 25–32}; 5[111]; 6[14].

105. Cf. Wolf, *KS* 820n; 5[82].

106. *Graiis — praeter laudem nullius avaris]* "The Greeks — who desired nothing more than praise" {Horace, *The Art of Poetry*, line 323. The full quote is: "*Graiis ingenium, Graiis dedit ore rotundo / Musa loqui, praeter laudem nullius avaris.*" ("The Muse gave to the Greeks their native character and let them speak in well-rounded tones, they who desired nothing more than praise.")}.

107. *nugari]* "to talk nonsense" {This term is used by Horace at *Epistles* II, 1, 93.}

108. *degree]* U II 8: extent

109. Cf. Wolf, *KS* 827n.

110. *triste]* "sad"

111. *gradual]* Lacking in Mp XIII 6b.

112. *by bad . . . intentions.]* Mp XIII 6b; *Le*, *Le*[2]: by bad and contradictory organization of the individual intentions.

113. *not knowing]* From U II 8, 200: faith

114. *readily]* U II 8, 200, Mp XIII 6b: perhaps

115. *still]* Mp XIII 6b; lacking in U II 8, 200 [as note 105]

[4 = N I 3b. Spring 1875]

1. On Oskar Peschel, cf. note to *CW* 4, 39[8]{: *Völkerkunde* (Leipzig: Duncker und Humblot, 1874)}.

2. N acquired Schopenhauer's works (Frauenstädt edition, 1873–74) on 25 June 1875.

3. There is precise information about the acquisition of natural science works by N in the years 1875–79: Karl Schlechta and Anni Anders, *Friedrich Nietzsche: Von den verborgenen Anfängen seines Philosophierens* {"Friedrich Nietzsche: On the hidden beginnings of his philosophizing"} (Stuttgart-Bad Cannstatt{: Friedrich Frommann Verlag}, 1962), 162ff.

4. Cf. N to Carl von Gersdorff, 8 May 1875 {*KGB* II:5, 47}; Ludwig Rütimeyer {(1825–95)} was a professor of zoology and comparative anatomy in Basel.

5. *Choephorae]* {A tragedy by Aeschylus, title typically translated as *The Libation-Bearers.*}

6. N had in his possession as of May 1875 a complete copy of Jacob Burckhardt's lectures on "Greek Cultural History," which his student, Louis Kelterborn {(1853–1910)} had prepared and dedicated to him; this copy is part of *NL*. Concerning it, N wrote to Overbeck on 30 May 1875 {*KGB* II:5, 58}: "Little Kelterborn has presented to me a richly bound book of 448 narrow quarto pages; it is the Greek Culture of Burckhardt; and indeed, it has advantages over Baumgartner's version, it is richer in material and better organized and an exceptional supplement, while Baumgartner has a keener eye for Burckhardt himself and great imitative skill." ⟨Baumgartner's copy is not in *NL*.⟩

7. Cf. *WB* 2.

8. *Uneasiness . . . positions.]* Cf. *WB* 3 {*CW* 2, 267, line 25–268, line 8}.

9. *W⟨agner⟩ the theater)]* Cf. *WB* 7 {*CW* 2, 294, line 35–295, line 1}.

10. Cf. 12[31].

[5 = U II 8b. Spring–Summer 1875]

1. Cf. 5[59].

2. *themselves]* *Ms*: *sibi* {Latin in place of the German *sich.*}

3. Cf. P II 12a, 21; 1874 {*CW* 11, 37[4], 381}: Sometimes one sees too many of the *bare bones* in Aristotle (although *leanness* is certainly *appropriate*).

4. Cf. *HAH* 261; 6[28, 47].

5. *upon] GA*; *Ms*: and

6. Cf. 3[15].

7. *Goethe and Leopardi]* Cf. *WB* 10 {*CW* 2, 325, line 5}; 5[109]; 14[3].

8. Cf. 5[27].

9. *Then . . . improved.]* Cf. *WB* 3 {*CW* 2, 272, lines 23–28}.

10. *Demopheles]* Cf. Schopenhauer, *Parerga 2*, 347ff.{/292ff., "On Religion: A Dialogue." In this dialogue, Demopheles defends the social and political utility of religious belief.} {Citations from Schopenhauer will provide the page from the Frauenstädt edition, followed by the page from the English translation.}

11. Cf. 5[19].

12. Cf. 7[6].

13. Added later in connection with the reworking of 7[6]; cf. *Pd* to 7[6].

14. Hermann Köchly (1815–76), in his text on Gottfried Hermann {*Gottfried Hermann: Zu seinem hundertjährigen Geburtstage* ("Gottfried Hermann: On his one-hundredth birthday") (Heidelberg: Carl Winter, 1874)}, which N borrowed on 3 April 1875 from the Basel University Library.

15. Cf. 7[6].

16. Cf. 5[146], *MM* §220.

17. *Pythian Ode]* {The *Pythian Odes* were the most famous poems of the Greek lyric poet Pindar. *Pythian Ode I was* composed in 470 BCE in honor of the Sicilian tyrant Hieron and celebrated a series of victories by Greeks against foreign invaders.}

18. Cf. 5[54].

19. *ἀριστεύειν]* "to be the best"

20. 5[41] and 5[42] were inserted later.

21. *Gymnasium]* {The German college–preparatory high school.}

22. Cf. 7[6].

23. Cf. 3[41].

24. *just as in marriage]* Added subsequently.

25. *The struggle . . . being.]* Added subsequently.

26. Cf. 5[37].

27. *up to now]* From: now

28. Cf. chap. 1 of 5[55].

29. Cf. chaps. 3 and 4 of 5[55].

30. Cf. 5[12].

31. *implanted!] Pd*: implanted?

32. *It is especially . . . another.]* Friedrich Anton von Hellwald, cultural historian, follower of David F. Strauss and Ernst Haeckel; N is referring to his best-known work, which was dedicated to Haeckel, *Kulturgeschichte in ihrer natürlichen Entwicklung bis zur Gegenwart* {"Cultural history in its natural development up to the present"} (Augsburg{: Lampart & Comp.,} 187{5}), especially its summary section, "Ideals and Science"; in summer 1881, N had Overbeck send him this work: cf. N to Overbeck, 8 {July} 1881 {*KGB* III:1, 100–101}. {*KSA* 14 has the wrong date of the letter to Overbeck, the wrong title of Hellwald's book, and the wrong date of this book's publication.}

33. Cf. 5[4].

34. *The] Pd*: the

35. *enclosure]* [?] *Le*: scarecrows; *Le*[2]: creatures; *Ms*: happenings {*Ge*[*sc*]*hege*}; see facsimile {U II 8b, 170}.

36. This and a number of the following fragments from U II 8 probably originated from the reading of Jacob Burckhardt's *Vorlesungen über griechische Kulturgeschichte* {"Lectures on Greek cultural history"}, according to the nonextant copy made by Adolf Baumgartner (cf. note to 4[3]). Parallel passages in Burckhardt, *Griechische Kulturgeschichte*, vols. 5–8 of his *Gesammelten Werke* {"Collected works"} (Basel, Darmstadt, and Berlin{: Wissenschaftliche Buchgesellschaft,} 1955ff.), are referred to when possible, using the abbreviation *GK*. In cases where such passages cannot be referred to, similar ones from the contemporaneous, still-extant copy made by Louis Kelterborn will be brought in; it is, however, possible that a number of fragments originated on the basis of passages from Baumgartner's copy, which can be identified neither in the edition of Burckhardt's works nor in Kelterborn's copy.

37. *Only . . . falsified one:]* Cf. Burckhardt, *GK* 2:348: "With regard to the ancient Greeks, we have believed since the great rise of German humanism in the previous century that we see our way clearly: in the reflection of their martial heroism and bourgeoisie, their art and poetry, their beautiful land and climate we assess them as fortunate, and Schiller's poem, 'die Götter Griechenlands' {"The Gods of Greece"} summarized their entire presumed condition in an image whose magic has still not lost its strength today . . . One of the very greatest falsifications of historical judgment that ever occurred." On this point, Burckhardt tended in his lectures to express himself somewhat more bluntly; cf. the corresponding passage in a later (1885) formulation of the lecture manuscript: "The former opinion that the Greeks must have leaped with joy every day to be living in the Periclean age stems in part from Schiller: The Gods of Greece," cited by Felix Stähelin in the introduction to his edition of Burckhardt, *GK* ("Jacob Burckhardt-Gesamtausgabe" (Basel, Berlin, and Leipzig{: Deutsche Verlags-Anstalt,} 1930), 8:xxxii).

38. Cf. 12[22]; *MM* 224.

39. Cf. 3[51].

40. Cf. Burckhardt, *GK* 1:12, 57, 20.

41. *as learners]* Cf. 11[45], *WB* 3 {*CW* 2, 269, line 12}.

42. *do not . . . how] Pd*: do not only know how not

43. Cf. 5[122]. Cf. Burckhardt, *GK* 1:28.

44. *This against Wolf]* Wolf, *KS* 817–19, cf. 3[7].

45. Cf. Burckhardt, *GK* 1:19.

46. Cf. Burckhardt, *GK* 1:28.

47. Cf. Burckhardt, *GK* 1:45.

48. *Sappho's invocation to Aphrodite]* Cf. *Poetarum Lesbiorum Fragmenta: Carminum Sapphicorum*, {ed. Edgar Lobel and Denys Page (Oxford: Clarendon, 1955),} fr. 1, 2, 194, 211.

49. Cf. Burckhardt, *GK* 1:12: "Hence they seem with their creativity and capability essentially as the ingenious people upon earth, with all the mistakes and suffering of such a one." Kelterborn's copy, 2: ". . . the ingenious people in itself with all the mistakes and suffering of such a one . . ."

50. Cf. 5[84].

51. *Their form . . . temperament.]* Cf. Burckhardt, *GK* 2:363: "Now the entire appearance of Greek pessimism attains its full noteworthiness due to the decisive optimism of the Greek temperament . . ."; Kelterborn's copy, 83, 84–84a: "The religion and reflection were pessimistic, but the temperament optimistic; hence the enormous productivity . . . The people were full of elastic energies, hence the lively, optimistic temperament that continually stimulated to new actions. The worldview, however, is completely pessimistic." The latter formulation — "pessimism of worldview and optimism of temperament" — is also to be found in Malwida von Meysenbug, *Der Lebensabend einer Idealistin* {"The evening of life of an idealist"} (Berlin and Leipzig{: Schuster and Löffler,} 1898), 50ff., where she reports upon the reading of Burckhardt's lectures during the "reading evenings" in Sorrento (cf. Chronology 1877 {*CW* 19}). In Sorrento it may have been Kelterborn's copy that was read.

52. *(The surveillability . . . whole.)]* Cf. Burckhardt, *GK* 1:73.

53. *The individual . . . polis.]* Cf. Burckhardt, *GK* 1:80.

54. Cf. Burckhardt, *GK* 1:91ff.

55. *Greek culture . . . people.]* Cf. Burckhardt, *GK* 1:147.

56. *the wager-earner . . . part draft-animal] Ms*: the wage-earner, the port⟨er⟩, the semi-draft-animal

57. *Opposition of . . . species.]* Cf. Schopenhauer, *Parerga* 2, 365{/310}, 681{/577}; *Nachlaß* 352{/*Manuscript* 4, 224}.

58. Cf. Schopenhauer, *World* 2, 433{/396}.

59. Cf. Schopenhauer, *World* 2, 434{/396}.

60. *Προμηθεῖα]* "*Prometheia*" {The *Prometheia* was the title of a trilogy of plays by Aeschylus about the Titan Prometheus, of which only *Prometheus Unbound* survives.}

61. *"Clarity of mind"]* "*Besonnenheit*"; Schopenhauer, *World* 2, 437{/399–400}.

62. Schopenhauer, *World* 2, 438{/400}.

63. Schopenhauer, *World* 2, 438{/400}.

64. Cf. Schopenhauer, *World* 2, 442{/404}.

65. Schopenhauer, *World* 2, 445{/406}.

66. Cf. Schopenhauer, *World* 2, 445{/406; N's citation slightly changes Schopenhauer's wording, in this case replacing Schopenhauer's *begabte Individuum* ("gifted individual") with *Genie* ("genius")}.

67. Cf. Schopenhauer, *World* 2, 445{/406; N's citation alters Schopenhauer's wording}.

68. Cf. Schopenhauer, *World* 2, 446{/407}.

69. Cf. Schopenhauer, *World* 2, 447{/407}.

70. *nugari]* "to jest"

71. *nugari . . . Hellenes]* Cf. 3[72].

72. Cf. Schopenhauer, *World* 2, 448{/408}.

73. *Bacon of Verulam]* {Sir Francis Bacon}

74. *infimarum . . . nullus]* "Among philologists there is praise for the Greeks' low virtues, wonder at the middle [virtues], and no sense at all of the highest"; {cf. Schopenhauer, "On Genius," *World* 2, 448{/408}; Bacon, *De Augmentis Scientiarum* L, vi, c3. {N here replaces Bacon's Latin *vulgus*, "the vulgar," with *philologos*, "the philologist," in the saying of Bacon quoted by Schopenhauer.}

75. Cf. 5[70]; Burckhardt, *GK* 1:28 (cf. Plato, *Timaeus* 22a); Schopenhauer, *World* 2, 451{/411}.

76. {Giuliano Campioni, *Nietzsche-Studien* 28 (1999): 369, suggests the following: cf. Jacob Burckhardt, *Der Cicerone: Eine Anleitung zum Genuss der Kunstwerke Italiens*, 2nd ed., vol. 1: *Architektur* (Leipzig: E. A. Seemann, 1869), 2–3; *NL*: "But nowhere are the lines mathematically rigid, as in the entire structure, so, too, in the columns; instead a gentle swelling {*Anschwellung*} of their inner creative life in the most beautiful way can be perceived. [. . .] A sharp eye perhaps views the individual sides along the profile and finds that there is not a single mathematically even line in the entire structure. [. . .] These are expressions of the same feeling that demanded the swelling of the columns and also sought to reveal everywhere a pulsation of inner life in the seemingly mathematical forms."}

77. *ratio]* "reason" {in the sense of reckoning or calculating}

78. *Lichtenberg says]* Cf. Georg Christoph Lichtenberg, {*Nachtrag zu den Beobachtungen über den Menschen* ("Addendum to the observations on human beings"), in} *Vermischte Schriften* {(Göttingen: Dieterich, 1867)}, 1:186, *NL*; the passage is underlined by N.

79. *That someone . . . spirit.]* Cf. Burckhardt, *GK* 2:374.

80. *The ten generals in Athens!]* {In Athens in the late sixth century BCE, ten στρατηγοί (*stratēgoi* "generals"), one from each tribal political unit, were elected each year to be the military leaders of the polis.}

81. *O. R. G. B. N.]* Probably the beginning letters of the names Overbeck, Rohde, Gersdorff, Baumgartner, Nietzsche.

82. Cf. 5[179].

83. *πόλις]* "polis"

84. *αἰὲν ἀριστεύειν]* "to be the best forever"; cf. *Iliad*, bk. 6, line 208; bk. 11, line 704; also cited in Burckhardt, *GK* 2:330, 360.

85. *symposion]* "a drinking party, often involving serious discussion" {"*Symposion*" is also the German translation of Plato's *Symposium*, to which N might here be alluding.}

86. Cf. Burckhardt, *GK* 2:29ff.

87. *⟨god⟩] Le*: god

88. Cf. Burckhardt, *GK* 2:31, 320.

89. Cf. 16[8].

90. *how hard . . . live]* Cf. 3[19].

91. Inserted later on the lower margin of the page; cf. 3[31]; 19[2].

92. *Word- and object-philology]* Inserted between the lines. {This dispute in the classical philology of N's era had to do with whether texts (words) alone or material objects (as in the field of archaeology) could best provide understanding of past cultures.}

93. Cf. *WB* 10 {*CW* 2, 324–25}.

94. *Goethe . . . poet-philologist]* Cf. 5[17].

95. *never . . . Wagner]* Cf. 12[1].

96. *Bentley . . . fidei]* Cf. 3[{31}] {*KSA* 14 mistakenly points to 3[37]}; Nietzsche is referring to the "Confutation of Atheism" of R. Bentley (1694); cf. F. A. Wolf, *KS* 1033–34.

97. *defensor fidei]* "defender of the faith"

98. Cf. *WB* 4.

99. *when observing] Ms*: for observing

100. *Müller . . . Welcker]* N is referring to Karl Otfried Müller, *Geschichte der griechischen Literatur bis auf das Zeitalter Alexander's* {"History of Greek literature up to the age of Alexander"}, vol. 1 {(Breslau: Josef Max, 1841)} (borrowed on 3 April 1875 from the Basel University Library), and to Friedrich Gottlieb Welcker,

Kleine Schriften, vol. 4: *Zur griechischen Litteratur* {"Brief writings, vol. IV: On Greek literature"} (Bonn{: Weber,} 1861) (borrowed on 18 February 1875).

101. {Modern European philology is often considered to have begun with Friedrich August Wolf's *Prolegomena ad Homerum* (1795), which used internal textual evidence to argue that Homer's epic poems were fundamentally oral, rather than written, products — the result of a long-standing tradition of oral poetry where no single author, no "Homer," had produced them. These collective or communal poems were then standardized and written down at a much later point in time than that of their initial composition and circulation. See Notebook 3 in this volume for N's detailed engagement with Wolf's work, especially his impact upon the field of philology.}

102. *Pd*: *HAH* 154; cf. Burckhardt, *GK* 2:326.

103. *desire to fabricate fables.]* Cf. Goethe, *Zahme Xenien*, bk. 6 {in *Goethe's Sämmtliche Werke*, 3:146. *NL*.}

104. Cf. 18[48]; cf. Burckhardt *GK* 2:97.

105. *pudendum]* "external genitals, especially female," hence, by extension, an "object of shame"

106. Cf. *HAH* 154.

107. Cf. 12[21].

108. *Xenophon, Socrates]* Cf. Xenophon, *Memorabilia* I, 3, 2.

109. *Pd*: 20[7].

110. *When their . . . tragoediam] Pd*: *HAH* 154; cf. *MM* 179; Burckhardt, *GK* 2:359.

111. *vide tragoediam]* "see tragedy"

112. Cf. 5[66].

113. *The genuinely . . . Greeks.]* {Cf. Wolf, *KS* 817–18.}

114. Cf. Burckhardt, *GK* 2:277.

115. Title of the first essay in Otto Jahn, *Aus der Alterthumswissenschaft: Populäre Aufsätze* {"From the study of the classics: Popular essays"} (Bonn{: A. Marcus,} 1868). *NL*.

116. Cf. in Kelterborn's copy, 76a: "It is completely false to believe that the Greeks were completely secular and not at all concerned with what lay beyond in general."

117. Cf. Burckhardt, *GK* 1:80.

118. Cf. Burckhardt, *GK* 1:80; 2:373; perhaps more like Kelterborn, 84: "we will never learn how often the highly gifted, passionate egoism has overcome itself in the service of something general . . ."

119. Cf. Burckhardt, *GK* 2:352ff. and the chapter on the "Greek Hero-Cult," 2:207–52.

120. Cf. 12[28].

121. *education] Bildung* {*Bildung* is usually translated as "cultivation" in the fragments from this period, but here the context makes "education" a better rendering.}

122. *Rienzi]* {Early opera by Wagner, first performed in 1842 and his first success.}

123. *in the best case!]* Added later.

124. Cf. 5[150].

125. Cf. *WB* 1, {*CW* 2, 262, line 3. *KSA* mistakenly points to p. 434, line 33; it should be line 8.}

126. Cf. *MM* 378.

127. Cf. 11[4]; *WB* 3 {*CW* 2, 272, lines 2–17}.

128. Cf. *HAH* 261.

129. *Degeneration . . . it.]* Cf. *HAH* 158.

130. *Something . . . stifled.]* Cf. *HAH* 158.

131. *The most fortunate . . . limits.]* Cf. *HAH* 158.

132. *The greatest . . . triumphed.]* Cf. 5[118]; *HAH* 262.

133. *The suppressing element . . . everything.]* Cf. 5[36]; *MM* 220.

134. Cf. *MM* 220.

135. *κάθαρσις]* "catharsis"

136. Cf. Kelterborn's copy, 78: "Atonements, καθάρσεις, we find already with Homer, later with all possible causes. Yet just consider how in that violent time almost everyone could get murdered, (as today in Italy), whereupon revenge had to be exercised!" But cf. also the elaboration of N in §2 of his lectures on *The History of Greek Literature* (pt. 3, winter semester 1875–76): *Le*[2] XVIII, 141.

137. Cf. 5[139]; *HAH* 114.

138. *symmachia]* "alliance"

139. *ἀναγνωρίσεις]* "*anagnorisis*"; "recognition" {a key term in Aristotle's theory of tragedy}

140. Numbers added later by N.

141. Cf. Matthew 8:22.

142. Cf. 19[120].

143. Cf. *HAH* 148; above the first line is the following start upon a revision, added later in pencil: "as easers of life they turn our gaze away from the present or let it {appear} in a brightest [?] light — — —

144. Cf. 18[33]; *HAH* 108.

145. *"being helpful and good"]* Cf. Goethe, "The Divine" {in *Goethe's Sämmtliche Werke*, 2:67. *NL.*}

146. For the lecture series "Antiquities of the Religious Cult of the Greeks" (winter semester 1875–76).

147. *Homer . . . event.]* Cf. *HAH* 262.

148. *Narcotics] Betäubungen* ("anaesthetics")

149. *Gent⟨ile⟩]* [?]

150. *Love . . . ambiguity.]* Cf. *MM* 95.

151. *the Jews . . . people.]* Cf. 17[20].

152. *The struggle with necessity]* Cf. 11[1].

153. *Either to live . . . the other.]* Underlined with pencil, perhaps in order to connect it with 5[162] and 5[163].

154. *know it!] Pd*: know it?

155. Cf. 23[82].

156. *Pd*: *HAH* 234.

157. Cf. 5[100, 197].

158. *ἀριστεύειν]* "to be the best"

159. Cf. *HAH* 163.

160. *Pd*: *HAH* 360; title, "14. Demeanor when praised," added later to the copy in M I 1, 8 (No. 14).

161. *Pd*: *HAH* 234; title, "19. Value of the middle of the path," added later to the copy in M I 1, 15 (No. 19).

162. Cf. 9[1].

163. *Pd*: *HAH* 235; title, "18. *fatum tristissimum*" {"the saddest fate"}, added later to the copy in M I 1, 13 (No. 18).

164. *the warmest]* Later crossed out.

165. *Fatum tristissimum generis humani!]* "The saddest fate of the human species!"

166. *Procemium]* "Preface" {Underlined by N.}

167. *Pd*: *HAH* 619; title, "15. Advantage in being disdained," added later to the copy in M I 1, 8 (No. 15).

168. Later connected by N with a loop to 5[194] on the copy in M I 1, as the second paragraph of the *Pd* of *HAH* 233.

169. *ἀνδραποδισταὶ ἑαυτῶν]* "the reduction of oneself as a free-born man to a state of slavery"; cf. Xenophon's *Memorabilia* I, 2, 6.

170. *Pd*: 18[47].

171. *Pd*: *HAH* 233; title, "16. Voice of history concerning the engendering of genius," added later in the copy in M I 1, 9 (No. 16).

172. *Frightful . . . you! —]* Cf. Goethe, *Faust* I:485 {in *Goethe's Sämmtliche Werke*, 11:23. *NL*.}

173. Variant in M I 1, 81–82 (No. 145); cf. *Le*[2] XI 136, 433: The Greeks of the age of the Caesars are feeble and very well appear as the types of future, fatigued humanity; they seem to be humanitarian, especially in comparison with Rome, and are alone among people of that time in detesting gladiator combats.

174. *Pd*: *HAH* 125; cf. 8[6], 11[18].

175. *Pd*: *HAH* 474.

176. *Pd*: 18[46].

177. Following, crossed out, "Language has — — —

178. *Pd*: 18[46]; cf. Burckhardt, *GK* 1:147.

179. Cf. *HAH* 474; cf. Burckhardt, *GK* 4:175–76.

[6 = U II 8c. Summer 1875]

1. *σωφροσύνη]* "*sophrosyne*"; "moderation"

2. Parentheses missing in *Ms*.

3. *One thing is necessary.]* Cf. Luke 10:42.

4. *everything is false.]* Cf. the "Assassins' saying": "Nothing is true, everything is permitted" in *Z* IV "The Shadow"; and *GM* III, 24; in Notebook W I 1 (spring 1884 {cf. *CW* 15, 25[505]}), this saying went: "Everything is false! Everything is permitted!" {N cites the "Assassin's saying" correctly in *CW* 15, 25[304], 26[25], 32[8]. Cf. Joseph von Hammer, *Die Geschichte der Assassinen, aus morgenländischen Quellen* ("The history of the Assassins, from Oriental sources") (Stuttgart/Tübingen: Cotta, 1818), 84.}

5. *Only where . . . gloominess? —]* Cf. Burckhardt, *GK* 1:27–28.

6. *Only where . . . own poems.]* *Pd*: *HAH* 261.

7. *Or rather . . . own poems.]* Added later.

8. Cf. 6[44].

9. *written note]* From: passage

10. *ancient Greek]* From: pre-Socratic

11. *Socrates is . . . death]* According to the narrative in the cyclical epic *Aethiopis*. {*Aethiopis* is the title of a lost epic of ancient Greek literature. It was one of the so-called Epic Cycle, that is, the "Trojan" cycle, which told the entire history of the Trojan War in epic verse.}

12. *the authority of the wonderful myth]* From: authority

13. *"the indecent . . . happiness"]* Cf. Johann Heinrich Merck, writing to . . . in the fall of 1777: "The indecent pretension to happiness, to the extent that we dream of it, spoils everything in this world," in *Briefe an und von Johann Heinrich Merck* {"Letters to and from Johann Heinrich Merck"} (Darmstadt{: Johann Philipp Diehl,} 1838), 1:100; cited in Schopenhauer, *Parerga 1*, 435–36{/359}.

14. *γνῶθι σαυτόν]* "know yourself"

15. Cf. *WB* 4, *CW* 2, 273, lines 25–32; 3[70]; 5[111].

16. Cf. note 13 above.

17. *vita practica]* "practical life"

18. *vita . . . contemplativa]* "contemplative life"

19. *Mimnermus]* {7th c. BCE Greek elegiac poet, known for the line "Would that my fated death might come at sixty, unattended by sickness and grievous cares."}

20. Cf. *HAH* 261.

21. *more witty]* From: cleverer

22. Cf. *HAH* 261.

23. Cf. *HAH* 261; 5[7]; and Burckhardt's comments about the Greek tyrants, *GK* 1:166–201.

24. *"he overturns . . . arbitrarily."]* {George Grote quotes these "pregnant words of Herodotus" in *A History of Greece* (London: John Murray, 1851), 3:16: "He subverts the customs of the country: he violates women: he puts men to death without trial." N read the book in German translation by Nicolaus Meißner, *Geschichte Griechenlands* (Leipzig: Dyk, 1851), 2:12. *NL*.}

25. *threnoi]* "ritual wailings at Greek funerals"

26. *μανικὸν πένθος]* "maniacal mourning"

27. *displeases Solon . . . itself.]* Cf. Plutarch, "Solon," 21.

28. *'altro diletto, che 'mparar, non provo.']* "I have no delight other than learning." {Petrarch, *Triumph of Love*, I, 21.}

29. Cf. Schopenhauer, *Parerga 1*, 439{/363}; cited by N from the Frauenstädt edition, with a small omission.

30. *the hunt for happiness!]* Cf. 6[14, 15].

31. Cf. *HAH* 92; Thucydides 5.85–111. {N is referring to Thucydides's account of how the Athenians offered the Melians nothing more than self-preservation if they submitted.}

32. Cited by N from Thucydides, 5.105, *Geschichte der Peloponnesischen Kriegs*, trans. Dr. Adolf Wahrmund, bk. 5 (Stuttgart{: Krais,} 1864), *NL*. {Cf. Thucydides, *The War of the Peloponnesians and the Athenians*, trans. Jeremy Mynott (Cambridge: Cambridge University Press, 2013), 382: "As far as good relations with the gods are concerned, we don't feel we shall be any worse off than you. There is nothing either in our principles or our practice at odds with human assumptions about the gods or with human purposes in their own sphere."}

33. Cf. Luther, *Werke* {*Works*}, Weimar edition, *Table Talks* 2 (Weimar: Hermann Böhlau, 1913). N follows here the popular version of the edition of Johannes Aurifaber (1566); the *Table Talks* date from January 1532.

34. *the apparent . . . fate]* Cf. Schopenhauer, "Über die anscheinende Absichtlichkeit im Schicksale des Einzelnen" {"Transcendent speculation on the apparent deliberateness in the fate of the individual"} *Parerga 1*, 215ff.{/178ff.}.

35. *people]* From: age

36. Cf. 6[49, 50].

37. Cf. *WS* 55.

38. *We . . . too swiftly.]* Cf. *HAH* 261, *CW* 3, 178, lines 7–9.

39. *(Their . . . existence.)]* Cf. 6[10].

40. Cf. *WB* 2, *CW* 2, 263, lines 1–5.

41. *daemon ex machina]* "divinity/demon from the machine"

42. *νοῦς]* "*nous*"; "mind"

43. *ἄθεος ex machina]* "nongod from the machine"

44. Cf. *HAH* 261.

45. *The tyrants . . . progeny.]* Cf. 5[7].

46. *Pd*: It occurs to me how humanly beautiful and worthy of imitation *all* of the signs of ancient philosophy are; no distorted and desolate figures at all are among them. No priestly visages, no fanatical desert[devil]-hermits, no scholastics, no stiff pedants, no

theologizing counterfeiters of thought, no common prettifiers of things: although the seeds for everything were there and only one evil puff of wind needs to come over it, and then all sorts of weeds are blossoming. Cf. 6[48]2: "Hence I . . . fellow human beings. — "

47. *energy . . . everything is]* From: sunshine and makes life possible anew,

48. *two . . . directions]* Cf. *WB* 2, *CW* 2, 264, lines 22–23.

49. *hostile . . . place]* From: hostile drives are here forced to serve each other; the one that wants to know must tear up [and] or undermine the ground upon which human beings live, and the drive that wants life must again and again find a place

50. N cites from Georg Christoph Lichtenberg, *Einige Lebensumstände von Capt. James Cook, größtentheils aus schriftlichen Nachrichten einiger seiner Bekannten gezogen* {"Some circumstances of the life of Capt. James Cook, drawn for the most part from the written accounts of some of his acquaintances"}, *Vermischte Schriften* 4:152. *NL.*

51. *have forgotten the best . . . put]* From: did not rediscover these. Compare the thinkers of other ages and other peoples with those [the pre-Greeks], indeed, compare

52. *depressed and pale scholars]* From: concept-spiders

53. *Poets and historians]* From: Thinkers

54. *we could let . . . mirror image]* From: posterity [—] should not allow them to slip away; we should not rest at all until we have re-created their images and if we have gotten this far — then we will certainly not rest. For our human beings lack precisely the discovery that those philosophers must have made: where else did their marvelous beauty come from! — For what is beauty, if not the mirror {reading *Spiegel* where *KSA* 14 has *Siegel* ("seal")} of nature

55. *into life?]* into life

56. Cf. 6[38].

57. Cf. 6[38].

[7 = Mp XIII 6a. 1875]

1. Cf. 2[3].

2. Words for the "Hymn to Friendship"? The corresponding note-pages have no text; the work on this composition stretched

from 24 April 1873 up to 19 December 1874; alongside, the metrical schema {*KSA* 14 corrected as per Mp XII 6a, 3}:

|— —|— —|— ◡|◡ ◡ ◡|—
|— —|— ◡ ◡ ◡|—|—|
—|— —|— ◡|◡ ◡ ◡|— —
— —|— ◡|— ◡|—|—
— —|— ◡ —
— —|— ◡ — ◡
— — ◡|— ◡|— ◡|— ◡ ◡|— —|—|—

3. *laws] Rechten* {Could also be translated as "rights."}

4. Cf. 3[31].

5. *Pd*: *For the beginning.* — The philologists have something in common with the theologians: in other respects, all other servants of science are differentiated from them: they instinctively protect their pedagogical status and take care that their own science does not endanger this. Thus a medical man wants first to become a doctor, then a scholar, thus a lawyer first a state employee, then a researcher. But the claim of the philologists to be *teachers* is *quite surprising*: why precisely *they*! This is by far not so obvious as that the medical man wants to be a doctor. What does it mean that the classical philologist advances the claim to be a teacher in the higher sense and to educate not only all scientific humans, but all cultivated ones as well? — In any case, he must credit *antiquity* with this force. — Now if the cultivation of our cultivated people actually is at a low level, this would be attributed *either* to *antiquity or to the interpreters of antiquity: the blame would lie either here or there. Either antiquity does not educate or the philologists do not understand antiquity* — or both. The former is what secondary school teachers assert.

6. *Pd*: We now understand a philologist to be a person who has knowledge of Greek and Roman antiquity and uses it to educate young people from 13–20 years of age. Naturally we require that he know something else, too, e.g., some mathematics or his mother tongue or modern languages, but his main thing is the former. We esteem it if he does understand a completely different language, too; we demand, for example, that he at least know his mother tongue. {We understand} a professor of philology in universities

to be a person who educates philologists; — — — The present class of philologists consists on the one hand of people who use their knowledge of Greek and Roman antiquity in order to teach youths from 13–20 years of age with it and of those who in turn educate teachers in this career. The philologists of the universities are thus the educators of educators; no higher authority exists over them; hence the responsibility is to be attributed to them if the education of the youth is badly directed. Government authorities who deal with matters of education do this only by utilizing former philologists or professors or they are ignorant people [to whom we should not pay attention] who must allow something to be whispered to them by those who do know; as is most often the case — — — We separate out the most talented youths, especially those upon whose education the parents can amply expend money, and then we turn them over to the philologists. Thus is our higher education provided.

First revised version of 7[7] in U II 8, 182–83: Anyone who is not in agreement with the cultivation that now goes along in full swing will have to look around for the creators who implant and promote this cultivation: and will catch sight among them of the *philologists* once again; either these want a false cultivation or they do not want it, but are too weak to make what they do want prevail. The guilt therefore falls upon either their insight and intention or their weakness, which hinders them from making their insights and intentions prevail. On the whole, therefore, contemporary cultivation occurs either with or against the will of the philologists: [and in both cases they are guilty] but it is quite questionable whether we can call them guilty. In the first case, they would say they did not know any better, in the second, they could not do any better. But in any case we would still like to hear what they say. Since I am myself a philologist and have lived sufficiently among them and with some reflection, I want to defend them and to speak for once in their name.

7. *Il faut dire la vérité et s'immoler.]* "It is necessary to speak the truth and to immolate oneself." added later in pencil. {Schopenhauer cites this remark from Voltaire in a letter to Julius Frauenstädt of 17 February 1853; cf. *Arthur Schopenhauer: Von ihm. Ueber*

ihn. Ein Wort der Vertheidigung ("Arthur Schopenhauer: By him. About him: A word of defense") by Ernst Otto Lindner and *Memorabilien, Briefe und Nachlassstücke* ("Memorabilia, letters, and legacies") by Julius Frauenstädt (Berlin: Hayn, 1863), 578.}

8. *do not understand . . . education] do not understand* how to make use of antiquity for creating a nobler cultivation; or instead, that antiquity is used mistakenly as the most important resource for education

9. *teachers mistakenly . . . antiquity? — — —]* teachers mistakenly. In order therefore to ascribe to the philologists their share in contemporary bad cultivation, we could {see} their guilt either in not understanding antiquity or [in the unsuitability] generally in the [use of antiquity] preoccupation with antiquity or in the use of the correctly understood antiquity. All reproaches against the philologists can be condensed in this sentence — either the philologists do *not* understand *antiquity or the present or themselves*. Conversely: if they wanted to prove their innocence — — —

[8 = U I 6b. Summer 1875]

1. *Mörike]* Mörike died on 4 June 1875; N is probably referring to a judgment about Mörike for this reason.

2. *Goethe]* Cf. 8[5].

3. Cf. K. Schlechta and A. Anders, *Nietzsche: Über die verborgenenen Anfänge seines Philosophierens* {"Nietzsche: On the hidden beginnings of his philosophizing"} (Stuttgart: Frommann-Holzboog, 1962), 155–56, where this fragment is, however, erroneously attributed to Notebook N I 6.

4. Acquired on 26 May 1875.

5. Eugen Dühring, *Cursus der Philosophie als streng wissenschaftlicher Weltanschauung und Lebensgestaltung* {"Course in philosophy as a strictly scientific worldview and form of life"} (Leipzig: E. Koschny, 1875), *NL*, acquired by N on 21 April 1875; traces of reading it in spring–summer 1875 — N read it once again in 1885 — on the first pages can be found; p. 2: "Philosophy is the development of the highest form of consciousness of the world and of life," underlined by N; p. 5: "With regard to this great task, it is not a question of disparaging natural disposition or, in

other words, the drives and feelings of human nature in favor of a one-sided culture of reason, but instead, in opposition to that, of completely liberating through reason these naturally emerging endowments of our being and allowing them to work in those directions where they are capable of living fully, with the least oppositional disturbance." Marginal comment by N: as if some form of disposition did not have to be there first in order to set such a task for reason! i.e., how weak and lame would the disposition (the "will") have to have become in order to let itself be led in this way! And what value would such a world then have?! p. 6: "The form of life besides the simply theoretical representation of worldview for which it [philosophy] intercedes is therefore related far less to the isolated private morality of an individualistic form, than instead to the socialitarian and political connection of universal and especially spiritual intercourse." Marginal comment by N: But we must start with the individual! And where is this *first thing!* p. 6: "It goes without saying that this cooperation must finally take on the form of the state; but the middle stages up to this goal may traverse a manifoldness that can begin with the loosest association, indeed, with the accidents of an unorganized literary communication and only later advance to regulated unions and at first, in fact, within the framework of the ordinary forms of collective action." N: Never! p. 6: "This highest form [of philosophical consciousness] means first of all that in comparison with it no higher instance can be encountered that could decide about the assessment and treatment of existence." N: I am thinking *development of the higher forms into the highest.* p. 9: ". . . similar to the chemical constitution of bodies, the general constitution of existence can also be traced back to basic elements and basic forms." N: Doubtful comparison! cf. the title of *HAH* §I.

6. *Reis]* No doubt Reidt, although in the *Ms* Reis is undoubtedly to be read (not Reidt, as in Schlechta-Anders); N is here confusing the two works with each other: Paul Reis, *Lehrbuch der Physik* {"Textbook of physics"} (Leipzig{: Quandt & Händel,} 1872), and Friedrich Reidt, *Die Elemente der Mathematik* {"The elements of mathematics"} (Berlin{: G. Grote,} 1868), both in *NL* and acquired on 22 June 1875.

7. Cf. 5[161, 165].
8. Cf. 9[1].
9. Here for the first time the *Unfashionable* on the philologists is postponed until after the one on Wagner.
10. *diadoche]* "succession"
11. Cf. the fragments in group 15 (= U II 11).
12. Cf. *WB* 2, *CW* 2, 263, lines 2–4.
13. Cf. 11[18]; 14[6].
14. Cf. N to Rohde, 8 December 1875 {*KGB* II:5, 126}; 23[140].

[9 = U III 1. Summer 1875]

1. Eugen Dühring, *Der Werth des Lebens: Eine philosophische Betrachtung* {"The value of life: A philosophical examination"} (Breslau{: Eduard Trewendt,} 1865), *NL*; henceforth abbreviated as *WL*.
2. *Bad style . . . style.]* *Le*[2] X 381, 1.
3. *"the strength . . . ignoring"]* *WL* 3.
4. *"piles . . . thinking."]* *WL* 4.
5. *In the field . . . knowledge.]* *WL* 5.
6. *misfortune]* *Übel* {In this notebook, *Übel* will consistently be translated by "misfortune."}
7. *emotion]* *Gemütsbewegung* {literally, "a movement of one's disposition"}
8. *Whether . . . possibilities.]* *WL* 9.
9. *"the adverse . . . misfortunes."]* *WL* 9.
10. *"World and . . . factual one."]* *WL* 10.
11. *"the idea . . . coherence,"]* *WL* 10.
12. *Only, . . . ideas.]* *WL* 12.
13. *Even . . . can shift."]* Cf. *WB* 3, *CW* 2, 272, lines 23–32.
14. *"The judgment . . . can shift."]* *WL* 12.
15. *between . . . can shift."]* Dühring: "between what is unalterable and what is accessible to human intervention."
16. *In short: . . . of existence!]* Cf. *HAH* 32.
17. *"he touches . . . distinction"]* *WL* 18.
18. *"the uprooting . . . feelings"]* *WL* 18.
19. *"bound up . . . alive."]* *WL* 19.
20. *"The individual . . . crime."]* *WL* 19.

21. *"If the bond . . . fate."]* *WL* 19; somewhat altered and condensed.

22. *"if the bond . . . cease."]* {Cf. *WL* 19.}

23. *"the mood . . . attitude"]* *WL* 20.

24. *"Our morality is]* Dühring: Now our morality is in part

25. *"Our morality . . . abstractions."]* *WL* 20.

26. *"Thus the false . . . of life."]* *WL* 22.

27. *"the higher . . . upon us."]* *WL* 26; somewhat altered.

28. *"Everything . . . equals."]* *WL* 26.

29. *"The sensations . . . injustice."]* *WL* 27.

30. *"lethargy of the life-drive"]* {*WL* 34.}

31. *"Where . . . temperament."]* *WL* 34; somewhat altered.

32. *"premature . . . life-energies."]* *WL* 34.

33. *"regaining . . . striving."]* *WL* 35.

34. *ἀνάγκη]* "*ananke*"; "necessity"

35. *(And yet . . . conscious!)]* Remark of N's.

36. Cf. *Laws* 803c, also 644d.

37. *"Life . . . pains"]* *WL* 62.

38. *Every stage . . . present.]* Cf. 5[186].

39. *The greatest . . . another]* *WL* 69.

40. *"crude . . . justice?"]* *WL* 78.

41. *A dismissive judgment.]* Cf. Dühring: ". . . the former [dishonor] is in contrast a dismissive judgment through which the constitution of our behavior is characterized." *WL* 82.

42. *honor] Ms*: marriage

43. *"Indeed . . . success."]* *WL* 86.

44. *Opposite . . . Aphrodite]* Cf. Plato, *Symposium* 180d–181e{, where Plato uses these two terms to distinguish between Uranian (heavenly) and pandemian ("of the people," so "public," often rendered as "earthly" or "common") modes of love}.

45. *"and in pleasure . . . desire."]* Goethe, *Faust* I:3250.

46. *Aphrodite . . . Eros] Ms*: Eros . . . Aphrodite; cf., however, Dühring: ". . . not only as Aphrodite, but also as Eros . . ."; *WL* 104.

47. *"striving . . . conjuncture."]* *WL* 106.

48. *"With . . . in two"]* Cf. Schiller, "Die Glocke" {"The Bell"}; *WL* 120.

49. *all that . . . destroyed]* Cf. Goethe, *Faust* I:1339–40.

50. *"giant . . . fears."]* *WL* 132.

51. Cf. Schopenhauer, *Parerga* 2, 333{/280}.

52. *"Who does . . . things?"]* {*WL* 142–43.}

53. *Hence the tragic . . . visible.]* *WB* 4, *CW* 2, 279, lines 34–35.

54. Cf. Dühring: "Now it would be deviating too far from the character of experience if we wanted to count upon a change of the periodicities themselves." *WL* 153.

55. *"the objective . . . drive"]* {Cf. *WL* 153.}

56. *"than"]* *Ms*: in; cf. *WL* 159.

57. *"a partial . . . life-energy"]* *WL* 159.

58. *"the play . . . have become before."]* *WL* 160.

59. *⟨do not⟩ wish for]* *⟨ver⟩wünscht*. Corrected from "wish for" {*wünscht*} in *Ms*, according to *WL* 173.

60. *strengthens]* confirms; *WL* 182.

61. *"The cloister . . . good sense.]* *WL* 182.

62. *If humanity . . . one?)]* *WB* 4, *CW* 2, 279, line 34.

63. *talio]* "retaliation"

64. *⟨not⟩ only]* Cf. Dühring: "dream images not only the causes, but . . ." *WL* 227.

65. *"Humans . . . guilt."]* *WL* 232.

66. *Therefore . . . affair.]* Cf. 5[188].

67. *The woe . . . themselves.]* Cf. *HAH* 292, *CW* 3, 191, lines 30–31.

68. *The belief in the value of life . . . upon the others. —]* *Le*[2] X 388, 11; *Le* X 492, 3.

69. Excerpt from Balfour Stewart, *Die Erhaltung der Energie* {*The Conservation of Energy: Being an Elementary Treatise on Energy and Its Laws* (London: Henry S. King and Co., 1873)} (Leipzig: Internationale wissenschaftliche Bibliothek IX, 1875), acquired on 20 January 1875; N excerpted from only the first twenty-two pages; *NL*.

70. *an individual molecule]* *Ms*: molecules

71. *a molecule]* *Ms*: molecules

72. *it]* i.e., "a self-moving body"; cf. Stewart, 22 {19 in the original English}: "We thus see that whether we measure the energy of a moving body by the thickness of the planks through which it can pierce its way, or by the height to which it can raise itself against gravity, the result arrived at is the same."

73. *it]* i.e., "a self-moving body"; cf. note 72 above.

[10 = N I 6. Summer 1875]

1. Cf. *WB* 7, *CW* 2, 294, lines 5–8; 11[47].

2. Cf. 22[109]; under the date 22 October 1875, on this day N wrote his letter to Paul Rée about his *Psychologische Beobachtungen* {"Psychological observations"} {*KGB* II:5, 122–23}.

3. Cf. *WB* 2; 11[6].

4. Cf. 12[14].

5. Cf. 11[18]; *WB* 7, *CW* 2, 294, lines 22–23.

6. Cf. *WB* 10; 11[32].

7. Cf. *WB* 2, *CW* 2, 266, lines 20–22.

8. Cf. *WB* 4, *CW* 2, 273, lines 8–10; 11[22] (variant U II 9, 43).

9. *Taking . . . up to now.]* Uncertain reading.

10. Cf. 11[35].

11. Note for *WB.*

12. Cf. *WB* 4, *CW* 2, 279, line 24–280, line 11.

13. Note for *WB.*

14. Cf. *WB* 5, *CW* 2, 282, lines 1–5.

15. Cf. *MM* 134, *CW* 4, 59.

16. *breaks]* [?]

17. Cf. 11[37].

18. Presumably for *WB.*

19. Keywords for *WB.*

20. Themes of *Unfashionable Observations*?

21. Motto in a small heraldic design of N's; cf. *Z* III "The Wanderer."

[11 = U II 9. Mp XIII 4, 6–8, 47. Summer 1875]

1. Cf. 11[20]; *WB* 4, *CW* 2, 278, lines 3–7.

2. *ἀνάγκη]* "*ananke*"; "necessity"

3. Cf. *WB* 8, *CW* 2, 299, lines 16–30.

4. *Religion] Ms*: Religions

5. *bestializes and]* Added later.

6. *"You heroic . . . that."]* Thomas Carlyle, *Geschichte Friedrich's des Großen* {*History of Frederick the Great*}, in Richard Wagner, *Einleitung zum dritten und vierten Bande* ("Introduction to the third and fourth volumes"): "The thousand-year Reich of anarchy; — abridge it, give your heart's blood to abridge it, you heroic

sages . . ."; *Gesammelte Schriften und Dichtungen* ("Collected writings and poetry") (Leipzig: E. W. Fritzsch, 1871–73), 3:2. {Hereafter, references to these texts will be cited as *WGS*, followed by volume number and page number.}

7. Cf. *WB* 10, *CW* 2, 325, line 35–326, line 21; 5[143]; 14[4].

8. *Hillebrand believes.]* Cf. Karl Hillebrand, "Schopenhauer und das deutsche Publikum" {"Schopenhauer and the German public"}, *Zeiten, Völker und Menschen* {"Times, peoples, and humans"} (Berlin{: R. Oppenheim,} 1875), 2:355, *NL* (discussion of *SE*): "To want not to perceive that Hegel brought German cultivation [that of historical development] into a system . . . means . . . to present Germany's contribution to European civilization as worthless."

9. *itself!]* Beside this in U II 9, 69, without mark of insertion: "to damage oneself by excess"

10. *σώφρων]* "moderate"

11. *modern] Le*: other

12. *The Empedoclean.]* Cf. 11[5].

13. *rocks]* Written above: "depths"

14. *wide]* Written above: "quick"

15. *He moves . . . weather.] Pd*: *WB* 9, *CW* 2, 316, line 35–317, line 11.

16. Cf. *Pd* in Mp XIII 4 to *WB* 9, *CW* 2; 11[15], pp. 173–74, the paragraph that begins "Thus with Beethoven"; 14[9].

17. Cf. *WB* 10, *CW* 2, 324, line 24–325, line 137; 14[9].

18. *"barbaric advantages."]* Cf. Goethe, *Anmerkungen über Personen und Gegenstände, deren in dem Dialog "Rameau's Neffe" erwähnt wird* {"Remarks upon persons and objects mentioned in the dialogue *Rameau's Nephew*": "Taste" {*Sämmtliche Werke in vierzig Bänden*, Vol. 29 (Stuttgart and Tübingen: J. G. Cotta, 1856), 332. *NL.*}; *HAH* 221; Cosima Wagner to N, 9 February 1872 {*KGB* II:2, 537–40}.

19. Cf. *WB* 8, *CW* 2, 308, lines 13–17; *CW* 4, 27[69], 30[147].

20. *Siegfried . . . deeds.]* Cf. Wagner, *Götterdämmerung*, Act 3, *WGS* 6:345ff.

21. Cf. *CW* 4, 28[6, 8, 9].

22. *Nirmsdorf]* Where the eldest stepbrother of N's father, Friedrich August Engelbert Nietzsche (1785–1858), was minister; N

writes about this already in his autobiographical juvenilia (composed in August–September 1858), "From My Life": "I still remember, too, my residence in Nirmsdorf, where my dear, blessed uncle was pastor. I still know well how the evening moon shone upon my bed and how I ⟨saw⟩ the golden meadow in silvery glow in front of me; how Aunt Auguste then spoke: 'The moon has arisen / The little golden stars sparkle etc.'"

23. *the moon has risen]* Matthias Claudius, "Abendlied" {"Evening song"}

24. *Plauen]* N was there in 1853 and 1857.

25. *Pobles]* Cf. *CW* 4, 28[8], hence in 1851; on the "loss of childhood," cf. *WS* 168, *CW* 4, 222–23.

26. *Naumberg]* Probably on the Windlücke {a peak in the Alps}; cf. *CW* 4, 28[6].

27. *"Wunderseliger Mann"]* "Wonderfully Blessed Man"

28. *When grandfather . . . to me.]* Grandfather David Ernst Oehler (1789–1859), minister in Pobles, supposedly explained to N during one of his frequent visits the poem "Das Landleben" {"Life upon the land"} by Ludwig Christoph Heinrich Hölty; the first and the final stanzas of this poem begin with the words "Wonderfully blessed man, who escaped the city!"; cf. L. Chr. H. Hölty, *Werke und Briefe* {"Works and letters"}, ed. Uwe Berger (Berlin and Weimar{: Aufbau-Verlag,} 19{6}6), 165.

29. *Wied (?)]* N no longer recalled the precise name of the river; cf. *CW* 4, 28[8].

30. *Near Bonn . . . childhood.]* During his trip to Bonn (October 1864), N traveled via Elberfeld to Oberdreis in the Westerwald with Paul Deussen to his parents' house and from there on 16 October (one day after his twentieth birthday) walked with Deussen to Neuwied, where the Wied River flows into the Rhine; cf. N to his family, October 1864; cf. also N to Gersdorff, 11 October 1866 {*KGB* I:2, 171}: "Some afternoons were so mild and sunny that I had constantly to recall that unique and irrecoverable time when I, free for the first time from the pressure of school . . . saw the Rhine with the free, proud feeling of an inexhaustibly rich future." Paul Deussen also wrote from Aachen on 14 October 1877: "If, like today, the October sun shines through the window,

I have to recall the old times when we hiked together to Bonn 13 years ago."

31. *Neugasse]* where N lived in the first years after he moved to Naumburg; cf. *CW* 4, 28[9].

32. *The story . . . told.]* perhaps in connection with this: *CW* 4, 28[13].

33. *Ice-skating . . . acreage.]* At the city limit of Naumberg.

34. *"what I . . . lyre."]* {N here recalls a German folk proverb: "Was ich des tages verdient auf meiner Leyer, das geht des Abends wieder in den wind." ("What I earn during the day from my lyre, by night is lost in the wind.")} Cf. *CW* 4, 28[6].

35. *Ravaillac]* [?] {No obvious connection. François Ravaillac was the French religious zealot who assassinated King Henry IV in 1610.}

36. *all music . . . his]* Cf. *WB* 9, *CW* 2, 306, lines 11–12.

37. *An immense . . . indeed.]* Cf. 12[6].

38. Cf. *WB* 9, *CW* 2, 314, line 10–315, line 35.

39. *ἦθος]* "ethos"

40. *swinging arc]* Written above: "arc-swing"

41. *circumstances]* Written above: "mood-music"

42. *there in the distance . . . thunder.]* Added later.

43. *(self-reflection . . . self-judgment)]* This parenthetic insertion is written above the following phrase: "with the vision . . . that"

44. *a human voice]* Written above: "the voice of a human being"

45. *Thus with . . . musical language.]* Cf. 11[8].

46. *he has . . . sculpture:]* Added later (1876?).

47. *modifying the tempo]* Cf. Richard Wagner, *Über das Dirigiren* {"On conducting"}, *WGS* 8:356–79.

48. *heart]* From: bull's-eye

49. *He has achieved . . . die down.] Pd*: *WB* 9, *CW* 2, 316, lines 8–22.

50. *the prolonged . . . passion]* Added later; cf. 11[7, 8].

51. *conviction]* Added later (1876?) above: "clarity"

52. *he could . . . miraculous]* Added later (1876?).

53. *(for sung . . . spoken)]* Added later (1876?).

54. Entered alongside 11[15] (U II 9, 57).

55. Corresponding to the last part of 11[15], entered alongside it with pencil (U II 9, 53).

56. *toads etc.]* From: etc. toads

57. Cf. 11[27].

58. *Chladni sand-figures]* {Chladni figures (or sonorous figures) are the figures formed by the accumulation of fine grains of dry sand along the nodal lines on the surface of a vibrating elastic plate or a similar mechanical system.}

59. *A word . . . his thinking.] WB* 9, *CW* 2, 309, lines 3–26.

60. *Aeschylus . . . pious.]* Cf. 8[6]; 14[6].

61. *flattery]* Written above: "anxiety"

62. *(With every . . . dully.)]* On the neighboring page (U II 9, 49), without insertion mark; cf. *WB* 7, *CW* 2, 294, lines 22–23; 10[7].

63. Cf. *WB* 10.

64. *Meyerbeer]* Cf. *WB* 8, *CW* 2, 298, lines 11–20.

65. *they stood . . . Faust]* Cf. Goethe, *Faust* I:785ff.

66. Cf. *WB* 4, *CW* 2, 277, line 35–279, line 23.

67. *ἀνάγκη]* "*ananke*"; "necessity"

68. *How unjustly . . . struggle.]* Cf. 11[1].

69. *the entire day]* {More literally, "from the early hour"} *Ms*: before the early hour; cf. *WB* 4, *CW* 2, 278, lines 19–20.

70. *begging . . . something]* Cf. 5[150].

71. *and religion]* Added above the line.

72. *injustice]* Written above: "immorality"

73. *This is what . . . religions.]* Cf. 9[1]; added on the side, with the final formulation of *WB* 4 (U II 9, 45): And even if all of humanity should have to perish — who could doubt this? — it has been charged, as its supreme task for future generations, with the goal of growing together into oneness and commonality so that it can confront its impending demise *as a whole* and with a *tragic disposition*. So at present, all future hope and guarantee for what is human lie in the tragic disposition not dying out. A cry of unequaled woe would have to resound across the earth if human beings [precisely] were ever to completely lose this disposition: and on the other hand, there is no more blissful pleasure than to know what we know: how tragic thought has once again been born into the world. For this is a wholly [im]suprapersonal and general pleasure, a rejoicing of humanity at the victory of what is fundamentally human. *Pd*: *WB* 4, *CW* 2, 279, line 30–280, line 11.

74. *Of theater . . . corrupt!]* Cf. 11[23].

75. *Wagner . . . astringent.]* Cf. *WB* 4, *CW* 2, 274, lines 22–26; 11[22].

76. *We . . . workers — — — —]* Cf. *WB* 4, *CW* 2, 278, line 27; 11[20].

77. *Wagner . . . coast]* Cf. 11[22].

78. *Fairy tale . . . women]* Cf. *WB* 8, *CW* 2, 301, lines 10–11.

79. *Pd*: *WB* 4, *CW* 2, 273, line 8–274, line 31.

80. *leaving aside . . . suffer]* Beside these lines (U II 9, 4), the following sentences without insertion mark (to 11[22]): Christianity itself is a piece of oriental antiquity, and indeed, one thought through and pursued with excessive diligence to its logical conclusion. Now the Alexandr⟨ian⟩ Hellenic turn is once again breaking more into the light: power-factors of every kind are putting on pressure and at the same time one also presents to oneself the fruits of culture as exchange and common property. The direction remained unaltered. Cf. 10[10]; *WB* 4, *CW* 2, 273, lines 16–20.

81. *So, then, . . . task.]* Beside these lines (U II 9, 4), the following sentence without insertion mark (to 11[22]): in order thus to bring [pull] together the most manifold often most distant points of knowledge, the most distant continents of talent; it truly requires eternal running and hunting and seven-league boots; in order to traverse and rule the entirety of this enormously expansive domain in all directions, speed and winged feet are necessary. Cf. *WB* 4, *CW* 2, 274, lines 11–15.

82. *Aristotle]* From: Humbold⟨t⟩

83. *I recognize . . . world.]* {Cf. *WB* 4, *CW* 2, 274, lines 22–31.}

84. *work.]* As conclusion (U II 9, 4), the following sentence without insertion mark: Just as German philosophy joins itself again to the Greek of the classical 6th and 7th centuries, to the Eleatics and [Pyth⟨agoras⟩] Empedocles, so Wagner to Aeschylus — — — ; cf. *WB* 4, *CW* 2, 273, lines 25–27.

85. *Pd*: *WS* 4, *CW* 4, 275, line 3–276, line 26.

86. *undisguised]* From: thoughtless

87. *they throw . . . creating.]* Added later; cf. 11[37]; *WB* 10, *CW* 2, 319, lines 30–31.

88. *Wagner manifests . . . Impossible!]* Cf. *WB* 10, *CW* 2, 319, lines 14–29.

89. *preoccupation with . . . fairy tale]* Cf. *WB* 8, *CW* 2, 301, lines 9–13.

90. *We must . . . fiber.]* Cf. 11[9]; *WB* 10, *CW* 2, 325, lines 9–10.

91. *diadochi]* "successors" {Underlined by N.}

92. *"to the strongest"]* Like Alexander.

93. *(If we . . . all sorts.)]* Added beside (U II 9, 35), without insertion mark; cf. *WB* 4, *CW* 2, 277, lines 20–26.

94. *With the name . . . them.]* Cf. *WB* 4, *CW* 2, 277, lines 1–3.

95. Crossed out by N.

96. *A great goal . . . found.] Pd*: *WB* 2, *CW* 2, 264, line 30–265, line 9.

97. *Wagner . . . demon.]* Beside these lines (U II 9, 35), without insertion mark.

98. *but can it not be felt . . . secret:] Pd*: *WB* 2, *CW* 2, 265, line 13–266, line 33.

99. *enticing, e.g., . . . so greatly?]* Cf. *WB* 9, *CW* 2, 318, lines 20–24.

100. *the oath . . . Brünnhilde]* Cf. Richard Wagner, *Götterdämmerung*, Act 2: "By the point of the spear / I say the oath"; *WGS* 6:321.

101. *life]* From: nature

102. *the relationship of the two . . . gone!]* Cf. *WB* 3, *CW* 2, 267, line 1–268, line 23.

103. *with Wagner . . . necessary]* Beside these lines (U II 9, 31) N's later note: the *symphonic* does not run away with him: *one page further* [that is, 11[27]].

104. *As musician . . . Wagner]* Cf. *WB* 9, *CW* 2, 312, line 36–313, line 24.

105. *just consider . . . into it?]* Cf. *WB* 9, *CW* 2, 317, lines 21–31.

106. *carefree]* Above it: "avoiding work"

107. *"people given over to quiet drunkenness"]* Cf. *WB* 5, *CW* 2, 295, line 21.

108. *who devote . . . self-satisfaction]* Added between the lines.

109. *Pd*: Wagner was the first to draw the conclusion about the emergence of drama from performative improvisation from the fact that Shakespeare as well as the ancient Greeks were masters of the dramatic art ⟨and⟩ actors: he feels their essence to be self-alienation.

110. *Wagner . . . improvis⟨ation⟩]* Cf. Richard Wagner, *Über die Bestimmung der Oper* ("On the destiny of opera"): ". . . In any case, we believe we are introducing a genuine facilitation for the solution of an exceedingly difficult problem when we characterize Shakespearean drama as a *frozen mimetic improvisation of the very highest poetic value* . . ."; *WGS* 9:172.

111. *"Self-renunciation"]* Cf. *WB* 7, *CW* 2, 291, line 24; Richard Wagner, *Über Schauspieler und Sänger* ("On actors and singers"), *WGS* 9:259ff.

112. *the bitter-joyful . . . Meistersinger]* Added later beside these lines, without insertion mark (U II 9, 27); cf. *WB* 8, *CW* 2, 303.

113. *renunciation]* Above: "temporary self-alienation"

114. *philosophiers]* {N's German noun here is *Philosophirer*, i.e., not the usual German word for philosophers, *Philosophen*.}

115. *listen . . . crawls!]* Cf. Richard Wagner, *Das Rheingold*, Scene 3: "Alberich: . . . bent and gray / crawl toad! . . . (. . . the gods preserve in stone a toad crawling toward itself)"; *WGS* 5:322.

116. Cf. Richard Wagner, *Das Kunstwerk der Zukunft* ("The Artwork of the Future"), *WGS* 3:60–62.

117. *Wagner is . . . new ideas.]* Cf. Wagner, "Introduction to the third and fourth volumes": "Where art once went silent, political wisdom and philosophy began: where the political sage and philosopher have now come to an end, there the artist begins once again." (Motto to the first edition of "Art and Revolution") *WGS* 3:3; cf. 14[7].

118. *The next . . . education]* Cf. *WB* 5, *CW* 2, 284; 11[26].

119. *"We . . . Wagner.]* Added later (U II 9, 25) without insertion mark; cf. Richard Wagner, *Eine Mittheilung an meine Freunde* ("A Communication to my Friends"), *WGS* 4:311; cf. also note 204 to 11[42].

120. *Pd*: *WB* 10, *CW* 2, 323, line 3–324, line 15.

121. *swollen]* From: burdened

122. *Necessity . . . example.]* Cf. Richard Wagner, preface to "The Artwork of the Future," 1st ed. (1850): "Not vanity, but instead an unavoidable necessity has made me — for a short time — into a writer . . . I preferred striving to attest to my willing only through artistic actions. Because I never managed to succeed completely

in this, I had to acknowledge that not the *individual*, but instead only the community is capable of achieving irrefutably sensory, really artistic actions. To acknowledge this means, as long as hope in general is *not* surrendered, so much as: to rebel from the ground up against our conditions of art and of life. Since I have laid hold of the necessary courage for this rebellion, I decided to become a *writer* as well." Cf. also "Music of the Future," *WGS* 7:152ff.

123. *These writings will be found . . . prose writings.]* Inserted later.

124. *— even . . . sparks —]* Added between the lines

125. *"clothed in content"] "verinhaltlicht"* {N's coinage}

126. Cf. 12[32]; *WB* 6, *CW* 2, 290, line 8–291, line 11.

127. *spectacle]* From: thing

128. *where it . . . blooming.]* From: a rosebush that never ceases to bloom

129. *is nourished]* Beside this (U II 9, 21) the words: To be said

130. *oldest . . . In this way]* From: primal experience: and it could almost be called a law. So

131. *an abyss . . . united]* From: [an abyss] a pairing of strength and goodness

132. *are we granted . . . possibility]* From: should it be embraced

133. Crossed out by N; cf. *WB* 1, *CW* 2, 260–62.

134. *Through . . . life]* Between the lines, added later: parody, in light of the really unmagical lantern of newspaper writers seems for Wagner — — —; cf. *WB* 1, *CW* 2, 260, line 36–261, line 7.

135. *modern . . . devalued]* From: arts are half and half devalued

136. *For many . . . come.]* Cf. 5[158].

137. *newly arisen]* From: true

138. *He yearns . . . ; for]* From: A need for purification and consecration is awakening;

139. *Prominent . . . communicating.]* Cf. Wagner, "A Communication to My Friends": ". . . But only *one* drive led me constantly in this direction, too, namely to communicate as clearly and understandably as possible to the view of others what I have seen . . ."; *WGS* 4:367.

140. *or significant]* From: and great

141. *and in order . . . skeptics.]* From: in the long run, he is right after all.

142. *the individual . . . one word]* Beside these lines (U II 9, 19) without insertion mark: His depiction of the cobbler apprentices — he is able to demonstrate to an apprentice how to rejoice, and to a giant dragon how to roar. Cf. *WB* 10, *CW* 2, 321, lines 24–25.

143. *princes . . . of him]* From: princes, who half shyly, half curiously felt themselves near him

144. *intentionally . . . ; and]* From: most confused, most disloyal; but

145. *Prominent . . . hear him.] Pd*: *WB* 10, *CW* 2, 320, line 22–322, line 1.

146. *While he . . . past.] Pd*: *WB* 10, *CW* 2, 318, line 35–319, line 2; cf. 11[37].

147. *and how great . . . thought]* From: there was no time to lose, the danger was all too great that something

148. *It is indeed . . . utopias]* Cf. Wagner, "Art and Revolution": "Utopias! Utopias! I hear them call, the great sages and sugar-coaters of our modern state- and art-barbarism, the so-called practical people . . . 'Beautiful ideal' that . . . unfortunately . . . shall not be attained! So the good-natured dreamer sighs . . ."; *WGS* 3:43.

149. *and basically . . . himself.]* Beside these lines (U II 9, 19) without insertion mark: even his *friends were his* dangers (*previous* page [i.e., fragment 11[37], numbered by N p. 36 in the notebook]), Afterward, chapter looking back {*WB* 11?}

150. *as though . . . dancers]* Written beside (U II 9, 17) without insertion mark

151. *He got over . . . mastery! —]* Cf. *WB* 8, *CW* 2, 306, line 12–307, line 24.

152. *But the person . . . taking.]* Cf. *WB* 1, *CW* 2, 259, lines 18–19.

153. *But the person . . . Wagner]* From: But in order to lift this treasure, he

154. *furrow] Ms*: fear

155. *We could . . . sooner.]* Cf. *WB* 10, *CW* 2, 318, line 26–319, line 11.

156. *and if . . . sooner.]* Cf. 12[11].

157. *The unfortunate . . . talents.] Pd*: *WB* 10, *CW* 2, 319, line 30–320, line 8.

158. *"Watch on the Rhine"]* {"Die Wacht am Rhein" was written in 1840 by Max Schneckenburger and put to music in 1854 by Karl Wilhelm. After the Franco-Prussian War of 1870–71, it acquired unofficial status as the German national anthem in the newly declared German Empire of Wilhelm I.}

159. *And then . . . music!]* Cf. 10[17].

160. *Pd*: *WB* 3, *CW* 2, 271, line 12–272, line 36.

161. *panting]* From: heavily breathing

162. *such an . . . and]* From: a reposing and [restful] peaceful

163. *there are moods . . . mellowness.]* say to myself with a rare mood *quid agitas* {"what is bothering you"} etc.; cf. Horace, *Carmina* II, 11, 11?

164. *for once . . . as it were]* From: and relax

165. *for]* Here at the bottom edge of the page (U II 9, 14), without insertion mark, the words: If the Germans act, then they immediately deny their history and philosophy.

166. *something . . . credit.]* From: one can turn to their praise and blame.

167. *a mark]* From: a sign

168. *in contradistinction . . . movements]* Added later.

169. *but for that . . . happiness]* Added later.

170. *beyond them, a creative]* From: over them and away, and every creative

171. *only when he has grown weary.]* From: in the lowlands

172. *and from . . . soul]* Added later.

173. *he is . . . because]* Added later.

174. *If history . . . theodicy]* Varies a sentence of Ludwig Feuerbach (philosophy is a disguised theology) that N came upon in Wagner; cf. Wagner, "Introduction to the third and fourth volumes," *WGS* 3:4.

175. *ardent]* Added later.

176. *all that . . . it is]* From: all that . . . to accomplish with it is

177. *its tranquilizing and comforting power]* From: its reassuring comforting character

178. *and even . . . exaggerated]* Beside these lines (U II 9, 13), without insertion mark: there are moments in Wagner, too, when he *rests*, recuperates in philosophy

179. *and quietistic]* Added later.

180. *philosophy]* From: their philosophy

181. *the most important question]* From: the main problem

182. *themselves]* Added later.

183. *them]* From: it

184. *for]* From: in

185. *no sleeping potions]* Added later.

186. *and heroic]* Added later.

187. *heroic and philosophical]* Added later.

188. *Siegfried's words . . . head]* Siegfried's expression

189. *"thus I . . . me."]* Cited from Richard Wagner, *Siegfrieds Tod* {"Siegfried's death"}, Act 3, Scene 1: "then life — look! — thus I throw it far away from me!"; *WGS* 2:282; in *Götterdämmerung*, Act 3, *WGS* 6:340, it goes: "Life and body — look! — thus I throw them far away from me!"

190. *on which . . . shatters.]* Cf. Richard Wagner, *Siegfried*, Act 3, *WGS* 6:228.

191. *Pd*: *WB* 3, *CW* 2, 270, line 23–271, line 4.

192. *tell future . . . about it]* From: as the late [en⟨ough⟩] erected monument of the nature of the German spirit, from which the German Reformation — — —

193. *always]* From: only

194. *in nuce]* "in a nutshell"

195. *Pd*: *WB* 9, *CW* 2, 310, line 10–311, line 15.

196. *sins . . . German.]* From: helping verbs, the losses of the case-designations; whereas he rejoices with deep pride in the German roots and their resonant strength; Wagner's poetry is full of a love of German that, with the exception of Goethe, no German has ever felt.

197. *and yet . . . Bold]* From: and when he struck the rock with his staff an abundant stream of water issued forth.

198. *almost unique]* From: quite great

199. *verbal expression]* From: language

200. *something at which . . . succeed]* Added later.

201. *rarest of all]* Added later.

202. *remain]* From: sound

203. *as the soul,]* Added later.

204. *(the Norn . . . "unsatisfied").]* Cf. Wagner, "A Communication to My Friends": "The one . . . gift of 'the never satisfi'd spirit who forever broods upon something new' is offered to us all at our birth by the youthful Norn, and through it alone could we all become 'geniuses' someday . . ."; *WGS* 4:310–11.

205. *A violent . . . fetters.] Pd*: *WB* 2, *CW* 2, 264, line 23–265, line 12.

206. *There were . . . way]* From: Now and then the doubt tormented him frightfully

207. *a few short hours]* From: moments

208. *Raphael's Cecilia]* {N refers here to Raphael's painting *The Ecstasy of St. Cecilia*, finished between 1516 and 1517.}

209. *Enough that . . . erudition.]* Cf. *WB* 9, *CW* 2, 313, lines 24–35.

210. *annihilation]* From: self-annihilation

211. *Pd*: *WB* 1, *CW* 2, 262, lines 11–29.

212. *poison]* [?]

213. Cf. *WB* 1.

214. Crossed out by N.

215. *The Germans . . . people]* Cf. 5[65].

216. *Wagner was a . . . innovate.]* From: To all the innovative and creative deeds of Wagner, however, there belongs as precondition the learning acquisition of the highest culture in every domain; beside these lines (U II 9, 5) without insertion mark: Questions in music

217. *poetic]* From: poetic and concentrating

218. *And yet . . . astray]* Beside these lines without insertion mark, the sentence: the logical tension passes over mighty spaces

219. *energy]* From: water-energy

220. *he is surrounded by]* From: there is in him

221. *can perhaps . . . off]* From: [has more something frightening] frightened more than enlivened

222. *The Germans . . . afraid."] Pd*: *WB* 3, *CW* 2, 269, line 12–270, line 18.

223. *"has not learned to be afraid."]* ⟨Like Siegfried.⟩

224. *He not only passes through fire]* ⟨Like Siegfried.⟩

225. *He not only . . . work.] Pd*: *WB* 3, *CW* 2, 272, line 36–273, line 6.

226. First outline for a cohesive presentation on the basis of the fragments in U II 9.

227. Cf. 11[43, 44].

228. Cf. 11[28, 18, 32, 29, 27, 6].

229. Cf. 11[25, 22, 12, 35].

230. Cf. 11[15] {p. 173: "— An example . . . that cause. — "}; 11[4, 3, 1].

231. Cf. 11[40].

232. Punctuation added; more comprehensive outline for a cohesive presentation on the basis of the fragments in U II 9; the numbers beside the key words were added by N after making a rubric (11[60]).

233. *From what . . . viewed?]* Cf. 11[44].

234. Cf. 11[34].

235. Cf. 11[43].

236. *The fundamental . . . music.]* Cf. 11[42, 27, 5].

237. Cf. 11[45, 39].

238. Cf. 11[6, 37, 19].

239. *The great . . . conclusion?]* Cf. 11[33].

240. Cf. 11[29].

241. Cf. 11[15, 7, 8].

242. Cf. 11[18].

243. Cf. 11[41].

244. *No cloud . . . first.]* Cf. 12[9].

245. Cf. 11[38].

246. Cf. 11[32].

247. Cf. 11[35].

248. Cf. 11[28].

249. Cf. 11[40].

250. Cf. 11[25].

251. Cf. 11[22, 39].

252. Cf. 11[12].

253. Cf. 11[9].

254. Cf. 11[33].

255. *Art and . . . 35.]* Cf. 11[20, 1].
256. Cf. 11[23].
257. Cf. 11[24]; instead of 18, N wrote 8 in error.
258. Cf. 11[26].
259. Cf. 11[2].
260. Cf. 11[31].
261. *Naturalism 27.]* Cf. 11[13].
262. Cf. 11[37].
263. Cf. 11[13].
264. Cf. 11[4].
265. *Ninth Symphony]* Cf. 11[15] {p. 173: "— An example . . . that cause. — "}.
266. *Anyone . . . contemporary.]* Cf. 10[1]; *WB* 7, *CW* 2, 294, lines 4–8.
267. Punctuation added; later outline of a plan probably written down after the composition of *WB* §§1, 2 (U II 10, 150–140).
268. Cf. 11[57]; *WB* 7.
269. Cf. 11[15].
270. Cf. 11[41].
271. Cf. 11[18].
272. Cf. 11[15, 28]; *WB* 9.
273. Cf. 11[25, 22].
274. The themes of this arrangement were only partly worked out by N
275. Written above: Greeks [?]
276. *caress]* [?]
277. *Eckermann p. 251]* N cites from his edition of the *Conversations* (Leipzig: Brockhaus, 1868); he is referring to the following saying of Goethe (5 July 1827): ". . . The understanding will get in the way of the French, and they won't reflect that the imagination has its own laws, to which the understanding cannot and should not have access . . ."
278. Context unclear.
279. At the beginning, above these lines, without context, the words: Other tones and more joyful; cf. the words to the recitative of the solo baritone in the fourth movement of Beethoven's Ninth Symphony

280. *imitation-world]* Written above *imitation-*: rhythm-

281. *teasing]* [?]

282. Punctuation added; at the beginning of lines normalization of the capitalization.

283. Cf. 11[15, 28]; *WB* 9.

284. Cf. 11[18, 40].

285. Cf. 11[32].

286. Cf. 11[24].

287. Cf. 11[25].

288. Cf. 11[29].

289. Cf. 11[35].

290. Cf. 11[37].

291. Cf. 11[26].

292. Cf. 11[37, 24].

293. *To conclude.] Ms*: to conclude; cf. 11[25].

294. Cf. 11[15, 28].

295. Cf. 11[18, 40].

296. Cf. 11[41].

297. Cf. 11[32].

298. Cf. 11[38].

299. Cf. 11[15, 28].

300. Cf. 11[18].

301. Cf. 11[35].

302. Cf. 11[32].

303. Cf. 11[37].

304. Cf. 11[26].

305. Cf. 11[47].

306. *What will . . . perish.]* Cf. *WB* 11, *CW* 2, 329, line 11–330, line 17.

307. Cf. *WB* 7.

308. Punctuation added, normalization of capitals at paragraphs; arrangement of the fragments in U II 9 and plan for a further elaboration, probably occurring to N after the first continuous writing out of five chapters (= second draft) in U II 10 (cf. 12[33]).

309. Cf. 11[29].

310. *But . . . passion.]* Cf. 11[15].

311. Cf. 11[15, 28, 41].

312. Cf. 11[18, 32, 35]; 12[19].

313. *the "friend of art" set aside.]* Cf. 11[28]; 12[19, 28].

314. *The great talent.]* Cf. 11[33].

315. *Diadochi.]* Written above: Misunderstandings; cf. 11[26].

316. *the apparently reactionary]* Cf. 11[4].

317. *the apparently naturalistic]* Cf. 11[13].

318. Cf. 11[56]; 14[1, 2]; *WB* 11.

319. Cf. 11[31]; Wagner, "The Artwork of the Future," *WGS* 3:60–62.

320. Punctuation added, normalization of capitals at paragraphs; rubricizing of the fragments in U II 9, which N undertook after numbering them; the numbers (1–36) are added in the text by N at the beginning of each fragment; on the back side (Mp XIII 4, 7a), the words "volcanic high flung upward," which relate to the neighboring page of the notebook, no longer existing, from which this sheet was torn.

[12 = U II 10. Mp XIII 4, 13–46. Summer–End of September 1875]

1. *Oresteia]* Cf. 5[109]; Richard Wagner on the *Oresteia*, *WGS* 3:35, 8:81; cf. in addition *Mein Leben* {ed. Martin Gregor-Dellin (Munich: List, 1969)}, 407 {*My Life*, ed. Mary Whittall, trans. Andrew Gray (Cambridge: Cambridge University Press, 1987), 342–43}: "Amid such renunciations and demands, this summer [1847], I managed, amid the pleasure of an almost complete seclusion and the great charm that my new establishment [in the Marcolini Palace in Dresden] granted me, to maintain myself in a highly favorable mood for the completion of my *Lohengrin*. What gave to this mood a cheerfulness that I had never enjoyed with such great intensivity were, along with the labor on my works, my most zealously pursued . . . studies. For the first time ever with mature feelings and understanding, I made myself master of Aeschylus. The eloquent *didaskalia* {teachings} of Droysen in particular helped me to present the intoxicating image of the Athenian performances of tragedies so clearly to my imagination that I could feel especially the *Oresteia*, in the form of such a performance, act

upon me with an unprecedented penetrating force. Nothing compared to the sublime emotion that the *Agamemnon* elicited from me: up to the end of the *Eumenides*, I lingered in a state of rapture from which I have really never again fully returned to reconciliation with modern literature. My ideas about the meaning of the drama and especially, too, of the theater, were definitively shaped from these impressions." {GH: my translation.}

2. *Predramatic part.]* Cf. *WB* 2, *CW* 2, 263, lines 14–15; 12[10].

3. *The line . . . composer.]* Cf. 11[47].

4. Cf. 12[28].

5. *now attach themselves] Ms*: they now attach

6. *fire of the spirit]* From: spirit of those truths

7. *humanity.]* Following, crossed out: I speak from experience, when I it — — —

8. *to confess . . . painful:]* From: I do not rightly know that it has nothing presumptuous or immodest to acknowledge this: for I truly wished more than anything just to have learned to speak far enough in order as artist — — —

9. *why precisely . . . duty]* From: [since I would wish simply to say thanks to the creator of the Bayreuth work by assisting in his work] [because it reminds me of how feeble a way in which I can thank him for having raised me above the offended people] why, I need say to no one, but indeed, this, that I a right to myself — — —

10. *bringing into . . . deception]* sketching an [apparently] continuous form, [after I have found myself incapable of doing this now] that would still only be an apparently complete one

11. Cf. 11[13].

12. *to write]* [?]

13. Cf. 11[1, 20].

14. *relationship to] Ms*: conduct toward

15. Punctuation added; crossed out by N; *Pd*: *WB* 2, *CW* 2, 263, line 6–264, line 19.

16. *at most]* [?]

17. Cf. *WS* 203.

18. Cf. 11[37]; 12[12]; *WB* 3, *CW* 2, 267, lines 13–30.

19. Cf. 11[45]; *WB* 3, *CW* 2, 269, line 10–270, line 18.

20. Cf. 12[11]; 11[37]; *WB* 3, *CW* 2, 267, lines 13–30.

21. Cf. *WB* 3, *CW* 2, 267, lines 10–11.

22. Cf. *WB* 8, *CW* 2, 296, line 28–298, line 11.

23. *stick to the stage]* Perhaps to *WB* 10, *CW* 2, 318, line 35.

24. First arrangement for *WB* 8 (chap. 3 of the first draft); *Pd* to: 12[15, 16, 17].

25. *Common need . . . civilization.]* Punctuation added, regularizing of capitals at the beginning of lines.

26. *He investigates modern civilization.]* From: there is almost something Romantic, a looking backward.

27. *Revolutionary on behalf of the theater!]* Cf. Richard Wagner, *Eine Mittheilung an meine Freunde* ("A Communication to my Friends"): "So from my artistic standpoint, especially, too, on the previously characterized path of thinking about the transformation of the theater, I had reached the point where I was in a position to acknowledge fully the necessity of the irrupting revolution of 1848 . . . I emphasize precisely this, however tastelessly it may be perceived by others who make fun of me as 'revolutionary on behalf of the theater . . .'"; *WGS* 4:378 and note.

28. *He thereby . . . world.]* Beside these lines, without context: *Danger through friends.* To dogmatize. But cf. the revised version toward the end of this fragment.

29. *the dramatic song]* Written above: of music

30. *Then, when . . . people.]* Cf. *WB* 8, *CW* 2, 300, lines 26–28 and note.

31. *the age seems futile to him]* Cf. *WB* 8, *CW* 2, 302, lines 26–29 and note.

32. *he completes . . . another]* Cf. *WB* 8, *CW* 2, 304, line 20 and note.

33. *renounces . . . far away.]* Added between the lines.

34. *giving shelter]* Cf. 10[5].

35. *he finds out . . . effect]* Added between the lines.

36. *Pd*: *WB* 8, *CW* 2, 300, line 26–304, line 36; cf. the notes to these lines.

37. *feels] Ms*: felt

38. *experiences] Ms*: experienced

39. *completes . . . another]* Cf. *WB* 8, *CW* 2, 304, line 20 and note.

40. *Striving . . . to be.]* Cf. *WB* 8, *CW* 2, 302, line 24–305, line 17.

41. *It was . . . future.]* Cf. *WB* 10, *CW* 2, 302, lines 18–21.

42. *If we now . . . can be.]* Cf. *WB* 11, *CW* 2, 330, line 34–331, line 5.

43. Cf. *WB* 8, *CW* 2, 299, line 20–300, line 25.

44. Transition to *WB* 5, with the following variant of it beside these lines: After this break, I can explain more precisely why I recognize in Wagner a simplifier of the world. First, the past appears in the illumination of Wagnerian thought shorter and specifically because a standard has been found according to which we can exclude what is objectionable failed and half-successful: and then, it is observation of the past from one visual angle: in its relationship to art.

45. *external appearance]* above: outer side

46. Punctuation added; abandoned plan, perhaps for the continuation of the first draft.

47. *Has . . . impoverished?]* Cf. 12[28].

48. *innocence]* Cf. Richard Wagner, *Beethoven*: "The same drive that directed Beethoven's rational knowledge to construct for himself the *good* human being led him into the production of the *melody* of this good human being. He wanted to give back to melody, which had lost its innocence from being employed by art-musicians, this purest innocence . . . Now it is a Scottish, now a Russian, now an old French popular mode in which he [Beethoven] recognized the dreamed-of nobility of innocence . . . But what mattered was to find the primeval type of innocence, the ideal 'good human being' of his faith . . ."; *WGS* 9:119–20.

49. Cf. Wagner, *Beethoven*: *WGS* 9:113; the entire passage is cited in 13[1].

50. Cf. 12[20]; *DS* 5.

51. *Drama . . . of art.]* Cf. 12[28]; in addition, Richard Wagner, *WGS* 3:132–33, 6:371, 9:371.

52. Cf. Richard Wagner, *Art and Revolution*: ". . . At the time of its blossoming, art among the Greeks was therefore *conservative*, because it existed for public consciousness as a current and adequate expression: with us, genuine art is *revolutionary*, because

it exists only in opposition to the current general public." *WGS* 3:35.

53. Cf. N, "*Mahnruf an die Deutschen*" (1873) {"Exhortation to the Germans" in *CW* 1}: ". . . Schiller's wondrous presentiment . . . that perhaps at some time tragic drama might develop from opera into a nobler form . . ."; cf. also Wagner, *Beethoven*: ". . . Both concurred, too, in the presentiment about the *essence of music*: only this presentiment was for Schiller accompanied by a deeper view than for Goethe, who conceived in it, corresponding to his entire tendency, rather only the accidental, plastic-symmetrical element of art-music . . . Schiller grasped more deeply the problem touched upon here with the judgment, to which Goethe likewise assented, and through which it was decided that the epic inclined toward the plastic arts, drama in contrast toward music . . ."; *WGS* 9:83; cf. Schiller to Goethe, 29 December 1797.

54. Cf. 11[58]; 12[28].

55. Cf. 12[19]; *WB* 6, *CW* 2, 289, lines 13–18; *DS* 5.

56. Cf. 5[119]; in N I 6, 108, under the date 27 October 1875, the note: Thucyd III 82.

57. *Book . . . genuine.]* Today, too, this chapter is still regarded as not genuine (H. W. Gomme).

58. *νεωτερισμός]* "innovation"

59. *where] Ms*: in which

60. *situation . . . injustice)]* From: peace-loving respect, harming no one

61. *τὸ κερδαίνειν; μὴ ἀδικεῖν]* "to gain advantage"; "not to judge"

62. *πόλις]* "*polis*"; "city-state"

63. *νόμοι]* "*nomoi*"; "customs, laws"

64. *φύσις]* "*physis*"; "nature" {Underlined by N.}

65. *διὰ πάθους ἐπιθυμοῦντες . . . διὰ παντὸς ἐπιφθονοῦντες — (διὰ παντὸς]* "desiring through suffering" . . . "bearing a grudge throughout everything" — ("throughout everything" {N is here arguing for Thucydides's use of the preposition *διὰ* in a temporal rather than a causal sense.}

66. *εὔηθες]* "well-disposed"

67. Title added later: 17. Value of *Wounding*; *Pd*: *HAH* 224.

68. *Degenerating . . . degenerations]* {N here uses two different German terms, *degenerirend* as an adjective, then *Entartung* for the noun.}

69. Added later between these lines: As the ancient world really had eventually used up language in rhetoric, so language is sickened by writing and printing, by literature — language a thing that can be made stupid. Cf. Wagner, *WGS* 3:125ff.; 9:139ff.

70. *individual]* From: modern

71. *paths.]* Beside these lines, added later: Consider how a young musician can still express himself individually: he tells us exactly what his personality is. A poet, in contrast, is a hundred-times veiled impossibility who cannot learn to know himself. Show how rich and deep nature is — if you abandon the word and entrust yourself to the musician

72. *expected.]* Beside these lines, added later: while he condemns the contemporary state just as unconditionally, and as most people already condemn the church. Cf. *WB* 5, *CW* 2, 284, lines 14–16.

73. *In order to explain . . . modern world.]* Subsequently reworked into *WB* 5, *CW* 2, 280–86, after the arrangement of 12[28]; here in the original form.

74. *as Beethoven . . . compassion.]* Cf. the citation from Wagner's *Beethoven* in 13[1].

75. *He grasps . . . music]* Cf. Wagner, "A Communication to my Friends": "I cannot grasp the spirit of music otherwise than in love"; *WGS* 4:325; cf. also *Oper und Drama* ("Opera and drama"), *WGS* 3:389ff.

76. *as a will . . . close to]* From: by going into

77. *since precisely . . . success.]* From: in the vehemence of his struggling, he is brought close to the sudden insight into the lack of success.

78. Related to 12[24].

79. *to expect . . . foolish]* Allusion to Karl Hillebrand; cf. 12[28].

80. *lack of . . . piecework.]* Cf. variant U II 10, 116 to *WB* 5, *CW* 2, 284, lines 31–32.

81. Cf. *WB* 7, *CW* 2, 293, line 4–294, line 24.

82. *Pd*: Anyone who does not set aside Plato's objections to [various] art with the habitual thoughtlessness or even with foolish

arrogance knows that the existence of a [great] powerful art also conceals a host of dangers within it and that the concern for the effects of a powerful artist must seem very serious to all those who know better the dangerous element of life. — We must perceive quite distinctly that even the greatest art should never itself direct the competition among goals in life and that the great artist is not suited to be the immediate educator.

83. *the greatest . . . effect]* From: the greatest artist can have an effect

84. *must instill]* From: is able to instill

85. *cross . . . We would]* From: cross life, but instead, beneath it — — —

86. *limiting the size]* From: the abolition

87. *to draw . . . therefore]* From: to declare that it is extremely

88. *is . . . dangerous]* Two words here crossed out by N: "is" and "dangerous," leaving the sentence fragmentary.

89. Cf. *WB* 4, *CW* 2, 277, lines 26–34.

90. Cf. 12[24].

91. Cf. 11[15].

92. Cf. 11[58]; 12[26, 19, 28].

93. *(to write what I suffer)]* Cf. Richard Wagner, *Censuren* (Preface): "If 'Tasso' therefore gives comfort in this way, that a god gave him the power to say what he suffers — whereby he designates his poetic talent — so I allow myself to rejoice in the fact that it was allotted to me to *write* about this, too." *WGS* 8:258–59. Cf. Goethe, *Tasso*, Act V, Scene 5, lines 3431–32. Wagner, like N in this fragment, too, quotes from the motto of the Marienbad elegy, with the change of "how" into "what": "Entangled in such torments, half-guilty, / a god gave him the power to say what he suffers."

94. *After the break]* I.e., after the insertion of *WB* 3, *CW* 2, 270, line 19–*WB* 4, 280, line 11, by which N is referring back to earlier notes in U II 9; cf. from *PmN*, the variants to *WB* 5, *CW* 2, 280, lines 13–16; this plan for *WB* 5, 6, 7 was also abandoned.

95. Cf. 12[18, 24].

96. Cf. 12[19].

97. *He purifies: . . . imagination.]* Cf. 12[25]; K. Hillebrand gave expression to his "hopes" in *Zwölf Briefe eines ästhetischen Ketzers*

{"Twelve letters of an aesthetic heretic"} (Berlin{: Richard Oppenheim}, 1874), *NL*; N's enthusiasm at the appearance of this text by Hillebrand was sternly condemned by Richard and Cosima Wagner, as Cosima wrote on 20 March 1874: "I have read Hillebrandt's {*sic*} little text at your recommendation, rejoiced in the correctness of the views, however found much blameworthy in it . . . I also find that the whole foundation of the text is a failed one . . . *His* formative hopes, too, seem quite paltry; these are decisively stimulated by *The Birth of Tragedy*, by opera and drama, art and politics, etc., but he does not have the spiritual force to link himself to these hopeful ones, and reserves a small place for himself and his plastic art, which appears just like a corner for sulking." {*KGB* II:4, 416.}

98. *Wagner . . . imagination]* Cf. 5[131]; 12[2].

99. Cf. *WB* 5, *CW* 2, 283, line 35–284, line 33.

100. *(drama . . . of literature]* Cf. 12[19]; on this, Richard Wagner, *WGS* 3:132–33; 6:371; 9:371.

101. *Schiller's presentiment.]* Cf. 12[19] and corresponding note.

102. *The modern . . . one.]* Cf. 12[19].

103. Cf. 12[29].

104. *The seemingly . . . civilization.]* Cf. 11[4].

105. *The seemingly . . . appearance.]* Cf. 12[24].

106. Cf. Goethe to Eckermann on 2 May 1824: "I have regarded all my works and accomplishments only symbolically, and I have basically been rather indifferent whether I made pots or bowls."

107. *From there . . . himself.]* Cf. 12[28].

108. This fragment followed immediately after *WB* 3, *CW* 2, 270, line 18, and is to be considered as a placeholder until the insertion of the text of *WB* 3–8, *CW* 2, 270, line 19–296, line 35 (cf. also the variants to these pages in *WB* from U II 10, 134–35).

109. *into that . . . intentions.]* Cf. 4[4].

110. *To reflect . . . developed.]* Cf. *WB* 9, *CW* 2, 308, lines 19–22.

111. *Such a truly . . . reflective.]* Cf. 11[33]; *WB* 6, *CW* 2, 290, lines 8–18.

112. *Pd*: I hold it to be possible gradually [—] to deepen the general impression of a great talent upon our sensation, so that we can infer backward (infer backward with sensation) from the real

certainty of the great artist-individuality once to the state in which he [is] forced into creating — — — in which he [—] — — — through recollection of one's own states — — —

113. *"Nature is . . . more real!"]* Cf. *WB* 6, *CW* 2, 289, lines 23–33.

114. *But the hand . . . free beings.]* Cf. *WB* 7, *CW* 2, 294, lines 16–18.

[13 = D 10a (PmN). Summer–Autumn 1875]

1. The incompletely preserved *PmN* to *WB* ends with this.

2. {Cf. Luke 23:43.}

3. *"Never has any . . . Symphony?"]* Citation from Wagner, *Beethoven*, *WGS* 9:113–14, with changes and omissions.

[14 = Mp XIII 4, 9–12. Autumn 1875–Spring 1876]

1. Cf. *WB* 11; punctuation added, normalizing of capitals at paragraphs.

2. Cf. *WB* 11; punctuation added, normalizing of capitals at paragraphs.

3. *But takes . . . eyes."]* Cf. *WB* 11, *CW* 2, 330, line 30 and corresponding note.

4. Punctuation added.

5. *His writings . . . "Faust").]* Cf. *WB* 10, *CW* 2, 324, line 20–325, line 9.

6. *Already . . . saying.]* Cf. *WB* 10, *CW* 2, 327, lines 6–9 {where N quotes a stanza from Schiller's poem "Die Künstler" ("The artists")}.

7. *Pd*: *WB* 10, *CW* 2, 325, line 35–326, line 20.

8. *"channeling . . . humanity."]* Cf. the note to *WB* 10, *CW* 2, 326, lines 9–12 {*CW* 2, 392}: "Nietzsche draws this quotation, which he has modified and adapted, from Wagner's 'Introduction' to the third and fourth volumes of his *Schriften*, 3:3, 7–8. In this passage, Wagner cites the historic role of the Germans, as the people of the Reformation, in turning the force of revolution to the good of humanity."

9. Cf. *WB* 10, *CW* 2, 327, lines 6–9 and note.

10. Cf. 11[4].

11. *He stands . . . unreligious.]* Cf. 8[6]; 11[18].

12. *Pd*: *WB* 11.

13. *Wagner's words . . . etc.]* Cf. 11[31] and corresponding note.

14. *Schiller's words.]* Cf. *WB* 10, *CW* 2, 327, lines 6–9 and note.

15. *Schiller's . . . history.]* Added later in pencil.

16. Final plan for *WB*; {the format of this fragment has been changed considerably from what appears in *KSA* 8 to more closely follow N's original formatting; cf. https://ores.klassik-stiftung.de, Signatur GSA 71/229, pp. 73–74}.

17. *Art-capacity . . . clarity]* Cf. *WB* 9, *CW* 2, 316, line 4.

18. *Poet . . . human beings]* Cf. 11[8, 9].

19. *talent . . . Faust)]* Cf. 11[35].

20. — *Writings . . . Faust)]* Cf. 14[3].

21. Cf. *WB* 11, *CW* 2, 329, line 32–330, line 17.

[15 = U II 11. Spring 1876]

1. From 15[5] to 15[14]: for the planned addendum to the *Unfashionable Observations*; cf. 16[12]. The page numbers in 15[5] relate to D. F. Strauss, *Der alte und der neue Glaube* (Leipzig: Hirzel, 1872), *NL*. {English translation: *The Old Faith and the New*, trans. Mathilde Blind (London: Asher and Co., 1873). N's citations appear on pp. 124, 49, 335, 277, and 55, though the translation has been altered considerably.}

2. *44]* {*KSA* incorrectly has 49.}

3. Cf. G. Chr. Lichtenberg, *Vermischte Schriften* {"Mixed writings"}, 1, 177; cf. *CW* 11, 27[12].

4. Cf. *CW* 11, 27[8].

5. *"poor in spirit"]* Cf. Matthew 5:3.

6. Cf. *CW* 11, 27[11].

7. *Aristotle's opinion]* Cf. *Politics* 1335b26–1336a2.

8. Cf. 5[125]; cf. *CW* 11, 27[10].

9. Cf. *CW* 11, 27[29].

10. *sentiments]* {N uses this term in French here.}

11. *factor . . . farceur] factor . . . Farceur* {While it is not clear precisely what N means by using *factor*, it may be that he is punning on the alliteration between the two words, and perhaps pointing to Hegel as someone who makes things or deals with facts, while Heine is someone who disrupts things in playing around with styles and words.}

12. After 1 Corinthians 13:2; cf. *CW* 11, 27[35].

13. Punctuation added; cf. *CW* 11, 27[51].

14. *Empedocles]* In Diogenes Laërtius VII, 63.

15. Cf. *CW* 11, 27[66].

16. Cf. 19[63]; *WS* 199; *CW* 11, 27[72].

17. Up to 15[26]: cf. 8[4].

18. {Fragments 15[15–26] deal with nuances of German grammar and are often impossible to translate in terms that make sense with regard to English grammar, which lacks case modifications and uses verb moods differently than German. Hence the oddity of some of what follows, where the reader is best referred back to the original German. N's analysis here of historical shifts in German usage is clearly related both to his critique of David Strauss's style in the first *Unfashionable Observation* and of Wagner's style throughout these notebooks. The philosophical or cultural force of N's account, though, seems aimed at aligning contemporary German usage more with classical Greek or Latin, where the range of available cases made the use of prepositions less frequent.}

19. Punctuation added.

20. *"mich dünkt" . . . "mir dünkt"]* {Both the German accusative case and dative case in these phrases meaning "it seems to me."}

21. *"es friert mich" . . . "mir friert."]* {Both the German accusative case and dative case in these phrases meaning "I am freezing."}

22. *"Ich schlage . . . ins Gesicht."]* {Both the German dative case and accusative case in these phrases meaning "I hit you in the face."}

23. Punctuation added.

24. *Christlichkeit der Theologie]* {Franz Overbeck, *Über die Christlichkeit unserer heutigen Theologie* (Leipzig: Fritzsch, 1873); *How Christian Is Our Present-Day Theology?*, trans. Martin Henry (London: T & T Clark International, 2005).}

25. *ἦθος]* "ethos"

26. *πάθος]* "pathos"

27. Cf. *HAH* 151; 17[1, 79].

[16 = N II 1. 1876]

1. Cf. 17[61]; this note is placed under the date 30.3.1876 in the *Ms*.

2. Cf. *HAH* 200.

3. Cf. 19[41].

4. *Pd*: 18[30]; cf. *HAH* 555.

5. *putting up with]* Written above: enduring

6. *ῥεῖα ζώοντες]* "those living easily" or "those living at ease" {i.e., as the gods live}; cf. *Iliad*, bk. 6, line 138; *Odyssey*, bk. 4, line 805; cf. 17[85]; 17[74].

7. Crossed out by N.

8. Original version had, following number 4 {The Artist}: 5. The Death of the Old Culture. 6. The Teacher. 7. Woman and Child. 8. Property and Work. 9. (The Easy Life) Means to l⟨ive⟩ at ease. 10. Path to Freedom.

9. *Pd*: *HAH* 589; cf. 19[9].

10. *"friend."]* {A pun by Nietzsche on the resemblance in German between "friend" (*Freunde*) and "joy" (*Freude*).}

11. *Pd*: *HAH* 76.

12. Cf. the fragments of group 15 (= U II 11).

13. Variant in U II 5, 169: There are various steps to freedom. If someone has a stubborn temperament, he may attempt a different one, e.g., with the sense for independence. There is one stairway for lovers and one for the loveless.

14. Cf. *HAH* 392.

15. Cf. 18[25]; written during the Bayreuth days.

16. Also in U II 5, 173; the citation is from Ralph Waldo Emerson, *Neue Essays* (*Letters and Social Aims*), trans. and intro. by Julian Schmidt (Stuttgart{: Abenheim,} 1876), 171; *NL*. {Cf. *The Collected Works of Ralph Waldo Emerson*, vol. 8: *Letters and Social Aims* (Cambridge, MA: Belknap Press of Harvard University Press, 2010), 97.}

17. *Consilia . . . habent.]* "The counsels of youth have something more divine about them."

18. Cf. *HAH* 151; 17[1]. Variant in U II 5, 171: The poet must first have seen a thing precisely and then make it imprecise, wrap it with a veil. Many attempt the latter — — —

19. Under the date 28 August, inferrable from the handwriting that it was written down during the train journey from Bayreuth to Basel; cf. *CW* 19, Chronicle of N's life 1876.

20. *Pd*: *HAH* 595.

21. {Cf. Isocrates's fictional defense of his teaching of rhetoric in his "Antidosis."}

22. Cf. 17[84].

23. *Pd*: *HAH* 272.

24. *Pd*: *HAH* 269. Cf. N to Marie Baumgartner, 13 May 1875 {*KGB* II:5, 52}.

25. *Pd*: *HAH* 456.

26. *Pd*: *HAH* 388.

27. *Pd*: 19[24].

28. Cf. *HAH* 206.

29. Cf. *HAH* 206.

30. *Pd*: 20[10].

31. *Pd*: 19[18].

32. Cf. 19[13].

33. *Pd*: *HAH* 283.

34. *vitam]* "mode of life"

35. Cf. 17[48].

36. *vita umbratica]* "sheltered or contemplative life"

37. *Pd*: *HAH* 283.

38. *Pd*: *HAH* 286.

39. *Pd*: *HAH* 286.

40. *Pd*: *HAH* 291.

41. Cf. 17[50].

42. *Pd*: 17[42]; cf. *HAH* 291.

43. Cf. *HAH* 284.

44. *Pd*: *HAH* 291.

45. *Pd*: 17[39].

46. *Pd*: 17[41]; beside this, the words: therefore *unfashionable*!

47. *esprit fort]* "strong spirit"

48. *Pd*: *HAH* 291.

49. Cf. 17[16].

50. Cf. *HAH* 159.

[17 = U II 5b. Summer 1876]

1. Cf. *HAH* 151, 279; 17[16, 18, 32, 79].

2. *Pd*: *HAH* 31.

3. For *WB*?

4. *Pd*: 18[34].

5. Cf. 18[34]; belongs to the written notes from which *HAH* 549 and 117 (= "Plowshare" 111) and 18[32] (= "Plowshare" 112) developed but were not used.

6. Cf. *HAH* 628.

7. Cf. *HAH* 289; beside this, the title *The Value of Illness for Knowledge* for the copy in M I 1, with the indication "v. p. s." {"*vide pagina supra*" ("see pages above")}, i.e., U II 5, 197, where *Pd* of *HAH* 289 (= "Plowshare" 11) is to be found.

8. *Pd*: *HAH* 405.

9. *Pd*: *HAH* 335; cf. 18[32].

10. Cf. *HAH* 549.

11. Cf. 17[1]; 16[53].

12. Cf. *HAH* 151; 17[1].

13. *Pd*: *MM* 95; cf. 5[166].

14. Cf. 5[166].

15. Cf. 22[48].

16. Cf. 17[30].

17. Cf. *WS* 332.

18. *Pd*: *HAH* 421.

19. Cf. 17[24]. *Pd*: It is to be explained why childhood and youth are idealized. People most often *become less free*.

20. Cf. N to Rohde, 18 July 1876 {*KGB* II:5, 177}; revised 1884–85.

21. Es geht ein Wandrer durch die Nacht
Mit gutem Schritt;
Und krummes Thal und lange Höhn
Er nimmt sie mit.
Die Nacht ist schön —
Er schreitet zu und steht nicht still,
Weiß nicht, wohin sein Weg noch will. —

Da singt ein Vogel durch die Nacht. —
— „Ach Vogel, was hast du gemacht?
Was hemmst du meinen Sinn und Fuß
Und gießest süßen Herzverdruß
Auf mich, daß ich nun stehen muß
Und lauschen muß,
Zu deuten deinen Ton und Gruß?" —

Der gute Vogel schweigt und spricht:
Nein Wandrer, nein! Dich grüß ich nicht

Mit dem Getön;
Ich singe weil die Nacht so schön.
Doch du sollst immer weiter gehn
Und nimmermehr mein Lied verstehn.
Geh nur von dann'
Und klingt dein Schritt von fern heran
Heb' ich mein Nachtlied wieder an
So gut ich kann. —
Leb wohl, du armer Wandersmann! —

22. Cf. 17[1]; *Pd*: Infidelity of memory necessary for the artist.

23. *He can . . . latter.]* Lacking in *Pd*.

24. Cf. *HAH* 619; 5[190].

25. Cf. *HAH* 291.

26. *Pd*: 16[50].

27. *Pd*: in individual species the will strives to die out.

28. *Pd*: 16[51]. Cf. *HAH* 284.

29. *esprit fort]* "strong spirit"

30. *Pd*: 16[47].

31. *Canon]* {The *Canon* is Epicurus's principal work on epistemology.}

32. *Pd*: The ages of active people work for us; a deepening and calming like never before must come over human beings, if they become *tired* of this rush.

33. *Pd*: 18[12].

34. *Pd*: 16[39].

35. Cf. *HAH* 267; 19[75]; *Pd*: Goal of linguistics is to discover a universal language: it is necessary as soon as the European universal human being exists. For what purpose, this awful learning of languages!!

36. Cf. 16[45].

37. Cf. 18[22].

38. *Pd*: *HAH* 285.

39. *Pd*: *HAH* 285.

40. *Pd*: *HAH* 285.

41. *Pd*: 18[17].

42. *Pd*: 18[16].

43. *νεμεσσητικόν]* actually νεμεσητικόν: "inclined to indignation (at the happiness and unhappiness of another)": cf.

Aristotle, *Nicomachean Ethics* 1108b3–4. Cf. *WS* 29, 30; *CW* 4, 41[10]; *D* 78.

44. Cf. 16[3].

45. Cf. 18[11].

46. Cf. *HAH* 637.

47. Cf. 18[61]; *MM* 288.

48. Cf. *HAH* 226.

49. Plan for "The Plowshare."

50. *Five] Ms*: 5

51. Cf. 16[8]; 17[85].

52. *Pd*: *HAH* 227.

53. *pudendum]* "external genitals, especially female," hence, by extension, an "object of shame"

54. Cf. *MM* 98; *CW* 4, 28[35].

55. Cf. 18[61].

56. Cf. *HAH* 151; 17[1].

57. Cf. 20[1].

58. Cf. *HAH* 284.

59. Cf. *HAH* 284.

60. *Pd*: 16[27]; cf. 17[25].

61. Cf. 16[8]; 17[74].

62. Cf. *MM* 407.

63. *out of my modest obscurity]* [?]

64. Cf. *HAH* 30.

65. Cf. *HAH* 284.

66. Cf. *HAH* 228.

67. Cf. *HAH* 481.

68. Cf. *HAH* 453.

69. Cf. 18[19].

70. Cf. 18[7].

71. Cf. 18[52].

72. *Swiss movement] Schweizer Bewegung* {N refers here to Switzerland's movement from a relatively loose confederation of cantons to the establishment of a federal state in 1848.}

73. *Pd*: 18[58].

74. *Pd*: 18[51].

75. *Pd*: 18[53]; 18[56].

76. Cf. 23[81]; *HAH* 611.

77. Plan for "The Plowshare."

78. *Easing . . . all too human.]* In addition to this, the later note: 9 maxims on woman and child 27 [On the various] professions and occupations (in this notebook) + 16

79. Plan for "The Plowshare."

80. The following notes were arranged thus by N in U II 5: 19[56]; *Pd HAH* 118; *Pd HAH* 75; 19[48]; *Pd HAH* 115; *Pd* 20[5]; *Pd HAH* 595; *Pd HAH* 88; *Pd HAH* 80; *Pd HAH* 589; *Pd HAH* 611.

81. Arranged thus in U II 5: *Pd HAH* 469; 19[55]; *Pd HAH* 191; 19[51]; *Pd HAH* 181; *Pd HAH* 189; *Pd HAH* 209; 19[32]; *Pd HAH* 454; 19[26]; 19[27]; 19[22]; 19[21]; *Pd HAH* 597; 19[19]; 19[20]; *Pd HAH* 573; 19[16]; 19[11]; 19[8]; *Pd HAH* 186.

82. Arranged thus in U II 5: *Pd HAH* 383; 19[53]; 19[52]; *Pd* 20[16]; 19[42]; 19[38]; *Pd HAH* 456; *Pd HAH* 388; *Pd HAH* 377; *Pd HAH* 407; 19[13]; *Pd HAH* 598.

83. Arranged thus in U II 5: *Pd HAH* 318; *Pd HAH* 322; *Pd HAH* 557; 19[50]; *Pd HAH* 561; *Pd HAH* 338; 19[43]; *Pd* 20[6]; *Pd HAH* 595; *Pd HAH* 505; *Pd HAH* 294; 19[12]; 19[9]; *Pd* 20[8]; 19[7].

[18 = M I 1. September 1876]

1. Cf. Wernher der Gartenaere, "Meier Helmbrecht," verses 544–50. {Cf. Linda B. Parshall's translation (New York: Garland, 1987), 36–39, where the German text differs from N's modernized version in the epigram: "That could be you, dear son, / if only you'd heed me now. / Till the fields with your plow, / and you will benefit many; / both poor and rich / will profit from you, / as will the wolf and eagle / and all other creatures / and everything that God / called to life here on earth."} The same passage, with changes, is quoted in *D* 202; see also *CW* 5, 329n102.

2. *Pd*: *HAH* 581.

3. *a view . . . for us]* *Pd*: a view: the fate is to be lonesome or twosome.

4. *protectionists and free-traders]* *Le*: protectionism and free-trade; cf. 17[97].

5. *Among . . . patriotism.]* Added by N.

6. Cf. 18[42]; *Pd*: Free spirit on the heights: all motives of the will have become faint. The will would indeed still like to bite — but its teeth are broken.

7. *overripe] Ms* M I 1: overrich

8. *more certain] Ms* M I 1: certain

9. Cf. 17[64].

10. *Pd*: 17[47].

11. *Pd*: 17[57].

12. *Pd*: 17[56].

13. *Pd*: *HAH* 83; cf. 17[92].

14. Cf. *HAH* 475; 17[96].

15. *castes;] Pd*: castes. But it is a movement that cannot stand still. It is not "race" that moves there, but instead prejudice. The only race-people, the Jews, are not at all affected by this tendency to build a state — they *have* the advantage.

16. *Pd*: Concerning the upside-down opinions that we have about *hard work*, especially among scholars (despite all the beautiful words, however, I know: you bore yourselves to death without your hard work).

17. Cf. 23[152]; *Ms*: Christianity and Larochef⟨oucauld⟩ are right to condemn human *motives*: knowledge of that is quite necessary in order to liberate from the vehement will.

18. Cf. 17[51]; *WS* 203.

19. Cf. *MM* 130.

20. Cf. 16[18].

21. *for example . . . attempts.]* Added later by N.

22. *Pd*: Goethe's saying: the animal lives on in the mussel.

23. *Pd*: 16[7].

24. *this Christian-like comfort]* "Plowshare" 111 (*Pd HAH* 117), which this fragment follows, concludes with the words: we are all of the same kind.

25. *Pd*: 5[163]; cf. *HAH* 108.

26. *Pd*: 17[16]{; cf. 9[1]}.

27. *Pd*: Beginning of "Woman and Child." To the question: "Where to? Why precisely thus?" I answer "because of father and mother"; let's leave it at that.

28. Cf. *HAH* 378.

29. Cf. *HAH* 393.

30. *even . . . this.] Pd*: even friendships are thus spoiled.

31. *Fathers . . . sons.] Sd: HAH* 382.

32. *continually . . . heart]* From: yearn for the birth of genius

33. Cf. *HAH* 539; 18[8].

34. *maintenance;] Pd*: maintenance, [sexual satisfaction];

35. *love] Pd*: marriage

36. *demands . . . friends.] Pd*: is monogamy; for sensuality alone is decisive for it.

37. *Pd*: 5[198].

38. *Pd*: 5[193].

39. *Pd*: 5[117].

40. *Pd*: Everything on which someone stakes his life is considered excused — so highly do we assess life?

41. *In no other way . . . life.]* From: We can assess the overall value of life perhaps no more highly than in this way.

42. *Pd*: *HAH* 66; *Pd*: 17[101].

43. Cf. 17[98].

44. *Pd*: 17[102].

45. *better . . . marriage.] Ms*: better, or of the rich person, that he becomes ever richer. The air will eventually become too pure to breathe; a little more sin makes it more tolerable.

46. *Pd* at the end: He should compensate for damage — nothing more. If he cannot do that — — —

47. *Pd*: *HAH* 568; *Pd*: 17[102].

48. Cf. 19[41].

49. *that everyone . . . nonexistence.] Pd*: that it is not a matter of "death" (reincarnation, "everyone can only deliver himself into nonexistence"). Nonsense!

50. Cf. 17[100].

51. *bites of conscience] Gewissenbisse* {In German, there are bites (*Bisse*), not pangs or stings, of conscience (*Gewissen*).}

52. Cf. *CW* 4, 31[7].

53. Cf. 17[70]; 17[78].

54. *will] Pd*: and knows how to transform it here into the higher one of purity, will

55. *Pd* at the end: Behind the plowshare goes the sower.

[19 = U II 5c. October–December 1876]

1. *Bex]* {A small municipality in southwest Switzerland.}

2. Up to 19[6], handwriting of Paul Rée with corrections by N.

3. Cf. 3[31]; 5[106].

4. *exc.] excudit* {"he made it"; in this context, *excudit* would mean that the reader feels he knows the text as though he had made or written it.}

5. *Anyone . . . is lucky.]* Unfinished correction from: Unhappy naïveté of the one who believes that he does not understand only the passages where the text is corrupt!

6. *Shakespeare]* From: Montaigne

7. *Pd*: *HAH* 499; *Pd*: Friends out of "fellow rejoicers," rejoicing with {*Mitfreude*} higher than compassion {*Mitleid*, literally "suffering with"}.

8. *Shared joy makes the "friend" (the one with whom we rejoice)] Mitfreude macht den "Freund" (den Mitfreuenden)* {Nietzsche's coinages here (*Mitfreude* and *Mitfreuenden*) create wordplay in German between *Freude* ("joy") and *Freunde* ("friends"), but also set up a counterpoint with the German term for compassion (or sometimes, sympathy), *Mitleid*; thus, "suffering with" pairs with "rejoicing with."}

9. Cf. *HAH* 226; *Pd*: as in a country producing wine one becomes a drinker of wine.

10. Cf. *HAH* 598.

11. *Pd*: *HAH* 295.

12. *Thus Socrates . . . listeners.] Pd*: Socrates Wagner

13. *Pd*: *HAH* 381; cf. 16[37].

14. *will be able to* {and} *; every human being is a medical history.]* Crossed out by N; beside it (U II 5, 104) is the *Pd* to *HAH* 306 {cf. *CW* 3, 343}.

15. Cf. 20[8]; 21[81].

16. *Pd*: 16[36]; crossed out by N and replaced with *Pd*: *HAH* 407.

17. *is . . . together.]* From: has the strange character that it can be seen through completely and yet still catch us again in its net: it is periodically incurable

18. Cf. *HAH* 439.

19. *among the rich . . . difference.] Pd*: Only there it is imposed and here a drive; this drive then imposes the overexertion of the workers as well.

20. *Pd*: *HAH* 188.

21. *their thoughts . . . sentence.] Pd*: their thoughts: "when one considers" "one adds on" — etc. Full sentences about a small thought are nothing other than the cackling of the hen about the laid egg.

22. Cf. 16[32].

23. Cf. 22[103]; *HAH* 372.

24. *is no longer of . . . country]* unfinished correction in *Ms*: is no longer the first soldier of his country

25. *we should . . . individual.] Pd*: we should get out of his way, as with all those who simply seem to be great.

26. *seriousness]* Written above later with pen: being active

27. *those active . . . labor.] Pd*: and the active people should maintain these idle people with their excess labor.

28. *If]* From: Therefore if

29. *experienced] Ms*: [ar]med and experienced

30. *Pd*: *HAH* 187.

31. *Pd*: *HAH* 613.

32. Cf. *HAH* 133.

33. *Pd*: *HAH* 192.

34. *to allow . . . occasionally.]* From: to collect his ideas like a miser and to lay them in a chest.

35. *Pd*: *HAH* 39, {*CW* 3, 49, lines 9–14}.

36. *Many . . . way.]* Cf. *HAH* 558.

37. *Pd*: Father and mother both.

38. *Pd*: *HAH* 39. *Pd*: Two forms of bad sensations.

39. *esse]* "being"; "essential nature"

40. *and suicide . . . for truth. —] Pd*: the fear of speaking out unconditionally in favor of suicide is the driving motive of Schopenhauerian ethics.

41. *"Become . . . are."]* Cf. Pindar, *Pythian Ode* 2.72; cf. *EH* title.

42. Cf. 18[57]; 19[39].

43. *Pd* crossed out by N up to the version of 19[42]; U II 5, 79–80: If women [say that they sighingly obey necessity, they

often mean only: "what people would say if— "] sigh that they are obeying fate, they mean by fate the tongue of the neighbor. U II 5, 80: The [honesty] virtue of women is preserved [even more] [less] not so much by the voice of conscience [|God's eye|] as the voice of the neighbor. — The virtue of women is not as securely preserved by the proximity of God as by the proximity of the neighbor.

44. Cf. *HAH* 546.

45. Cf. *HAH* 546.

46. *Pd*: *HAH* 583.

47. Cf. *MM* 170.

48. *"in him . . . being."]* {Cf. Acts 17:28.}

49. *Pd*: *HAH* 198.

50. Cf. *HAH* 596.

51. *casus belli]* "a case for war"

52. *presumed]* From: false

53. *Pd*: *HAH* 119.

54. *no longer . . . unburden.]* From: begins to trouble the heart.

55. *If formerly . . . deadly:]* Perhaps based on Schopenhauer, *Parerga* 2, 573n{/486n}.

56. Cf. *MM* 181.

57. Cf. *WS* 199; 15[14].

58. *Pd*: *HAH* 123.

59. Cf. *HAH* 482 and corresponding note.

60. *we live . . . to culture.]* Cf. *HAH* 520.

61. Attempt at an arrangement of the materials from M I 1, pp. 1–96 ("The Plowshare") and U II 5c, 114–59; for this purpose, N entered beside each key word the numbers of the corresponding fragments from both notebooks; cf. the descriptions in *KGW* IV:4, 515–16 and 552ff.

62. M I 1: 39, 34, 30.

63. N deleted the following fragment numbers from M I 1: 106, 36, 35, 74.

64. M I 1: 11, 20–22, 25, 26, 28, 29, 37.

65. M I 1: 40–47.

66. M I 1: 17.

67. M I 1: 76, 27.

68. M I 1: 75; U II 5c: 36.

69. M I 1: 130, 2, 14, 123, 15, 84.

70. *Production of genius]* U II 5c: 30, 31, 29, 110, 105, 82, 73, 51, 47.

71. *Middle of the way]* M I 1: 16, 19.

72. M I 1: 119.

73. U II 5c: 60, 57; M I 1: 12, 106, 144, 150, 166, 173.

74. U II 5c: 92, 93, 78, 79, 62, 49, 50, 45, 35, 28, 20–22, 9, 1–6; M I 1: 6, 13, 57–59, 64, 67, 68, 72, 90, 91, 94.

75. U II 5c: 118, 98, 42, 11.

76. U II 5c: 109, 95, 88, 94, 80, 81, 40, 25–27, 12, 14, 118–20; M I 1: 159, 160, 171.

77. U II 5c: 97, 99, 77, 34, 37, 24, 19, 121; M I 1: 93, 116–41.

78. U II 5c: 112, 113, 115, 102, 103, 100, 53, 43, 44, 41, 32; M I 1: 5, 10, 24, [48, 49], 62, 65, 69, 77, 81, 95, 142, 154, 157, 158, 164, 163, 174.

79. U II 5c: 116, 117, 108, 111, 107, 89, 84, 66–69, 63, 48; M I 1: 33, 70, 80, 82, 147, 148.

80. U II 5c: 101, 104, 87, 90, 91, 85, 86, 83, 72, 74–76, 70, 71, 64, 61, 58, 55, 46, 38, 39, 33, 16, 17, 18, 7, 10; M I 1: 7–9, 12, 48–56, 60, 61, 63, 66, 71, 78, 79, 88, 89, 96–100, 143, 149, 151, 153, 152, 175, 38.

81. U II 5c: 13; M I 1: 73, [82], 87, 101–105, 107–113, 115, 155, 170, 122.

82. *fatum tristissimum]* "the saddest of fates"

83. M I 1: 18.

84. Cf. 5[194].

85. *stroll]* [?]

86. *Homo . . . est.]* "A free man thinks of nothing less than of death, and his wisdom is a meditation on life, not on death." Cf. Spinoza, *Ethics* IV, Prop. LXVII {trans. Edwin Curley in *The Complete Works of Spinoza*, vol. 1 (Princeton, NJ: Princeton University Press, 1985)}.

87. *like the aesthetic]* [?]

88. Cf. 17[49].

89. *Thou shalt prefer . . . world.]* first version, not crossed out: Thou shalt think the truth, but speak it only to friends. / Thou shalt let the world be.

90. Cf. 19[77].

91. *Il maudit . . . compagnie.]* "He spoke ill of the scholars and wanted henceforth to live only in good company."

92. *mean nothing] Ms*: do not matter

93. *needs] Ms*: would need

94. *uncertain]* Cf. 21[2].

95. *storyteller] Le*: storytelling; there follows this, crossed out by N, *Pd*: *HAH* 167, 168.

96. Cf. *HAH* 224.

97. Cf. 19[113].

98. Cf. *HAH* 120.

99. *Aristotle . . . again.] Pd*: *HAH* 212.

100. *Perhaps . . . knowledge.]* Cf. Phillip Mainländer, *Philosophie der Erlösung* ("Philosophy of redemption") (Berlin{: Grieben,} 1876), *NL*.

101. *Pd*: *HAH* 110.

102. *sensu allegorico]* "in an allegorical sense"

103. *consensus gentium]* "consensus of the people"

104. Cf. 5[175]; 23[82].

105. Cf. *HAH* 436; 19[110]; 23[10].

106. Cf. *HAH* 73.

107. Cf. 23[144].

108. *ἐπέχω]* "I hold back"

109. *Pd*: *HAH* 532.

110. *houses built on stilts]* {For the purpose of staying above tidal flows or river currents.}

111. Cf. 19[104]; 23[10].

112. {Cf. Schopenhauer, *World* 2, chap. 44, "Metaphysics of Sexual Love."}

113. {Cf. Schopenhauer, *World* 2, chap. 44, "Metaphysics of Sexual Love," 565; cf. also *JS* §354.}

114. *Plato]* Cf. *Symposium* 206b–209e.

115. *the causa . . . speeches."]* Cf. *Symposium* 210a.

116. Cf. 19[93].

117. Written to separate what follows from the other notes in U II 5, 21; pp. 1–20, with the exception of p. 13, contain earlier notes (1874).

118. Cf. Goethe, *Maximen und Reflexionen* (*Maxims and Reflections*), 499: "If I am to listen to the opinion of someone else, it must be expressed positively: I have myself enough that is problematic in me." (*Sämmtliche Werke in vierzig Bänden* [Stuttgart: J. G. Cotta, 1853], 3:159. *NL.*) {Cf. also 841: "Our opinions are only supplementary to our existence. A person's way of thinking shows what he lacks. The emptiest people think very highly of themselves, the first-rate are mistrustful, a vicious person is impertinent and a good man is anxious. So everything is set in balance; everybody wants to be whole or to appear whole in their own eyes."}

119. Cf. *HAH* 35; 22[15].

120. Cf. 17[1]; 17[79].

[20 = Mp XIV 1a (Brenner). Winter 1876–1877]

1. Cf. 17[80].

2. *Pd*: 19[39]; originally continuation of *HAH* 39.

3. *Pd*: *HAH* 545; cf. *HAH* 89.

4. *Pd*: 5[120].

5. Cf. 19[17]. *Ms*: Two forms of vanity: two boys in front of the fruit-seller, the one has money to buy; two fruit-sellers and one buyer: the one has more beautiful fruit.

6. *let them . . . In an exchange,]* *Ms*: make it seem more desirable. Possessions are so intensely esteemed and defended in order to have good means of exchange [of power]. In an exchange,

7. *power . . . claims;]* From: As long as human beings do not yet know the limits of their talents and energy, they take them as the highest and make the highest claim in an exchange;

8. *capacity; jealousy]* *Ms*: capacity. Competition or war, the good and the evil *eris* {"strife"}! *Jealousy*

9. *Pd*: 16[35].

10. Follows immediately upon *Sd HAH* 224 (after "its refinement visible"; *CW* 3, 154, line 31), was therefore originally the conclusion of *HAH* 224; *Pd*: 12[22].

11. *Pd*: M I 1, 13 (as beginning of *HAH* 235); cf. 5[188].

12. Cf. *HAH* 351.

13. Cf. *HAH* 304.

14. N's handwriting, crossed out.

15. Seemingly written by N after the dictation to Brenner, so, too, 20[19–21].

16. Cf. 20[21].

17. Cf. *CW* 4, 28[27].

18. *philanthropist]* [?]

19. *l'idée fixe musicale]* "the fixed musical idea"

20. *operetta melody]* Cf. 20[19].

21. *or]* [?]

[21 = N II 3. End of 1876–Summer 1877]

1. Cf. 22[131].

2. Perhaps in connection with *Pd*: *HAH* 211.

3. *it is]* In noticeably smaller writing, inserted after "style"; perhaps not belonging here.

4. *filigree]* After this, a perpendicular line.

5. *criminal]* [?]

6. *viewpoint]* [?]

7. Cf. *HAH* 95; written very unclearly.

8. Cf. *HAH* 162; Thucydides 2.35.

9. *nature]* [?]

10. *blind man]* From: deaf and dumb man

11. *Pd*: *MM* 319.

12. Following this, without context, the words: [philology] treat⟨ise⟩

13. Cf. *MM* 213.

14. *Mammal engendering-animal] Säugethier Zeugethier* {Something of a play on words, given the similarity of the two terms, the second a coinage of N's.}

15. Cf. *HAH* 330.

16. In C. A. Bernoulli, *Franz Overbeck und Friedrich Nietzsche: Eine Freundschaft* {"A friendship"} {Jena: Eugen Diederichs Verlag, 1907}, 1:72, Overbeck reports upon this dream of a toad: "He once recounted to his dinner partner, 'I recently dreamed that my hand, which lay before me upon the table, suddenly acquired a glassy, transparent skin: I saw clearly into its bone structure, into its tissue, into the play of its muscles. All at once I saw a fat toad sitting on my hand and felt at the same time the irresistible compulsion

to swallow the animal. I overcame my appalling reluctance and choked it down.' The young woman laughed. 'And you laugh about this!' Nietzsche asked with dreadful seriousness and held his deep eyes directed toward his neighbor, half questioningly, half sorrowfully." Cf. *CW* 4, 28[42].

17. *Pd*: 23[159]; cf. 21[66].

18. Cf. *HAH* 340.

19. *Pd*: 23[106].

20. Cf. Aristotle, *Nicomachean Ethics* 1166a1ff.; *Eudemian Ethics* 1240a23ff.; *Rhetoric* 1361b36–37, 1381a1ff.

21. Cf. 23[109].

22. *Pd*: In the final quarter.

23. *a . . . friend or beloved] Ms*: a [?] friend [?] or beloved; *Le*, *Le*[2]: a friend or a beloved

24. Cf. *HAH* 35; *Pd*: Mouthful of pleasantness.

25. Cf. *HAH* 102, 104.

26. Cf. 18[7].

27. Cf. *HAH* 94; 23[109].

28. Cf. *HAH* 13.

29. Plan for a pseudonymous publication of *HAH*; crossed out at the end: history.

30. Cf. *HAH* 566.

31. Cf. 23[21].

32. Cf. *Pm* variants to *HAH* 251.

33. *Executioner]* Written above "Desmoulins"

34. Cf. 23[25].

35. Cf. *HAH* 257.

36. Cf. *MM* 31.

37. *fata morgana]* {Unusual superior mirage seen just above the horizon.}

38. Cf. *HAH* 500.

39. *Pd*: *HAH* 141 {*CW* 3, 108, line 35–109, line 1}; cf. *MM* 208.

40. *Pd*: 23[147].

41. Above this, three illegible, almost invisible scrawled words.

42. List written in red ink of the themes to be dealt with; cf. e.g., *HAH* 87; above this, two illegible, almost invisible scrawled words.

43. Cf. *HAH* 251.

44. *We]* After this, an illegible scrawled word, added later.

45. *Pd*: *HAH* 131.

46. Cf. 23[145]; *HAH* 272.

47. *Pd*: 23[64].

48. Cf. *HAH* 11.

49. Cf. 23[65]; *HAH* 630; perhaps also 21[42]?

50. Cf. 23[136].

51. On the same page (N II 3, 63) where 21[63] and 21[64] are found, a scrawled fragment that is unclear to the point of illegibility: Song [— — —] itself moreover because of sickness [— — —]

52. *every]* [?]

53. *years]* [?]

54. Cf. 21[23], 23[159].

55. *Pd*: *HAH* 274.

56. Cf. 16[2]?

57. Cf. *HAH* 28.

58. Cf. *HAH* 99.

59. Cf. *HAH* 102.

60. Cf. *HAH* 27; page torn at the edge.

61. *Pd*: *HAH* 212.

62. Cf. *HAH* 241.

63. Cf. *MM* 90.

64. Very unclear, scrawled almost illegibly; uncertain reading.

65. Cf. 22[20].

66. Cf. 19[17].

67. Probably in connection with ideas for *HAH* 292, with which N originally wanted to conclude his work.

[22 = N II 2. Spring–Summer 1877]

1. Cf. *MM* 134; page torn.

2. Cf. *MM* 121.

3. Cf. *HAH* 49; 23[54].

4. Cf. *HAH* 594.

5. Punctuation (periods) completed.

6. *need . . . father]* Cf. *HAH* 389; the image perhaps from Plato, *Symposium* 203b–d; so, too, Schopenhauer, *Ethics* I, 36.

7. Cf. 8[4], 111–12, "5) to pursue . . . philosophers.'"; 21[82], p. 342: IV, VI; to Cosima Wagner 19 December 1876 {*KGB* II:5, 209–11}.

8. *Conjectanea]* "Conjunctions"

9. Punctuation (periods) completed.

10. *Pd*: *HAH* 472.

11. Cf. *HAH* 35.

12. Cf. *HAH* 472.

13. N's drawing in the *Ms.*

14. Cf. *HAH* 134, 135; 21[80].

15. Cf. *HAH* 473, *CW* 3, 256, line 34?

16. *thinks . . . directs.]* {This does not capture N's wordplay with *denkt* ("thinks") and *lenkt* ("directs"). N doubtless has in mind the German proverb *Der Mensch denkt, aber Gott lenkt*, often loosely translated into English as "{A} human being proposes, but God disposes."}

17. Cf. *MM* 171.

18. *. . . in life]* Cf. Schiller, "Die Götter Griechenlands."

19. Cf. *MM* 126; 23[138, 190].

20. Cf. *HAH* 27, 148.

21. *to become wise]* Cf. 23[160]; *HAH* 292.

22. *Pd*: *HAH* 20.

23. *reason for why science]* Written by N over on p. 33 because he had cut off the bottom half of pp. 31–32.

24. Cf. *Pd* of the variants to *HAH* 633 in Mp XIV 1, 30.

25. Cf. *HAH* 16; 23[125].

26. *Cave of Salamanca] Zwischenspiel* {"Interlude"} by Miguel Cervantes, in vol. 2 of the collection *Spanisches Theater* {"Spanish theater"}, ed. Moriz Rapp, Hermann Kurz, and Ludwig Braunfels {Hildburghausen: Verlag des Bibliographischen Instituts, 1868}; this collection became known to N in Sorrento at the beginning of 1877; cf. Malwida von Meysenbug to Olga Monod, 16 January 1877.

27. Sentence fragment, the context of which is unknown.

28. *Pd*: *HAH* 145.

29. Cf. *HAH* 152.

30. Cf. *HAH* 473?

31. Crossed out by N.

32. Cf. *HAH* 69; Matthew 5:45.

33. Cf. *HAH* 292; above, scrawled very unclearly and crossed out by N: it is necessary [?] to do something that we do not need [?]; then another likewise very unclearly scrawled line, the beginning of which has been erased: [t] is better than [— — —]

34. Cf. *HAH* 628; 23[197].

35. *the tune of time]* Cf. 22[55].

36. *now]* [?]

37. *earnest chimes . . . serious bells] Glockenspiel . . . Glockenernst*; cf. the similar play on words in *Z* I "On Reading and Writing": "tragic-plays . . . tragic-seriousness" (*Trauer-Spiele . . . Trauer-Ernste*) {*Trauerspiel* is the German word for tragic drama.}

38. Cf. *HAH* 599.

39. Cf. 17[22].

40. *which ⟨were⟩ . . . in that]* Uncertain reading.

41. Context unknown, perhaps to 22[48]?

42. *even . . . credulity]* From: in case this were not an intentional misleading of German credulity and as such would quite usefully prove precisely that

43. *The] Pd*: the

44. *We]* From: "It wills in me" means "it must" we

45. Context unknown.

46. Cf. variants to *HAH* 27 in Mp XIV 1.

47. Context unknown.

48. Cf. variants to 23[194] and 25[2] in U II 5, 76; 22[45].

49. Cf. 22[58]; 22[113]; 23[3].

50. Cf. 22[57]; 22[113]; 23[3].

51. Cf. *HAH* 292.

52. Cf. *HAH* 365.

53. Dedication to Malwida von Meysenbug.

54. Ist von Sorrento's Duft Nichts hängen blieben?
Ist alles wilde, kühle Bergnatur,
Kaum herbstlich sonnenwarm und ohne Lieben?
So ist ein Theil von mir im Buche nur:
Den bessern Theil, ihn bring ich zum Altar
Für sie die Freundin Mutter Arzt mir war.

55. *cool]* From: cold

56. *The better . . . to me.]* Variant: The other part I have kept for myself / And for friends —

57. Cf. *HAH* 13.

58. *a]* [?]

59. Cf. *HAH* 414, 416.

60. Cf. *HAH* 205.

61. Probably relating to Siegfried Lipiner's *Prometheus*; cf. 22[78].

62. *that is]* [?]

63. Context unclear: D. F. Strauss was also the author of works about Ulrich von Hutten and Voltaire; perhaps for the planned new edition of the *Unfashionables*?; cf. 22[48].

64. *Schwabians]* {A Grimms' fairy tale, where events mock the supposed courage of the title characters.}

65. Cf. *HAH* 625.

66. *in]* [?]

67. *and]* [?]

68. Cf. *HAH* 11.

69. Mag Vernunft den Vernünftigen erbauen
Der Künstler soll nur die Kunst verdauen
Und doch hat ein Künstler dies Buch *geschrieben*!
Nicht seine Vernunft that's, es that sein *Lieben*.

70. Cf. *HAH* 160.

71. Related to Siegfried Lipiner's *Prometheus*; cf. N to Rohde 28 August 1877 {*KGB* II:5, 277–78}; punctuation completed.

72. *drunken . . . s⟨ound⟩]* Uncertain reading.

73. Cf. 22[95].

74. Im bairischen Walde fieng es an
Basel hat was dazu gethan
In Sorrent erst spann sich's gross und breit
Und Rosenlaui gab ihm Luft und Freiheit
Die Berge kreissten, am Anfang Mitt' und End'!
Schrecklich für den, der das Sprichwort kennt!
Dreizehn Monat bis die Mutter des Kinds genesen —
Ist denn ein Elephant gewesen?
Oder gar eine lächerliche Maus? —
So sorgt sich der Vater. Lacht ihn nur aus!

75. Cf. 24[10]. Draft of a dedication to Jacob Burckhardt, the same dedicatory verses for *MM* to F. Overbeck in Bernoulli, *Franz Overbeck und Friedrich Nietzsche*, 1:276.

76. *shame]* From: avidity

77. *Until . . . one day]* From: That a tree one day

78. *blooms]* From: bloomed

79. *Already now . . . one]* From: (1) Shame, too, that I took a risk and did not follow the greater one; (2) Indeed I enjoy in advance the happiness that I am following the greater one

80. *rejoices . . . planting.]* From: one day, eager hand on the good enclosure

81. *Pd*: *HAH* 171, 172.

82. Perhaps relating to Siegfried Lipiner's *Prometheus*; cf. 22[78].

83. Cf. *HAH* 91.

84. *art.]* Written underneath: (in stories)

85. Dedication to someone unknown, perhaps Louise Ott or Isabelle von der Pahlen; the draft of a letter to the latter can be found in N II 2, 92: "It was at the Turino train station that I promised you something in an obscure expression (for I am shy about speaking of children who are not yet born). In short: what I meant at that time was this book. Take it, please, like myself, as occasional travel companion and may you be well-disposed — — — " Fr. v. d. Pahlen

86. Cf. *HAH* 477; 23[154].

87. *than he — — —]* Above this line an unreadable word, perhaps: Lipiner.

88. Dedication to Cosima and Richard Wagner, somewhat altered in Elisabeth Förster-Nietzsche, *Große Biographie* I, 2, 294; *Der einsame Nietzsche* {"The solitary Nietzsche"}, 50; also in F. Nietzsche, *Gedichte und Sprüche* {"Poems and sayings"}, 71. Variants: N II 2, 95: It wants, before other earthly fates / First to look into the master's true eye, / To meet with the mistress's shrewd good will / Before the clouds of ill will rain; N II 2, 95–96: Yet before we send it into the world / (1) It should ⟨look into⟩ the master's true eye (2) May it, blessing, look into the master's true eye / May the mistress with shrewd good will; And surely some day of its street / And of its travels here and there; May henceforth follow him only / The shrewd good

will of the mistress; Only may, for protection from sulfur steam / the shrewd good will of the mistress follow it!

89. Dem Meister und der Meisterin
Entbietet Gruss mit frohem Sinn,
Beglückt ob einem neuen Kind,
Von Basel Friedrich Freigesinnt.
Er wünscht dass sie mit Herzbewegen
Auf's Kind die Hände prüfend legen
Und schauen ob es Vater's Art
— Wer weiss? selbst mit 'nem Schnurrenbart —
Und ob es wird, auf Zween und Vieren
Sich tummeln in den Weltrevieren.
In Bergen wollt' zum Licht es schlüpfen
Gleich neugebornen Zicklein hüpfen
So gleich zu suchen eignen Gang
Und eigne Freude Gunst und Rang
Oder vielleicht Einsiedlers Klaus
Und Waldgethier sich wählet aus?
Was ihm auf seinem Erdenwallen
Beschieden sei: es will gefallen
Nicht Vielen: Fünfzehn an der Zahl
Den Andern werd' es Kreuz und Qual,
Dass nur, zur Abwehr ärgster Tücke
Des Meisters Treuaug segnend blicke!
Dass nur den Weg zur ersten Reise
Der Meisterin kluge Gunst ihm weise!

90. Newly reworked: 1884–85.

91. Dies ist der Herbst.
Sonne schleicht zum Berg
Und steigt hinauf
und ruht bei jedem Schritte.
Auf müd gespannten Fäden spielt
Der Wind sein Lied:
Die Hoffnung flieht,
Er klagt ihr nach.
O Frucht des Baums,
Du zitterst, fällst!

Welch ein Geheimniss zeigte dir
Die Nacht,
Dass eis'ger Schauder deine Wange,
Die purpurne, verhüllt? —
Ich bin nicht schön,
So spricht die Sternenblume,
Doch Menschen lieb' ich,
Und Menschen tröst' ich,
Sie sollen jetzt noch Blumen sehn,
Nach mir sich bücken,
Ach! und mich brechen —
In ihren Augen glänzet dann
Erinnerung an schönre auf
Und Glück.
Ich seh's und sterbe dann,
Und sterbe gern.
Dies ist der Herbst. —

92. *veiled . . . one?] Ms*: [covers], the crimson [covered] veiled?

93. *Ah! . . . off —]* From: as if I were beautiful

94. Newly reworked: 1884–85; cf. *CW* 15, 28[60].

95. Um Mittag, wenn
Der junge Sommer in's Gebirge steigt,
Da spricht er auch,
Doch sehen wir sein Sprechen nur:
Sein Athem quillt wie eines Wandersmanns
In Winterfrost:
Es geben Eisgebirg und Tann und Quell
Ihm Antwort auch,
Doch sehen wir die Antwort nur.
Denn schneller springt vom Fels herab
Der Sturzbach wie zum Gruss
Und steht als weisse Säule horchend da.
Und dunkler noch und treuer blickt die Tanne
Als sonst sie blickt.
Und zwischen Eis und todtem Graugestein
Blickt plötzlich Leuchten auf:
Wer deutet dir's?

In todten Mannes Auge
Wird wohl noch einmal Licht:
Sein Kind umschlang ihn harmvoll
Küsst' ihn.
Da sagt des Auges Leuchten:
„Ich liebe dich"
Und Schneegebirg und Bach und Tann
Sie sagen auch
Zum Sommerknaben nur
Dies Eine Wort:
Wir lieben dich!
Wir lieben dich!
Und er — er küsst sie harmvoll,
Inbrünstiger stets
Und will nicht gehn:
Er bläst sein Wort wie Schleier nur
Von seinem Mund — ein schlimmes Wort. —
Da horcht es rings
Und athmet kaum:
Da überläuft es schaudernd wie
Ein Glitzern am Gebirg
Rings die Natur:
Sie denkt und schweigt. —
Um Mittag war's
Mein Gruss ist Abschied
Ich sterbe jung. —

96. *My greeting . . . young.]* Added later.

97. Cf. 22[79].

98. *So all . . . harmony.]* Written on the adjoining page, not certain it belongs here.

99. Cf. *HAH* 292; 21[84].

100. Cf. 22[106].

101. Cf. *HAH* 234, *CW* 3, 161, lines 1–3.

102. *Pd*: *HAH* 550.

103. Cf. 22[85].

104. Cf. 23[114].

105. Cf. *HAH* 372; 19[25].

106. *culinary art]* [?]
107. Cf. *HAH* 373; punctuation completed.
108. Cf. 22[97].
109. *lazy]* [?]
110. Cf. *HAH* 37; 23[114].
111. Context unknown.
112. Cf. 10[3].
113. Cf. *HAH* 216.
114. Cf. 22[57, 58]; 23[3].
115. Context unknown, perhaps cf. *HAH* 224?
116. *from]* [?]
117. The following poetic fragments (22[119–27, 129, 130, 132]) deal with: The blind man on the path. The soul gives no shine; cf. 23[197]; the writing of these fragments is very unclear.

118. Nun ich seh' mehr als ihr
Will's euch erzählen

119. ein blinder [—], doch in Schuh und Rock
[—] das ist, [— — —]
[— —] als Ziege und Ziegenbock

120. Nun ist doch sonnenklar
Ein Mensch hat Leib und Seele, ein Paar

121. Ich weiss was Schatten ist und Licht
Was Leib und Seele — ihr wisst's nicht

122. Zieg an Ziege ohne Zagen
Drängt an meinem Knie vorbei
Leckt die Hand und scheint zu fragen
Was ich blind und einsam sei.

123. Da steckt wohl das Seelchen drin
Er schont es auf Reisen das ist der Sinn

124. Doch hinter seiner viel werthen Gestalt
Hat jeder ein Bündel angeschnallt
Da steckt er die Seele wohl hinein
Er schont sie auf Reisen wie ich vermein'

125. Wie der Leib den Schatten wirft
Wirft die Seele Licht
Schatten haben sie allgesamt
Seele aber nicht

126. Er kommt dann heim und packt das Seelchen aus
Dasselbe — — —
127. Wenn ich so am Wege sitze
Bis der Schatten kälter wird,
Bis Ziegenherden ohne Furcht an meinem Knie vorbei
128. Cf. 21[1].
129. Sitz' den ganzen Tag am Wege
Bis der Schatten kälter wird,
Und in tieferem Gehege
Abwärts zieht Herd und Hirt
Alle Ziegen drängen trau⟨lich⟩
Sich an meinem Knie vorbei
Lecken mir die Hand
dass ich blind und einsam sei
130. Cf. 23[197]; also *CW* 4, 40[2]?
131. *Ecce ecce homunculus]* "Behold behold the homunculus {tiny human being}"

[23 = Mp XIV 1b. End of 1876–Summer 1877]

1. *while . . . climbing]* From: amid dangers
2. Cf. 22[57, 58, 113].
3. *partie honteuse]* "shameful part"
4. *pudendum]* "external genitals, especially female," hence, by extension, something shameful
5. *Aristotle]* Cf. *Nicomachean Ethics* 1141a1–6b3.
6. *σοφός]* "*sophos*"; "wise"
7. *Why . . . at all?]* From: I no longer assume a *drive for preservation.*
8. *fore;]* fore; [it is chemical laws according to which health is regulated]
9. *just as] Ms*: as
10. *The word . . . laws.]* From: there really are no drives; a full bladder causes pressure pain, is recalled, but no drive to urinate exists
11. Cf. 19[110].
12. *ἀνάμνησις]* "*anamnesis*"; "recollection"
13. Cf. *HAH* 127.

14. *Pd*: Expression "will to life."

15. *It was . . . expression,]* From: The expression "will to life" must be examined. If we assume a single principle concerning all individuals, the expression may be valid. But without that sort of metaphysical hypothesis, the individual human being does not enter into life through such a will, since before he exists, his will, too, does not yet exist: what should this then be? Expressing itself in life, it is not a "will *to* life," but instead a will to stay alive:

16. *continually changing.]* continually changing. [Nothing at all is known immediately to us about a characteristic of this feeling of willing, of striving toward something.]

17. *This universal . . . intellect.]* From: This must in the very end be a chemical process. But it is not a will to life.

18. *be observed . . . however,]* From: be considered as an animal fact,

19. *It is not . . . price,] Ms*: |It is not true that| We do not want existence at any price,

20. At the end, the note: cf. following two pages.

21. Cf. 23[114]; *HAH* 132.

22. *Lagarde]* Cf. *Ueber das Verhältnis des deutschen Staates zu Theologie, Kirche und Religion* {"On the relationship of the German state to theology, church, and religion"} (Göttingen: Dieterichsche Verlagsbuchhandlung, 1873), §§9 and 10.

23. *indeed, . . . along.]* From: he brings his own wind with him like a great conflagration, which increases him and carries him farther.

24. Cf. *MM* 179.

25. *Nevertheless . . . pathos.]* Crossed out by N.

26. Cf. *HAH* 2; *MM* 5.

27. *Pd*: 21[41]; cf. *HAH* 40, 519.

28. *"Just . . . unconditionally."]* Cf. Goethe, *Faust* I:1851–55.

29. *Pd*: 21[43]; cf. 25[1].

30. {Cf. note to 19[109].}

31. *just] Le, Le*[2]: however

32. *Sd*: *HAH* 365 follows this.

33. Cf. *HAH* 60.

34. *Pd*: The reason why we cry is not clear. Someone said, with *Hermann und Dorothea* and with Homer — — —

35. *Hermann und Dorothea]* {Epic poem written by Goethe in 1796–97.}

36. *Pd*: Derivation of the unegoistical drive from the social instinct. This from fear, compulsion, habituation, first softened (tempered with joy).

37. *"the ruling . . . society."]* {Julius Fröbel, *Aus Amerika: Erfahrungen, Reisen und Studien* ("From America: Experiences, travels, and studies") (Leipzig: Weber, 1857), 1:24.}

38. Cf. *HAH* 141{, *CW* 3, 109, lines 12–16}.

39. Cf. *HAH* 271; *MM* 33.

40. *"The insight . . . rest."]* Cf. Schopenhauer, *Ethics* 182{/178}.

41. *"the ultimate . . . acting."]* Cf. Schopenhauer, *Ethics* 109{/116}.

42. *"all . . . judging."]* Cf. Schopenhauer, *Ethics* 114{/121}.

43. Cf. *HAH* 629–37; 23[65]; at the end, a later note by N: To tie in here: Two kinds, the one a conviction, the other knowledge.

44. *Winkler puts it.]* Paul Winkler; cf. 23[158] {and the corresponding note}.

45. *real perversity . . . metaphysics.")]* Cf. Schopenhauer, *Parerga* 2, 214–15{/183}.

46. Cf. *MM* 18.

47. *his relatives]* Lichtenberg's writings were first published by his brother, Ludwig Christian Lichtenberg (1799–1800), later by his sons Christoph W. and Georg Christoph (1843–46).

48. *Pd*: *HAH* 36, cf. *HAH* 37; 23[75, 161, 152].

49. *author . . . Observations]* Paul Rée

50. At the upper edge of the page: The *Memorabilia*. {Likely Xenophon's *Memorabilia* of Socrates.}

51. *cultivated]* Cf. 23[7].

52. *is resisted . . . soul."]* From: resists the "chastity of the soul," so to speak, a little mischievously.

53. Cf. *MM* 181.

54. *move unsteadily]* From: balance

55. *national . . . contradictions.]* Cf. *CW* 4, 36[2].

56. Cf. *MM* 320.

57. *the aversion . . . metaphysically]* Schopenhauer, "On the Metaphysics of the Beautiful and Aesthetics": ". . . the shock and horror . . . at the sight of these animals . . . seems to be grounded

in a much deeper, metaphysical and mysterious connection." *Parerga* 2, 457{/382}; similarly also, *Nachlaß* 350{/*Manuscript* 4, 384}.

58. *when . . . species]* Cf. 24[7].

59. Cf. *HAH* 36; 23[41].

60. Cf. *MM* 323.

61. *Pd*: At the beginning: Feeling of indignation at a purely naturalistic view of the world: or of the deepest need.

62. *geniuses] Pd*: richly bestowing geniuses

63. *restored Catholicism] Pd*: Catholicism (after the Council of Trent)

64. Cf. *HAH* 215.

65. *⟨we find fault with⟩]* In *Le*.

66. *un bon homme]* "a good fellow"

67. *Mügge]* {"Am Malanger Fjord," novella by Theodor Mügge, German author of adventure and romance novels.}

68. *Pd*: Broadened concept of abortion. The human being is continually born. Anyone who detaches himself from tradition is an abortion.

69. *One]* From: *My*

70. Cf. 23[181]. *Pd*: Happiness more moving than unhappiness.

71. *will to power]* {This is the first appearance of this concept in N's notebooks.}

72. *Pd*: 21[59].

73. *Pd*: 21[61]; cf. 23[38].

74. Cf. *CW* 4, 28[21].

75. At the end, crossed out: most dangerous among renegades

76. Cf. *WS* 326. N II 3, 7: nail bent problem crooked; N II 3, 8: Many people hit the nail, but not on the head and make the problem hopelessly crooked: it is better to miss something completely.

77. Cf. *HAH* 381.

78. *many or all]* Written above: (multitude) {In German, *Vielsamkeit* in contrast to *Einsamkeit*, so multitude in the sense of socialness, as the opposite of solitude.}

79. Cf. *HAH* 378.

80. Cf. note to *WA* 9.

81. *factum . . . fictum]* "in fact . . . in fiction"

82. *formerly]* Written above: so one [believed] formerly

83. *know]* Written above: have

84. *explanation . . . fact]* From: knowledge about it

85. At the end, crossed out: (whores etc.)

86. *the ego, the person]* From: the human being

87. *decisive sign]* From: characteristics

88. At the end (bottom edge of the page), without insertion mark: no longer as usual in relation to all actions, but instead even in relation to feelings

89. At the lower edge of the page without insertion mark: so that it *now for the first time* has become something great and venerable where a monogamous instinct has emerged. The impossible [—]

90. *shame]* Cf. 23[6].

91. *we should . . . even]* From: we ought not to think of a moral origin. Even

92. *Hence jealousy . . . house-slave]* From: Hence so frightfully strong, it is inherited from the animal kingdom. In political states, the instinct of monogamy then becomes sanctioned in the interest of the securely organized family; if women actually originally a piece of property, slave

93. *no longer . . . polygamy.]* From: has changed. We should guard against *solemn hypotheses* when simple ones suffice. Too shallow and too deep of an explanation is of no use. — Where the natural basis is different, monogamy moreover will really not exist, but instead polygamy; although the state holds on to it and places the lawfully married woman and her children under its sanctification.

94. Cf. 5[175].

95. *that is . . . humanity))]* Cf. *HAH* 517.

96. *admittedly]* In different handwriting (Gast).

97. *Pd*: Night old city moonlight a singer

98. *appeared . . . to us]* From: wanted to speak once again to the present

99. *in all . . . theme.]* From: in yearning: that is the theme.

100. Cf. *HAH*, 145, 155.

101. {Plutarch's life of Lycurgus, legendary lawgiver of Sparta, recounts that newly born children in Sparta were brought to a

triage where it was determined whether they were healthy enough to be allowed to live or should instead be exposed to die.}

102. Cf. *HAH* 23.

103. *"the highest . . . energies!"]* Cf. Goethe, *Faust* I:1852.

104. Cf. *HAH* 96.

105. *bound up . . . good.]* From: bound up with pleasure, of course, after lengthy inheritance produces goodness, to be good.

106. *Judge not!]* Cf. Matthew 7:1.

107. *As the boy . . . emphasis.]* Crossed out by N.

108. *Pd*: *HAH* 496; crossed out and covered over by *Pd HAH* 418.

109. Cf. *MM* 271.

110. Cf. *HAH* 242; *MM* 179, 180, 181.

111. *Henceforth . . . culture]* From: A wholly new kind of education and educators must emerge, this is my new view!

112. *The prudence . . . lost.] Pd*: *MM* 163.

113. {Pedro Calderón de la Barca's *El principe constante* was written in 1629. August Wilhelm Schlegel translated it into German as *Der standhafte Prinz* (Vienna: Sollinger, 1826).}

114. Cf. *HAH* 96.

115. *without custom (the indecent one).] ohne Sitte (der unsittliche)* {Nietzsche here plays with the similarity of the German terms *Sitte* ("custom," but also "morality") and *unsittlich* (literally, "immoral" or "uncustomary," but typically meaning "immoral" or "indecent").}

116. *stands] Le*: is

117. Cf. *HAH* 131.

118. Cf. *MM* 323; 23[145].

119. Cf. *HAH* 629.

120. Crossed out at the end: childhood.

121. *Pd*: Free-spiritedness from bites of conscience

122. *poisonously and inwardly enraged]* From: poisonous and malicious

123. *Pd*: 21[26].

124. *Aristotle]* Cf. *Nicomachean Ethics* 1166a2–6.

125. *afflict . . . interpretation]* From: deal with . . . hermeneutics

126. *diagnostics]* {Cf. *MM* 35 for N's other use of the German term here, *Nierenprüfen*: an unusual German word, used first by Herder — literally meaning "examination of the kidneys" — in

a more figurative sense: a close examination of the inward seat of someone's life force and affects. Used three other times in the published works: *Z* II "On the Land of Culture"; *JS* 308, 335.}

127. Cf. *HAH* 236; *Pd*: We have freed ourselves from the representation of a god, of an eternal life, of a requiting justice, of sin, of the savior and of the salvation-easing of life — Duty? Free will?

128. *Compare . . . spirit?]* Added later.

129. Cf. *WS* 215.

130. Cf. *HAH* 152.

131. *sublime] Pd*: sublime, like the ugly

132. *Pd*: *HAH* 140.

133. In part revised for *HAH* 37, 38; here, the original version; cf. 22[107].

134. *Admittedly . . . task.)]* Cf. *HAH* 132; 23[13].

135. *but instead . . . nature]* Cf. 22[101].

136. *Pd*: Critique of delight in nature — stimulation of the nerves upon mountains is delightful

137. {N is referring here to the second movement of Beethoven's Seventh Symphony.}

138. *Hope]* From: Art

139. *Pd*: Kant's verbose and not completely clear manner, in which we note the thinking along with the writing (and not before the writing). He lacked time. He did not present his ideas in the best way.

140. First version of *HAH* 16; *Pd*: 22[33].

141. *logicians]* N means Afrikan Spir, *Denken und Wirklichkeit* {"Thinking and reality" (Leipzig: J. G. Findel, 1873)}, especially the exposition in vol. 1, bk. 3, chap. 3, "Das Verhältnis der Welt zu dem Unbedingten" {"The relationship of the world to what is unconditioned"}; cf. note to *HAH* 18, *CW* 3, 28, lines 23–27; *CW* 19, Chronicle of N's life "1877, Sorrento, January–beginning of May."

142. *Pd*: *Philosophizing in Germany* now a dangerous symptom, a turning away from science.

143. Cf. *HAH* 140.

144. *pleasure . . . in itself.] Pd*: emotion of fear as pleasurable.

145. *self-renunciation]* Allusion to Wagner; cf. 11[29].

146. *morning-fresh]* From: lively

147. *It is . . . women.]* From: Likewise the thinking spirit of women.

148. *himself competed]* From: worked

149. *Even . . . cameos.] Pd*: *HAH* 35.

150. *time to time; —]* From: time to time; [just as to educate a child] —

151. *Only in . . . pleasure.]* Cf. 23[168].

152. At the end, in red pencil: monsters; cf. 23[59].

153. Cf. 21[63].

154. Cf. *MM* 126; 23[190]; 22[25].

155. *Wagner]* Cf. "On the Performance of Beethoven's Ninth Symphony," *WGS* 9, esp. 277–82.

156. *Is . . . possible?]* From: There is no historical performance.

157. *Pd*: Isn't he, too, making fun, when he recounts how they made fun of D⟨on⟩ Quixote in the baron's court?

158. *nature, . . . success]* From: artist-nature, rarely praise what is praiseworthy and what seems good to the artist. Quite the reverse.

159. *its victims . . . idealists]* Crossed out with red pencil, and above: against the chivalric novels

160. *Imperceptibly]* From: Unconsciously

161. *seem wise . . . conclusion.]* From: seem wise. He belongs to the decadence of Spanish culture, he is a national misfortune. He was contemptuous of human beings. They were delighted by the insane man, at the baron's court and they laughed to scorn even the heretic being burned at the stake. Cf. 8[7].

162. *Goethe . . . Schiller.]* Cf. Goethe to Eckermann, 18 January 1825.

163. Cf. 19[107].

164. Cf. *HAH* 272; 21[56]; 23[100].

165. *he passes . . . human being.]* From: e.g., as religious, as artistic, as scientific human being.

166. Cf. *HAH* 176.

167. *We are . . . completely]* From: With the question, how *Shakespeare* could have his heroes speak so appropriately each time, with such *profound utterances* and the like, whether such speeches are a mosaic of *opportunisti⟨cally⟩ discovered individual sentences*, I said: No. The continual habit of finding every remark appropriate

only out of the mouth of a particular person, or indeed, to a single situation, is really a completely different one from ours, to make the remark for the sake of the truth,

168. Cf. 21[49].

169. Cf. *HAH* 141, *CW* 3, 110, lines 24–26.

170. *Pd*: Art does not belong to nature, instead only to human beings. {N here decides to underline the title, a stylistic *choice* that he will adopt for *HAH* and after.}

171. *so that . . . a thing]* and, to be sure, cutting successively through a thing with the gaze, therefore transversely

172. *⟨it⟩] Le*[2]

173. *⟨that⟩] Le*[2]

174. *We are . . . abiding.]* From: We divide what is moved and movement; but it is originally false; what is moved, the thing is invented, imagined in, since our organs are not free enough to perceive the movement here. There is nothing abiding.

175. Cf. 18[21]; 23[41, 161, 167].

176. *It is a great . . . intellect.]* From: All of that is false, in themselves there are only actions of a specific character, what is moral has nothing to do with the thing in itself, but is instead "opinion," belongs in the realm of the quite variable intellect.

177. *Aristotelian⟨ism⟩]* Uncertain reading.

178. Cf. *HAH* 25; *Pd*: There was more morality in trade than in Christianity, the love of humanity from fear of God or the Kantian "what you do not want" — ecumenical goals.

179. *"do as . . . done unto"]* Cf. Matthew 7:12.

180. *"love . . . of God."]* Cf. Leviticus 19:18.

181. *The pathos . . . things,]* From: The bow of feeling has been stretched all too tautly by certain views of things,

182. *The pathos . . . themselves]* Cf. Epictetus, *The Handbook* V; *HAH* 141, *CW* 3, 110, line 5.

183. *indicates . . . suffering]* From: expresses as basis for his suffering

184. *that is, . . . mood.]* From: metaphysically fabricated; if he perceives that, the pathos is lacking in his mood.

185. *Yet if all . . . them.]* Separated by N by two vertical strokes before "Yet" and after "them" and by a horizontal line under the

final lines of the remaining text, because fully taken up in *HAH* 630, *CW* 3, 297, lines 10–25.

186. In the original version, this fragment follows *Sd HAH* 513; after the composition of *HAH* 513, it was worked on by itself; the original version read: However far a human being may stretch, however objective he may seem, in the end he nonetheless carries nothing away from this except his own biography. But life becomes astonishingly lightened through such a liberation of the spirit, which experimentally calls into question all the representations that burden life so much, make it so unbearable: so that we have our joy in this disburdening and prefer the simplest life that this joy grants to us.

187. *Paul Winkler]* Cf. *Zwey Tausend gutte Gedancken zusammen gebracht von dem Geübten* ("Two thousand good thoughts brought together by the experienced") (Görlitz{: Christoph Zippern,} 1685), no. 1034: "Der Mensch ist so lange Weise / als er die Weißheit sucht / wenn er aber meinet / er habe sie gefunden / so wird er zum Narren." {"Human beings are wise as long / as they seek wisdom / but if they think / they have found it / they become fools."} Cf. 23[38].

188. *Pd*: 21[23]; cf. 21[65].

189. Text written over with *Sd HAH* 292.

190. Cf. 23[41, 152, 167].

191. Cf. 23[41, 152, 161].

192. Cf. 23[132].

193. *acquire . . . exaggerate] Ms*: acquire and hold on to | and exaggerate |

194. *media] Le, Le*[2]: medium

195. Cf. *HAH* 3.

196. *relatives]* From: cousins

197. *schools]* From: etc.

198. *the personalities and]* From: those

199. *pensum]* From: work {A *pensum* is a school task assigned as a punishment, i.e., as an occasion for reflection upon a mistake.}

200. *exhausted]* Written above: thirsty

201. Cf. 23[156]; *HAH* 164. *Pd*: Schopenhauer unfortunately smuggled mysticism into the concept "intuitive knowing," as if a hole in the cloak — — —

202. *image] Gleichniss* {*Gleichniss* can be translated into English in various ways according to context — "allegory," "analogy," "simile," "parable" (in biblical contexts), or others. Its core meaning is "likeness."}

203. *these] Ms*: all

204. *our experience . . . us.]* From: feeling.

205. Cf. 23[61].

206. Cf. *HAH* 26.

207. Cf. *MM* 225.

208. *Faith . . . mountains.]* Cf. 1 Corinthians 13:2.

209. *Pd* at the end: Against Empedocles

210. *judging]* From: knowing

211. *The intellect . . . feeling.]* From: Pain is fled in both cases.

212. *Pd*: dreams *unexperienced* conditions e.g., floating. Cf. on this Friedrich Maximilian Klinger, *Betrachtungen und Gedanken über verschiedene Gegenstände der Welt und der Literatur* ("Reflections and thoughts on various objects in the world and in literature"), no. 700. {In *F. M. Klingers sämmtliche Werke in zwölf Bänden* ("F. M. Klinger's collected works in twelve volumes") (Stuttgart and Tübingen: Cotta, 1842), 11:215.}

213. *Pd*: Yearning for death like someone who is seasick looks for land, early night the harbor lights.

214. *Pd*: we are carried away by sensual pleasures most easily when we are sorrowful — why?

215. *"if a person . . . animal."]* Cf. Cervantes, *Don Quixote* II, chap. 11; the same passage is cited in the letter from Cosima Wagner to N, 19 October 1869 {*KGB* II:2, 62}.

216. Cf. 22[25]; 23[138]; *HAH* 172; *MM* 126. *Pd* at the end: "all energy works to elevate"

217. *Ms*: philologist — scholar of writing; U II 5: *poets* who cannot read — opposite of philologists

218. *"to dictate"] diktiren* {N's etymological point is clearer in German, where the word for poet is *Dichter*, the one who dictates words.}

219. *Pd*: In all blaming and praising, a human being behaves according to the principle: the purpose sanctifies.

220. Cf. 25[2]; p. 440, "Play of ideas, . . . necessity."

221. Motto:
Tanz der Gedanken, es führt
eine der Grazien dich:
o wie weidest den Sinn du mir!–
Weh! Was seh' ich! Es fällt
Larve und Schleier der Führerin
und voran dem Reigen
schreitet die grause Nothwendigkeit.

222. From the complex for *HAH* 35–38 (first thought of as preface, cf. the variants to that); at the bottom edge of the page, without marks of insertion, the sentence also belonging to it: so he must give himself the answer: for the benefit of the thinker who for Germany, at least, the great — — — . At the bottom edge, surrounded by the notes to *HAH* 35, 37 and 23[195], the date: Ragaz, May and June 1877. {The text to which N refers here is Paul Rée's *Der Ursprung der moralischen Empfindung* (*On the Origin of the Moral Sensations*).}

223. *for]* [whom he especially wishes to have as reader and] for

224. *his]* From: these

225. *immodest . . . for himself]* so immodest as to name that thinker to whom we owe the investigations on the origin of moral sensations

226. *that also . . . book.]* which this book also acknowledges [as guiding star].

227. Beside this, in pencil: acceleration of "time"

228. *nature of travel]* Crossed out.

229. *afterword.]* Crossed out at the bottom edge: 28 July [June] Mazzini's birth⟨day⟩. Giuseppe Mazzini was born on 22 June 1805; N found the incorrect statement of Mazzini's birthday in his notebook calendar for 1877 (= N II 8).

230. *the phantom . . . itself]* Uncertain reading.

231. *Mornings . . . death]* Perhaps a memory of the boat trip from Sorrento to Genoa (8–10 May 1877); cf. N to Malwida von Meysenbug, 13 May 1877 {*KGB* II:5, 235}. Cf. also 23[188].

232. Cf. 22[119–27, 129, 130, 132].

233. *Ecce homunculus]* "Behold the homunculus {tiny human being}" Cf. 22[135].

234. *chimes]* Cf. 22[45].

235. Cf. *Z* II "The Prophet." Reporting on his encounters with N in summer 1877, Reinhart von Seydlitz writes: "Nietzsche recounted with laughter that in a dream he had to climb an endless mountain path; at the very top, under the peak of the mountain, he wanted to pass by a cave, when from the dark depths a voice called out to him: "Alpa, Alpa, — 'who is dragging his ashes to the mountain?' — " Cf. R. v. Seydlitz, *Wann, warum, was und wie ich schrieb* {"When, why, what, and how I wrote"} (Gotha{: Perthes,} 1900), 36.

[24 = Mp XIV 1c. Fall 1877]

1. The numbers 1–43 refer to aphorisms that were in part taken up in *HAH* or *MM*, or to fragments, in any case, to texts, which were all written down in Mp XIV 1b, the content of which is rendered by key words in this categorization; N supplied the corresponding texts in Mp XIV 1b with these numbers:

1 = *HAH* 157; 2 = *HAH* 161; 3 = *HAH* 3; 4 = *HAH* 155; 5 = 23[74]; 6 = *HAH* 156; 7 = *HAH* 199; 8 = 23[131]; 9 = *HAH* 146; 10 = *HAH* 147; 11 = *HAH* 236; 12 = *HAH* 219; 13 = 23[146]; 14 = *HAH* 162; 15 = *HAH* 170; 16 = *HAH* 201; 17 = *HAH* 160; 18 = *HAH* 150; 19 = 23[138]; 20 = 23[140]; 21 = *HAH* 207; 22 = 23[150]; 23 = *HAH* 250; 24 = *HAH* 159; 25 = *HAH* 215; 26 = 23[84]; 27 = *HAH* 130; 28 = 23[101]; 29 = 23[142]; 30 = *HAH* 260; 31 = 23[167]; 32 = 23[168]; 33 = *HAH* 212; 34 = *HAH* 176; 35 = *HAH* 164; 36 = *HAH* 149; 37 = *MM* 171; 38 = *MM* 165; 39 = *HAH* 165; 40 = *HAH* 223; 41 = 23[81]; 42 = *HAH* 222; 43 = *HAH* 213.

2. Grouping of the fragments numbered in 24[1] into six chapters.

3. *survival]* N's English.

4. Themes for *HAH*.

5. *Friendship]* This key word is marked by N with three vertical blue lines, as are the following notes in Mp XIV 1 and M I 1: 23[106], *HAH* 368, *HAH* 296, 20[15], *HAH* 499, *HAH* 378, 18[44].

6. *Woman and child]* Marked with two vertical blue lines, as are the following notes in Mp XIV 1 and M I 1: *HAH* 412, *HAH* 455, 23[20], *HAH* 410, *HAH* 387, *HAH* 394, *HAH*, 419, *HAH* 141,

HAH 389, 23[72], 23[79], *HAH* 418, *HAH* 424, *HAH* 409, *HAH* 398, *HAH* 416, *HAH* 402, 23[121], *HAH* 396, *HAH* 259, 23[128], *HAH* 384, *HAH* 385, *HAH* 423, *HAH* 421, *HAH* 411, *HAH* 158, *HAH* 407, *HAH* 598, *HAH* 406, *HAH* 404, *HAH* 413, *HAH* 388, *HAH* 379, *HAH* 392, *HAH* 400, *HAH* 401, *HAH* 393, *HAH* 377, 18[35], 18[41], 18[43], *HAH* 405.

7. *Education]* Marked with four vertical lines, as are the following notes in Mp XIV 1 and M I 1: *HAH* 479, *HAH* 268, 23[29], *HAH* 251, *HAH* 267, 23[43], 23[44], *HAH* 395, *HAH* 72, *HAH* 254, *HAH* 263, *HAH* 242, 23[94], *HAH* 592, 23[136], *HAH* 250, 23[151], *HAH* 203, *HAH* 244, 23[160], 18[2].

8. *The writer]* Marked with two horizontal blue lines, as are the following notes in Mp XIV 1 and M I 1: 23[7], *HAH* 201, 23[31], 23[40], *MM* 113, 23[42], *HAH* 207, 23[91], *HAH* 176, 23[98], *HAH* 178, *MM* 227, *HAH* 199, 23[132], 23[134], 23[137], 23[139], 23[146], *HAH* 202, 23[162], 23[171], *HAH* 191, *HAH* 181, *HAH* 189, *HAH* 187, *HAH* 186, *HAH* 184, *HAH* 188, *HAH* 192, *HAH* 180, *HAH* 200, *HAH* 206

9. *Thoughts of discontent]* Marked with one blue cross, as are the following notes in Mp XIV 1: *HAH* 351, 23[61], *HAH* 40, *HAH* 590, 23[83], *HAH* 68, *HAH* 542, 23[113], *HAH* 516, *HAH* 60, *HAH* 352, *MM* 212, *HAH* 277, *HAH* 513, *HAH* 628, 13[188], 23[189], *HAH* 629.

10. Arrangement for *HAH.*

11. Arrangement for *HAH.*

12. Cf. 23[46].

13. *The parents . . . parents] Pd:* Schopenhauer goes so far as to describe the parents simply as the accidental causes, so that the will can newly individualize itself in a child. In truth the children could more rightly be described as the opportunistic effects of the parents.

14. Cf. *HAH* 498.

15. *shall]* From: ca⟨n⟩

16. *Since . . . harvest.]* Cf. 22[81].

17. Seit dies Buch mir erwuchs, quält Sehnsucht mich und Beschämung,

Bis solch Gewächs dir einst reicher und schooner erblüht,

Jetzt schon kost' ich des Glücks, dass ich dem Größeren nachgeh',
Wenn er des goldnen Ertrags eigener Ernten sich freut.

[25 = Mp XIV 1d. (Gast). Fall 1877]

1. Cf. 23[25].

2. *Fourth . . . exist.]* Cf. *HAH* 446.

3. Copy (with N's corrections) on the basis of a first draft by N in Mp XIV 1, 387, lines 397–99.

4. *Play . . . necessity.]* Cf. 23[194]; *Pd*: Come friends and view a new / play today / Me with the pipe of time / [— — —] to a wild dance / the whirring of the wind with damp blows of its wings / boat, your course is necessity. Cf. also 22[55].

5. Spiel der Gedanken, es führt
eine der Grazien dich:
O wie weidest den Sinn du mir! —
Weh! Was seh' ich? Es fällt
Larve und Schleier der Führerin,
und voran dem Reigen
schreitet die grause Nothwendigkeit.

6. Headings for the nine chapters of *HAH*.

7. Became the fifth chapter, with the title "Signs of a Higher and Lower Culture."

8. Became the first chapter.

[26 = D 11. Winter 1877–78]

1. Variants to *HAH* 63; crossed out in *Pm*, following from *HAH* 599.

Overview of Nietzsche's Manuscripts 1875–1877

N = small notebooks, classified by the Nietzsche Source Digital Archive as jotters
U = larger notebooks, generally quarto- or octavo-sized
M = quarto notebook
Mp = dossiers of loose sheets, mostly quarto-, some folio-sized; clean copy transcriptions
D = print-ready manuscript

More detailed information on the manuscripts of this period can be found in *KGW* IV 4, 93–106. Digital copies of many of these manuscripts (nonduplicative ones) and general descriptions of them can be found online at: http://www.nietzschesource.org/DFGA/. Also worth mentioning is that Nietzsche typically wrote in his notebooks from back to front, hence the reversed pagination in some of these notebooks below.

• •

1 = N I 4 (Winter–Spring 1875; Basel): Casual jottings, the draft of a letter to Richard Wagner, philological material, and preliminary notes for *UO*. 110 pages, sparsely written on.
2 = U II 8a (up to the beginning of March 1875): Small preliminary studies for "The Pre-Platonic Philosophers," mostly notes

for "We Philologists," with a few *HAH*-style aphorisms. U II 8 ≐ 240 pages.
3 = Mp XIII 6b (March 1875): The bulk of U II (pp. 239–100) transcribed by Carl von Gersdorff as the basis for the never-published fifth *Unfashionable Observation* "We Philologists"; further revised and supplemented by N with additional fragments; also reading notes on F. A. Wolf's *Kleine Schriften*. 11 quarto sheets page-numbered 1–22.

— — — —

4 = N I 3b (Spring 1875): Casual notes and work plans, also material from 1872 and 1879. N I 3 = 100 pages.
5 = U II 8b (Spring–Summer 1875), pp. 198–108: Material for "We Philologists," partially transcribed and revised in Mp XIII 6a.
6 = U II 8c (Summer 1875): Notes on pre-Socratic philosophy.
7 = Mp XIII 6a (1875): Transcribed by N; final work toward "We Philologists." 12 pages.

— — — —

8 = U I 6b (Summer 1875): Reading and writing projects. U I 6 = 148 pages.
9 = U III 1 (Summer 1875): Quotations from and notes on Eugen Dühring's *Der Werth des Lebens*; brief notes on Balfour Stewart's *The Conservation of Energy*. 180 pages.
10 = N I 6 (Summer 1875): Casual jottings, notes for lectures, and preliminary notes for *WB*. 178 pages.
11 = U II 9 (Summer 1875): Preliminary Work for *WB*; numbered (in reverse order) by N in 11[60], with numbers then added to the work plan for *WB* in 11[47]; parts dictated to Adolf Baumgartner in Mp XIII 4, 6–8, 47; Sections 11–13 also contain miscellaneous entries on other topics, such as Thucydides, Darwin, etc. 72 pages.
12 = U II 10 (Summer–End of September 1875): First version of initial sections of *WB*; sheets from back half of U II 10 torn out and contained in Mp XIII 4, 13–46. 162 pages.

13 = D 10a (Summer–Autumn 1875): Clean copy (*PmN*) of chapters 1–6 of *WB* dictated to Peter Gast from U II 9–10; only additions by N included in *KGW*.
14 = Mp XIII 4, 9–12 (Autumn 1875–Spring 1876): Notes and organizational plans for *WB*.
15 = U II 11 (Spring 1876): Notes on German language; not included in *KGW* is the clean copy of the final three chapters of *WB* prepared by Gast, based on U II 9. 236 pages.

WB published July 1876.

— — — —

16 = N II 1 (1876): Preliminary notes for Chapter 11 of *WB* and for *HAH*, along with various other entries from later in 1876, including multiple plans for expanding the *UO* project, as in 16[10–11]; first brief aphoristic entries. 278 pages.
17 = U II 5b (Summer 1876; Bayreuth/Klingenbrunn): Notes for "The Plowshare," project for revitalizing European culture and education, first "free spirit" entries. U II 5 = 250 pages.
18 = M I 1 (September 1876): Dictated to Peter Gast based upon U II 5b, N II 1, and other Summer 1875 material; some aphorisms already in form of mini-essays. 100 pages.
19 = U II 5c (October–December 1876; Bex/Sorrento): First plans for "The Free Spirit," retrospectively numbered with reference to *HAH*.
20 = Mp XIV 1a (Winter 1876–1877): Mp XIV 1 is known as the Sorrento papers, although some entries date from after N's stay there; second clean copy of "The Plowshare" transcribed by Albert Brenner, also Peter Gast, with some entries by N.
21 = N II 3 (End of 1876–Summer 1877): Philosophy-related jottings and aphorisms. 86 pages.
22 = N II 2 (Spring–Summer 1877; Ragaz/Rosenlauibad): Mainly notes for *HAH*. 154 pages.
23 = Mp XIV 1b (End of 1876–Summer 1877): Aphorism drafts for *HAH*.

24 = Mp XIV 1c (Autumn 1877): Organizational plans for notes in Mp XIV 1b from period when N and Gast were preparing *Pm* for *HAH*.
25 = Mp XIV 1d (Autumn 1877): Transcribed by Peter Gast, also during *HAH Pm* preparation.
26 = D 11 (Winter 1877–1878): For *HAH*, written by Peter Gast, with N's corrections.

HAH published April 1878

Chronicle of Nietzsche's Life While Writing These Notebooks

1874
15 February 1874: letter to Erwin Rohde with first critique of Bayreuth excesses (*KGB* II:3 202–3)
October 1874: plans for ten more *UO*; N teaching only one course, on Greek literature
1875
January 1875: in Basel
January–April 1875: work on "We Philologists"
30 March: start of dictation of "We Philologists" to Carl von Gersdorff
April–mid-July 1875: ill
16 July–11 August: in Steinabad for cure
August: Basel, with sister Elisabeth
September: work on *WB* and course preparations
13–30 September: ill
October: Heinrich Köselitz (aka Peter Gast) attends N's lectures; N reads Paul Rée for the first time; N reads the *Sutta Niputa*
1876
January: Basel
January–March: on medical leave
6 March–April: trip with Gersdoff to Veytaux on Lake Geneva
11 April: marriage proposal to Mathilde Trampedach

April–July: Basel; N requests one-year leave from the university, approved 2 June
May: meets Heinrich von Stein
May–June: finishes last three sections of *WB*
July 1876: *WB* published
23 July–27 August: in Bayreuth for rehearsals
6–12 August: "flight" from Bayreuth
27 August: return to Basel
August–September: dictation of *Pm* of "The Plowshare" to Albert Brenner (M I 1)
October 1876: trip to Sorrento via Bex. Geneva, Genoa, Naples
October: visit with Wagner family, Wagner's critique of Rée and *Parsifal* discussion

1877

January: Sorrento, with Brenner and Malwida von Meysenbug
April: Meysenbug conveys to N Cosima Wagner's critique of him
May–June: in Ragaz for cure
June–August: Rosenlauibad
September–October: Basel, living with sister; dictation to Brenner of second *Pm* of *HAH*
September–January 1878: N and Gast working on *Pm* for *HAH* (see Notebook 25 for a full sketch of chapter titles)
3–7 October: extensive consultation in Frankfurt about N's vision with Drs. Eiser and Krüger

1878

3 January: score of *Parsifal* reaches N
10 January: N finishes correcting Gast's *Ms* of *HAH*, sent to Schmeitzner for printing
Mid-April: proof page corrections of *HAH*
April 1878: publication of *HAH*

Translator's Afterword

Gary Handwerk

The maxim as theme of sociability.

—19[119]

A maxim is one link out of a chain of ideas; it requires that the reader reconstruct this chain with his own devices: that means it requires a great deal. A maxim is a presumption. — Or it is a warning: as Heraclitus knew. In order to be enjoyable, a maxim must first be stirred up and mingled with other materials (example, experiences, stories). Most people do not understand this and one can therefore express objectionable things unobjectionably in maxims.

—20[3]

I

The notebooks contained in this volume of *The Complete Works of Friedrich Nietzsche* have been dated (by the Colli-Montinari edition) to the period from Winter 1875 to Autumn 1877. These are the years when Nietzsche was finishing the composition of *Richard Wagner in Bayreuth* (published in July 1876) and doing the writing and final preparation, along with Heinrich Köselitz, of the manuscript for *Human, All Too Human I* (published in

April 1878). Like other periods in Nietzsche's life, he was during these years contemplating a frequently shifting variety of future projects; the notebooks provide a fascinating record of these rapidly proliferating possibilities.

The afterwords that I have previously written (for volumes 3 and 4 of *The Complete Works*) provide extensive biographical context for Nietzsche's work during this period: his increasingly fraught relationship with Richard Wagner, his perpetual struggles with health, the interruptions of his professional career, and the transformation of his personal and professional identities as a result of the unsparing self-examination forced upon him, in part, by his circumstances.[1] I will not repeat that material here, but have provided as guidance for dating and making use of the notebooks two additional resources: a timeline of this period in Nietzsche's life and a manuscript history, the latter based upon the material contained in *KGW* IV 4, especially pages 9–40, 93–105, and 491–572.

Here I want to concentrate instead upon the issue of the value, both for scholars and for general readers, of Nietzsche's notebooks.[2] From the start of the Stanford University Press Nietzsche project, the utility of the notebooks for English readers has been seen as a paramount justification for undertaking the translations — both the original press editor, Helen Tartar, and the original general editor, Ernst Behler, shared this view. Newly translating Nietzsche's published works for an edition based closely upon the Colli-Montinari edition was seen as having considerable value in itself, but also as being indispensable

1. In writing those sections of the afterwords, I relied very much upon the *Chronik zu Nietzsches Leben* in vol. 15 of the *Kritische Studienausgabe* (*CW* 19) and Curt Paul Janz's remarkable three-volume biography of Nietzsche's life (*Friedrich Nietzsche: Biographie* [Munich: Hanser, 1978]), which is based upon a very thorough acquaintance with Nietzsche's correspondence. Also of considerable value to me in this regard were the two afterwords written by Richard Gray for vols. 2 and 11 of *CW*.

2. For this topic, I have benefited immensely from Alan D. Schrift's essay "Nietzsche's *Nachlass*" (in *A Companion to Friedrich Nietzsche: Life and Works*, ed. Paul Bishop [Rochester, NY: Camden House, 2012], 405–28), and Adrian Del Caro's afterword to *CW* 16, which extends the discussion in Schrift's essay. See esp. pp. 478–80 of Del Caro.

for allowing readers to make reliable use of the notebooks, where cross-referencing multiple variants perpetually occurs and translation consistency across published and unpublished texts is a vital objective. As the SUP project has proceeded, however, it has become clear that the notebooks offer considerable value independently of the published works, as a window into Nietzsche's thought processes and compositional methods. They open up new ways of seeing Nietzsche — especially as the remarkably self-aware author that he was. In making use of them, readers should bear in mind the distinct differences among the different categories of notebooks; the varied N, U, M, Mp, and D sections capture quite different stages of Nietzsche's thoughts and presentation strategies. Detailed information about the nature of the individual notebooks can be found in *KGW* IV 4, 489–572, and online at the Nietzsche Source, http://www.nietzschesource.org/DFGA/. English readers of this volume can refer to a condensed overview of the different manuscripts provided on pages 449–52.

Although all are of great interest, the notebooks clearly have quite differential values at different moments of Nietzsche's career. They are an indispensable substratum for Nietzsche's never-completed works, and a necessary corrective, as Schrift and Del Caro and others have argued, to Elisabeth Förster-Nietzsche's amalgamation of Nietzsche's late writings into her invented *Will to Power* text. Notebooks prior to *The Will to Power*, however, from when Nietzsche was still actively publishing (the 1880s), also contain a wealth of fragments, ideas, and work plans for future projects that never came to be. Earlier notebooks, like these from 1875–77, on the other hand, were extensively mined for Nietzsche's published works. Indeed, those in this particular volume were doubly mined: initially for *Human, All Too Human I*, then again for the two works that became *Human, All Too Human II*, *Mixed Opinions and Maxims* and *The Wanderer and His Shadow*. As a result, one finds in these particular notebooks less that is novel or unexpected.[3]

3. For instance, the extensive reformulation of a conclusion in 23[250] into the final section (§292) of chap. 5 of *HAH* (*CW* 3, 194–96) is a striking instance of Nietzsche's stylistic and communicative decision-making.

To a large extent, the entries in this particular set of notebooks can be divided into five categories, albeit with considerable overlap in some of the notebooks of different kinds of entries. (1) The first category includes preliminary work on the *Richard Wagner in Bayreuth* essay, contained especially in Notebooks 11–14 (1875–76). These entries show Nietzsche formulating his stance toward Wagner as man and as musician, and as the prototypical modern artist; they come from an interval of time when he had entirely broken off work on the manuscript, as well as the months in 1876 when he resumed work upon it at the instigation of Heinrich Köselitz and brought it to completion. During the first half of that year, Nietzsche reworked earlier sections of *Richard Wagner in Bayreuth* and wrote the bulk of the final four sections. While still largely laudatory, the notebook entries from this time also show traces of his mounting skepticism about the cultural and artistic value of Wagner's works . . . and indeed, about art generally as a culturally revitalizing force for the modern era. Thus, 12[26] takes up in detail Plato's objections to the artist as participant in a stable society, applying the lessons of the *Republic* specifically to Wagner. "It is extremely natural and therefore dangerous *not* to understand Wagner *as* an artist, or to express it differently: to want to infer from his artworks specific hints for the shaping of life." Translation of these notebooks involved steady consultation of Richard Gray's translation in *CW* 2 of the Wagner essay, during which I sought to conform as consistently as possible to his rendering of the final published version of that work.

(2) These notebooks also contain Nietzsche's intense reflections upon philology, not only as an academic discipline but as a hermeneutic method. For much of this period, Nietzsche entertained the idea of writing an *Unfashionable Observation* that would be entitled "We Philologists," especially during the months when he had deferred finishing the Wagner essay.[4] These entries can be found particularly in Notebooks 3–5, then again in 7,

4. On this, see Richard Gray's comments in his afterwords at *CW* 2, 405, and *CW* 11, 470–76 and 489–91.

10, and 16. This essay was conceived as part of a major extension of the *Unfashionable Observations* project, with a dozen or more possible titles for different essays listed at various points in the notebooks. The varying tone of Nietzsche's analysis of the academic enterprise of philology is striking, often vociferously critical, at other moments imbued with the more nuanced genealogical stance and more empathetic tone that Nietzsche's writings can also display. Nietzsche's critique of the academic enterprise of philology is mingled throughout with his equally uncompromising critique of himself as a philologist, of both his professional background and his own intellectual biases. These are entries that contemporary scholars, humanists (and antihumanists) alike, might want to read with particular attention. For much of what Nietzsche says about scholars and the scholarly enterprise applies all too well to the current practices of academia. Vital as critical perspectives on culture (and the rest of human affairs) may be, they do not exempt us from constant reflection about what the *impact* of those critiques upon society as a whole is likely to be. All scholars, perhaps, incur the risk of becoming the disciplinary philologists whom Nietzsche mocked, so intent upon their immediate tasks that wider historical vision escaped them.

(3) Long stretches of these notebooks contain extensive notes taken from specific texts that Nietzsche was reading intently, plus his commentary on those texts. Reading Friedrich August Wolf's *Kleine Schriften in lateinischer und deutscher Sprache* (1869) and his *Deutsche Aufsätze* (1869), for instance, sparked reflections on philology and its history as a discipline (especially Notebook 3, but see also note 4 to Notebook 2 in this volume, p. 452). Similarly, receiving Louis Kelterborn's transcript of Jacob Burckhardt's lectures on Greek cultural history (in May 1875; see note to 4[3], p. 460) initiated a series of reflections on the relationship between classical Greek and contemporary history, both in relation to philology and to Nietzsche's prospective university courses. One of the lengthiest set of reading notes includes Nietzsche's quotations from

and comments on Eugen Dühring's *Der Werth des Lebens* (1865, *NL*) (Notebook 9). These notes, never used in any publication, illuminate Nietzsche's thoughts on this topic just as he was beginning to reformulate his own ideas concerning the value of life in general and the direction his own life should take. The range of Nietzsche's reading interests is impressive, leading him for instance to launch, but then ultimately break off, a close reading of the German translation of Balfour Stewart's *The Conservation of Energy* (1875) (*Die Erhaltung der Energie* [Leipzig: Brockhaus, 1875], *NL*) immediately after his work on Dühring.

(4) Along with these other projects, Nietzsche imagined for a time (mid-1876 through early 1877) producing a volume of aphoristic works to which he gave the tentative title "The Plowshare" (notably Notebooks 17–18 and 20).[5] Much, but by no means all, of this material came to be integrated into *Human, All Too Human I*. Fragment 17[105], for example, contains a table of contents where "The Plowshare" is the provisional title for a work that includes several chapter titles that do eventually show up in *Human, All Too Human I*. Amid these entries one can trace important themes such as Nietzsche's emerging focus upon the idea of the free spirit (as in 16[25]).

(5) For many readers, the greatest interest of this particular volume of notebooks is likely to be the material from which Nietzsche drew in composing *Human, All Too Human I*, the inaugural work of Nietzsche's aphoristic orientation. Notebooks 19–31, written from late 1876 into very early 1878, show Nietzsche firmly on the path toward his own distinctive aphoristic enterprise. "Human, All Too Human" appears as a title (one apparent chapter title among others) in 17[72] (so as early as summer 1876) and then as a book title in 19[119] (with the subtitle there, "Sociable Sayings"). These aphoristic forays, however, were initially conceived in relation to the *Unfashionable Observations* project (16[10–12]), and specifically described in 16[12] as "Addenda to the unfashionable observations (aphoristic)." That

5. See Richard Gray's discussion of this project in *CW* 2.

entry mentions seven *Unfashionable Observations*, each essay conceived as having an addendum that would provide a stylistic counterpoint to thematically organized longer essays. In these fragments in particular, one can find occasional gems or omitted topics that already have the electric intensity of Nietzsche's published aphoristic works. Many more, however, are thoughts in process, testimony to the unfinished and shifting nature of both Nietzsche's ideas and his work plans.

II

Access to these notebooks has particular pertinence in allowing us to track in very close detail Nietzsche at work crafting his distinctively original usage of the literary-philosophical aphorism.[6] His fragmentary mode of writing for himself already appears in *CW* 11 and indeed dates back to the earliest notebooks of 1869. But it was during the years 1875–78 that he sharpened his awareness of the possibilities of the stylistically flexible aphoristic structures that appear in his later works. Starting with *Human, All Too Human I*, he transformed his habit of writing in fragments from a private method of intellectual inquiry into a carefully modulated mode of public communication . . . a mode that Nietzsche intriguingly described in the epigraph above as "sociability [*Geselligkeit*]."

We can trace this compositional shift with precision. Thus, Notebooks 16 and 17 (dated midyear 1876) contain predominantly shorter aphorisms much like those of the French aphorists whom Nietzsche read carefully with Paul Rée, Albert Brenner, and Malwida von Meysenbug in Sorrento later that year. Notebook 18 (dated only slightly later, in September 1876) and following notebooks already exhibit at the notebook stage

6. Without entering deeply into the earnest and extensive scholarly debate on this topic — whether to call Nietzsche's literary form "aphoristic" at all — I consider the aphorism, and Nietzsche's fascination with it during this period, to be the foundational block for the style and structure throughout his later periods. As I said in *CW* 3, 377, however, "Nietzsche made the aphoristic form very much his own" — reinventing it for the modern era as completely as Rousseau reinvented the genre of confessional literature.

a large number of more extended aphorisms as well, some as long as a page and a half — essentially mini-essays rather than traditional aphorisms. Titles begin to appear with some of the aphorisms as early as Notebook 23 (dated Summer 1877), but not before then. As the record of Nietzsche's reading and references from these years indicates, Goethe, Rée himself, and Schopenhauer (especially his *Parerga and Paralipomena*) were also among the writers whose use of this form Nietzsche studied in detail and on whom he modeled his own efforts.

These notebooks, then, offer a close-up view of Nietzsche as a *stylist* and *composer*. It is evident in them how Nietzsche thinks in fragments, lightning flashes of ideas that sometimes show stylistic flair in their very first formulation, while in other cases going through considerable honing before finding a rendering that satisfied their author. The notebooks make equally clear how crucial a step the composition, the basic putting together of his works, was for Nietzsche. I use "stylist" and "composer" in a strong sense here, in order to capture two distinct aspects of Nietzsche as a writer. Finding a structure that would make individual fragments resonate against one another, a key step in honing the fragments for publication, was much more than a matter of devising thematic categories into which he could loosely group related fragments. As I wrote in the afterword to *CW* 4, it was from his experiences in these years that "Nietzsche began forging a new style and a new identity, an identity based in part on the realization that for him style and identity would henceforth be one and the same thing" (558).[7] In a quite literal sense, his novel aphoristic structures are a manifestation of Nietzsche's emerging philosophical principles and spirit — most obviously, of his perspectivism. They make visible his

7. Among the many valuable scholars who have contributed to this discussion, I have found works by Alexander Nehamas, *Nietzsche: Life as Literature* (Cambridge, MA: Harvard University Press, 1985); Robert Pippin, *Nietzsche, Psychology, and First Philosophy* (Chicago: University of Chicago Press, 2010); and Henry Staten, *Nietzsche's Voice* (Ithaca, NY: Cornell University Press, 1990) of particular value for my thinking about Nietzsche as stylist.

characteristic ways of seeing and his habitual modes of thought. This means that one needs — even in reading preliminary versions in the notebooks — to attend to features such as voice, tone, and mood, for such features are clues to any writer's stance toward the particular topics or questions he is discussing. Reading through the notebooks provides steady reminders of how carefully Nietzsche thought about the basic structural principles of language — the centrality of syntax, for instance, in weighing different clauses within a given sentence.[8] While word order in German is frequently more prescribed by grammar than in English, as a translator one still needs to pay close attention to Nietzsche's construction of clausal order and to his placement of individual words and phrases. Equally important for a translator of Nietzsche is to remain steadily aware of and seek to retain wherever possible his highly purposive, often idiosyncratic usage of punctuation. Nietzsche's marked preference for the dash and for emphases of various kinds is crucial in providing explicit indications of the tempo at which a reader should proceed.

In addition, these notebooks highlight what I have called the "interruptive mode" of Nietzsche's thought,[9] its perpetual tendency to redirect or even to reverse itself, for which the aphorism model was especially congenial. Fragment 20[3], cited above, offers a good instance of this. It begins with a relatively simple hermeneutic principle, one at the core of modern reader-response theories. Novalis (an author whom Nietzsche also very much admired, and one who, like the other German Romantics, utilized the aphorism form extensively) formulated this idea in terms of the role of a reader as *erweiterte Autor*, an "extended author" who plays an essential role in completing the thoughts presented upon the page.[10] Yet Nietzsche quickly

8. Notebook 15, from the *WB* period, includes a long set of linguistic entries analyzing the logic and the historical development of the German language.

9. *CW* 3, 378.

10. "The true reader must be the extended author. He is the higher tribunal, which receives the subject matter from the lower tribunal already reworked."

gives this broadly cognitive idea specifically rhetorical and ethical implications: a maxim (*Sentenz* in German, a term that I would restrict to the shorter, pithier versions of the aphorism) is both a "presumption" and a "warning" (here citing Heraclitus, yet another of the stylistic influences upon Nietzsche). Then another turn, this time to the affective element of the experience, the pleasure a maxim "arouses," but only when it is "mingled," either by author *or* by reader, or indeed by both, with other, quite distinct elements ("example," oddly singular in the German, but also "experiences" or "stories," so narratives of one kind or another). Then a final turn, not to the reader successful at this, as one might expect, but to the unsuccessful reader, the one who reads it without mixing it with other components and who as a result completely misapprehends the real force of the maxim, how objectionable the idea being presented may actually be. As analyzed here by Nietzsche, maxims are an ideal mode for communicating selectively with diverse audiences or saying different, even contradictory, things at one and the same time. All extended authors, in other words, will not recompose the same version, or even a consistent version, of the import of a given aphorism, and that is the right outcome for an author to pursue.

Among the stylistic and conceptual revisions that the notebook entries undergo on the way to published form, several distinct kinds can be distinguished: a given entry can be expanded or it can be contracted, but it can also be restructured, joined with other entries, or divided into multiple parts. Fragment 23[85], for instance, contains a very short formulation of Nietzsche's thoughts about the advantages that modern people have as a result of being able to recollect and compare

---

Novalis, *Schriften: Die Werke Friedrich von Hardenbergs*, ed. Paul Kluckhohn, Richard Samuel, et al. (Stuttgart: W. Kohlhammer Verlag, 1960), 2:470 (fr. 125). This idea is also central to twentieth-century reader-response criticism, both the German and Anglophone versions of it. For the German Romantics, the "fragment" form, as they called it, was also an entry point into producing genuinely collaborative, multiauthored texts.

the products of diverse cultures across different historical periods. Fragment 23[160] expands this brief thought into a two-paragraph entry entitled "In Conclusion" (which would structurally heighten the prominence of this idea), where the "good fortune" of moderns is linked more specifically to their ability to psychologically traverse or live through entire stretches or expanses of human experience. In 23[160], however, this idea is reformulated specifically in terms of Nietzsche's own autobiographical trajectory, casting this as a truth learned from his personal experience that will contribute to the wisdom that he aspires to reach by his sixtieth year. That this idea is related (or perhaps better, relatable) to evolutionary theory becomes evident in the published form of these entries in *HAH* §23. Among the "forms of morality, of customs, of cultures" envisaged there, some will live on, but many others will die off. Moreover, *HAH* §23 sharpens the idea by defining the capacity for comparison and assessment of these cultural-historical variants, and thus the basis for conscious selection among them, as "aesthetic" in nature. It is by virtue of "feeling" that modern people will become able to "select" among alternative forms of "higher" and "lower" moralities, proceeding then to a blending or hybridization that moves human culture beyond the "isolated, original cultures of individual peoples."[11] Rather than concluding a section of *Human, All Too Human I*, though, as the title in 23[160] anticipated, this aphorism now appears within a series devoted to discussion of the possible progress of human culture that further underscores the evolutionary resonance latent in this line of thought from the beginning.[12]

11. This point is highly relevant to Nietzsche's analysis of Wagner as well, whom he repeatedly describes as a "counter-Alexander," bringing together the disparate strands of European and Asian cultures, though in artistic rather than political form. See Nietzsche's discussion of this idea in *WB* §4 (*CW* 2, 273–80) and in the many notes in this volume that expand upon that presentation of it.

12. These notebooks contain one long entry on Darwinism (not Darwin), 12[22], which bears on the issue of individual-society relations that I discuss later. "Unconstrained, much more uncertain and *weaker* individuals, who

A stylistic move in the opposite direction, toward contraction, is equally common and can be seen by comparing the more developed version of an idea in 19[37] with the maximally brief *HAH* §558, where Nietzsche retains only the terse final sentence of the original fragment. Here the notebook version helpfully allows us to unpack the meaning of the published aphorism. The latter provides only minimal context, highlighting the dependence of moral "goodness" upon circumstantial opportunity. Its title there neatly underscores the ironic force of Nietzsche's observation, suggesting that "many people" wait their whole lives for such an opportunity — perhaps in vain, never quite managing to find a suitable situation to put their potential goodness into action. In the notebook entry, however, the maxim's personal, psychological orientation is framed by a more general discussion of the historical development of morality, added context that gives sociocultural force to what might appear a more narrowly conceived psychological observation. That framing ties it more clearly to the long historical perspective of *HAH* §23, a linkage that a cross-referential reading of the notebooks allows us to recognize.

The process of splitting a given entry is nicely visible with 23[94] and the multiple end points this idea finds in *HAH* §242 and *MM* §§179–81. The topic in all of these entries is education or upbringing (*Erziehung*). *HAH* §242 takes up the notebook's interest in the negative effects that a metaphysical ("miraculous" in *Human, All Too Human I*) perspective can have upon human education, but in contrast to the notebook entry, *HAH* §242 emphasizes the countervailing value of this process and the risks of suddenly upending it. Sections 179–81

attempt new things and attempt many different things, are the ones on whom progress depends: countless individuals of this kind perish without effect, but in general they *loosen things up* and thus inflict from time to time a *weakening* upon the stable element, introduce something new in one spot or another that has grown weak. This new thing is gradually assimilated by the overall intact collective being." On Nietzsche's understanding and use of Darwin, see John Richardson's *Nietzsche's New Darwinism* (Oxford: Oxford University Press, 2004).

of *MM* develop instead the notebook's imagined alternative, an "ecumenical," multicultural education that would transform the haphazard, constraining outcomes of a narrower, monocultural upbringing. The *MM* trio also extends the core idea in multiple metaphorical directions (metaphysics is like living beneath a bell that blocks one's wider view of alternative, nonmetaphysical perspectives; the future task of pursuing ecumenical goals is akin to bees seeking out bitter nectars). Section 180 of *MM* lays out components of a more positive educational path not fully envisaged in the notebook entry, while *MM* §181 turns again to a metaphor. The lack of consistency in present educational methods is there imaged as having the effect of contorting a plant's natural growth, deforming the educators responsible for transmitting cultural heritage.

Notebook entry 19[39], with its analysis of how the pangs of conscience arise, reappears in *HAH* §39, but in an extended and wholly reformulated fashion. The published version lays out in considerably more detail a discussion of the effects of belief in free will. It sharpens the description of how conscience emerges into a four-stage process by which society assigns responsibility successively to a person for the effects of an action, then to the actions themselves, then to the motives behind it, and finally to the very nature of that person. Thus, the aphorism concludes, a moral "being" has been invented, with that idea shaped into a compact maxim that leads off a new, traditionally aphoristic concluding section that begins with the line: "No one is responsible for his actions, no one for his nature [. . .]"

Fragment 23[21] takes up the relationship between humans and animals, arguing that without the mental errors induced by metaphysical explanations of human development, people would — despite their technological and cultural advances — have remained animals. This theme recurs in both *HAH* §40 and *HAH* §519. The first aphorism, though, has gained the intriguing title "The Ueber-Thier," and takes a different tack. Without the development of moral (not metaphysical) errors in judgment, humans might well have torn themselves to pieces

— so these errors are a positive gain: a gain, however, that the aphorism argues has produced a secondary error, a division of humans into supposed superanimals and lower beings, such as slaves. *HAH* §519 pushes the idea further, though in the very condensed form of a single maxim with the title "Truth as Circe" (thus mingling in an illustrative story of precisely the kind that 20[3] recommends). It also adds a further potential developmental stage to this process, pondering whether the replacement of error with truth might produce a reversion to an animal state.

III

The topic of Nietzsche as stylist is a well-trodden path to which many scholars have made valuable contributions; much can be said about that issue strictly from attentive reading of his published works, while variants in the notebooks allow us to probe more closely the nuances of meaning that pervade Nietzsche's prose. With the aid of these notebooks, though, I want to offer some preliminary thoughts about the related but also quite different idea of Nietzsche as *composer*. This, too, is not a new idea, but it is one that is hard to examine with the same analytical precision, for it has at one and the same time a looser, more metaphorical musical sense derived from Nietzsche's reflections upon Wagner and a quite literal, rhetorical signification. Nietzsche was, of course, deeply steeped in the lessons of classical rhetoric; one finds in these notebooks and throughout all of his works regular reference to various Greek rhetoricians who made up a significant subject for Nietzsche's university lectures.[13] This topic was for him naturally linked to music, as well as to other components of what he viewed as a superior, because integrated, classical Greek (especially Athenian) educational culture. There, music was considered to have an essential role along with gymnastics in training mind, spirit, and body toward harmony with one another.

13. Nietzsche's lectures for 1874–75 included two separate courses on Aristotle's *Rhetoric*; his summer 1876 course dealt with pre-Platonic philosophy.

While the raw materials had long been at hand, the task of *building* a lengthy aphoristic work was new to Nietzsche in the 1870s. The notebooks strongly reinforce one's sense of how deeply Nietzsche was influenced as an author by his reflections on musical forms and composition, how he sought to transpose lessons from Wagner, Beethoven, and others into principles for the construction of prose texts, where the relation between sound and sense is different than in opera. Where stylistic analysis focuses primarily upon issues of tone or voice at the level of individual words and sentences, composition is a matter of structural form in a broader sense, involving questions of the modulation of varying tones or moods across the entirety of a larger aesthetic artifact. Reading the notebooks (in conjunction with *Human, All Too Human I* and *II*) sheds considerable light on how Nietzsche (to shift metaphors) laid out his notebook fragments as building blocks with all of the attention of a skilled mason to the placement of individual stones.

Janz's biography deals extensively with the idea of Nietzsche's quasi-musical mode of composition, quite specifically in relation to the "Plowshare" project. Janz astutely relates this compositional method to the necessity forced upon Nietzsche by his ailing eyesight of dictating his draft of this projected essay to Heinrich Köselitz, a compositional method common to many of his aphoristic works.[14] Janz describes the process in this way: "Dictating means that the thoughts, up to [the point of] their formulation, were already worked through by Nietzsche mentally (*im Geist*) to a relatively complete form, similarly to how he had improvisationally come upon his compositions on the piano. This compositional technique becomes from here on determinative for his literary mode of production as well. 'The Plowshare' . . . formed the starting point for notes [*Aufzeichnungen*], 'improvisations,' from the abundance of which, over time, something extrinsically new can be supposed to have

14. The oral nature of this process of dictation, very common for Nietzsche throughout this period, offers another entry point into discussion of his sensitivity to the sound and music of words.

come into being: the first aphorism collection" (1:713–14). Janz takes this shift quite seriously, describing it as a shift in both "thematics" and "philosophical standpoint" compared to the *Unfashionable Observations* essays, yet still, perhaps, not as seriously as one might take it in structural-compositional terms.

Del Caro takes up Janz's perspective in his afterword to the 1885–86 notebooks, offering a richer sense of the implications of this idea. He quotes Janz in asserting, "'In music there is the possibility of retrograde variations, of gradual unveiling of the theme: from an entire sequence of variations the theme in the end bursts forth.'"[15] Del Caro quite usefully goes on to discuss this theme-and-variation idea in terms of a set of "seven clusters or strands" of meaning, relying for his organizational matrix particularly on Nietzsche's drafts for titles of books. But neither he nor Janz pursues very far the implications of this idea with regard to the moods or emotional registers of a text, the rawly visceral dimension of music to which Nietzsche was always attentive. Aesthetics as affect offers an alternative, decidedly nonconceptual way of imagining organizational structure, one that might well echo the cognitive movements of a given text but might also intersect with that cognitive content in a variety of different ways. To imagine Nietzsche as an improvisational artist (if somewhat anachronistically) is to imagine him analogously to a jazz artist in relation to classical or popular music traditions.

While this is not the place to pursue this idea at length, I would like to take up a particularly suggestive pair of published and notebook entries that deal explicitly with musical composition and its relation to audience effects. One of the lengthiest drafts for the *Wagner in Bayreuth* essay (almost seven continuous pages in length) occurs in 11[15], a draft for the ninth section of that essay, composed in summer 1875 (thus, prior to the interruption in the writing of *Wagner in Bayreuth*). This section returns to the very first theme of *Wagner in Bayreuth*,

15. Del Caro, *CW* 16, 498; Janz, *Friedrich Nietzsche* 2:415.

§1's account of the crucial relationship between artist and audience. *Wagner in Bayreuth* begins by stressing this tie. "For an event to be great, two things must come together, the great sensibility of those who create it, and the great sensibility of those who experience it" (*CW* 2, 259). Section 9 echoes this idea in its second sentence: "If art is nothing other than the ability to communicate to others what one has experienced, then every work of art contradicts itself if it cannot make itself understood" (*CW* 2, 308). That section goes on to examine Richard Wagner's talent as a musician of poetic effects, a composer who can "think mythically," which Nietzsche glosses as the ability to think "in visible and palpable events" (*CW* 2, 309), that is, in dramatic form. Accomplishing this required Wagner to "force language back into a primal state in which it conceives almost nothing with the help of concepts, a state in which it itself is still poetry, image, and feeling" (*CW* 2, 309). Accessing and communicating passion, Nietzsche goes on to argue, means realizing that "the real passion of life does not speak in maxims" (*CW* 2, 311),[16] but instead requires a mixture of "verbal expression, gesture, and music" (*CW* 2, 312).

Nor does passion speak episodically. Communicating human passions directly and effectively turns out immediately to be a problem of structural and temporal sequence, of what Nietzsche terms "the rhythmic sense of its architect" (*CW* 2, 312), which he contrasts in turn with the "intentional complexity and confusing multiplicity of architectural style" typical of lesser composer-artists. With Wagner, "Language abandoned rhetorical expansiveness and returned to the concision and power of a language of feeling [. . .] now internal events, which until then had been banished from the stage by the verbal dramatist's fear of what is allegedly undramatic, compelled the listener to passionate participation, while the accompanying language of gesture needed to be expressed in only the most delicate modulation" (*CW* 2, 312). Pre-Wagnerian music,

16. A point worth stressing when considering Nietzsche as aphorist.

the essay contends, "had spoken an alienated, constrained, and unfree language" (*CW* 2, 313).[17] Wagner's music, in contrast, thanks to its different nature, attunes its audiences in deeper and more complex ways.

Here is where *WB* §9 inserts the opening section of 11[15], which takes up the question of precisely how Wagner managed to use music to transcend the limits of traditional staged drama. Nietzsche praises Wagner's skill in avoiding the "epic-lyrical" tendencies of prior music (*Wagner in Bayreuth* terms these instead "narrow limits"), a skill that manifests itself in quite specific structural terms. The following historical account (in 11[15], but not incorporated into *Wagner in Bayreuth*) of European music prior to Wagner emphasizes the crucial impact that Beethoven had in devising ways for a composer to manage or modulate a listener's moods over an extended length of time. Like Wagner, Beethoven is praised for his ingenuity in allowing language to speak "the forbidden language of passion." Both knew how to compose, that is, how to uncover what one might term the logic of a series of moods, and then to orchestrate the "trajectory" of this sequence or modulation of moods as it passed through multiple registers of feeling and aligned them into "a coherently structured artistic totality." "Every passion has a dramatic course," as Nietzsche writes in *Wagner in Bayreuth*, praising Beethoven's "last and greatest works" because "[h]e truly discovered a new means for reproducing the great sweeping arc of every passion [*den großen geschwungenenen Bogen jeder Leidenschaft*]" (*CW* 2, 315). Though Nietzsche will go on to subject to critique the transformation of discord into harmony for which he praises Wagner here (*CW* 2, 316), his account of structural integrity has considerable relevance to his own production of "well-orchestrated" long aphoristic texts. Section 9 of *Wagner in Bayreuth* culminates (unlike the notebook entry) with an explicit musical/rhetorical parallel.

17. An interesting conjunction of adjectives in light of *HAH*'s theme of the free vs. constrained spirit.

Wagner turns out to be akin to Demosthenes, the great Athenian orator.

These two texts in combination provide, of course, a very astute analysis of how Wagner accomplished his musical effects, of precisely why they worked. But as one reads in the notebooks Nietzsche's comments on music, philology, philosophy, and form in proximity, one can see more exactly how Nietzsche was in the process of transferring his understanding of musical form into his own practices of prose composition. These notebooks, then, facilitate consideration of Nietzsche's aphoristic works aesthetically, in the basic sense of that term, as "coherently structured totalities" that are unified by the force (improvisational force, Janz would say) of their author's skill in attuning readers by modulating *disparate* "registers of feeling." Works like *Human, All Too Human I* have modal (or "moodal," an etymological affinity that Nietzsche might have appreciated) structures, not simply thematic ones — important as an analysis of themes or strands of meaning remains for the large-scale architecture of a work. The local twists and turns of thought that Nietzsche admired in the aphorists he was reading in this period, in the structures of their individual maxims, could be translated to the larger structural form of aphoristic texts, held together by a Wagnerian modulation of registers of feeling. Attuning readers, that is to say, involves consciously or improvisationally (though how much difference would there be in these two terms for Nietzsche?) employing a structural affinity that plays out in similar ways across the individual sentence, the individual aphorism, the individual chapters, and the textual wholes.

In addition, the notebooks add to an understanding of *Wagner in Bayreuth* simply by including elements that the finished essay leaves out. Thus, Nietzsche provides in 11[15] the sort of "examples" that add pleasure and clarity to an aphoristic assertion. He adds a brief negative comment about Schubert's Eighth Symphony in C major (deemed "boring"), but also an explication of Beethoven's Ninth Symphony that does not appear in *Wagner in Bayreuth*. 11[15] explores the "arc of passion" in that symphony as it moves from one register to another, a coldly analytical account that would suit the tone of *Human, All Too Human I*, but which is replaced in *Wagner in Bayreuth* by expanded panegyric praise of Wagner's uniqueness. That concluding portion of *WB* §9 is one of the most rhetorically intensified (indeed, perhaps overwrought) passages in the essay. Wagner is described in godly terms, "Subduing turbulent, resisting masses into simple rhythms, asserting one will throughout a confusing multitude of demands and desires — these are the tasks for which he feels himself formed, in which he feels his freedom" (*CW* 2, 317).

Along with material for speculation about aesthetic form, of course, we find in the notebooks and published works of this period numerous direct comments by Nietzsche himself on the aphorism or maxim (*Sentenz*, but also *Spruch*, as in the title to *Mixed Opinions and Maxims*). Fragment 20[3] terms the aphorism sociable or interactive, as I have noted, and elsewhere Nietzsche offers advice to potential readers in an entry not carried over into any published text. In an abandoned preface (likely to *Human, All Too Human I*), fragment 23[196], Nietzsche offers advice to a prospective reader about the kind of book he was composing — advice here much more in accord with a conventional assessment of the aphorism.

> There must be books that we do not read through, but frequently open up: we remain with one or another sentence today, attach ourselves to a different one tomorrow, and reflect once again from the depths of our heart: for and against, within and out beyond, however the spirit moves us, so long as every time we thereby become cheerful and clear-headed. Gradually there emerges from this sort of animated — genuine, because not forced — reflection a certain general *remodulation* [my emphasis] of views: and with it that general feeling of spiritual recuperation, as if the bow were again strung with new string and could be drawn more strongly than ever. We have traveled usefully.

An interruptive or segmental mode of reading fits what this preface terms a "travel book," to be read while underway on a trip with all of the disruptions that those circumstances entail. Here, too, however, Nietzsche alerts us to the importance of a "remodulation of views" that comes from a different source, not immediate experience with a single work, but repeated encounter with a well-remembered single passage.

By 1876–77, Nietzsche clearly already sees the aphorism as suitable for serious philosophical speculation. He specifically rebukes Kant for his mode of writing in 23[122], another unutilized entry.

> Even Kant allowed himself to be determined by the scholarly manner of making books (which is even considered by the traditional judgment as an academic obligation) into that verbose kind of communication, which is doubly lamentable with him because he was always lacking for time (because of his academic duties): during the writing he frequently had first to think himself back into his train of thought. Had he been satisfied, in Hume's way, to communicate in the shortest form what he had established *prior to* the writing (perhaps on a walk), the entire conflict about the correct understanding of Kant, which still lives on today, would have been superfluous.

Kant as aphorist . . . an intriguing thought, indeed.

IV

The Colli-Montinari *Kritische Gesamtausgabe* is a truly masterful and massive philological project of precisely the sort that Nietzsche himself might have viewed with great caution. Its meticulous cross-referencing (duplicated in notes to the SUP edition) allows readers to track Nietzsche's shifting perspectives upon issues such as socialism (taken up in 21[43], 23[25], and 25[1], then pursued further in published aphorisms such as *HAH* §473). Thematic reading of this kind with respect to the 1875–78 notebooks produces valuable clusters of meanings around themes that persist throughout Nietzsche's authorial career.

Of particular significance for *Human, All Too Human I*, for instance, are the many aphorisms that deal with the contrast between a "free" and a "constrained" spirit.[18] The cultivation of free spirits is one of the key tasks that Nietzsche sets forth for contemporary philosophers and their societies, a backing off from the heretofore evolutionarily valuable binding of disparate individuals into cohesive social wholes. Nietzsche's comments about race with regard to classical Greek history, particularly in Notebook 5, have independent value as one perspective on this key topic. Fragments elsewhere bear directly on this theme as well, such as 17[55]: "Meanwhile the observant free spirits have their mission: they remove all the barriers that stand in the way of a blending of human beings: religions states monarchical instincts, illusions of wealth and poverty, prejudices about health and races — etc." Related to these themes are persistent observations about the relationships among German, European, and global cultures.[19]

During this period, Nietzsche was persistently writing as well about the relationships between individuals and collectivities (societies on some occasion, species on others). These relationships are complexly assessed by him, rarely formulated in an either/or fashion. As with artist/audience relationships, each side depends upon the other in crucial ways; there is a necessary synchronicity in their emergence if either side is to thrive. Geniuses, Nietzsche notes elsewhere, do not flourish in or even emerge from societies plagued by *ressentiment*. Entries like 19[115] look forward to Nietzsche's later discussions of the interplay of egoistical and unegoistical impulses (*Regungen*). Of particular interest on this theme is 20[11], taken up in part at *HAH* §224, but with the free and constrained spirits treated

18. For the tricky German adjective *gebunden*, I have consistently used "constrained" rather than the more literal "bound." Both have advantages, but "constrained" captures for me the sense of social constraint that Nietzsche sees human societies imposing upon individuals.

19. See Del Caro's discussion of this theme in *CW* 16, 521–23.

there in a more oppositional way. Entry 20[11], in contrast, is more nuanced, stressing at its end the complementary value of the two kinds of spirits: "From this entire observation, the free spirit can take the proof that he is useful for the constrained spirits, too: for he helps so that the productions of the constrained spirits, their state, their culture, their morality do not become fixed and die out; he permits the invigorating sap of rejuvenation to flow ever anew into stem and branches." That observation, interestingly, grows out of an analysis of how the Romans "inoculated" the Germans, an instance of cultural-racial hybridization that "wounded" the Germans, yet opened productive new avenues of development for them as well. Entry 20[11] offers a cautionary comment as well, in terms of relating this process of human "evolution" to animal history: "I want with this observation intentionally to remain with human beings and to guard against drawing conclusions about animal natures and their laws from the laws concerning human improvement on the basis of weaker and degenerate natures."

V

One salutary effect of reading through Nietzsche's notebooks, independently or alongside his published works, is the persistent reminder of how the artist-philosopher's projects were perpetually in motion — incomplete, and in fact, *imprevisible*. Nietzsche's notes to himself remain a process of constant exploration, self-critique, and revision. Trying to imagine or anticipate the completed shapes of these projects and individual ideas (what "The Plowshare" might have looked like, for instance) may be an amusing game, but remains a fundamentally speculative one.[20] In a very basic way, the core value of Nietzsche's notebooks may lie in this opening to multiplicity, the additional intellectual lines of flight that they encourage us to pursue in reading his works.

20. In this regard, see Gray's perceptive and cautionary comments about *Übertragung* in *CW* 11, 485ff., with their reminder, once again, of how the forms and contents of thought perpetually intersect in Nietzsche's analysis.

As a result, the notebooks put pressure on interpretations of Nietzsche (or indeed, of any author) that want to stress his organic development, the phases of his thought, and thus on our predilection for giving interpretive primacy to neatly chronological lines of emergence. The notebooks enact in intriguing ways the idea of recurrence as an alternative to progressive or regressive models of history. This is not to say that such recurrences are ahistorical or antihistorical (though they are surely anti-Hegelian). But they do run counter to explanatory hermeneutics that find their modern formulations in Schleiermacher, whose ordering of Plato's philosophical texts has carried immense interpretive power over our sense of Plato's purposes and over the methodologies of philosophy in general. A strongly linear mode of viewing development does persist through the *Unfashionable Observations*, which rely heavily on a genetic framework that is organic and one-directional. Strauss, Schopenhauer, and Wagner are all conceived by Nietzsche as individuals engaged in an agonistic struggle toward the clarity of self-realization. Thus, projected titles for multiple versions of the *Wagner in Bayreuth* essay organize the analysis around how and why Wagner became who he had become, "[w]hat he is and how he developed into [or became] it," as 11[46] puts it. In this regard, all of the *Unfashionable Observations* offer testimony about Nietzsche's autobiographical sense in those years of his own development and prospects. But just as Nietzsche's confidence in Wagner's emblematic status for future cultural development began to wane, so, too, did his confidence in the explanatory framework that had underpinned his earlier perspective. At the same time, the entries in these notebooks reconfirm that Nietzsche did continue steadily to employ the mode of blended philosophical-cultural-biographical critique that the *Unfashionable Observations* had devised and deployed. That concern for the ways and byways of development, education, cultivation, *Bildung* lies at the heart of his genealogical approach to human, all too human issues, the mix of critique and compassion that characterizes his most telling observations.

Index of Persons

Subject Index

The Complete Works of Friedrich Nietzsche

IN NINETEEN VOLUMES

1 The Birth of Tragedy/Unpublished Basel Writings (Winter 1869/70–Fall 1873)
2 Unfashionable Observations
3 Human, All Too Human I
4 Human, All Too Human II/Unpublished Fragments from the Period of *Human, All Too Human II* (Spring 1878–Fall 1879)
5 Dawn
6 The Joyful Science/Idylls from Messina/Unpublished Fragments from the Period of *The Joyful Science* (Spring 1881–Summer 1882)
7 Thus Spoke Zarathustra
8 Beyond Good and Evil/On the Genealogy of Morality
9 The Case of Wagner/Twilight of the Idols/The Anti-Christian/Ecce Homo/Dionysus Dithyrambs/Nietzsche Contra Wagner
10 Unpublished Fragments from the Period of *The Birth of Tragedy* (Fall 1869–Spring 1872)
11 Unpublished Fragments from the Period of *Unfashionable Observations* (Summer 1872–Winter 1874/75)
12 Unpublished Fragments from the Period of *Human, All Too Human I* (Winter 1874/75–Winter 1877/78)
13 Unpublished Fragments from the Period of *Dawn* (Winter 1879/80–Spring 1881)
14 Unpublished Fragments from the Period of *Thus Spoke Zarathustra* (Summer 1882–Winter 1883/84)
15 Unpublished Fragments from the Period of *Thus Spoke Zarathustra* (Spring 1884–Winter 1884/85)
16 Unpublished Fragments (Spring 1885–Spring 1886)
17 Unpublished Fragments (Summer 1886–Fall 1887)
18 Unpublished Fragments (Fall 1887–Winter 1888/89)
19 Editors' Afterwords/Chronology of Nietzsche's Life/General Index

Library of Congress Cataloging-in-Publication Data

Names: Nietzsche, Friedrich Wilhelm, 1844–1900, author. | Handwerk, Gary J., 1954– translator, writer of afterword. | Nietzsche, Friedrich Wilhelm, 1844–1900. Works. English. 1995 ; v. 12.
Title: Unpublished fragments from the period of Human, all too human I (winter 1874/75-winter 1877/78) / Friedrich Nietzsche ; translated, with an afterword, by Gary Handwerk.
Description: Stanford, California : Stanford University Press, 2021. | Series: The complete works of Friedrich Nietzsche ; volume 12 | Includes bibliographical references and index. | Translated from the German.
Identifiers: LCCN 2020035337 | ISBN 9780804728850 (cloth) | ISBN 9781503614840 (paperback)
Subjects: LCSH: Nietzsche, Friedrich Wilhelm, 1844–1900—Notebooks, sketchbooks, etc. | Philosophy, German—19th century.
Classification: LCC B3312.E5 H36 2021 | DDC 193—dc23
LC record available at https://lccn.loc.gov/2020035337